The Ascendancy of
in Sout

The Ascendancy of Theravāda Buddhism in Southeast Asia

Prapod Assavavirulhakarn

SILKWORM BOOKS

First edition published in 2010 by
Silkworm Books
6 Sukkasem Road, T. Suthep
Chiang Mai 50200 Thailand
info@silkwormbooks.com
http://www.silkwormbooks.com

ISBN: 978-974-9511-94-7

Typeset by Silk Type in D Garamond 11 pt.
Cover photo by Woralun Boonyasurat
Printed in Thailand by O. S. Printing House, Bangkok

10 9 8 7 6 5 4 3 2 1

To Her Royal Highness Princess Maha Chakri Sirindhorn
for her kindness and unfailing support

Contents

Preface

Every book has its own "history." Mine has a long one. It was initially conceived as a thesis for my doctoral degree in Buddhist Studies at the University of California at Berkeley, and took twenty years to be transformed into a book. Suggestions that it should be published came right after it was finished, but the difficulty of turning my dissertation into a book was enormous. I was lost in other work, mainly university teaching and then administration. At times it has seemed that this project was a lost cause, but with help from friends it finally materialized.

The manuscript for this volume has passed through several editors who helped shape the style and language. The content, however, remained mostly the same. Over the course of twenty years, new evidence has certainly emerged, but, in my opinion, it does not contradict the main thesis of the book. Where necessary, I have added additional information in the notes and bibliography.

The book is intended to be a history or, perhaps more to the point, a proto-history of Buddhism in mainland Southeast Asia. The idea for this as a research subject arose from the moment I began to read books on the history of Buddhism in the region. Born and raised traditionally as a Buddhist in Thailand, we study Buddhism in school. Students know Buddhism as their *sāsanā*, or their teaching. Apart from the biography of the Buddha, the history of Buddhism was scarcely mentioned in school. At home being of Chinese descent, our prayer room was populated with Chinese gods and goddesses, Buddhist images, and paraphernalia from many beliefs—Hindu gods and goddesses, as well other sacred or holy objects of other creeds. All seemed to get on very well under the loose nomenclature of "Buddhist." The distinction between Hīnayāna or Theravāda and Mahāyāna, if it ever existed, was very remote to us. We knew more of these terms when we were in college studying civilization in class. These were terms we only came to know from books on Buddhism by Western scholars. Actually Thai scholars, even up until very recently, happily followed Western scholarship and referred to Buddhism in Thailand as Hīnayāna, unaware of its pejorative connotation.

Books on the history of Buddhism in Southeast Asia are rare. Those written by Southeast Asian scholars that I came across were mainly based on legends. Almost every book traced Buddhism in this region back to Aśoka's mission to Suvarṇabhūmi, thought to be a country or the whole region of Southeast Asia. Each book seemed to make an effort to identify the author's country of origin as Suvarṇabhūmi, that is, the first place in Southeast Asia that became Buddhist. The Buddhism brought by Aśoka's mission was believed to be of Theravādin or Pāli Buddhism and was later supplanted by Mahāyāna or Sanskrit Buddhism according to the writings of Southeast Asian scholars, followed by Vajrayāna and culminating in the ascendancy of Pāli-Theravāda Buddhism, presumably from Sri Lanka. This paradigm is, in fact, influenced somewhat by Western scholarship and flavored with Pāli or Theravāda "patriotism."

The more I read, the more I became baffled. The strict line drawn between the different denominations of Buddhism did not seem to make sense. Identification of Southeast Asia as Suvarṇabhūmi was equally doubtful. Did Sri Lankan Theravāda really supersede other kinds of Buddhism, Brahmanism, or indigenous beliefs? These doubts and questions urged me to research the history of Buddhism in Southeast Asia, using a variety of sources in the hope of, maybe, getting a clearer picture of how Buddhism became the "normative" creed in the region. Of course, no matter how diligent one is, one will never have complete evidence. Moreover, historical evidence prior to the eleventh century is not as "historical" as we would like; hence, the word "protohistorical" seems more appropriate.

In the long time it took to bring out this book, there were those all along the way who were kind enough to provide critical as well as supportive comments and suggestions. First and foremost is Her Royal Highness Prince Maha Chakri Sirindhorn who has unceasingly bestowed upon me all the material necessities and moral support for my education and livelihood. It is to her that I beg royal permission to dedicate this book, as a small token from a humble and loyal servant in whose life she has become "Sāvitṛ" And, if I may be so presumptuous, I believe Her Royal Highness will probably be happier than I to see this book materialize. My old friend and mentor, and, so often, the driving force behind my work, Peter Skilling has always firmly believed I should publish my research findings. He was one of the first editors of the manuscript, among many (most of whom he helped find), to go through the laborious process of editing my clumsy English and presentation. To him I owe my deepest gratitude. Bruce Evans kindly converted the old electronic file into a more updated one. Justin McDaniel and Steven Collins were both kind enough to endure the tortured task of correcting and copyediting the work. Their great labor will always be remembered with gratitude. I would also like to thank Lilian Handlin for thoroughly reviewing the manuscript. She pointed out my clumsiness and other awkward reasoning. Regrettably, due to time constraints, I have not followed all of her advice. My publisher, Trasvin Jittidecharak of Silkworm Books, was adamant to get this work published, even though there is little to no financial prospects in it. I accumulate great debt to Lisa S. Keary, my editor at Silkworm, who has done her job meticulously, superbly, and tirelessly. The research for this book could not have been done without the knowledge kindly imparted to me by my teachers and professors, as well as all the scholars of Buddhism. To them I offer my respect. Lastly I would like to thank the Ananda Mahidol Foundation for giving me the opportunity to widen my academic horizons.

The picture of Buddhism in Southeast Asia presented here is still very vague. There remains a good deal of uncertainty and supposition, but I hope this book sheds some light on how we should look at Buddhism and its development in Southeast Asia. Perhaps the merit of this book, if there is any, is not in discovering something new but in searching and becoming more perplexed.

Source Materials

PRIMARY SOURCES

Epigraphic and archaeological data constitute the primary sources used in this study, but they are by no means complete. Data from the various countries of Southeast Asia are published in different places and in different languages. There are also problems arising from uneven scholarship among Southeast Asian scholars; scholarship from colonized countries is often more comprehensive. Even though the period under study is not concerned with present political boundaries, nevertheless, these sources have been profoundly affected by the political situation in the countries of Southeast Asia.[1] Much of the data made available from Burma, Cambodia, and Vietnam dates from the colonial era. But in the postcolonial period, due to unrest in these countries, studies of epigraphic and archaeological data became much less. On the other hand, data obtained in Thailand has received increased attention by scholars in recent decades.

EPIGRAPHIC DATA

The series *Epigraphia Birmanica* provides a substantive portion of the epigraphic data on Burma used in this study. Unfortunately, religious inscriptions consisting of short passages or verses from texts were not included in this series, and they do not appear in the list of inscriptions found in Burma called, *Inventaire des inscriptions pālies, sanskrites, mon et pyu*, prepared by Charles Duroiselle (1912). This list is essential to this study because it includes earlier inscriptions (fourth century on), while those published in *Epigraphia Birmanica* date from the eleventh century. At present, we do not have any reports on recently discovered inscriptions in Burma. Some of the earlier studies of inscriptions found in Burma appear in the *Annual Report of the Archaeological Survey of India* (ARASI), *Annual Report of the Archaeological Survey, Burma Circle*, (ARASB) and in the *Journal of the Burma Research Society* (JBRS). Some studies are also listed in the selected bibliography in Nihar Ranjan Ray's, *An Introduction to the Study of Theravāda Buddhism in Burma* (1946).

Epigraphic data from Thailand has been studied and published by George Cœdès, but Cœdès edited only two parts of the series entitled *Prachum silacharuek* (Collection of Inscriptions). These contain the only data available in a Western language, in this case, French. The Thai government has published the succeeding volumes; however, the inscriptions were transcribed into Thai script and translated only into Thai. Our main sources are contained in these first three volumes. The National Library of Thailand has published a series called, *Charuek nai Pratet Thai* (Inscriptions in Thailand), arranged by script in five volumes, which incorporates both previously published inscriptions and the newly discovered ones (the former, in some cases, re-deciphered and retranslated). The first volume is comprised of inscriptions in Pallava and Late Pallava scripts (sixth to eighth century CE); the second volume in Pallava and Mon scripts (sixth to fifteenth century CE); the third, Khmer script (ninth to tenth century CE); the fourth, Khmer script (eleventh to twelfth century CE); and the fifth, Dharma and Thai scripts (fifteenth to eighteenth century CE). We shall consult only the first three. Inscriptions of the Sukhothai era have been reprinted in a volume entitled *Charuek samai Sukhothai*. All of these publications are in Thai. The primary source in English for inscriptions found in Thailand is the series, "Epigraphic and Historical Studies," by A. B. Griswold and Prasert na Nagara, published in the *Journal of the Siam Society* (*JSS*). Most of these inscriptions date from the later period, primarily the thirteenth century onward.

Khmer and Cham inscriptions have been extensively published in French. Inscriptions from Cambodia and neighboring countries have been edited and translated by Cœdès in his monumental seven-volume work, *Inscriptions du Cambodge* (1937–1966). An eighth volume includes an inventory of all inscriptions from these two cultures, including inscriptions appearing in other publications. This eighth volume is essential for any study of the history of Southeast Asia. Other studies of individual inscriptions appear in several series of essays in the *Bulletin de l'École Française d'Extrême-Orient* (BEFEO): "*Études épigraphique*," "*Notes d'épigraphies*," "*Études cambodgiennes*," "*Études indiennes et indochinoises*," and so on. For newly discovered inscriptions and further analysis of those previously published, the works of Claude Jacques will be consulted, which appear mostly in *BEFEO*. Jacques also edited a collection of articles on Cham inscriptions by Louis Finot, Édouard Huber, George Cœdès, and Paul Mus entitled, *Études épigraphiques sur le pays Cham*. Later, some of the inscriptions from these French collections were translated into

English and published in the *Journal of the Siam Society*. In addition, there are works in English by R. C. Majumdar, D. C. Sircar, and Philip N. Jenner.

For Indonesia, our main source is *Prasasti Indonesia I* and *Prasasti Indonesia II* by J. G. de Casparis (1950 and 1956), supplemented by Louis-Charles Damais's "Études d'épigraphie indonésienne" that appears serially in BEFEO beginning with volume 45. Inscriptions found in the Malay peninsula are published in the *Journal of the Royal Asiatic Society, Malaya Branch* (JRASMB).

ARCHAEOLOGICAL DATA

The primary archaeological data for Burma comes from the *Annual Report of the Archaeological Survey, Burma Circle*, along with detailed archaeological studies published in the *Annual Report of the Archaeological Survey of India*. Reports on Burma in the latter series ceased after Burma's independence in 1948. There are some relevant reports in the *Journal of the Burma Research Society*. Gordon Luce's *Old Burma-Early Pagan* also provides a great wealth of data, but mainly from King Aniruddha's reign in the eleventh century on. Knowledge of the current state of Burmese archaeology is poor due to the political situation in that country. In 1990 Janice Stargardt published *The Ancient Pyu of Burma*, which also provides a detailed study of Burmese archaeology from prehistoric times. A collection of articles on Burma appears as *Études birmanes en hommage à Denise Bernot* in the Études thématiques series published by the École Française d'Extrême-Orient, and also includes an extensive bibliography on Burma.

For Thailand, we have more published data and studies. In addition to the classic inventories done by Lunet de Lajonquière in the early twentieth century, there are works by George Cœdès, Pierre Dupont, and Jean Boisselier. The proceedings of two conferences on the archaeology of Thailand also proved to be very useful. They are the *Premier Symposium Franco-Thaï, la Thaïlande dès débuts de son histoire au XVème siècle* (1988) and the *Research Conference on Early Southeast Asia, Bangkok and Nakhon Pathom* (1985). The latter focuses on archaeological studies in Thailand for both prehistoric and protohistoric periods. One of the most comprehensive studies, covering almost all the countries of mainland Southeast Asia, is Charles Higham's *The Archaeology of Mainland Southeast Asia from 10,000 B.C. to the Fall of Angkor* (1989). New discoveries are regularly reported in two Thai periodicals: the *Silpakorn Journal* published by the Department of Fine Arts and *Muang Boran*. Both journals are mainly in Thai, but *Muang Boran* supplies English synopses of articles. A comprehensive work on the very early period in Thailand is Higham's *Prehistoric Thailand: From Early Settlement to Sukhothai* (1998). Even though the book gives an exhaustive survey of all the sites excavated in Thailand, regrettably, there is little attention given to beliefs and religions. For general reports on archaeological sites in Thailand, see *Thailand: Culture and Society*, edited by Sanit Samakkan (in Thai, with abstracts in English). In addition, there are inventories and archaeological reports of Thailand published by region, which have been issued by the Department of Fine Arts.

For Cambodia and Khmer art, in general, articles in *BEFEO* are the main source. There are also several monographs on the subject, most of them published by the École Française d'Extrême-Orient. Among them are the works of Pierre Dupont, Louis Malleret, and Jean Boisselier. The latter has written a book on Cambodian art from the earliest period entitled, *Trends in Khmer Art* (1989). A collection of articles on Cambodian culture appears as the first volume of the series, *Recherches nouvelles sur le Cambodge* (Études thématiques).

For archaeological data in Indonesia several works were consulted, including the conference proceedings published by SEAMEO's Project for Archeology and Fine Arts.[2]

LOCAL CHRONICLES

Chronicles and local legends also serve as a type of primary source material. Although these appear later (no earlier than the fifteenth century), they are still useful because they usually contain some data on both Buddhist practices and indigenous beliefs. David Wyatt has examined this type of literature in his "Chronicle Traditions in Thai Historiography" in *Southeast Asian History and Historiography: Essays Presented to D. G. E. Hall*, ed. by C. D. Cowan and O. W. Wolters (1976). A monograph on the subject, *The Buddhist Annals and Chronicles in South-East Asia with Special Reference to India and Ceylon*, has been written by Kanai Lal Hazra (1986). Some of the chronicles, such as *Cāmadevīvaṃsa*, *Jinakālamālinī*, and *Sāsanavaṃsa*, have been translated either into French or English.

SECONDARY SOURCES

Few studies are devoted to the ancient history of Buddhism in Southeast Asia, which is usually dealt with only in passing in general histories of the region. A complete history of Buddhism in Southeast Asia from the beginning to the present has yet to be written. While some topics have been perennially popular, for example, the precise location of Suvarṇabhūmi or the historicity of Aśoka's mission, the nature of Buddhism in that early stage has held little interest for scholars. As a result, the picture of early Buddhist history is distorted and misrepresented.[3]

Nihar Ranjan Ray's studies, *Brahmanical Gods in Burma* (1932), *Sanskrit Buddhism in Burma* (1936), and *An Introduction to the Study of Theravāda Buddhism in Burma* (1946) are the only works that come close to what may be called the "history of religion." Ray, however, confines his study to Burma in the geopolitical sense—the Burma at the time of his writing. This, as noted earlier, is inadequate since the Burma known today is a postcolonial entity, a construction of nineteenth century imperial mapmaking. Ray apparently does not see any connections between Brahmanism,[4] Sanskrit Buddhism, and Theravāda Buddhism. Some of his conclusions are now out of date, especially those regarding how and when Buddhism was introduced into Burma. A more recent study on Pyu Buddhism can be found in Janice Stargardt's, *The Ancient Pyu of Burma* (1990).

Two books published in the Éditions des Cahiers de France series *Le bouddhisme des Thaïs* (1993) by François Bizot and *Le bouddhisme au village* (1998) by George G. Condominas give accounts of Buddhism in Thailand and Laos, respectively.

Even though the word "Buddhism" does not appear in the title of Kamaleswar Bhattarcharya's *Les religions brahmaniques dans l'ancien Cambodge* (1961), it is a rich source of information on Buddhism in ancient Cambodia. Unfortunately this study does not take into account Buddhism in other countries of the region, and so, like Ray's, it does not reflect a broad perspective of the history of Theravāda Buddhism in Southeast Asia.

For changes and developments in religious concepts and in cultural relations between India and Southeast Asia, Paul Mus's *Barabudur* (1935) and "Cultes indiens et indigènes au Champa" (originally published in *BEFEO* in 1933) are essential sources for this study. Mus provides numerous insights on religious concepts in India and Southeast Asia; however, in many cases he fails to supply adequate data to support his theories.

In addition to these works, there are many articles and books on the history of Southeast Asia itself, but the authors are often vague with regard to religious issues. Studies on religion are done, for the most part, from the perspectives of sociology and anthropology, and thus only describe the present state of Buddhism in Southeast Asia, which represents a Western approach to the study of the religious situation in Southeast Asia. Since contemporary religious practices are found to differ in many aspects from the Buddhism prescribed in Buddhist scriptures, sociologists and anthropologists must explain how it is that these practices and beliefs can exist together. These scholars tend to explain this coexistence either as examples of syncretism or as multilayered functions. However, if one takes the structure of religious phenomena in ancient Southeast Asia into account, then these two concepts do not emerge as the best answer to the question. Instead, the answer must be sought from the perspective of the peoples of Southeast Asia.

While there has been an effort to integrate historical perspectives with sociological and/or anthropological studies, the full history of Buddhism in Southeast Asia has not been fully studied. Although Tambiah's admirable work *World Conqueror and World Renouncer* (1976) purports to examine the history of Buddhism, historical data is taken from the *Aggaññasutta* and the history of Buddhism in Sri Lanka, rather than from Thailand, despite the book's subtitle: "A Study of Buddhism and Polity in Thailand against a Historical Background." One would expect Tambiah to use data from the Dvāravatī, Sukhothai, and the Ayutthaya periods, but such evidence is wholly absent.

Two bibliographical articles by Frank Reynolds are useful: "From Philology to Anthropology: A Bibliographical Essay on Works Related to Early Theravāda and Sinhalese Buddhism" (1972), and "Tradition and Change in Theravāda Buddhism: A Bibliographical Essay Focused on the Modern Period" (1973). Volume three of Heinz Bechert's *Buddhismus, Staat und Gesellschaft in den Ländern des Theravāda-Buddhismus* provides valuable and comprehensive information on works on Theravāda Buddhism.

There are, on the one hand, a number of works that deal with the introduction of Buddhism to the region, usually beginning with the Aśokan missions before the leap across the centuries to the time of Aniruddha and Ramkhamhaeng. On the other hand, there is a wealth of works on modern Theravāda Buddhism. What is missing here is the story of Buddhism from its initial introduction until the eleventh century.

Since this is a historical study, we shall not deal with the practices of Buddhism in detail, and since data on Burma and Cambodia can be found in the works of Ray and Bhattacharya, we shall provide, in most cases, data found in Thailand. The book will demonstrate that the religious situation in this period had a profound impact on the subsequent period. Its structure and development are crucial for understanding the development of Buddhism in Southeast Asia. Without this understanding, scholars have misunderstood the meaning of the "ascendancy" of Theravāda Buddhism and its practice in the so-called "Theravāda Buddhist countries of Southeast Asia."

Note on Transliteration

The transliteration of Pāli and Sanskrit words and terms follow the form found in Appendix X of A. L. Basham's *The Wonder That Was India.* The system of the Royal Institute will be adopted for Thai, but without diacritical marks. Cambodian words will be transliterated following usage in the publications of the École Française d'Extrême-Orient. For Chinese, the Pinyin system will be adopted throughout. In quotations, however, terms will be left as they are spelled in the original source.

1
Introduction

This volume was written as a response to existing literature on the history of Buddhism in Southeast Asia, which tends to present Theravāda Buddhism either in terms of a "revival" or an "introduction" of Buddhism in Southeast Asia. Within the literature, this is said to have occurred in the eleventh century in Burma and in the thirteenth century in Thailand, and is believed to be connected with two great kings: King Aniruddha of Pagan and King Ramkhamhaeng of Sukhothai.

Broadly speaking, there are two theories regarding the status of Theravāda Buddhism in Southeast Asia. The first holds that prior to the eleventh century the Theravāda was but a small, non-influential school among several other schools of Buddhism in the region. Only later, when Theravāda Buddhism was adopted by these two great kings, did it become the "national" or "state" religion of Burma and Thailand. The second theory maintains that Theravāda Buddhism did not reach Southeast Asia until the beginning of the eleventh century when it was introduced to these two kings and then became the state religion.

In both cases it is clear that the ascent of Theravāda Buddhism in Southeast Asia is seen as beginning from the eleventh century, a date that dictates the writing of the history of Buddhism in Southeast Asia. If a book on this subject were to be written, and if it mentioned the period before the eleventh century at all, that period would be divided into two parts. The first part would treat what is usually called "early" Buddhism in Southeast Asia; the second part would deal with the history of Theravāda Buddhism from King Aniruddha's reign in the case of Burma, and from King Ramkhamhaeng's in the case of Thailand.

Regrettably, most studies of the history of Buddhism in Southeast Asia do not include the period of early Buddhism. If such a history were to be written, it would, in all likelihood, begin with the introduction of Buddhism from the time of Aśoka, an issue extensively discussed in the literature. However, those discussions usually center upon the problem posed by trying to identify Suvarṇabhūmi, whose location was said to be somewhere in Southeast Asia, and the supposed site of the missions sent in the Aśokan period. However, the nature of Buddhism subsequent to its introduction has never received the attention it deserves, or if it is mentioned at all, it describes a period right before its ascendancy. This period is regarded as the "wane of Buddhism" by Gordon Luce. I quote Luce extensively below, and other authors will be similarly quoted at length, in order to illustrate in detail the various arguments and analyses that have been made about Buddhism in Southeast Asia:

> About this time Buddhism was almost everywhere on the wane. In Sung China, during the 11th century, the recoil from Buddhism set in with the rise of Neo-Confucianism. In Tibet, the 'Red Hat' sect of Padmasambhava had relapsed into demonolatry, before the Paṇḍit Atīśa (an older contemporary of Aniruddha) came and introduced Tāntric Mahāyānism of Pāla Bengal. In North India, Muslim armies were continually raiding from the west. In 1033–34 the Ghaznavid general Ahmad sacked Benares. In 1039 the Chedi prince Karnadeva invaded the Buddhist Pāla kingdom of Bihar (Magadha). Kyanzittha's latest Prome inscription (c. 1105 A.D.) says that (at some date, unspecified) the Vajrāsana temple of Bodhgayā, the very heart of Buddhism, had been "irremediably destroyed by other kings." In East Bengal (Samataṭa, 'the level country'), from the beginning of the 11th century, says Bhattasali, "Buddhism had begun to decline with the fall of the Candras." In the Deccan, Buddhism was yielding almost everywhere before the revival of Brahmanism; and the split between Mahāyāna and the southern schools of Theravāda, etc., was ever widening. In South India, early in the 10th century the Śaivite Coḷa empire arose, holding for a time most of the country south of the Kistna. The Coḷas were strong at sea. Between 1017 and 1070 they ruled most of Ceylon; but from about 1050 the Singhalese prince Kīrti (afterwards Vijayabāhu I) led a desperate revolt against them, from the south and the centre of the island. In 1025 the Coḷas conquered Palembang (Srī Vijaya), including the north of Sumatra and the mainland up to the Isthmus of Kra.
>
> Of all the great Buddhist kingdoms which I-Tsing had admired so much in the 7th century, little remained except Nagara Srī Dharmarājā (Ligor) on the east coast, just south of Kra. Dvāravatī, the Theravāda stronghold in Lower Siam, the source of Mon inscriptions 400 hundred years before the first in Burma, fell to the Khmers early in the 11th century. The Śaivite court of Angkor (Mahānagara), under Sūryavarman I, occupied Lopburi; and between 1002 and 1050 extended Cambojan rule over much of Siam. There is no evidence, I think, that they persecuted Buddhism; but they are not likely to have supported it. They even tried, as we shall see, to invade Burma. In this perilous period

> Buddhism was saved only by such valiant fighters as Vijayabāhu in Ceylon and Aniruddha in Burma, and by such ardent reformers as Paṇḍit Atīśa in Tibet, and in Burma by Shin Arahan.[1]

In short, the presence of Buddhism, especially Theravāda before Aniruddha and Ramkhamhaeng, was insignificant, according to Luce. If one agrees with this, then such alleged state of affairs supports the theory of the precipitate rise of Theravāda Buddhism in the eleventh century, along with the fame of the two kings. Yet Luce's account is woefully inaccurate. The word "decline" cannot be applied to the Buddhism of Sung China. In that dynasty we see the beginning of the printing of the *Tripiṭaka*, and at the time China was still the source of Buddhism for Korea and Japan. Neither can it be said that in Dvāravatī, Mahāyāna Buddhism superseded Theravāda Buddhism while it was under Khmer influence. Inscriptions show that the Khmer king recognized Theravāda Buddhism as one of the major creeds of his kingdom, which in time became the paradigm for the entire history of Southeast Asia. The paradigm begins with the presence of Hīnayāna schools, which sometimes included Theravāda and sometimes not, followed by Mahāyāna, and culminating in the ascendancy of Theravāda Buddhism.

However, when we read local Buddhist chronicles such as the *Sāsanavaṃsa*, the *Cāmadevīvaṃsa*, or the *Jinakālamālinī* an entirely different picture emerges: Theravāda Buddhism is presented as a continuity of tradition, not simply as an introduction.

In order to come to a clearer understanding of these issues one must study the situation prior to the eleventh century. If such an event did occur at that time, the best way to understand it is to examine the circumstances that preceded it. This study shall demonstrate that the prevailing paradigm of the religious situation in Southeast Asia described above does not accord with the data.

DEFINITION OF TERMS

In conducting research on Theravāda Buddhism in Southeast Asia, one immediately confronts the two terms, "Southeast Asia" and "Buddhism." Because these two terms have been used in different contexts, their meanings are varied and nuanced. With this comes misunderstanding and misinterpretation due to the fact that these terms are rarely defined when they are used. For the purpose of this study, we shall try to narrow the meanings of these terms as they are used herein.

"SOUTHEAST ASIA"

The term "Southeast Asia" was first used in an Austrian geographical magazine as early as 1900, but it became widely accepted only after World War II. It was used first as a geographical term, and later it was appropriated by scholars of other disciplines, principally history, sociology, and anthropology. The area covered by the term includes countries with different ethnic groups and cultures, raising the question of whether it can be studied as a single region. Harry J. Benda, a pioneer in Southeast Asian studies, notes the problems with trying to delineate Southeast Asia:

> What is it? Is it merely a geographic convenience, or was it born of the need to define operational theatres during the Second World War? What should it include, what exclude? By commonly, if tacitly, accepted definition, Southeast Asia has nowadays apparently come to embrace Burma, Thailand, Laos, Cambodia, Vietnam, Malaya and Indonesia. The Philippines appears to constitute the borderline case, seeing that they are excluded from Professor Hall's massive standard work. Pakistan has found its way not only into the so-called Southeast Asia Treaty Organization but also into some recent books devoted to 'Southeast Asia', while Ceylon, which might be a far more appropriate candidate, has usually been left to our 'South Asian' colleagues.
>
> This uncertainty is ample proof of the difficulty, or even the impossibility, of subsuming Southeast Asia in terms of an integral civilization, like those of India, China, Korea and Japan. The perplexing ethnic, linguistic and religious divisions which prevail throughout the area only underline the difficulties confronting us. However, diversity in and of itself need not be an insurmountable barrier to our efforts at generalization, since the diversity of Europe has not prevented more or less meaningful generalization about the general—and the generic—course of its history.[2]

The term "Southeast Asia" is commonly used differently among scholars, even those from the same field. In fact, for the so-called "Southeast Asian peoples" themselves, the term and its designation has never been a conscious part of their identity. There was no such entity as "Southeast Asia" or "Southeast Asian" until a very recent effort to define the region, mainly as an economic unit within the regional organization known as the Association of Southeast Asian Nations (ASEAN). However, this definition is meaningful only for the governments of ASEAN countries and essentially meaningless to its people.

Geographically, Southeast Asia is usually divided into two regions: mainland and archipelago. The main difficulty here lies with the application of the term to regional cultural studies. There is an attempt to divide Southeast Asia into two parts, using its different cultures as the guiding principle. The first consists of the modern countries of Burma, Thailand, Laos, Cambodia, and the insular region; the second consists of Vietnam. Since the first grouping is considered culturally "Indian," it, therefore, has been considered "Indianized," and since Vietnam is culturally "Chinese," it has been considered "Sinocized." For many reasons this division is both simplistic and inaccurate. For example, much of Vietnam was also "Indianized" but in different periods and in different contexts.

For want of an adequate principle to delineate the area of Southeast Asia, we shall rely on our own. Since this work proposes to examine ancient Buddhism in the area, we shall use Buddhism itself as the norm to limit the area. We shall deal only with those regions where Buddhist culture is present. This area includes Burma, Thailand, Laos, and Cambodia, which are now regarded as "Theravāda Buddhist countries," with some additional reference to the other areas influenced by Indian Buddhism, namely, parts of Vietnam and island Southeast Asia. However, there is one pitfall. The political boundaries of the present era cannot be used, for in that earlier time the ancient civilizations of Southeast Asia were yet to be designated as Thailand, Burma, Laos, and so forth.

"BUDDHISM"

The use of the term "Buddhism" gives rise to another set of problems since it is a cultural as well as a religious term. Any attempt to define it must take into consideration its historical context. This book is primarily concerned with the importation of Buddhism into Southeast Asia, but in order to study the process of its acculturation, an understanding of its Indian cultural roots is essential. Hinduism cannot be neglected, nor can indigenous beliefs be disregarded. The process of the spread of Indian cultures as a whole has been referred to as "Indianization," a term which is also problematic.

Even if we limit our scope to "Buddhism" or even "Buddhism in Southeast Asia," we do not find ourselves in an easier position. Buddhism has a long and complex history. It comprises not only the Theravāda school, but also numerous other schools. These schools have been grouped and designated under various names in different periods, and most difficult of all, there is certainly no single principle to differentiate among them.

The most generally accepted division in most modern studies on Buddhism is the one between Hīnayāna and Mahāyāna. The first is a derogatory term understood to be used by Mahāyānists to designate schools other than the Mahāyāna one. However, the word "Hīnayāna" is not used consistently in all Mahāyāna scriptures.[3] Terms used to refer to schools other than Mahāyāna are "Śrāvakayāna" and "Pratyekabuddhayāna." In place of Mahāyāna, a commonly used term is "Buddhayāna."[4]

Traditional accounts list eighteen schools of Buddhism that existed before the rise of the Mahāyāna school, which are divided into two main groups: the Sthavira and the Mahāsāṃghika. These two, in turn, are divided into subgroups of different schools, one of which is the Theravāda school. Usually, Theravāda is synonymous with the Buddhism of Sri Lanka. But there is confusion here as well. Some scholars are reluctant to use the word "Hīnayāna" because it signifies the "Lesser" Vehicle. They instead use the word "Theravāda" to signify Buddhist schools which do not belong to the Mahāyāna. In this case, Theravāda has the same meaning as its Sanskrit counterpart, Sthaviravāda. However, because the term Theravāda does not include the Mahāsāṃghika, it is an inadequate term, if the purpose is to contrast it with other schools from Mahāyāna. The word "Hīnayāna," derogatory or not, can serve a useful purpose here, by separating all other schools of Buddhism from Mahāyāna.[5]

Furthermore, if, as a principle of clarification, we look at the languages used in the scriptures, there are three to take into account: Sanskrit, Buddhist Sanskrit, and Pāli. Pāli is used exclusively by the Theravāda, and Sanskrit and Buddhist Sanskrit are used by different schools within Hīnayāna and Mahāyāna. One might assume that in that case, it could be said that Theravāda is Pāli Buddhism. The situation is, however, not that simple, because some inscriptions have been found using Pāli that may or may not belong to the Theravādins.[6] Moreover, if the term "Theravāda" is used to denote Sri Lankan Buddhism, which had three main schools, the Mahāvihāra, Abhayagiri, and Jetavana, then one must consider that the Abhayagiri school is reported sometimes to have used Sanskrit as a sacred language. Therefore, to equate Theravāda with Pāli Buddhism does not resolve the confusion.

The term "Theravāda Buddhism" will be used throughout this study when there is evidence that the practices are derived from the Pāli canon, especially from the *Abhidhammapiṭaka*. When the evidence considered is in Pāli, but cannot be definitively shown to be a citation from the Pāli canon, then the term "Pāli Buddhism" will be used. To specify the Theravāda of Sri Lanka, the words "Sri Lankan" or "Sinhalese" will be prefixed to Theravāda.

Even though the title of this volume uses the term "Theravāda Buddhism," this study will not deal exclusively with this particular school of Buddhism, but rather, the ascendancy of this school as substantiated by scholars will be taken as a culminating point or temporal limit for the study. This investigation will focus on the history of Buddhism as a whole, with particular emphasis on Theravāda Buddhism.

"ASCENDANCY"

Thus far, this work has been limited geographically and conceptually; the word "ascendancy" limits it temporally. Since the prevailing belief is that the advent of Theravāda Buddhism in Southeast Asia began somewhere around the eleventh to thirteenth centuries,[7] our focus will be on the period beginning with the introduction of Buddhism in Southeast Asia up until its proclaimed ascendancy.

The aim here is to discern the development and the structure of Buddhism, especially of Theravāda Buddhism in order to examine the circumstances under which Theravāda came to attain its present status in Southeast Asia. In so doing, we shall be better placed to evaluate Luce's account regarding the "wane of Buddhism" in the period prior to its ascendancy.

PERIODIZATION OF SOUTHEAST ASIAN HISTORY

Only the periods in the history of Southeast Asia from the earliest times until the thirteenth century will be examined, since this constitutes the scope of the study. This particular time span can be roughly divided into two periods: prehistoric and protohistoric. Here "prehistoric" means the period before any written records, and by "protohistoric," the period where written records occur but are either historically insignificant or cannot be used as accurate historical documents. The protohistoric period in Southeast Asia is considered by most scholars to be the result of "Indianization." The states or kingdoms in this period are referred to as "Indianized states," which is quite misleading, since it suggests that if it had not been for Indian civilization, then these states would not have come into existence.

PREHISTORY IN SOUTHEAST ASIA

There are at least three systems for dividing prehistory into periods. The old system divides prehistory on the basis of materials used to make artifacts. For example, if the artifacts are made from stone, they are classified as "lithic," with further divisions into Paleolithic, Mesolithic, and Neolithic. If the material is bronze, the artifacts are classified as belonging to the Bronze Age, followed by those made in the Iron Age. A second system is based on living and social conditions, for example, the society of hunter-gatherers, the society of agricultural villages, and lastly, a society of urban dwellers. A third system bases the division on the geological ages. For our purposes the last system is too complicated and not useful for studying belief systems. Higham provides a summary of the prehistory of mainland Southeast Asia in terms of culture and society. His terminology differs from the three systems mentioned above. Higham appears to combine the first two systems. For instance, he divides the span of time from 10,000 BCE until the fall of Angkor into six periods.[8] For our purposes here, only the first five will be used, as the sixth and last period concerns Indianization, which belongs to a later part of our study.

Higham's Prehistory Periodization System[9]

10,000 B.C. Early Hunter-Gatherers

At that time the sea level, originally much lower than today, rose about three meters above its present level, submerging early coastal settlements. The main surviving sites were inland rock shelters. A limited range of stone tools were found at these sites, and wooden implements for hunting and gathering were probably used as well. Small, nomadic groups collected wild plants and shellfish, as evidence of hunting, fishing, and trapping.

5000–1500 B.C.[10] Coastal Settlement

The sharp rise in sea levels from about 7000 to 4000 BC in all likelihood destroyed coastal settlements. In 4000 BC, the sea level stabilized at a higher level than it is today. Evidence for rich sedentary coastal settlement involving ranking, exchange and elaborate mortuary rituals has been found at Khok Phanom Di in Thailand. From pollen found there, there is evidence that the area was settled by 4700 BC. Marine sources were important for food, and rice was consumed. Rather than cultivated rice, this rice may have been harvested from natural stands found in fresh water swampland.

3000 B.C. General Period A

Settlements expanded into the tributary streams of the Khorat plateau, the middle Mekong delta, and the Chao Phraya River valley. These settlements were small and social organization loosely ranked. Stone implements and shells were exchanged between communities, and rice was probably cultivated along the swampy margins of river deltas.

2000–500 B.C. General Period B

During this period bronze working began to spread among autonomous lowland settlements. Ore was mined in the hills, ingots were traded, and implements cast in lowland communities. An increase in ranking within small communities was beginning to occur. Some family groups assumed a high rank, signified by jewelry and bronze implements. Subsistence farming was now wide-ranging and included rice, which was probably cultivated.

500 B.C. General Period C

Iron working, settlement centralization, and the formation of chiefdoms are characteristics of this period. Initial contact began with Indian traders and Han Chinese armies, concomitant with increased exchange, ranking, and agriculture. Specialized bronze workers produced ceremonial drinking vessels, decorative body armor, bowls, and immense decorative drums. Burials were chiefly in boat-shaped coffins.

By the time of initial contacts with Indian and Chinese civilizations, the Southeast Asian region had already attained an advanced state of development in important areas such as rice cultivation, regional trade and exchange, and metallurgy.[11] Over the years debates have raged as to whether or not rice domestication and metallurgy originated in Southeast Asia.[12] We are not in a position to discuss these issues here, except to note that these technologies evolved at an early stage when outside influences had not yet reached the region.

Since paddy rice growing demands control over water resources, it can be assumed that knowledge of irrigation techniques was known and utilized, especially in areas of recurrent flood or drought. Drought was avoided by moving down to river valleys, where some rivers could be controlled to prevent flooding.[13] The difference between highland and lowland cultures became increasingly marked in the late prehistoric period when initial contacts between the region and Indian civilization took place.[14]

This contrast seems to have occurred also among lowland settlements. Not every valley provides a perfect ecology for paddy rice growing, because in some areas water was more readily accessible, while other areas were prone to flood. This situation seems to have affected the development of the classical states of mainland Southeast Asia. The area that would become the Khmer kingdom was forced to develop a complicated system to control water, which evolved into a "temple-building" culture with complex social and political structures. In contrast, the Chao Phraya valley remained a loosely organized political structure, made up of small city-states or clusters of cities, usually surrounded by moats and walls but without the grand scale building projects of the Khmer.[15]

Another contrast in Southeast Asia history can be noted between the mainland and the coast. Because river valleys are scarce in the archipelago, paddy or watershed rice growing could not easily develop, and consequently, coastal societies were incapable of sustaining major political growth. And yet this part of Southeast Asia played a major role in both intra- and extra-regional trade. There is evidence that before the coming of the Indians and the Chinese, there had been a gradual evolution of trade and cultural relationships between different areas of the region itself, as indicated by bronze drums found scattered throughout many parts of Southeast Asia.[16]

Therefore, we may conclude that around the second half of the first millennium BCE, Southeast Asia had already advanced in a number of areas: material civilization, as evidenced in rice growing, metallurgy, and pottery making; political civilization, as evidenced in the concept of "men of prowess" (leaders of protohistoric chiefdoms) as well as the potential for developing advanced political entities;[17] and a social civilization that was agrarian with concomitant beliefs or religious systems.[18]

These facets of local civilization offered favorable circumstances for the implantation of Indian civilization. Lea E. Williams has rightly observed that:

> It is certain that outsiders who first came from India and China to Southeast Asia were met by settled agricultural peoples living within the established social order, not by scattered bands of forest dwellers. Clearly, without the requisite material and institutional infrastructure, aspects of higher cultures could not have been so successfully transplanted to the region. Nor would so much that is neither Indian nor Chinese have endured had indigenous cultures not possessed vitality and been both receptive to enrichment and able to maintain distinctiveness.[19]

The same situation had, in fact, occurred in India itself when Buddhism, and sometime later the modified forms of Brahmanism and Hinduism, emerged and spread. At that time central India had become a rice-growing agrarian society. With the use of iron, agriculture could easily be expanded and intensified, allowing small kingdoms to develop.[20] We may safely speculate that this was the culminating point of Aryanization, which is another misleading term, since it refers only to the Aryans and omits the local people. In fact, it was the Aryans whose concepts of religion, society, and politics were dramatically changed by the encounter with and challenge from indigenous cultures. The transformation effected upon religion is probably the most conspicuous: the Vedic religions changed in the course of time whereby old gods were dethroned and new gods and new styles of worship appeared. But this does not mean that Aryan cultures had no part in the evolution of Indian cultures, but rather, it means they formed one of the two intertwined threads of the civilization that was eventually to expand to the lands beyond India's shores.

PROTOHISTORY IN MAINLAND SOUTHEAST ASIA

The much-discussed issue in Southeast Asia's protohistoric period is Indianization. The concept has dictated the studies of Southeast Asian culture for a century. It cannot be denied that Indian civilization helped shape Southeast Asian culture, but it is incorrect to regard the region as "Indian."

Process of Indianization

As we have seen, even though the term "Indianization" has the defect of ignoring the indigenous aspects of the process, nonetheless, we must use the word for the sake of convenience, keeping in mind that it refers to a reciprocal process, and that Indianization was not the sole dynamic in the development of Southeast Asian civilization. In any case, the word "Indianization" is preferable to "Hinduization," which is misleading because it excludes Buddhism, a crucial factor in Indianization. It is also better than "Sanskritization," which seems to limit the process to the sphere of language and better than "Brahmanization," which suggests that the process was dominated by the Brahman caste, or even that Southeast Asian society adopted the Hindu caste system, as Cœdès indeed suggests.[21]

What then is this process of Indianization? In light of available data, we can safely say that it is a process of acculturation, or rather, a process of cultural relations between India and Southeast Asia. When we observe the historical evidence, we find that at first Indian cultures seemed to exert strong influence in almost every field, but before long the indigenous cultures begin to absorb, transform, and blend the two cultures into one that reflects local or regional characteristics. Therefore, different areas in the region produced different schools of art, adopted religions and beliefs in different ways, and used Indian concepts to enhance or heighten their concepts in singular ways.

The fact that art, crafts, and architecture as well as local languages existed side by side with standard Indian languages suggests that there were multiple ethnic groups in the area when the process of Indianization began. It is clear that Southeast Asia was inhabited by different ethnic and linguistic groups, however, the question of whether or not the individual states were connected to single ethnic groups remains controversial and undetermined. The standard view that students are taught is that the region is Tibeto-Burman to the north, Mon-Khmer in the center and the southeast, and Malay to the south, including the islands of the archipelago. This view also states that the Tai peoples slowly migrated to the south, a migration supposedly intensified by pressure from the expanding Mongol Empire. According to this line of thought, Dvāravatī was a Mon kingdom that was superseded by the Khmer Empire, and finally by the Thai.

Early scholars of Southeast Asia held that these ethnic groups formed separate nations or states, creating a political situation that will be shown to deviate from the facts. Frequently, the designating of a specific area with a specific ethnic group was work done by scholars of the colonial era that had the political implication of claiming territories that supposedly belonged to the great ancient empires, such as the Khmer Empire. At its height, scholars claimed that the Khmer Empire held sway over most of the central and northeastern parts of present-day Thailand.[22]

While it is true that inscriptions in Mon, Khmer, Pyu, and so on were found in different regions, it does not follow that all people in the areas in which the inscriptions were found belonged to one and the same race. For example, Khmer inscriptions are found in central Thailand in an area supposedly belonging to Mon-speaking peoples. Would this suggest that around that time people in the area in question became Khmer?

Analysis of skeletal remains excavated from prehistoric sites shows that the inhabitants were of mixed types. Studies of blood types reveal that Thais and Malays are closely related.[23] However, studies of this nature will probably not yield results significant for the understanding of either the history or culture of Southeast Asia. Instead of following these scientific studies, we should concentrate instead on the relations among the different cultures whose continuity persists up to the present day, regardless of which race or ethnic group inherits them.

There are no satisfactory or conclusive sources that describe precisely how the process of Indianization unfolded in history. Available epigraphic and archaeological data reveal Indian influences. We have inscriptions in Indian languages, not only in Sanskrit, but also in Pāli and perhaps other Prakritic languages. Neither do we lack inscriptions in local dialects. Both Indian and local languages were often used in the same inscription, although for different purposes.[24] Objects of art have been found, such as statues of Hindu gods, images of the Buddha and bodhisattvas, which at first closely resembled their Indian prototypes, but then progressively evolved into local styles. From such data, scholars extrapolated the effects of Indianization, but unfortunately, their efforts focused mainly on determining what is Indian, rather than by looking at the dynamics of the mutual process of transformation and the effect on indigenous culture, for example. This aspect of the process will be dealt with later in a discussion about the effects of Indianization.

Initial contact between India and Southeast Asia began in the late historic period from about 300 BCE.[25] Since then, these contacts have been constant, involving a process continuing even to the present day. It is pointless to try to determine an exact moment Southeast Asia became "Indianized," since the process was not one that was prompted by military force or colonial imperative, but rather, one that developed naturally and peacefully throughout history. If we accept this premise, then there could not have been an abrupt moment in the transmission or adoption of Indian culture. The people of Southeast Asia never regarded Indian culture as an alien culture. On the contrary, it was highly regarded, and probably thought by commoners to be a culture signifying royalty or nobility. However, those ruling elites were indigenous ones rather than foreign.[26] The process must be seen as occurring in three ways: diachronically, with cultural waves coming from India; synchronically, with a process of selection made by kings or elites; and as a natural transformational process of acculturation of the masses. No conflict between the two cultures seems apparent. This may be explained because the enthusiasm came from the local side, or because the Indians who came to Southeast Asia were few in number. It has been proved that no grand scale migration from India occurred, as scholars of the Greater India Society might have argued. Another reason may be that circumstances were favorable for Indian civilization to develop in this area, as was pointed out earlier.[27]

The area affected by Indian civilization poses no geographical difficulty, as almost all parts of Southeast Asia were affected, except for the northernmost region, which later became Sinocized, a process beyond the scope of this study. On the contrary, the question as to what part of India these cultures came from does pose a problem, mainly because of regional bias among Indian scholars.[28] Present knowledge allows us to say that the cultures were mostly from South India, and to some extent from Central Asia—areas in which strict Brahmanism was not prevalent.[29]

Trade has been singled out as the main factor that spurred this acculturation. We have archaeological evidence that extra-regional trade took place between India and Southeast Asia long before the impact of Hinduism or Buddhism could be observed. However, certain characteristics of the process, such as inscriptions composed in highly ornate Sanskrit, suggest that the honor of introducing new cultural trends did not belong exclusively to the merchants.[30]

Trade is not a static, unchanging activity; its components of routes, goods, traders, buyers, and markets vary over time. Several routes, both land and sea, allowed the two regions to communicate with each other. At first, contact centered on mainland Southeast Asia, accessible both by land and sea, perhaps initially because the sea routes of maritime Southeast Asia were often unsafe due to piracy. Later, when Śrīvijaya controlled the maritime regions, trade shifted to maritime Southeast Asia. These conditions also affected the process of Indianization, since they allowed more time for the mainland to assimilate and thus indigenize Indian cultures on a greater scale than in the maritime areas.

If merchants did not play a leading role, then, who did: the priests and teachers (brahmans) or the rulers and warriors (*kṣatriya*)? Both inscriptions and Chinese sources relate the legendary origins of the royal families of classical Southeast Asian states. However, the legend seems to be based on the foundation myth of a South Indian dynasty, and may have been adopted by a local king in order to claim the prestige of a lineage that could be traced back to India.[31]

A question worth asking here is how could caste-bound Indians, especially brahmans who were forbidden to travel outside India, come to trade with Southeast Asia? And, it cannot be denied that both brahmans and members of other castes traveled to the region. Moreover, there is evidence that they intermarried with local women. It could be that the rules prohibiting foreign travel did not exist at that time, or that the caste system was differently interpreted and observed. But most likely the urge for wealth was so strong that the rules were not followed strictly.

In fact, Indian society around the time of the spread of Buddhism was undergoing a profound transformation. Conversions among the upper classes were common,[32] and merchants were the most generous supporters of the new religion. These people brought with them their beliefs and objects of reverence, making Buddhism a "portable" religion, and it was through the acceptance of Indian religions that the process of Indianization materialized.

The last point is whether or not there were migrations on a grand scale from India. Some scholars have tried to connect waves of Indian cultures to massive migrations of either the princely or the merchant caste from India. The *kṣatriya* migrations were supposedly caused by political upheavals such as Aśoka's invasion of Kalinga or Kaniūka's invasion of northern India. Other scholars have proposed a link between the accession of new Southeast Asian dynasties and the fall of Indian dynasties, with the assumed emigration of refugee rulers to Southeast Asia. But there is no evidence to support this theory, and the theory is now considered obsolete.[33]

The presence of high-caste Indian brahmans and *kṣatriya* in Southeast Asia was mostly linked to royalty. They acted as advisors, administrators, or royal priests who performed rituals for the prosperity of king and realm. This phenomenon of ritual performance came later than the earlier trading contacts, occurring at the height of the process when communications and travel between the two centers were frequent, as evidenced by records of pilgrimages to India by Southeast Asians,[34] in all probability from the upper rather than the lower classes. Therefore, it is reasonable to assume that Southeast Asian kings invited brahmans from India to be their advisors, a practice that persisted until the nineteenth century, after which advisors were imported from the West.

We may safely conclude that merchants could have made the initial cultural contacts, but that process could not have been intense, since members of the trading castes would not have been adept masters of statecraft or political philosophy. However, neither were these merchants illiterate, and as devout Hindus or Buddhists traveling with their faith, they would have been exemplars of Indian high culture. Furthermore, we should not forget that the merchants involved were not only Indians but also Southeast Asians. D. G. E. Hall rightly observed that the Malays were a sea-going people *par excellence* that resorted to the ports of India and Ceylon every bit as much as India and Ceylon used the ports of Southeast Asia.[35] Other factors were the efforts of regional chieftains or kings, who sought to strengthen their rule and prestige by employing brahmans as advisors and making pilgrimages from Southeast Asia to India. As for missionary zeal as a factor in Indianization, this is not evident for the brahmans, who were mainly court functionaries; but it did play an important role in the spread of Buddhism.

Effects of Indianization

The impact of Indian cultures in a sense pervades all cultural and social aspects of Southeast Asia. Since the process was long and varied in concentration according to place and time, the impact also varied in different parts of Southeast Asia. Moreover, the different social and cultural institutions that were affected cannot be treated entirely separately; they are interrelated. Politics, religion, and the arts reflected and influenced each other. Since this section attempts to propose a historical framework for further research in the field of religion, we will take up only those topics that are relevant to our purpose.

The arts, architecture, and literature will not be examined in detail, except to note that they reflect not just an Indian but also an Indianized influence, meaning that it implies the work of native peoples. Another important gift from India was the alphabet, the importance of which cannot be underestimated. The alphabet ushered in the historical era to Southeast Asia. Government and the enforcement of laws became more effective, and cultural relations were facilitated. This alphabet, which probably came from South India, is the prototype for all scripts used in ancient Southeast Asia. The scripts in use today evolved from these ancient scripts.[36]

We will concentrate here on the political and social impacts of Indianization, in order to become familiar with the names of the political units and their important centers that will be cited in subsequent chapters.

Cœdès makes Indianization the determining factor in the founding of the ancient or classical states of Southeast Asia, to which he gives the name, "Indian states." He claims that:

> From this Indianization was born a series of kingdoms that in the beginning were true Indian states: Cambodia, Champa, and the small states of the Malay peninsula; the kingdoms of Sumatra, Java, and Bali; and, finally, the Burmese and Thai kingdoms, which received Indian culture from the Mons and Khmers. Through reaction with the indigenous substratum, however, each of these states developed according to its own genius, although their cultures never lost the family resemblance that they owed to their common origin.[37]

Cœdès's statement has influenced historians up to the present. He distinguishes these states according to race and sees the similarity among them as rooted in Indian culture. Using his divisions, there are six broad political entities: (1) present-day Burma, the kingdom of Śrīkṣetra of the Pyu people, south of which was the Mon kingdom of lower Burma, which would supersede the former prior to being overthrown by Pagan, located to the north of Śrīkṣetra; (2) central Thailand, the kingdom of the Mon of Dvāravatī, which later would be invaded by the Khmer or the Angkor Empire; (3) Cambodia and the Mekong delta, where the kingdoms of Funan, Zhenla, and the Khmer flourished successively; (4) coastal Vietnam and northern Cambodia, the kingdom of the Chams that became weakened through wars with the Khmer Empire, to be finally taken over by the Vietnamese; (5) southern Thailand, an area of small kingdoms mostly known from Chinese sources and later dominated by the empire of Śrīvijaya, which supposedly originated in Sumatra; and (6) the East Indies, the area dominated by Śrīvijaya and the Śailendras of Java.

The time span of these states ranges from the first to the thirteenth centuries. In Cœdès's view, the Mongol invasion, which pushed the Tai peoples south from China, caused the decline of these classical kingdoms, bringing in its wake the destruction of Pagan, the advent of Thai kingdoms in the north of Thailand, and the invasion of the Khmer kingdom by the Thai kingdom of Ayutthaya, all of which brought an end to the Indian kingdoms.[38]

The names of the early kingdoms are, for the most part, "reconstructed" from Chinese sources. Only Dvāravatī and perhaps Śrīvijaya have epigraphic support.[39] Only three names appear to be Sanskritic: Śrīkṣetra, Dvāravatī, and Śrīvijaya. Śailendra is a dynastic name, not that of a kingdom. The others—Funan, Zhenla, P'an-p'an, Tun-sun, and so forth—seem to be Chinese interpretations of local names,[40] which in all probability were names of cities and not kingdoms. In their inscriptions, the people of Southeast Asia used the names of their capitals to identify themselves, a practice that persisted until the nineteenth century.[41]

To support his picture of the classical kingdoms of Southeast Asia, Cœdès relies upon epigraphic and archaeological data and interprets them with the help of Chinese sources. Consequently, his concept of these states is colored by the Chinese concept of territorial states. A closer look reveals that these kingdoms did not have definite boundaries and were never really centralized, certainly not according to the Chinese concept of a great empire.[42]

Cœdès himself does not explain why he calls these polities, "Indian states." They definitely were not a part of India, not politically "Indianized," nor were they ruled by Indian princes or colonies of Indian merchants. O. W. Wolters believes that if we avoid thinking in terms of the Chinese concept of "state," we will be able to accept that political units, such as states, can evolve through an indigenous process.[43] The fact that foreign merchants traded with inland cities rather than coastal areas suggests that some sort of political organization such as city-states ruled by kings was already in place; otherwise, the states or centers would have developed only along the coasts where the first contacts took place. It is certain that the consolidation of these states was aided by Indian concepts of a supreme monarch that included "*mahārājā*," "*sarvabhauma*," and "*cakravartin*."[44] These concepts reflect only an inspiration or an ideal; they were not the primary cause for the foundation of these states. Had there not been an indigenous concept of "man of prowess,"[45] the Indian concepts would have never taken hold.

Around 500 BCE, the period of initial contact between the two areas, Southeast Asian societies had become increasingly centralized due to advances in agriculture and the use of iron. Tribal units were growing in size and in cultural complexity. Higham writes:

> The most signal variable, however, was the organisation of people. Basically, what we find is this. Successive leaders of elite local families in different areas sought an unrivalled position of eminence. To achieve this, they needed to attract followers. We have already encountered this in General Period C, but the difference as we proceed, during General Period D, into the first millennium A.D., is that these overlords sought universal acknowledgment of their superior status.[46]

To obtain this acknowledgment, these overlords had to attract loyal followers, and that was done by establishing a central court filled with large, beautiful buildings with enclosed sacred precincts that served as the foci for rituals, ceremonies, and display. Added to this was the ability to deploy military force.[47] Some overlords succeeded in manipulating all of these factors and thus established political units whose sphere of influence expanded beyond the boundary of chiefdom. The result was not, however, a state with a central capital or clearly defined boundaries, but rather, a political unity which was fluid in terms of territory and the ability to endure.

Scholars beginning with I. W. Mabbett use the Sanskrit term "*maṇḍala*" to describe this type of political entity.[48] Higham describes a *maṇḍala* as:

> a political apparatus fluid in terms of territory and therefore without fixed frontiers. It centres on the court of the overlord, whose sway turns on attracting

> deference and obligations from other lords in his orbit through his ability to win alliances and overtake enemies. . . . In Mabbett's terms, such *maṇḍalas* had, at their fringes, a shading off of areas of influence. Southeast Asia, then, had no Hadrian [centralized empire], but centres whose edges were fluid and of uncertain durability.[49]

The development of these *maṇḍala*s can be seen as the result of both an original continuity of Southeast Asian culture along with influences from India and China.

In mainland Southeast Asia, the areas that sustained these *maṇḍala*s can be described as mainly riverine and lowland. They were situated at strategic points, mostly at the nodes of intra- or extra-regional trading centers, and usually located at the controlling point of a river valley that acted as a gateway to the hinterland beyond. In the maritime region, including the south of Thailand, the development of *maṇḍala*s seemed to depend upon control of the trade routes.

These claims do not, in fact, greatly differ from what Cœdès outlined in *The Indianized States of Southeast Asia.* However, scholars today look at the political and cultural situation in a totally different manner. Either the original situation changed, or it was regarded as a natural process of social development influenced by numerous factors. These *maṇḍala*s were not considered nation-states in the Western sense, neither were they considered to be "Indian" nor "Indianized," if the implication is that without Indian civilization these political entities would never have arisen. Leaders and elites of Southeast Asia indeed drew heavily on Indian concepts of government, but their adoption must be seen as a long and varied process, which would not have been successful without significant modification, experimentation, and interaction with other factors.[50]

During the course of development, these areas sustained numerous *maṇḍala*s that can be arranged into three periods: the early *maṇḍala*s from circa first to ninth century CE (ending in 802, if we use the date of the establishment of Angkor); the great *maṇḍala*s from circa ninth to thirteenth century; and the premodern *maṇḍala*s of the Burmese and the Thai from the twelfth century until the era of Western colonization. It would be inappropriate to give a detailed history of these *maṇḍala*s, as this is not a book on Southeast Asian history. Instead, we will name the *maṇḍala*s and their centers and explore their common features since they will be referenced throughout the study.

Early *Maṇḍalas*

The *maṇḍalas* located in the lower Mekong delta were known by the name "Funan," to the Chinese. Inscriptions refer to their center as Vyādhapura. Funan flourished from circa 100 to 550 CE.[51] Later, the center of activities seems to have shifted into the middle Mekong delta and the Tonle Sap plains, which were known to the Chinese as "Zhenla."

The Zhenla *maṇḍalas*, formerly understood as a kingdom that overthrew Funan, were, in fact, comprised of a number of centers competing for overlordship. "Zhenla" is used here to denote the area and not a kingdom. Centers mentioned in inscriptions include Isānapura and Mahendrapura.[52] The names usually resemble those of kings or overlords. These *maṇḍalas* lasted until 802 CE, when the great Angkorian *maṇḍala* was established.

The Dvāravatī *maṇḍalas*, 200–950 CE, which expanded over almost all of modern Thailand, appear to have been less unified than the aforementioned *maṇḍalas*. Their centers were U Thong, Nakhon Pathom, Khu Bua, Lopburi, and Si Thep. Dvāravatī cultures also penetrated into the Khorat plateau, but archaeological data shows both strong localization and influences from the areas aforementioned.

The *maṇḍalas* of central and lower Burma, that is the Pyu *maṇḍalas* known as Śrīkṣetra, appear to have had close relations with the Dvāravatī *maṇḍalas*. Their centers were Hmawza, Maunggan, and Beiktano.

Maṇḍalas in the Malay peninsula mentioned in Chinese sources later came under the overlordship of the great Śrīvijaya *maṇḍalas*. Important centers were Chaiya and Nakhon Si Thammarat.[53]

In the middle coastal regions of Vietnam were located the Cham *maṇḍalas* of Champa and their important centers of Amarāvatī, Vijaya, and Panduranga.

Great *Maṇḍalas*

By the eighth or ninth century, the process of centralization intensified and reached its apogee. *Maṇḍalas* were greater in extent and more complex in organization, and they attained significant cultural development in art and architecture. The monuments of Angkor and Barabudur date from this period. The three great *maṇḍalas* were: (1) the Angkorian *maṇḍala*, covering the whole Mekong delta, modern Cambodia, and perhaps parts of central and northeastern Thailand, with major centers concentrated in what is now central Cambodia, (2) the Śrīvijaya *maṇḍala*, covering the lower southern part of the Malay peninsula and Sumatra with centers at Chaiya and Nakhon Si

Thammarat in Thailand and Palembang in Sumatra, and (3) the Śailendra *maṇḍala* of Java, covering central Java.

Premodern Burmese and Thai *Maṇḍalas*

These *maṇḍalas* were the ones that would develop into the modern states of mainland Southeast Asia. Their advent is believed to have coincided with the expansion and the adoption of Sri Lankan Theravāda Buddhism.

The *maṇḍalas* share several common features: geographic, political, social, and cultural. Geographically, the mainland *maṇḍalas* were all concentrated in areas favorable to agriculture, with complex systems of irrigation for controlling floods and regulating the water supply, such as those found in the Mekong delta and the Tonle Sap plains.[54] Agriculture on this scale necessitated a highly organized network for control of labor, which together with the system of using temples as governmental units, eventually created the great Angkorian *maṇḍalas*. The early *maṇḍalas* were situated at the nodal points of intra- and extra-regional trade. Archaeological finds from Dvāravatī *maṇḍalas* revealed trade goods, including a second-century lamp from the Roman Empire. Because most of the centers were accessible by sea, Nakhon Pathom was probably a seaport.[55]

Politically, the early *maṇḍalas* were inspired by Indian concepts of government. Scholars differ on how these *maṇḍalas* developed. Some scholars advocate that large scale irrigation was the primary reason; others claimed it was trade and warfare. Without entering into that debate here, it is important to note that the factors were many and varied in different situations and time periods.[56] The central concepts that made such a development possible seem to have been a fusion of Southeast Asian concepts of kingship with Indian ideas of a supreme monarch, with the addition of Hindu and Buddhist beliefs. We have shown above that the leader or king was regarded as a religio-political person. By adopting universal religions such as Hinduism or Buddhism—faiths that go beyond local tribal beliefs—a ruler's legitimacy extended to his vassals and a broader public.

On the social level, we see the rise of elite groups who made use of Indian civilization. Cœdès goes so far as to say that the adoption of Indian civilization was not possible without adopting the Indian social system, that is to say, the caste system. While it is true that the word "*varṇa*" appears in Khmer inscriptions, there is no evidence that Khmer society was organized into what could be called a caste system. The word was borrowed to denote classes of Khmer society rather than castes per se.[57]

Culturally, art and architecture do show Indian influence, but not without modification through indigenous contributions. Some Southeast Asian monuments, such as Angkor and Barabudur, go beyond their Indian inspiration in scale and complexity. Sanskrit and Pāli were used in inscriptions, but local languages also are present. For instance, in the *maṇḍalas* of the middle Mekong and the Tonle Sap deltas, ancient Khmer was used in inscriptions alongside the Sanskrit ones; in the Dvāravatī *maṇḍalas*, ancient Mon; and in Śrīkṣetra, Pyu. But Indian and local languages were put to different uses. The former was used for eulogizing gods, the Buddha, and kings, while the latter was used for lists of offerings and of names of persons designated to take care of sanctuaries. In areas where Buddhism prevailed, there were also inscriptions using only vernacular scripts to record meritorious deeds. Sanskrit and Pāli were both used in the service of the king and religions. In instances where Pāli Buddhism prevailed, Pāli appears to be the religious language and Sanskrit the royal language.

There is evidence that the *maṇḍalas* maintained regular contact with each other. Art and architecture reflect influences from neighboring regions: the Khmer style is found in central Thailand; and the Dvāravatī style is found in Śrīvijayan art in the south of Thailand. Most likely, these relations were peaceful.

Judging from the volatility of their political situation, the expansion of these *maṇḍalas* should be regarded as cultural rather than as territorial. However, this does not mean that territorial expansion did not occur, only that its activities and impact lasted only for a short time, usually confined to the reign of a particular, ambitious, and powerful overlord. We can safely say that these *maṇḍalas* were culturally centralized areas, and that at times one or the other of them became culturally dominant beyond solely local spheres. Therefore, when we use the names of these *maṇḍalas* in this study, it is the cultural sense that is intended. The study of these relations can perhaps be called re-localization or sub-regionalization.

Broadly speaking, in terms of religions we can discern two axes: the first from Burma in the west to Thailand in the east, where Hīnayāna Buddhism seems to have dominated; the second from Cambodia to the southern regions of greater Southeast Asia, the archipelago, where Hinduism and Mahāyāna Buddhism dominated.

Without these religions, Indian culture in Southeast Asia would not have endured and flourished until the present day. If the Hindu and Buddhist faiths had not been adopted (and manipulated) by local and regional overlords, these faiths could have never exerted such a strong influence in the region. It was through Hinduism and Buddhism that language and its scripts, literature, law, and political concepts came to Southeast Asia. And, it was through them that the peoples of Southeast Asian elevated their cultures, applying Indian culture to different fields in such a way that it is possible to study this region as a whole.

2
Early Belief Systems in Mainland Southeast Asia

There are many kinds of traditional beliefs that play important roles in shaping Southeast Asian history, but for the most part, these beliefs have been left unstudied. In this chapter we shall try to disentangle and understand the beliefs that can be termed "unsystematic" or "prehistoric."[1]

What we mean by "early belief system" is the belief system that existed before the advent of Indic religions. This system could be referred to as "prehistoric" in contrast to the "historic" religions of Brahmanism and Buddhism. In most instances, these religions should be considered as a cultural, rather than as a purely religious phenomenon.[2] Hence, the term "belief system" here means a system of cultural beliefs rather than religious beliefs per se. In other words, these are beliefs that arose between the local traditions and the imported religions, and were transmitted from one generation to the next by the social processes of education and enculturation. Cultural beliefs, in this sense, are inseparable from the societal, political, and economic spheres of a community. Even in the case of the historic religions, Southeast Asians seem to have integrated them rather unconsciously as part of their culture or tradition. For this reason, some Southeast Asians might profess that they belong to a specific religion but in actual fact might practice different faiths simultaneously without any misgivings.[3]

In this context, mainland Southeast Asia will be limited to what are now called the Theravāda countries of Burma, Thailand, Laos, and Cambodia. Even this is a presumption that there is unanimity for the term "Southeast Asia" and that "Theravāda" Buddhism is a clear-cut category. The term "Southeast Asia," as noted in chapter 1, poses many problems, as the term was first used to designate a political entity, and then later became a geographical designation rather than a cultural one.[4] When the term is applied to cultural studies, one is confronted with many diverse languages, social structures, beliefs, and so on. Even if a religious division or grouping is relatively easy to assert, it masks differences in local perception, acculturation, and the transformation and development of belief systems. To complicate the task even further, there was and continues to be intra- and/or extra-regional contact.

If our concern is only with a pre-Indic or a prehistoric belief system, problems still abound. The term "prehistoric" usually means that this pre-Indic or indigenous belief belongs solely to prehistory and has long since disappeared. In fact, as a traditional phenomenon, it never disappeared completely; it is both a part of the historic past and remains part of contemporary history. It is possible that the belief system remained the same, or that it was transformed, adapted, affected by, as well as affecting, the historic religions. Indigenous beliefs are generally considered to belong to the time before Indianization. Even though indigenous beliefs originated in the prehistoric period, they continue to be present today. Those beliefs might have been modified by Indian culture, but they also took an active part in modifying Indian and other historic cultures. Indigenous beliefs should not be considered a substratum of Southeast Asian culture as compared to the Indianized belief system; on the contrary, there was a mutual exchange between them.

Archaeological data from the prehistoric period is scant and interpretations of it are, in most cases, speculative. The data might belong to groups of people different from present ones. The migration patterns of these people are unknown, but it can be assumed that even if they were different people, racially or ethnically, still their culture belongs to the region and has been passed on. There are also anthropological studies based on legends, myths, and folklore, as well as studies based on the present cultures whose traditions, originally thought to be non-Indic, persist. This data provides additional knowledge of an indigenous belief system, even though it remains speculative.[5]

Besides interpretative issues, there is the problem of the uneven quality of the data, both archaeological and anthropological. Studies in these two fields have been more abundant in Thailand, while elsewhere in the region data is more limited. A cautionary approach must be taken since this data cannot be generalized and assumed to have occurred in every area under discussion. Even sites described as a Paleolithic or hunter-gatherer society could very well have existed at the same time as Neolithic sites.

ARCHAEOLOGICAL DATA

Burial rites and customs are one important source of data that can provide clues about early belief systems. Archaeological reports give us various descriptions of prehistoric burial grounds. In addition to the general description of the site, details of the skeletal remains found are described primarily in terms of bodily position, head orientation, body ornaments, and burial offerings.

This data provides a general idea of life and society in the particular community excavated. These burial practices show little change over time.

For the hunter-gatherer period, certain data exists for Burma and Thailand. The sites belong to the Hoabinhian culture, an archaeological designation for this period in mainland Southeast Asia.[6] In Burma no burial sites from this period have been found, but there are sites in Thailand that are described as Paleolithic or hunter-gatherer. One exceptional site shows evidence of a long successive burial tradition. Instinctively, one might think that hunter-gatherer burial sites would be rare, however, the coastline area at Khok Phanom Di was continuously occupied by a hunter-gatherer community for four hundred years from 2000 BCE to 1600 BCE, a sufficient length of time for these people to have developed burial rites.

The designation "hunter-gatherers" suggests a community that relocates often in the search of food. Higham's comments on this point are worth noting:

> Most people, when asked how they imagine life must have been as a hunter-gatherer, reply that it meant being constantly on the move in small groups, in order to find sufficient food. This is a myth. Particularly when occupying rich environments, hunter-gatherers rarely if ever need to move, have little if any concern for their food supply, can develop large communities and are known to have distinctions in rank and wealth. In Thailand we have identified hunter-gatherer sites in upland caves, beside rivers and along former shorelines.[7]

If these hunter-gatherers advanced into large communities with social distinctions of rank and wealth as well as a burial tradition, then can it be assumed that they had or shared a belief system that governed or directed those burial rites? The graves seem to suggest that there was a discernible pattern in interring the dead. With knowledge of agriculture, the Neolithic Age began, allowing communities to become larger, growing more foodstuffs, which eliminated the constant need to hunt and gather. This change allowed time for creating ritual objects and developing rites to bury the dead. Even so, Neolithic, Bronze, and Iron Age burials differ very little in principle from the Paleolithic ones, which suggests a consistency in the belief system regardless of whether people hunted and gathered or cultivated crops.

Gravesites that date from the Paleolithic and Neolithic Ages were usually located on high ground or in mounds. Some sites were found with postholes indicating the presence of structures built over the graves. Higham is cautious here, saying only that postholes indicate the presence of structures built over grave clusters." Janice Stargardt in her description of a Neolithic-Iron Age site in Burma is more precise. She regards burial sites as dwelling places, and concludes that the burial pits were dug among the postholes of these ancient houses. In such a way, she suggests, the dead remained in close proximity to the living.[8]

Each site follows a uniform pattern in terms of body position and the orientation of the corpse's head. In a site with evidence of a lengthy occupation, there might be several layers of graves, which shows some evolution in the development of the pattern, but most of the differences are in the kind of offerings found in the graves and who was buried there, males, females, or children.[9]

It is evident that these graves had been carefully prepared, not just crudely dug out. A procedure was followed to prepare the corpse for interment that included wrapping the remains in cloth shroud. The position of the body and the orientation of the head are uniform with some variation among different sites. Before placing the corpse on a wooden bier, some rituals must have been performed because the corpses were found sprinkled with red ochre. This strongly suggests that funeral rites or some well-established tradition for burying the dead at Khok Phanom Di existed and, by extension, at other sites as well with, of course, some variants.[10] This leads us to the conclusion that there was a belief system that prescribed specific rituals. The custom of painting the corpse red or scattering red ochre over the body is found in other burial sites around the world.[11] Some scholars think that the red ochre powder functions as a symbol for fire, or perhaps this custom comes from a deeper stratum of beliefs combined with a universal cosmological dichotomy, in which red denotes the world beyond. Painting the corpse red would lead the deceased from the world of the living to the world of the dead. Others suggest that because red is the color of blood, the red ochre powder symbolizes vitality and life. In some cases, it can be established that burials in the same sites belong to the same family, which could make a strong case for ancestor worship. However, it is only conjecture to draw any conclusions from such meager data.

In most of the excavated sites, the corpses were positioned with the head to the east. There appears to be no discernible difference between males and females, with the exception of one site where the males and females were positioned in different directions. In one instance, two corpses were buried in a cross-shaped grave. Usually corpses were inhumed in a supine, extended position. In some other sites, the bodies were placed upright but in a crouching position.[12]

At Khok Phanom Di six mortuary phases of graves were discovered. Beginning from the second phase on, there is the first hint of a different treatment for males and females. At this site, a male was interred with a turtle carapace ornament, and a female with a clay anvil. This set a pattern that was found in other burial sites. At another site, the distinction was made between males and females by placing them in different directions.[13] Little difference could be found in the kinds of burial objects interred with the corpses. Children were accorded the same burial rites as adults, but in most sites, infants were buried in jars.

Ornaments and burial offerings differed according to a specific site. At some sites imported objects were found, which suggests a pattern of preplanning. The most common burial objects found were pottery and stone implements, which continued to be placed in graves at much later periods. During the Bronze and Iron Ages, bronze or iron vessels and utensils were rarely found as grave offerings. Some Dvāravatī gravesites are reported to have stone implements from prehistoric times. Other burial objects include shell disc beads, shell beads, and even barrels of shells. The shells indicate wealth and rank, because shells, especially cowries, were used as a means of monetary exchange. Cowries as currency have a long tradition and only became obsolete a hundred years ago in Southeast Asia.

Some graves contain more objects and more exotic items, which could be an indication of high status in the community. In one Neolithic grave, a skeleton of an old man was found with a perforated stone disk and an antler with the tines sawed off. Per Sørensen, the archaeologist who excavated this site, suggests that these items could be parts of a shaman headdress. This, in my opinion, is dubious.

Bones of animals or other parts of animals often were found interred or placed close to a particular part of a corpse. This seems to suggest a belief in animal worship at some of these sites. In a hunter-gatherer society the bond between humans and animals was very important and must have been integral to the belief system, but the available data is too scanty to draw any conclusions.[14] In one site, a female was interred with a crocodile skeleton and a child was wrapped in a crocodile skin. For Higham, this suggests a totemic culture, but the practice was insufficiently widespread to generalize that this find is evidence of totemic beliefs. Furthermore, some pottery vessels were intentionally broken and scattered under and around the corpses. In one grave, a stone phallus was found, and at Ban Don Ta Phet, an Iron Age site, a carnelian lion was found.

With all of these grave offerings as evidence, it is possible to conclude that a belief in life after death existed. Could it be that these objects, such as vessels, were intended for use in the world of the dead as they were used in the world of the living? Or, perhaps these utensils belonged to the deceased and were buried with them.[15] Children and infants were buried with grave offerings like pottery vessels, even though infants had no use for them in this world. However, the fact remains that these objects were gifts for the dead to use in the next world. Intriguing as this evidence is, it cannot be extended to the concept of transmigration or rebirth.

In other sites, a different type of inhumation was practiced side by side with primary burials. Even reburials were discovered. The corpse was exposed to be *décarnisé* or cremated before being interred in either a dolmen or a clay jar. In earlier sites inhumation in a jar usually was confined to infants. Considering that large stones were used for this type of grave, requiring a lot of manpower, this suggests that a strong leader who exercised control over a sizeable community was essential. Could it be possible that such stones were used for the burial of the chief, the "man of prowess"? In the twentieth century, there are reports of this practice for a chief of an island.[16] Therefore, Megalithic culture cannot be called prehistoric in this region, but instead, should be considered part of history, which is more or less still extant.

Not all Megalithic cultures buried their dead. In Thailand, some megalithic structures appear to be monuments or shrines linked to an earth cult.[17] The *sīmā* or boundary stones found in northeast Thailand and elsewhere could be remnants of an old megalithic cult. Furthermore, people consider *sīmā* to be not only a boundary stone (*nimitta*) used to demarcate the area for *saṅghakarma*, but also a stone with magical powers that needs to be propitiated.

In Burma and northern Laos, megalithic burial sites have been found alongside cremated remains, which were then reburied in a dolmen or a jar. Some scholars interpret cremation as evidence for a Buddhist cult, and regard Buddhism as the sole factor that transformed the burial rites of this region from burials to cremation.[18] However, this ignores the fact that cremation precedes the Buddha's time, and that the pre-Buddhist *stūpa* cult can also be regarded as a reburial. Considering this, it is possible that the Buddhist *stūpa* cult could be seen as megalithic. Funeral rites, for burials or cremations, did not result from Buddhism. The Buddhist practice of making merit for the dead was a later addition. However, the custom of preparing the corpse for interment or cremation seems to have predated Buddhism and remains unchanged.

Bronze drums may well be further evidence of a Megalithic culture of Southeast Asia, one that continues from prehistoric times. Bronze drums may have originated in the area of northern Vietnam around the middle of the first millennium BCE during the late Bronze Age. But whether or not they originated with the Vietnamese remains a debatable issue.[19] Bronze drums are still being cast and used in Laos and some islands of Indonesia. Old bronze drums also are still in use in various ceremonies in the court of Thailand, in Burma, and among the hill tribe peoples in Cambodia and Laos.

The drums' designs reveal religious and cultural beliefs. The designs are found on two parts of the drums: the tympan and the mantle, even though the drums themselves vary in type and vary when and where they were cast. Regardless of drum type, the center of the tympan is uniformly depicted with what is called the "solar star," featuring one or more concentric bands of geometric shapes, animals, flying birds, and sometimes scenes with figures. The solar star or the sun was thought to be the center of the universe and the concentric bands seem to suggest a cosmological pattern. On one of the drums found in Bali (but thought to be cast in the area near the China-Vietnam border) there is an inscription in Chinese. The decipherable characters read *san jie*, meaning the "Triple World," a Buddhist term. This inscription seems to suggest that the pattern on the tympan of this drum represents the Buddhist cosmology, although this is not true of all the drums.

Bernet Kempers and August Johan, who studied different types of bronze drums from different locations of Southeast Asia, classified the designs into two categories: geometric patterns and figure scenes. Some of the drums have been found with both designs. The figures usually consisted of feathered warriors, dancers, or musicians in procession between houses of a village. Kempers and Johan theorized that these houses formerly were ordinary houses that were later transformed into a kind of "primeval village" where the deceased, borne in the procession, would return. If Kempers and Johan's theory proves correct, then the design would seem to depict funeral rites within the context of a cosmological map.

The source for Kempers and Johan's interpretation may come from Hans Schärer's study of the cosmological maps used in the funeral rites of the Ngaju Dayak of Borneo. Schärer, a Swiss Protestant missionary, wrote his doctoral thesis on the topic, and studied the drawings of four cosmological maps, which depicted the upper world (heaven) and the underworld (hell) together with a village of the dead. Schärer identified associated objects with these places that included a boat for the soul used to transport the dead to the underworld, a boat used by the supreme deities for their journey to earth, a "tree of life," and an individual house within the upper world, among other associated objects. These maps were used as visual mnemonics in the ritual.[20]

The style and the design of these maps are not comparable to those of the bronze drums. The figured scenes thought to be a funeral procession lacked a corpse. The only remote resemblance to the drum's designs was the shape of the house, which, again, was similar to those found in Indonesia. This meager data is of little use in making any conclusion or interpretation of the figure scene on the bronze drums.

In China's Yunnan Province, some drums have a three-dimensional decorative design on the tympan. The Yunnan bronze drums are among the most evocative and remarkable examples of bronze casting in non-Chinese East Asia. They depict scenes of human sacrifice, horse riding, offerings of allegiance to a lord, women weaving on back-strap looms, houses, and many kinds of animals. Later examples feature three-dimensional frogs or toads. If these frogs are shown copulating, it is said that they are connected to fertility or rain cults.

Not only are the drums an example of a prehistoric artifact, but they are a protohistoric one as well. Bronze drums probably were cast during a period of time from 600 BCE until 500 CE, and in some parts of highland and insular Southeast Asia, they continue to be part of the lived tradition. The designs on the drums may trace their origins to a Neolithic community of bronze casters. Other groups could have appropriated the drums for their own use. That they were used in funeral rites is undeniable. However, we should not limit their function solely to this use.

Drums were used in a variety of functions in different traditions. In and of themselves, the drums possessed an aura of magic and sacredness. Bronze was a new metal that was introduced at the end of the Stone Age. The skilled knowledge to forge and the accompanying power of owning bronze utensils was awe inspiring. Bronze drums must have been the sole prerogative of the chief or the leader, rather than the common folk. The drums could have originated as a musical or rhythmic instrument, no doubt for ceremonial purposes, gradually acquiring their magical and sacred qualities. Drums served, and in some places still serve, as the emblem of the chief and the center of the community. And, they have been used in fertility and rainmaking cults.

Depictions of ships on the drums suggest that seafarers might have used them as sacred objects to ward off the dangers of the sea, or perhaps they were used simply as instruments to sound a rhythmic beat for the oarsmen. Could these ships represent vessels that would transport the dead to an original, primeval, heavenly land? It is purely speculative and hypothetical, unless one believes that contemporary bronze casters are the direct descendants of the original bronze drum casters. Designs on the drums reveal that they were used for other than funerary rites, and music may have played a role in such ceremonies.

During the Bronze Age in Southeast Asia, bronze drums were closely connected through trade and commerce within the region, and perhaps the world beyond. They represented multiple meanings, different values, and were put to various uses in the various societies in Southeast Asia, both mainland and insular. What cannot be certified is any definitive meaning or how significant these drums were as religious objects.

On the basis of the data gleaned from archeological sites, we can conclude with some certainty that funeral rites existed in various prehistoric communities. The postholes found above the graves suggest that there were some kind of structures built over the graves. These structures might have served as shrines erected for sacrificial or ceremonial purposes. Bones of animals found scattered around the graves or animals buried with the bodies are suggestive of sacrificial offerings. If this is the case, then one can postulate there was some form of ancestor worship or perhaps a priest-chief. In other places where a Megalithic culture was present, we may be more confident in suggesting the existence of ancestor worship. Later on, the cults of great monuments and the *sīmā* cult of northeast Thailand arose. The belief in an afterlife and the practice of ancestor worship adapted quite well to the Buddhist concept of merit transfer.

Did other rites exist for birth, marriage, or fertility? There is no strong evidence to assume that such rites existed, unless one considers the different burial positions for males, females, children, and infants. That difference might be social or religious; but at this point, it cannot be interpreted.

The fact that the dead were carefully buried suggests that these people had a belief in an afterlife or a world of the dead that paralleled the world of the living. This assumption is reinforced by various offerings found in graves, which were intended for the dead to use. One could also speculate that the utensils interred belonged to the deceased and a taboo was in place that prevented continued use by the living. In the case of infants buried in miniature clay jars, it is clear that these jars were made specifically for the inhumation of an infant who never had a chance to use it. Some vessels were found that were intentionally broken, so can we infer that they were meant for the other world? This practice of intentional breaking of vessels used in funerary rituals can still be found in many cultures of Southeast Asia.

Whether or not prehistoric peoples believed that life continued after death but in a different form, or if there was a place where the dead could live as they had lived on earth, no one can say with any certainty. Both cases presuppose a belief in some entity that could be passed on for another life or to be used in another world. Could they have had a concept of the dichotomy between body and spirit? Given the fact that people in Southeast Asia today believe in many kinds of spirits, even spirits inhabiting inanimate objects, it is reasonable to assume that these prehistoric people could have held similar beliefs.

In some burial sites, corpses were found with extravagant offerings and ornaments. Some archaeologists speculate that these corpses, whether male or female, might have been shamans. Others say that they were just wealthy members of the society, or individuals belonging to the "founder line." If they were shamans, then this is a religiously significant fact, for the rites and ceremonies would need a leader to perform them. But were they shamans whose function was to control and contact the spirits, or were they mediums possessed and controlled by the spirits? We cannot know for certain exactly who they were because one cannot rely solely upon the basis of offerings and ornaments to extrapolate what functions they might have performed. These corpses could be shamans, spirit mediums, clan chiefs, or simply wealthy elites. Given that a chief would be wealthy and may have possessed an air of mystery or charisma, he could have fulfilled both the role of priest and village head.[21]

A stone phallus was found at one site, suggesting that a fertility cult or a phallic cult existed there. However, since only one example was found, no assumptions can be drawn on only a single piece of evidence. Similarly, in a grave of an Iron Age site, a carnelian lion was found as a grave offering. Higham and Thosarat Rachanie have theorized that the lion in this context can be interpreted as a Buddhist object:

> The location of Ban Don Ta Phet would have facilitated its participation in a trading network for, in a sense, it lies at the Thai gateway to India. The Three Pagodas Pass to the west connects the rich lowlands of Kanchanaburi with the Andaman Sea and so to India. Glover (1989, 1990) has emphasized the strong evidence in favor of exchange contacts between these two regions from at least

> the fourth century BC which brought not only the new range of exotic ornaments, but also ideas. We have noted the presence of a carnelian lion: the lion was an early means of representing the Buddha before it became acceptable to portray him in human form. So here, in the early Iron Age cemetery, we can detect the first seeds in the spread of Buddhism into Thailand, which were to provide for such strong and vigorous growth over the ensuing millennia.[22]

However, this interpretation seems to be suspect, because a stone lion alone cannot be interpreted as a symbol of the Buddha; more evidence than that is required.

In some instances of Bronze Age burial sites, clay figurines of humans and cattle were found as grave offerings. Even though these human figurines do not appear to be gods or goddesses, the possibility that they might have had a religious function cannot be ruled out. Cattle figurines might represent food, and human figurines might represent servants. Because this is a common practice in China, there could be a cultural connection between the two regions, but, for want of any comparative studies or direct evidence, this is only an assumption.

The most common head orientation in the burial sites is to the east, with some exceptions to the northeast. This seems to be nearly universal since it is found in almost all prehistoric sites worldwide. If corpses are found with the head oriented in a different direction, it could be due to gravesite movement by rivers or streams flowing into that particular location.[23] Was there any special attachment to the sun? Even though bronze drums were not cast in the Stone Age, they often feature a solar star in the center of their tympan. This could suggest a belief in the sun as a god or as the center of the universe.[24] It was common practice to build or dig graves on high ground or mounds. Was the reason to avoid the floodwaters or does it signify some mystical aspect of the gravesite? It has also been noted that burials found on high ground suggest a belief in the protective power of the dead over the community. If Stargardt is right, then the interment near houses might suggest the protective power of the dead over the living and, hence, the presence of a belief in ancestor worship.

ANTHROPOLOGICAL DATA

When considering the anthropological data for clues to our inquiries, one notes that this data is also incomplete. Myths and legends from Burma and

Cambodia are protohistoric, that is to say, they emerge from the first contact between the region and Indian civilization. We find among the Tai people that their cosmogonic tales relate how human beings of different groups were created and how different cultures developed. Yet there is no certainty that these myths are pre-Indic. The only known criterion is that if a myth or legend is not found in India, then it should be considered indigenous.

Siraporn (Thitathan) Nathalang in her research on the Tai, which also includes other ethnic groups and Laos, concludes that creation myths comprise three types of cosmogonic tales, which are also found among some tribes in Burma.[25] She describes them as follows: "First, stories about 'Pu Sanggasa-Ya Sagasi' (Grandfather Sagasa-Grandmother Sagasi) as the world and human creators; second, stories about the sacred gourd as the origin of the people; third, stories about 'Devada' (Hindu or Buddhist deities) eating the fragrant soil and becoming the ancestors of human beings."[26]

The first two types are Tai or indigenous in nature, but in some versions they are "buddhisticized" by having the Buddha narrate the stories. The third story, a modification of the *Aggaññasutta*, is obviously of Buddhist origin. The first type features a creator who creates the primordial pair, who in turn, creates or generates human beings, animals, and other physical objects. The pair teaches people to grow rice. In some versions, the primordial pair is regarded as the first creators and in other versions human beings and animals made of clay or earth are said to become alive with *cittaviññaṇa* (living force) given by the primordial pair. In another version, the gods send their descendents to rule the world by climbing down a ladder from the sky, or have the elders of the world ask the gods to send down the leaders, who then teach the people how to grow rice and produce fine crafts.

The second type of creation myth relates the story of human origins. There are several versions, but the main theme is that human beings emerged into the world out of a gourd of divine origin. As the story goes, different ethnic groups come out of the gourd successively, usually beginning with the oldest tribal groups with the Tai being the last. This might reflect an actual historical event that the Tai were indeed the last group to migrate to the area. In some versions, the gourd event occurs after a great flood when the god, Thaen,[27] brings the gourd to earth, whereupon he drills a hold in it to let out the human beings and animals he had placed inside. In other versions, the gourd just appears and the god, who wonders what is inside, breaks the gourd. Some scholars attribute the cause of the flood to the failure of the people to give food offerings to the god, who then became angry and caused the flood.

Later the god causes the waters to subside and sends a buffalo so the people could work the rice fields. When the buffalo dies, a gourd comes out of its mouth. An elder then drills a hole in the gourd, and all races of people emerge.

From these various versions, Siraporn suggests that two ideas are significant. The first, which is extant among the northern Tai, emphasizes the celestial origin of Tai people and thus legitimizes the Tai and its rulers as supreme over all others. The concept of the ruler or the chief as descending from the gods or of celestial origins reinforces the status of the king, or to use Wolter's terminology, the "man of prowess," as sacred among the Tai. The second idea symbolizes the contact between the Tai and other tribes in the area of northern Laos and northern Vietnam who also have a story of the flood and the gourd. The main theme or point here is that all the races have the same origin.

The gourd has been interpreted as a symbol of fertility. The story of the god punishing people by causing the flood is seen as the dichotomy between the earth and the sky. Whereas the sky stands for righteousness and order, the earth or human beings represents disorder and disobedience; all becomes chaos. Because the god has the power to create, so, too, the god has the power to destroy. The emphasis seems to reside on the authority of the ruler who in his very person embodies both religious and political elements. He is the mediator between the realm of the seen and the realm of the unseen.

Rice culture is another component of these stories. All of the versions tell how the knowledge of rice growing comes into existence. They also relate how the god(s) or the primordial pair creates other cultural activities and crafts, a concept not unlike the Chinese myth of creation.

Belief in spirits or "forces" exists in all traditions of Southeast Asia. In general, these beliefs are absorbed under the term "animism." As with all the "-ism" terms, animism has various levels of meaning, and each society seems to have different ideas and concepts of the particular spirits in which they believe. In mainland Southeast Asia, the belief in spirits is ancient yet still very much alive today. Spirits are known by different terms in different traditions. Among the Tai they are called, *phii* (in Thai, *phi*), and in Burmese, *nat*, but basically, the concept is the same. These terms encompass not just the spirits of the deceased, but also divinities of all kinds that later became designated by the words, *deva* and *devatā*, and came to be applied to all celestial or benevolent spirits.

These various forces or spirits are more or less amorphous, existing as a form of energy, but nevertheless, a tangible form involved with and revolving around human beings. But because they are formless, they are believed to reside in places and objects.

The deceased generally are regarded as spirits. They travel to the other world and become *phii.*[28] Whether or not this includes a belief in a soul that migrates to the other world is not clear. Later the term used is the Pāli word, "*viññāṇa,*" a Buddhist term for consciousness. This is an example of how a Buddhist term replaced what was originally an indigenous concept. The deceased's *viññāṇa* leaves the body and goes to the other world. In some cultures the deceased takes the symbolic form of a butterfly, and is treated as an ancestor that receives due respect and sacrificial offerings. If the deceased belongs to the family of the chieftain or was a member of a royal line, he is regarded as the ancestor of the entire tribe or nation. It is normal for founders of dynasties and great kings to be revered as ancestors often with a cult of their own.[29] The main objective of ancestor worship is to perpetuate tradition and family lineage. This is clear in birth and marriage rites. In Tai languages, the violation of marriage vows is called *phid phii,* i.e., to offend the *phii.* The ancestors of a tribe or a nation by extension are responsible for or guard the laws and ritual traditions of that tribe or nation. This is evidence for the close relationship between ancestor worship and the law. Ancient laws of Southeast Asia were derived primarily from tribal customs and were legitimized by ancestor worship.

A different kind of spirit is a divine being. Everything has a divine aspect residing in it or guarding it. These are the spirits that reside in special places like houses, villages, towns, cities, countries, rivers, mountains, oddly-shaped rocks, mounds, trees, forests, rice fields, land, a pier, and so on. The characteristic of these spirits comes very close to the concept of energy or a force residing in or intensifying some entity. The locality is usually specified. For example, in a house, the spirit of a house is located in the main post, or, in a village, the spirit is located at the main crossroad. A city or a capital has a city pillar and some special divinities such as Phra Chua (a lineage divinity) and Phra Song Muang (lord of the city).[30] Later, many of these spirits were Indianized and became Hindu deities or Buddha images. Some spirits such as Chao Thii (Chao Thi) (lord of the land),[31] who is supposed to guard the land on which a house is built, have been supplanted by Phra Bhumi (Phra Phum), lord of the earth. A shrine for the Chao Thii will be placed somewhat lower than the Phra Bhumi shrine, because the latter governs the entire world. Locality divinities are closely connected to the leader of a particular community. The order of importance goes up hierarchically from the divinity of the village with its leader up to the divinity of the nation with its ruler or king.

The reason why a belief in spirits is so important in an agricultural society is due to the uncertainty of nature that leads people to offer sacrifices as a means to gain favor of the spiritual powers that are believed to control fertility and all life. The leaders who organize the sacrifices are not only esteemed highly by their subjects, but they gain spiritual powers as well. Such tribal chiefs are assumed to be similar to "men of prowess" who were the leaders of protohistoric chiefdoms.[32] What is noteworthy about these tribal chiefs, and presumably about early leaders of the same type, is that because of the vagaries of life, their potency could never be firmly established. Attempts were made to secure this potency by making the remains of these "men of prowess" objects of cultic attention, especially by those who succeeded them. Affirmation took place by identifying with or taking over the divine spirit that belonged to that locale. Perhaps because of the dual character of its leaders, Southeast Asia never developed a priestly class. As the ritual effectiveness of "men of prowess" waxed and waned, so too did the relative power of the polities they ruled.

Spirits of the deceased also could become powerful and localized to such a degree that a chief or a king, in order to control other tribes or regions with which the spirit is identified, had to accept its higher authority and pay due respect. In some instances, a king might try to control the spirits by limiting their authority, as in the case of Aniruddha of Burma, who by trying to limit the cult of the *nat*, systematized it and unintentionally elevated it, whereas among the Tai and the Khmer, local spirits were allowed to flourish and were never structured into a cult like the *nat* in Burma.[33]

It is noteworthy to observe that not all spirits are powerful, or equally powerful. Before they became amorphous, these spirits were considered to be a force or energy abiding in all places and things, but not every place or thing was filled with a spirit. There are many conditions that make spirits forceful. In the case of local spirits, the specific locality seems to be one of the chief factors in making that spirit powerful. Later on, this concept was applied to Buddha images. In the same way as spirits, not every image is powerful, but certain images are considered to be powerful and thus more important than others. It was not infrequent that the image of a vanquished country was appropriated or destroyed by a conquering state to indicate a shift in political power. And that is how some spirits, a shrine, a Buddha image, or a *stūpa,* which were regarded initially as locally sacred, became regionalized, nationalized, or even internationalized through the patronage of a leader or a king, raising the status of that place to be a capital or an important city.

Among the Tai, a powerful spirit is said to be *raeng* (strong, mystically powerful) or *saksit*, from the Sanskrit, *śakti* and *siddhi*, which have come to mean having the power to accomplish, i.e., the power to grant boons. *Raeng* or *saksit* also convey the sense of the sacred and magical, and have a mystical quality. Divine spirits are *saksit* by nature, although not equal. Spirits of the deceased become *raeng* or *saksit* but for different reasons. For example, the spirits of those who died a violent death, or a mother with a stillborn child, or individuals who were killed unjustly—all are considered to be powerful. A great king who dies usually becomes an object of veneration and *saksit*. In Thailand, the king himself, even when he is alive, is considered *saksit*, and his head is called "*phra cao*," which means god. An image of the Buddha also can become *saksit* due to the particular materials used in fashioning the image. Likewise, a legend, or the reputation of some important monks or kings to grant a specific boon, or a specific locality—all can become *saksit*. Once spirits became *saksit*, titles such as *chao* (*pho* or *mae*), *naek ta*, or *nat* are prefixed to the names that in time came to be regarded as Indianized ones. These titles are mostly kinship terms, which suggests a close relationship or intimacy between the spirits and people. It is these powerful spirits that must be propitiated and paid respects to, since they can affect us either beneficially or malevolently.

There is another spirit, which comes neither from the dead nor from a divine being. It can be seen as the life spirit or vital force within either an animate or an inanimate being. Known as *khwan* among the Tai, it may cognate with *hon* in Vietnamese, *pralu'n* in Khmer, and without a doubt, *hun* in Chinese. One does not die when this vital force leaves the body, but one does become ill. This vital force is believed to reside in all human beings, animals, houses, rice fields, and so on. It promotes a sense of well-being and from time to time leaves the body for some reason, making it necessary for a ritual to be performed to call it back into the body. In addition to calling the *khwan* back into the body, there are the rites of making *khwan* to reinforce the *khwan*, and *su khwan*, which is part of the welcoming ceremony. This ritual of calling the *khwan* is also performed for weddings, ordinations, at the beginning of the planting season, and other important occasions. However, when it is performed at the beginning of the agricultural cycle, the ritual is used to reinforce the vital force residing in the earth, so that it remains fertile.

Regarding the first type of spirit that has the characteristics of force or energy and has the capacity to become powerful, the connection with human beings is quite interwoven. It is possible, therefore, for an object considered to be "powerful" to be owned by someone who possesses equal or greater "power." This idea connects easily to the adapted meaning of *pāramī*. A leader or a king possesses the *pāramī* or force to own or control the powerful places and objects within that place because he is the Lord of the Land, and he is the Lord of the Land due to all the good deeds he did in the past to perfect his *pāramī*. If one's power is not equal to the power of the place or the object, the king or leader can also propitiate the spirits with the proper rituals and invite them to be his own. It is possible to learn how to control these powerful spirits or even make a normal spirit or place powerful by means of *vidyā-āgom* or *vijjā-āgom,* from Pāli, or in Sanskrit, *vidyā* and *vijjā*, with *āgama* meaning the knowledge of spells and magic. *Vidyā-āgom* can come in the form of magical spells, certain vocal sounds, a diagram or magical design, rituals, charms, or amulets. In times past, this type of mystical knowledge was considered to be the highest form of knowledge.

This notion also can be applied to a *devarūpa*, a Buddha image, and amulets and charms, which can be made powerful or empowered by rites performed according to magical knowledge. It may also be done through the chanting of a special Buddhist mantra using a special text or by fierce concentration to draw power into the objects in question, like amulets. The words in Thai are *sek* (from *abhiṣeka*) and *pluk sek* (*pluk* meaning to wake something up). When consecrating a Buddha image, the ritual is called *buddhābhisek*. If amulets and charms are to be empowered, they are usually put into an oil casket used for lighting in a temple, so that when the monks chant, the power of the chants will be fixed into the amulets.

When speaking about traditional beliefs in mainland Southeast Asia, it is impossible to avoid a discussion of the word "superstition." It is generally believed that particular superstitious practices will help overcome uncertainty or unforeseen events.[34] Some superstitions are in the form of prohibition. The reasons for this are many, yet simple. For example, one avoids stepping directly on the threshold of a door opening; this is based on the necessities of house construction. The threshold is an integral part of the structural frame of the entire house. If it is removed or broken, the structural integrity of the house is compromised (i.e., the house will collapse). The prohibition against cutting one's nails at night has its origin in the simple fact that using a crude sharp instrument at night was dangerous before the age of electricity. Other superstitions originate from astrological beliefs. One must consult an astrologer in order to pinpoint the precise auspicious moment for all ceremonies to begin. In marriage rites, a bride and groom must be astrologically compatible. Other superstitions are concerned with the loss of *vidyā-āgom*, i.e., magical knowledge. Some believe that all magical and powerful objects will lose their potency if touched by a woman, or even if they pass beneath women's clothes.

Beliefs in the spirits, in *khwan*, and in superstitions become expressed or translated into rituals and ceremonies either to propitiate or empower or to prevent bad omens and ill luck. These beliefs are also expressed in *khrueng rang khong khlang* and *sing saksit*, i.e., such magical things as amulets, charms, magical diagrams, and body tattoos.

Rituals usually include offerings of food, especially meat and alcoholic beverages. Over time brahmans came to officiate at these rituals, but the offerings remained the same even when the rituals were not strictly in accord with Brahmanical rites. For ancestor worship, there were periodic rites for the funeral of the deceased, and annual rites were performed for ancestors collectively. Rites for paying homage to teachers could be considered ancestral as well. The ritual offering of food and wine is consistent with the concept of the transferring of merit to the dead. Powerful spirits and important Buddha images have specific dates for annual rites, some more than once a year.

Agricultural rites also constitute a major part of ritual life of a Southeast Asian. In Tai culture, rituals are performed before planting crops, during the growing season, during the harvest, and after the harvest. These rituals mainly concern rice growing, however, other crops warrant rituals as well. Rituals occur at national ceremonies such as the Royal Plowing Ceremony in which the king presides over the first plowing that ushers in the annual planting season.

Closely connected with agricultural rites are the fertility cults, heavy with sexual symbolism, and usually performed before the planting season begins. Phallic symbols function as charms to ward off bad luck and evil spirits. Later this merged with Indian phallic cults introduced into Southeast Asia. Sometimes spirits are called to ensure that the weather will be favorable for the growing of crops. Spirit possession is also undertaken to heal the sick or search for lost items. Rituals performed with or for the purpose of black magic and curses are not uncommon. These rituals should be seen as acts performed according to traditional beliefs, whereas chants and cultic or magical objects are tangible and portable materials that people can access for protection, prevention, or to repulse bad luck and ill omens. These objects include amulets, charms, tattoos and *yantra*s (magical patterns), which later drew upon Brahmanical and Buddhist power sources to add to their efficacy. The power residing in these things are drawn out, intensified, or fortified by means of magical knowledge.[35]

It is clear that pre-Indic influences existed in Southeast Asia with a long tradition of beliefs well before the advent of Indic religions. These traditions included beliefs in the world of the dead, ancestor worship, a concept of the "man of prowess," and many kinds of spirit cults. Rites, rituals, and ceremonies were well established before they were altered by or prefixed with Indian culture, which added its own layers of cosmological and cosmogonic concepts.

3

Introduction of Buddhism into Southeast Asia

Books on Southeast Asian Buddhism usually begin with the arrival of Buddhism in the region.[1] The problem is not, perhaps, Buddhism's entry into the region itself, but rather how, when, by whom, from which part of India, and to what part of Southeast Asia was Buddhism first introduced. The last question sometimes involves nationalistic pride concerning which country can claim to be the first to have become Buddhist.[2]

In this chapter we shall try to answer these questions, keeping in mind that the introduction of Buddhism did not occur in a single moment, nor as a single act, but during a long process over time. Buddhism was a living faith that flourished in India for more than fifteen centuries, developing and changing over the course of time. Religious contacts between India and Southeast Asia would have been affected by these developments. Therefore, it is likely that there was more than simply one introduction, but rather, multiple introductions. And, there was not the introduction of just one single kind of Buddhism, but of numerous schools of Buddhism. This fact, together with the extensive area exposed to Indian cultures to which Buddhism belongs, makes the issue even more complicated, because this allows for the possibility that different places were exposed to different types of Buddhism at the same time. And it is probable that some regions did not adopt Buddhism directly from India.

Sri Lankan chronicles attribute the introduction of Buddhism into Southeast Asia to the mission sent from India during Aśoka's reign.[3] However, there is no indisputable evidence to support this claim, either from archaeological or epigraphic sources. If one accepts the traditional account, the introduction of Buddhism would have been a very simple and straightforward event, involving only two monks who came to the region and converted the inhabitants. But historically speaking, the introduction of Buddhism was not an independent process but rather part of an overall process of Indianization in which trade, missions, and pilgrimage—as well as initiatives from within Southeast Asian culture itself—all played important roles.

Yet the problems related to the location of Suvarṇabhūmi and the mission as recorded in the Sri Lankan chronicles still must be confronted, because contemporary scholarship remains mired in misconceptions concerning these two matters. They shall be dealt with under the topics of trade relations and Buddhist missions, respectively.

TRADE RELATIONS BETWEEN INDIA, SRI LANKA, AND SOUTHEAST ASIA

The importance of trade as an agent of cultural innovation has been acknowledged by previous scholars, some of whom have made trade the sole agent of Indianization. However, with a better understanding of epigraphic and archaeological data, this claim is rendered inadequate.[4] The main objection to giving trade such a prominent role arises from the fact that Indianization entailed the introduction of a high culture beyond the ken of itinerant merchants, a culture that included the use of Sanskrit with all its poetic embellishments. But whatever the case may be, contact between these areas would have been impossible without trade, which provided not only the means of transporting brahmans and monks, i.e., the human factors in the acculturation process, but also the material objects of worship.

The nature of trade relations between India and Southeast Asia was crucial to the spread of Buddhism. The same may be said for the spread of Buddhism to Central Asia and China.[5] Nevertheless, because circumstances differed, the specific characteristics of Buddhism in the two regions differed as well. In order to understand how trade operated between these regions, it is necessary to examine the dynamics of that trade, looking at ports of departure, destinations, routes, and merchants.

THE NATURE OF TRADE RELATIONS IN SOUTHEAST ASIA

Southeast Asia has long been considered to be both a bridge and a barrier to trade between India and China.[6] Perhaps this notion has been overemphasized, causing us to see Southeast Asia as a mere stopover for merchants, rather than as their final destination. According to Indian sources, Southeast Asia was a primary destination, not simply a means of access to China. The same sources show that not only Indian merchants but also Southeast Asian ones were involved in trade.[7] Intra-regional trade, which evidently flourished around the second half of the first millennium BCE,[8] must also be taken into account.

In ancient times, when knowledge of navigation was not advanced, trade between India and China probably involved a progression of stages rather than just single trips. Indian ships sailing to Southeast Asia used cities along the western coast of the peninsula as entrepôts. Ships from other countries, Southeast Asian states, or China, would continue along the other half of the route. This was a common practice recorded by Chinese monks who went to India by sea.[9]

Indian literature, whether Buddhist or Brahmanical, does not give a complete description of these ancient trade routes,[10] but mention is made of the seaports from which the merchants departed. The *Jātaka,*[11] *Mahāniddesa,*[12] and *Milindapañha*[13] name as ports: Bharukaccha, Suppāraka, and Kālacampaka; the *Mahākarmavibhaṅga* names Mahākośalī and Tāmralipti.[14] Ships thus set sail from both coasts of India. If the *Jātaka, Mahāniddesa,* and *Milindapañha* are regarded as the earlier texts, dating no later than the second century or, for the *Mahāniddesa*, the third century CE,[15] then the most frequented seaports would have been ones on the west coast, namely, Bharukaccha and Suppāraka. These two ports are also identified as seaports in classical accounts to the Western world.[16] The trade between the West, the Indian subcontinent, and Southeast Asia has left evidence at some archaeological sites, not only seaports but also inland towns.[17] Even though artifacts found at these sites were not religious in nature, the possibility of religious contacts cannot be ruled out. While there are no artifacts that date from the third century BCE,[18] which would set them in the age of the Mauryan Empire in India, in view of the scant archaeological findings within India itself, one can hardly expect much evidence to be found beyond India. The only way to trace these relationships is through art forms that seem to reveal continuities with that early period. One such example is the *dharmacakra*s placed atop pillars found in central Thailand, which are reminiscent of the Aśokan pillar at Sañcī.[19] If place names—in many cases borrowed from important sites in India—can be used as evidence, then the names Dvāravatī and Kambujadeśa suggest contact with the western coast of India.

Later, seaports on the east coast of India, especially the southern part, become more prominent in the records, especially Chinese ones.[20] Evidence of South Indian influence, both epigraphic and archaeological, is abundant.[21] When we refer to South India in this context, we must include Sri Lanka, as it lies astride the east-west sea trade routes.[22] Nihar Ranjan Ray's contention that the Pāli Buddhism of the Pyu kingdom had South India as its only source of contact would be too narrow, since we cannot rule out early contacts between Sri Lanka and the Pyu.[23] Moreover, evidence for relations between South Indian and Sri Lankan Buddhism can be found in an inscription at Nāgārjunakoṇḍa, which states that missionaries from Sri Lanka had spread Buddhism to several places in India.[24]

Traders coming either from Sri Lanka or the east coast seaports of India would cross the high seas to the Nicobar Islands, also known as the Nāga Islands, which served as a convenient way station. From there traders continued on to Southeast Asia, primarily to the peninsula, either by following the coast to the archipelago or taking the trans-peninsular route and crossing both land and waterways to the east coast of the peninsula.[25] It is a geographical fact that only a few bays along the western side of the Malay peninsula provide a safe harbor for ships, but these sites were too small to sustain large communities. All the sizeable city-states were located on the east coast of the peninsula. The fact that the merchants kept using these trans-peninsular routes shows that these cities were well established long before trade relations began.

When the merchants reached Southeast Asia, the most frequently used route seems to have been along the upper part of the Malay peninsula, termed by Paul Wheatley as the "Isthmian part." This route led to central Thailand and continued eastward along the coast and along the river valleys. If merchants sailed to the lower part of the isthmus, then they would use the trans-peninsular routes to the east coast.[26] From there they had two choices: either continue northward along the coast, or cross the Gulf of Thailand to the Mekong delta and beyond.

Sites along these routes were the earliest ones to feel the influence of Indian culture. At least fifteen sites belonging to the so-called "Funanese culture," the earliest Indianized culture of Southeast Asia, are located in what is now central Thailand.[27] Since religion is part of a culture, the influence of Buddhism as well as Hinduism must have been felt soon after the initial contacts between India and Southeast Asia were made.

Trade followed the land and river routes to inland settlements and eventually to the hinterland. In such a way, Indian religion spread to other parts of Southeast Asia. The inland cities became centers of trade and culture in their own right.[28] There is also evidence of international contacts. For example, two votive tablets inscribed in Sanskrit and Chinese were found at Si Thep, an ancient site in the Pa Sak valley in the northern part of central Thailand.[29]

Navigation in the Indian Ocean depended upon the annual rhythms of the monsoon. When setting out from India, mariners usually followed the northeast monsoon, which blows from north to south. Then they waited for the southwest monsoon before continuing further east. As a result of the seasonal winds, the Malay peninsula was the area most exposed by Indian culture, and the one that first felt the changes and developments in India. By way of contrast, the inland areas of central Burma, central Thailand, and Cambodia would appropriate Indian culture somewhat more gradually, and thus develop more distinctive local styles.

In Indian and Sri Lankan sources, the land to their east is referred to as Suvarṇabhūmi. Some scholars identify Suvarṇabhūmi as the Mon kingdom in southern Burma. Others have suggested central Thailand, the Malay peninsula, or maritime Southeast Asia. Because the location of Suvarṇabhūmi directly relates to the introduction of Buddhism to the region, this question will be examined next in some detail.

WHERE WAS SUVARṆABHŪMI?

There are numerous references to Suvarṇabhūmi in Indian literature.[30] The impression they give is of a land to the east of India, where adventurers traveled to seek their fortunes. Suvarṇadvīpa, Suvarṇakūḍya, and Dvīpāntara are other names that refer to the same area or neighboring regions.[31]

Scholars agree on one point: Suvarṇabhūmi was situated in Southeast Asia. But here agreement ends and arguments as to the exact location of Suvarṇabhūmi begin. The Indian references are shrouded in myth and fantastical language, and do not answer the question. Some of the *Jātakas* do name the routes and ports frequented by the merchants at the time, but the destination is always given simply as Suvarṇabhūmi without any further details. In some Buddhist texts, lists of place names along with the one of Suvarṇabhūmi give some idea of where and what Suvarṇabhūmi was considered to be.

The earliest mention of Suvarṇabhūmi is probably the one from the *Mahāniddesa,* a canonical work dating around 250 BCE. A passage from this text reads as follows:

> Overwhelmed by greed, [people] seeking wealth would set sail across the great ocean in quest of riches . . . going to Gumba, Takkola, Takkasīla, Kālamukha, Maraṇapāra, Vesuṅga, Verāpatha, Java, Tamalī, Vaṅga, Eöavaddana, Suvaṇṇakūta, Suvaṇṇabhūmi, Tambapaṇṇi, Suppāra, Bharukaccha, Suraṭṭha, Aṅgaṇeka, Gaṅgaṇa, Paramagaṅgaṇa, Yona, Paramayona, Allasanda . . .[32]

Perhaps the author of the *Mahāniddesa* had some vague notions of where the places were located. Takkasīla, for example, is in India and accessible only by land; other sites are seaports in India. The list does not follow any logical geographical sequence. In his "Ptolémée, le Niddesa et la Bṛhatkathā,"[33] Sylvain Lévi attempts to identify these place names with those mentioned by Ptolemy. He locates Takkola in the Kra isthmus. For Lévi, Takkasīla poses a more serious problem if he wants to retain the sequence in Southeast Asia because Takkasīla is located in northwest India. Ptolemy comes to his rescue by providing the name, Tokosanna, a place that came to be identified as being in Burma. By equating the two names, Lévi identifies the Takkasīla of the *Mahāniddesa* with Ptolemy's Tokosanna. As for Vaṅga, this is an old name for Bengal, but since this does not fit into the proposed sequence, Lévi identifies it as Banka, an island near Sumatra, and in such a way excuses the author of the *Mahāniddesa* for a lack of geographical knowledge. Levi identifies the other names that follow with locations in maritime Southeast Asia. He takes great care, however, in identifying Suvarṇabhūmi, saying only that it must be in the area east of the Bay of Bengal, and that the term should be treated as a directional name and not a regional one.[34]

There are discrepancies in Lévi's account caused by his attempt to treat the list as geographically sequential. That the list cannot be taken sequentially is clearly shown by names such as Takkasīla, identified by Lévi as Tokosanna, which is to the north of Takkola. This violates Lévi's own sequence, which should run southward from locations on the western coast of the Malay peninsula down the entire archipelago.

In addition, Takkola, Suvaṇṇakūṭa (Suvarṇakūḍya), and even Tambapaṇṇi (generally agreed to be Sri Lanka) can be located also on the Indian subcontinent. B. C. Law identifies both Suvarṇakūḍya and Suvarṇabhūmi as Suvarṇakūḍya and Suvarṇagiri in India. Were it not for the fact that the *Jātaka* and other sources clearly describe Suvarṇabhūmi as a place that could be reached by sea from India (even if there is no indication that it was a seaport), one would have to agree with Law.[35] But this objection can be easily set aside, as it was common practice in Southeast Asia to give Indian names to local sites.[36]

The only guide that points to these places being outside of India is the phrase, "set sail in the ocean."[37] But since Lévi accepts Suppāra, Bharukaccha, Suraṭṭha, and so on to be Indian cities and seaports, the statement fails to carry any weight. Hence, one cannot fully agree with him when he concludes that the *Mahāniddesa* list conforms to Ptolemy's description.

Now let us consider the Indian seaports on the list, all of which are situated on the western coast of India, but the destinations of the merchants who set out from them, if Lévi's identification is correct, are located on the east coast. From Lévi's account, one would expect the seaports to be on the east coast of India, otherwise we would have to assume that the author of the *Mahāniddesa,* as well as the authors of the *Milindapañha* and *Jātaka,* lived in western India and had no geographical knowledge of eastern India. Perhaps the trading activities were between India and Southeast Asia and the Western world, i.e., the Middle East and the Roman Empire. After stopping at a west coast Indian seaport, a ship would sail around Cape Comarin, passing Sri Lanka, and then crossing the ocean directly toward Southeast Asia.

From other sources, such as the *Mahākarmavibhaṅga,* the Pāli commentaries, and collections of tales from Sri Lanka, Tāmralipti, an east coast Indian seaport, is mentioned as the point of departure for merchants traveling to Suvarṇabhūmi. This supports the theory that Suvarṇabhūmi was a region to the east of India. Nevertheless, the author of the *Mahākarmavibhaṅga* always mentions the name Suvarṇabhūmi before Sīhaladvīpa (Sri Lanka). If this is regarded as a geographical sequence, then Suvarṇabhūmi would have to be closer to the author than Sīhaladvīpa, and Law's suggestion that Suvarṇabhūmi was Suvarṇagiri, a viceroyalty in Aśoka's time, would make sense. However, the author might be simply giving Suvarṇadvīpa and Sīhaladvīpa as examples of faraway places about which he had only sketchy knowledge. In this case, the sequence would have no significance in identifying the location of Suvarṇabhūmi.[38]

In Indian geographical terminology, a region is usually designated when the suffixes *deśa* or *patha* are attached to a place name, as in, for example, Madhyadeśa or Dakṣiṇapatha. For cities, only the name is given. In the *Mahāniddesa,* lists of regions and cities are mixed together. Nevertheless, names such as Suvarṇakūḍya and Suvarṇabhūmi, being affixed by "geographical terms," should be regarded as names of regions rather than cities or seaports.

Therefore, according to Indian sources, Suvarṇabhūmi or Suvarṇadvīpa should indicate an area either in India proper or a region to the east of India, but not a state or a city. If these sources do not describe an actual route, one cannot be entirely confident that Suvarṇabhūmi is a land beyond the confines of India. If the route mentioned indicates that Suvarṇabhūmi can be reached only by sea, then one can be more secure about locating it in Southeast Asia.

The region was well frequented by Indian merchants sailing to and fro in their own ships as well as in ships from Suvarṇabhūmi. The description of the area as rich in gold might have some truth in it, as the region from the southern part of present-day Thailand down the archipelago to Malaysia is, in fact, rich in gold and other minerals.[39] Despite that fact, one must conclude that Indian authors had only a vague idea of what Suvarṇabhūmi was and where it was located.

With regard to other names that appear in Sanskrit literature, such as Suvarṇadvīpa, Suvarṇapura, and Kāñcanapura, Majumdar observes:

> Thus, in addition to the generic name Suvarṇabhūmi, or gold-land, we have references to gold-island, gold-peninsula, and gold-city. It seems to be quite clear, therefore, that Suvarṇabhūmi was used primarily as a vague general designation of an extensive region, but, in course of time, different parts of it came to be designated by the additional epithets of island, peninsula [*dvīpa*], or city [*pura*].[40]

However, after Majumdar reviews the Western classical and Arabic sources, he concludes that Suvarṇabhūmi was a common designation for Burma, the Malay peninsula, and Sumatra, whereas the name, Suvarṇadvīpa, was applied only to Sumatra and the other islands in the archipelago.[41] This conclusion coincides with the two terms used in classical sources (presumably translations of Suvarṇabhūmi and Suvarṇadvīpa): Suvarṇabhūmi is called Khryse Khora, and Suvarṇadvīpa is called Khryse Khersonese. These classical sources only assure us that Suvarṇabhūmi was a region in Southeast Asia. It is obvious that Ptolemy uses the two terms to designate regions, not states or cities, for later on he describes specific towns and seaports of the region.[42]

Chinese records also contain numerous Southeast Asian place names. The only one that comes close to being Suvarṇabhūmi is Jin-lin, which can be translated as "Frontier of Gold."[43] This could be a translation of either Suvarṇakūḍya or Suvarṇabhūmi. Lévi suggests that the word, *jin,* is a translation of *suvarṇa,* and *lin* is a phonetic transliteration of *kūḍya.* Combined translation-transliterations are uncommon, but not an impossible method of rendering foreign names into Chinese. Wheatley suggests that both words are transliterations of a local vernacular name. If he is correct, then Jin-lin cannot refer to Suvarṇabhūmi.[44]

Local sources, all of which are dated much later than Indian ones, also do not offer any help in determining the exact location of Suvarṇabhūmi.[45] The Kalyāṇī inscription, written in the fifteenth century (1476 CE), identifies it with Rāmaññadesa, the Mon kingdom located in what is today Lower Burma.[46] The *Sāsanavaṃsa,* composed in the nineteenth century CE, pinpoints it at Thaton.[47] The author, Paññāsāmi, may prove to be the greater scholar by making his identification through inference based on distance and location, for he writes:

> And among those nine places, the one named Suvarṇabhūmi is the present city of Sudhammạ (i.e., Thaton) itself. If it be asked: "How then is this to be known?" . . . [the reply is] by inference based on distance [lit., route], or by inference from the location. How by inference based on distance? It is said that Suvarṇabhūmi was at a distance of seven hundred *yojanas* from here. Ships sailing on one breeze would get there in seven days and nights. Now, as it is said in the Commentary, once a ship sailed in this manner for seven days, as if on the back of a long and giant fish (that from Sīhaladvīpa to Suvarṇabhūmi). Thus, the distance from Sīhaladvīpa to Suvarṇabhūmi would be the same as that from Sudhammapura to Sīhaladvīpa. It is said that the distance from Sudhammapura to Sīhaladvīpa is seven hundred *yojanas*. A ship sailing with a favorable wind would arrive in seven days and nights. This is the inference based on distance. How by inference based on location? It is said that Suvarṇabhūmi is close to the ocean. It is a great harbour resorted to by merchants of different countries. Therefore, a great multitude of people like princes, etc., from cities such as Campā, etc., would come by ship to Suvarṇabhūmi to trade. Now the city of Sudhamma is indeed near the ocean. This is the inference based on location.[48]

However, Paññāsāmi's inferences are not viable. First of all, the distance should be calculated from India, not Sri Lanka. Second, the location described could, in fact, be one of the many harbors of Southeast Asia. The author was aware of divergent opinions at that time, for he adds:

> But some say that Suvarṇabhūmi is the state [*raṭṭha*] of Haribhuñja, reasoning that it possesses a lot of gold. Others propose that it is the state of Siam. All these should be investigated.[49]

Unfortunately, most modern scholars fail to heed his recommendation.

In Thailand, the inscription of King Ramkhamhaeng (1292 CE) of Sukhothai mentions Suvarṇabhūmi, which can be identified with the area of Suphanburi (Suvarṇapurī) Province in central Thailand.[50] Inscriptions from the Angkorian *maṇḍala* also mention Suvarṇapura, which is equated again with modern Suphanburi.[51] In other inscriptions Sumatra is called Suvarṇabhūmi or Suvarṇadvīpa. Mujambar has argued that the exact location of Suvarṇabhūmi seems futile, as it is clear that the name was used broadly to denote a vast region lying to the east of India. However, some scholars have tried to limit the area as follows: *Lower Burma*: in the region of Martaban Bay with Thaton/Sudhammavatī and Pegu/Haṃsavatī as its centers; *Central Thailand*: in the region of the Bight of Bangkok with Nakhon Pathom and the area around Suphanburi (Suvarṇapurī), U Thong (cradle of gold), and Kāñcanapurī as its centers; *General theory*: that Suvarṇabhūmi comprised the whole of Southeast Asia, or central Thailand and the Malay peninsula.[52]

Majumdar may have been the first scholar to openly assert that Suvarṇabhūmi was lower Burma. He reasons that

> Ptolemy's Chryse Chersonesus undoubtedly indicates the Malay Peninsula, and his Chryse Chora must be a region to the north of it. Now, we have definite evidence that a portion of Burma was known in later ages as Suvarṇabhūmi. According to the Kalyāṇī inscriptions (1476 A.D.), Rāmaññadesa was also called Suvaṇṇabhūmi, which would then comprise the maritime region between Cape Negrais and the mouth of the Salwin.[53]

The identification of Ptolemy's two terms as described by Majumdar is generally accepted. However, the region to the north of the Malay peninsula is central Thailand, not lower Burma, which lies to the west rather than north of the peninsula. Why would Majumdar equate lower Burma with Suvarṇabhūmi? The use of epigraphic data is anachronistic, as no inscriptions from the earlier period refer to lower Burma as Suvarṇabhūmi. Local texts refer to the area as Rāmaññadesa, not Suvarṇabhūmi. Had it been called Suvarṇabhūmi earlier, then that name should appear or be preferred in these documents, because it would link the region directly to the legend of Aśoka's mission. It is risky to use these later sources, especially those of the Mon kingdom of lower Burma, because they were written to prove that the Mon kingdom, Thaton to be exact, was the Suvarṇabhūmi that was converted to Buddhism by the Aśokan mission. If this kind of evidence is accepted, then central Thailand, where the names of several towns suggest a connection with Suvarṇabhūmi, stands a better chance of being identified as Suvarṇabhūmi. Moreover, the place names were not listed in order to claim primacy in being converted to Buddhism in the same way as the records of lower Burma. Lower Burma has always been called Rāmaññadesa, a Pāli name for the land of the Mon, which is identified with Suvarṇabhūmi only once, in the Kalyāṇī inscription. This identification was then followed by the author of the *Sāsanavaṃsa.* In any case, Rāmaññadesa is not a strictly geographical term, but rather a cultural-geographical term like Kambujadesa. In this light, wherever Mon culture predominated could be called Rāmaññadesa. This designation is found in a Thai chronicle that calls central Thailand Rāmaññadesa when Mon culture flourished in the area, a name that was later changed to Kambujadesa when Khmer culture gained supremacy over the Mon.[54]

From an archaeological point of view, lower Burma, and especially Thaton, has yielded few sites of ancient ruins, a situation that has long perplexed scholars. The difficulty stems from their acceptance of the *a priori* idea that Suvarṇabhūmi was lower Burma. The oldest archaeological evidence of Indianized civilization in Southeast Asia comes from central Burma, central and southern Thailand, and the lower Mekong delta. These finds belong to the period of Funan, which was the first *maṇḍala* established in Southeast Asia. If one takes into account the epigraphic and archaeological evidence, then the Suvarṇabhūmi mentioned in the early texts must be identified with these areas and not lower Burma. If one insists on claiming that it was in Burma, then Suvarṇabhūmi would be located in the Pyu *maṇḍala* in central Burma, an area rich in early epigraphic and archaeological finds.

These problems could be easily resolved if we accept, as the texts suggest, that Suvarṇabhūmi was a broadly used general term applied to all the regions to the east of India. Instead of asserting that Suvarṇabhūmi is located specifically in lower Burma or central Thailand, it would be more correct to say that lower Burma and central Thailand were in Suvarṇabhūmi, the generic name for the lands east of India. Over time, when more was known about the region, specific names arose, such as Yāvadvīpa and references to other vague areas beyond, such as Kārpuradvīpa.[55] But the use of the term, Suvarṇabhūmi, remained unchanged even in the later texts. This supports the theory that Suvarṇabhūmi was a region. The term did not refer to a historical or a political entity, but a geographical area. Suvarṇabhūmi could not be the Mon kingdom of lower Burma, because the Mon kingdom did not come into existence until the ninth or tenth century.[56]

The issue has been complicated further by the fact that the Pāli texts composed in Sri Lanka do refer to the conversion of Suvarṇabhūmi to Buddhism by a mission sent by Emperor Aśoka. The importance of the precise location of Suvarṇabhūmi now involves the national pride of claiming to be the first Buddhist state in Southeast Asia. But as shown above, Suvarṇabhūmi cannot be defined as a nation or a political entity, but only a region comprised of many cities and centers with extensive boundaries that varied over the centuries.

MERCHANTS AS MISSIONARIES

It is a widely accepted fact that a close relationship existed between Buddhism and merchants. Yet it is obvious that ordinary merchants, who in most cases were not highly educated people, could not have been the vehicle of a high culture, yet without these merchants Southeast Asia might not have come into contact with the outside world. While these merchants were not the agents who introduced the Sanskrit language and its literature, they did give the region its first contacts with Indian culture, especially with Buddhism.[57]

According to the *Dharmaśāstras*, traveling abroad was strictly forbidden for brahmans, so only the merchant caste was able to seek wealth in distant lands. Abundant examples can be found in the *Jātaka* stories and other sources. Canonical literature relates many conversions of the merchant caste, and in some instances, merchants show a profound knowledge of the religion. In fact, in Buddhism it is possible for a layman to teach doctrinal points to monks, a practice recorded in the diary of Fa Xian and still practiced in Thailand today. This type of layman was apotheosized in the person of Vimalakīrti. Of course, not all laymen were merchants, for some were converted brahmans. Because we find in the Pāli canon learned individuals like Cittagṛhapati and others who obviously belonged to the merchant community, it is possible to argue that learned merchants did indeed propagate the doctrine in India and elsewhere.[58] This argument is supported by epigraphic data, such as the inscriptions of the *ye dharmā* and other stanzas left by Mahānāvika Buddhagupta, the great mariner.[59]

Buddhist missions were not solely dependent upon monks.[60] When one considers the harsh circumstances of travel and the specialized knowledge required for sea navigation, monks were incapable of undertaking missions on their own and had to rely on seafaring traders.[61] The earliest known artifacts from India found in Southeast Asia, including inscribed seals, are unrelated to religion, so it is likely that any formal mission undertaken by monks came later.[62]

Not all merchants were like Buddhagupta. Most of them probably were common folk and their beliefs, even Buddhist ones, were likely to have been those prevalent in India at that time. In the early phase of Indian Buddhism, belief in local gods and spirits remained strong, and such beliefs can be found in the Pāli canon in the *Āṭānāṭiyasutta*, and the *Mahāsamayasutta* of the

Dīghanikāya.[63] It is likely that the merchants carried with them images of the Buddha or Gaṇeśa as protective amulets to ward off danger.[64]

Recent studies have identified a number of artifacts as merchants' amulets. These include images of a standing Buddha, claimed to be the Dīpaṅkara Buddha with the hand position of "calming the waves;" a seated female figure holding lotuses in both hands and flanked by elephants, claimed to be Gajalakṣmī; Kubera, the god of wealth; and Gaṇeśa, the elephant-headed god.[65] These artifacts did not necessarily belong to the merchants; they could equally have belonged to pilgrims or missionary monks. The standing Buddha image could be any Buddha, not specifically Dīpaṅkara, because Dīpaṅkara has no connection with the "calming the waves" *mudrā*, and thus would have no connection with seafarers or maritime traders.[66] The Gajalakṣmī in all likelihood is not Lakṣmī, the goddess of wealth, but rather a representation of the birth of the Buddha.[67] The only sound contender is Kubera, who does appear to belong to the community of merchants. Above all, it must be remembered that these objects were not originally Indian, but creations of local Southeast Asian artists. The one exception is a standing Buddha image found in the Celebes, which scholars more or less agree is of Indian origin.[68] Therefore, to describe all standing Buddha images as Dīpaṅkara, or Gajalakṣmī as the goddess of wealth, or label these artifacts found in Southeast Asia as amulets carried by Indian merchants distorts the intrinsic importance of them. This is not to say that Indian merchants did not carry amulets; they very well might have done so, and in so doing provided models for local artists to imitate.

The merchants came from all parts of India, and even though some were Buddhists and belonged to Indian culture, that is, to a Brahmanical or (later on) Hindu society, the Buddhism that they introduced would have reflected a religious pluralistic society that existed at that time in India. For example, inscriptions from Bharhut describe the Buddha as "Mahādeva" or "Pitāmaha," which are epithets for Hindu gods.[69] This attribution persists as a prominent feature of Southeast Asian religion as a whole.

Trade also affected the way Indian religions became distributed throughout Southeast Asia. The evidence for this assertion, which will be discussed in the next two chapters, is that Hīnayāna Buddhism reached Southeast Asia first, followed in the seventh century by the Mahāyāna school and Brahmanism. However, these creeds did not develop in the same regions. Hīnayāna Buddhism was strong in the western zone of the mainland areas, and Mahāyāna Buddhism and Brahmanism were dominant in the eastern zone and maritime regions. One reason for this difference was due to changes in the trade routes, which began to shift from the coastal and trans-peninsular ones to sea routes in the beginning of the seventh century. This occurred about the same time that Mahāyāna Buddhism was becoming active in the area. And close to the same time, there was a revival of Brahmanism. Therefore, both Mahāyāna Buddhism and Brahmanism became influential in the maritime regions and on the mainland for the Cham and the Khmer, who maintained close relations with maritime cultures.[70]

While trade and merchants were indeed important in introducing Indian religions to Southeast Asia, they were not the only agents. The presence of monks, monasteries, and religious texts requires another kind of mediator, namely, the missionaries. It was the Buddhist missions that laid the foundation for the spread and establishment of Buddhism in Southeast Asia.

BUDDHIST MISSIONS

It is generally accepted that Buddhism is a missionary religion, and that is the reason why it spread so effectively both within India and beyond. In fact, Buddhism was the only Indian religion that was able to flourish outside the confines of the subcontinent. Even though Hinduism reached Southeast Asia at about the same time as Buddhism, it never became the principal creed of the common people. This does not mean that Hinduism did not play a role in Southeast Asian religion, but by its very nature Hinduism was unable to attain a status equal to Buddhism. The success of the Buddhist missions also reveals the "portable" sanctity of Buddhism. Its sacredness was not bound by territory as was Hinduism, which forbade its chief representatives, the brahmans, from traveling abroad.

On a social level, Buddhism proved more flexible than Hinduism, as it is not defined or limited by the concept of caste. While anyone can become a Buddhist, one must be born into the Hindu religion. By this rubric, no one outside of Indian society could become a true Hindu. But in Buddhism, anyone anywhere could become a lay follower or, if qualified, as prescribed in the Vinaya rules, could be ordained as a monk. Thus the influence of Hinduism in Southeast Asia was confined to the religio-political sphere and did not spread as a creed or belief for the masses. What did occur was that Hinduism was absorbed into Buddhism, which did not reject but incorporated the important beliefs common to all Indian religions, such as transmigration, *karma*, and cosmology. Although Buddhism assimilated and adapted indigenous beliefs, it never lost its character as Buddhism because it had an institutionalized form in the Sangha. The Sangha needs the support of both the masses and the nobility. It did not and could not remove itself from the common people, yet simultaneously it was able to exert an influence in the political realm. In this way Buddhism was able to change while at the same time maintaining its uniqueness as a religion.

This is possible for a religion with a well-organized community that can preserve its original doctrines, confront changes, and adapt to new situations. It was the members of this community, the monks, who implanted and established the religion far and wide.

The missionary spirit of Buddhism was evident very early in its history, for it is related in the *Vinayapiṭaka* that the Buddha sent forth his first group of disciples to spread the Dharma.[71] This could well be the first religious mission in world history. Even during the Buddha's lifetime, his teachings had already spread beyond Magadha to as far afield as Avanti and Sunāparantaka.[72] This process of spreading the Dharma must have intensified in the ensuing centuries, because by the third century BCE Buddhism had already spread throughout India.[73]

The Pāli chronicles of Sri Lanka attribute this initial diffusion to the nine missions sent by Moggalītissa Thera during the reign of Aśoka Maurya.[74] Since our primary interest is in Southeast Asia, we will examine here only the eighth destination enumerated in the Sri Lankan sources, namely, the mission to Suvarṇabhūmi.

AŚOKA'S MISSION: HISTORY OR MYTH?

The connection between Suvarṇabhūmi and Buddhism or, to be more precise, the introduction of Buddhism into Southeast Asia is found not in Indian literature, but in the Pāli literature of Sri Lanka: the *Dīpavaṃsa,* the *Mahāvaṃsa,* and the *Samantapāsādikā.* These texts give the following information in verse form:

Dīpavaṃsa VIII, 11

Suvaṇṇabhūmiṃ gantvāna Soṇuttaro mahiddhiko
dametvā pisācagaṇe mocesi bandhanā bahū.

Mahāvaṃsa XII, 44–45

Saddhim Uttaratherena Soṇatthero mahiddhiko
Suvaṇṇabhūmiṃ agamā, tasmin tu samaye pana.
jāte jāte rājagehe dārake ruddarakkhasī
samuddato nikkhamitvā bhakkhayitvāna gacchati.

Samantapāsādikā I, 63–69

Suvaṇṇabhūmiṃ gantvāna	Soṇuttarā mahiddhikā
pisāce niddhamitvāna	brahmajālaṃ adesisuṃ.

The connection between the verses is obvious. If one accepts that the *Dīpavaṃsa* was composed before the *Samantapāsādikā*, then the latter must be quoting from the former. The verses appear in the account of the missions sent at the time of Aśoka after the convening of the Third Buddhist Council. From the missions we learn that Soṇa and Uttara went to Suvarṇabhūmi, tamed the local people—described as demons in the text—and thereby released them from the bondage of the world, so that they might become enlightened. The *Samantapāsādikā* adds that the two monks preached the *Brahmajālasutta,* the first *sutta* in the *Dīghanikāya* of the Pāli canon.

The *Mahāvaṃsa* has more to say about the demons. At the capital of Suvarṇabhūmi around the time when the two Theras, Soṇa and Uttara, arrived, whenever a child was born, it was said that a female *rākṣasa* rose up from the ocean and devoured it. The Theras, who must have reached Suvarṇabhūmi by sea, were mistaken for friends of the demon, causing the people to threaten to kill them. The Theras explained their mission, subjugated the demon, and then preached the *Brahmajālasutta.* The mission concluded with a great mass of people taking refuge in the "Three Jewels" (the Buddha, the Dharma, and the Sangha) with the result that thousands of men and women were ordained.[75]

If this is an accurate historical account, then we must assume either that the Theras were well versed in the local language or that the local people were well versed in Pāli, since it is recorded that the Theras preached the *Brahmajālasutta* upon their arrival. The fact that the *sutta* is a philosophically difficult text and ill suited for beginners makes the story even more implausible.[76] Moreover, at the time of the missions, the *Tripiṭaka* had yet to achieve the form that we know today, but the sermons said to have been preached by Soṇa and Uttara and by the missionaries sent to other lands are all present in the final compilation of the *Tripiṭaka.*[77]

The *Dīpavaṃsa* and the *Samantapāsādikā* accounts may be more accurate, in that the subjugation of demons could be seen as a mythologized version of indigenous people being subdued and converted. However, it is the conclusion of the mission in the *Mahāvaṃsa* that rightly reflects the establishment of Buddhism. Being a religion that has strict rules for the administration of the Sangha, the community of monks, and the application of these rules to an ordination ceremony that requires a Sangha, the establishment of Buddhism certainly required more than two monks. As Richard Gombrich observes:

> We must remember that in Buddhist estimation the Doctrine is only established where the Sangha is established, and, in turn, that is considered to be the case only when a monastic boundary has been duly established, for without such a boundary no formal act of the Sangha, whether *prātimokṣa* or ordination ceremony, can take place. The establishment of a monastic boundary requires lay support: the land has to be given to the Sangha. Alternatively, Buddhism can be considered to have taken root somewhere only when a local recruit has been properly ordained there. These considerations would apply just as much to the spread of Buddhism within India as to its diffusion into foreign parts.[78]

If this is correct, then other Buddhist monks would have had to be already present in Suvarṇabhūmi before Soṇa and Uttara arrived because the participation of other monks was required if higher monastic ordination was to be conferred. The account expressly tells us that the Theras ordained a multitude of people. The Vinaya prescribes that the ordination ceremony, a formal act of the monastic order, requires not only the Sangha—a group of at least five fully ordained monks—but also a fully established monastery with an assembly space demarcated by *sīmā* or boundary stones. Otherwise, we must assume that the two Theras were accompanied by other monks, and together set up the boundary stones within which the new ordinations could take place.

The introduction of Buddhism to Suvarṇabhūmi is also mentioned in a Buddhist Sanskrit text, the *Mahākarmavibhaṅga,* which ascribes the agent of conversion to Gavāmpati.[79] This would push the event back to the Buddha's lifetime. The enlisting of Gavāmpati is not unsuitable, since he was said to be foremost among the Buddha's disciples in teaching people of faraway lands and is a well-known figure in Southeast Asian Buddhism today.[80] Even if the list of missions given in this text includes both actual and mythical places, like Sri Lanka and Pūrvavideha, it reflects a more accurate situation than the Pāli sources with regard to the point that the spread of Buddhism began during the lifetime of the Buddha, which gradually progressed further and further beyond the land of its birth.[81]

It is worthwhile to compare Aśoka's inscription with the ones from the *Dīpavaṃsa* and the *Mahāvaṃsa.* The four inscriptions that mention Aśoka's missions agree, for the most part, in content and vocabulary. The relevant part reads as follows:

> In the opinion of the [king], the Beloved of gods, the most esteemed conquest is the Dharmavijaya (conquest of Dharma). And that conquest has been achieved by [the king], the Beloved of gods, both here (in his own dominions) and among all the border (or neighboring) regions as far as six *yojanas* where dwells the Ionian (or Greek) king named Antiochos, and beyond that Antiochos (i.e., in the north-west) [where live] the four kings named Ptolemy, Antigonos, Magas and Alexander and also downward (i.e., in the South) among the Cholas and Pandyas as far as the Tāmraparnī (river) people and thus also in the king's own provinces viz., in the countries of the Ionians and Kambojas, the Nābhapantis of Nābhaga, the Bhojas and the Pitinikas, the Andhras and the Pulindas. . . . Even where the envoys of the Beloved of gods do not go, they on hearing of the ordinances preached on the Dharma . . . follow and will follow the Dharma.[82]

The inscriptions do not state specifically that Aśoka sent monks abroad as missionaries; the word used is simply *dūta* (messenger, envoy). Nor do they state that he sent these messengers to propagate Buddhism, as the word "Dharma" in the inscriptions is a general word for norms of conduct that are common to all Indian religions.[83] There is no suggestion that the areas in question were converted. The purpose of sending the envoys was not to convert these kings and peoples to Buddhism, but rather to spread the notion of "Conquest by Dharma."

As for the geography of the inscriptions, areas to the north are mentioned in greater detail, but areas to the south rather sparingly. Scholars now generally agree that Tāmraparṇī does not refer to Sri Lanka, but instead to a river in the southern Deccan.[84] Thus, there is no supporting evidence for an Aśokan mission to Sri Lanka or Suvarṇabhūmi, regardless of whether or not it indeed means Southeast Asia.

However, the story of the missions must have some truth in it because not only do the chronicles of Sri Lanka preserve the story, but it appears, albeit in a different form, in the *Mahākarmavibhaṅga,* a Buddhist Sanskrit text. Still, the identification of the place names remains problematic. Suvarṇabhūmi and Siṃhaladvīpa are both mentioned in the *Mahākarmavibhaṅga.* The Thera who goes to Sri Lanka is Mahendra, which agrees with the Pāli chronicles, but the Thera who goes to Suvarṇabhūmi is Gavāmpati, rather than Soṇa and Uttara. The order of the names, in which Suvarṇabhūmi comes before Siṃhala in both the Pāli and the Sanskrit sources, seems to suggest that in this context Suvarṇabhūmi is not the overseas Suvarṇabhūmi, but instead the Suvarṇagiri region in southern India, as Law has suggested. The confusion did not originate in Sri Lanka but in Burma, where the effort was made to equate Suvarṇabhūmi with the Mon kingdom,[85] as no Sri Lankan source interprets Suvarṇabhūmi to be Southeast Asia.

Nevertheless, on the combined evidence of the texts and the inscriptions in the Brāhmī scripts found in abundance in Sri Lanka, it is likely that Buddhism arrived there in the Aśokan period or shortly thereafter. But whether or not this was due to the emperor's efforts in sending a mission to Sri Lanka cannot be certified by sources other than those written in Sri Lanka's own tradition. In fact, the chronicles themselves credit the initiative to Moggalītissa Thera, the patriarch who presided over the Third Buddhist Council.[86] It appears, then, that the missions described in the chronicles were probably not the same ones as those mentioned in the Aśokan inscriptions, but belong instead to the history of the Buddhist church, rather than the general history of regional politics.

As for Suvarṇabhūmi, there are no ancient inscriptions or archaeological data to support the claim that the Aśokan mission referred to in the Sri Lankan chronicles ever reached the island. The tradition that the two Theras traveled to Burma and converted the people is no older than the fifteenth century and is not found in any sources other than those from the Mon-Burmese tradition.

For these reasons, the Suvarṇabhūmi mentioned in the ancient sources cannot be located with any indisputable certainty. Even if it can be identified with Southeast Asia, as modern scholars argue with the help of classical and Arab materials, the mission to Suvarṇabhūmi described in the Sri Lankan chronicles still remains dubious. As seen from Gombrich's remark quoted above, to establish Buddhism meant to establish the Sangha, which cannot be accomplished overnight. It is more accurate to look at the introduction of Buddhism into Southeast Asia as a gradual process that involved many factors and dynamics. This does not mean that missions played no part in the spread of Buddhism into the region; on the contrary, they played a crucial role because only through them did Buddhism become firmly established.

The point to note here is that in the accounts of the missions drawn from Pāli sources, the conversion process is oversimplified. It is inconceivable that the whole of India would have been converted at the same time; some parts may have been converted during the Buddha's lifetime, while other parts would have been converted over time. Buddhist missionary activity must be seen as a continuous process carried out by members of the Sangha. Consequently, it is impossible to trace every step of these missions, except where evidence has survived intact, which is rare, because most sites have been altered and reconstructed wherever Buddhism remained a living faith.

NON-CANONICAL TRACES OF BUDDHIST MISSIONS

Except for a few references in canonical works, there is scarcely any mention of Buddhist missions. Even in the Sri Lankan chronicles, the missions were mentioned only in connection with an account of the Third Buddhist Council, most likely, more as an effort to confirm the authenticity of the direct lineage of the Sri Lankan church rather than to describe the history of the missions per se.

In Southeast Asia, local tradition seems to have exclusively followed and reproduced the accounts of the two Sri Lankan chronicles. However, there are numerous legends that relate visits made by the Buddha to the region. This could be interpreted to mean that there were Buddhist monks traveling about, preaching the doctrine in Suvarṇabhūmi,[87] a situation that is probably more in accordance with the facts than the chronicle accounts. If we accept that these legends and chronicles were written in order to affiliate the Buddha with regional sites, the chronicle authors probably intended for these texts to be taken literally. We must look elsewhere for evidence that monks from India and Sri Lanka visited the area. After relations between Sri Lanka and Southeast Asia intensified, there are references in Southeast Asian texts about Theras coming from Sri Lanka but, for the most part, Sri Lankan sources are silent on the matter, except with regard to relations between kings on religious matters.[88]

The silence could be due to the nature of the missions themselves, which were carried out gradually by the community of monks without any support from the state. If so, then it stands to reason that such records would be absent from the official chronicles. In a later period, when Theravāda Buddhism from Sri Lanka was ascending to the status of a national religion, histories of the Buddhist church written in Southeast Asia were entirely dependent upon Sri Lankan sources.

Chinese sources provide more extensive and more reliable information about the travels of monks and missions.[89] It is evident that the sea route between India, Sri Lanka, Southeast Asia, and China was in use at least by the beginning of the early part of the first century CE,[90] if not earlier. It became more frequently used due to political unrest in Central Asia in the fifth century.[91] Our evidence rests on the records of missionary monks from India and Sri Lanka going to or passing through Southeast Asia en route to China and, in some cases, later returning to Southeast Asia or India.[92] In some sources, there are accounts of monks residing in Southeast Asia who were invited to China to propagate the religion.[93] In one instance, a monk traveled in the service of a king as an ambassador to the Chinese court, carrying with him objects of worship and numerous sacred texts.[94]

These records are convincing evidence for the presence of monks from India and Sri Lanka in Southeast Asia. They could have traveled on their own accord to spread the Dharma or perhaps they were invited by local Buddhists to teach or establish a monastic community in the area. This leads us to discuss another factor in the introduction of Buddhism into Southeast Asia: pilgrimage.

PILGRIMAGE

If the missions to Southeast Asia demonstrate the theory of Buddhism's "portable" sanctity, then pilgrimage manifests Buddhism's "fixed" side.[95] Buddhist pilgrimage has its roots in the oldest Pāli text, the *Mahāparinibbānasutta* of the *Dīghanikāya*, in which we are told how the Buddha himself sanctifies the four great biographical sites—his birthplace, the site of his enlightenment, the site of his first sermon, and the site of his *nirvāṇa*—as places to visit in his memory. The merit gained by visiting the four sites will lead to the attainment of happiness in heaven.[96] These four great sites, as a result, have become the most popular sacred sites for pilgrimage.

After the Buddha entered *nirvāṇa*, his relics were divided and distributed among the princes of those days[97] and later redistributed during the reign of Aśoka.[98] The relics are usually set within *stūpas*, mound-shaped structures or tumuli. The four great sites together with the *stūpas* enshrining relics became centers of pilgrimage. These holy shrines were adorned by the faithful with elaborate gates and bas-reliefs depicting *Jātaka* stories and other scenes. Pilgrimage became a major factor in development of these arts.[99] Regions outside India naturally sought to acquire their own relics and to imitate what they had seen in India. In time, this impetus to possess relics led to the creation of pilgrimage sites in Southeast Asia proper. These pilgrimage sites usually had legends of their own associated with the history of their special relics that can provide insight into the attitude of the masses towards relics and religion.[100]

There is little hard evidence about pilgrimage from Southeast Asia, the earliest being from the ninth century. In a document from Nālandā (c. 849 CE), it is recorded that a king, Bālaputradeva of Suvarṇabhūmi, which in this case means Sumatra, sent an ambassador to the court of the Pāla king, Devapāladeva (c. 810–850 CE), proposing that an endowment be provided for a monastery he had built at Nālandā.[101] Later inscriptions record the building of monasteries (*vihāras*) in Negapatam in South India.[102]

These records reveal that at that time pilgrims (no doubt more monks than laymen) were sufficiently numerous if monasteries had to be built to house them. It leads us to assume that numerous pilgrimages had preceded the establishment of these *vihāras*. In those days, it was a common practice to build *vihāras* at pilgrimage sites, as there is evidence that a Sri Lankan king built monasteries for Sri Lankan monks at Bodhgayā and elsewhere.[103] (In the case of Nālanda, it could well be that monks went there as students and not solely as pilgrims.)

There are no extant sources that tell us precisely what Southeast Asian pilgrims did in India. We can assume that they visited the famous, holy pilgrimage sites in Magadha, like the Chinese pilgrims who traveled to India for the primary purpose of seeking out the holy texts but who also visited the sacred sites. There is no evidence that Southeast Asian pilgrims had the same goals as the Chinese, but there is evidence that Funan, Śrīvijaya, and other areas possessed large collections of sacred texts that could have been brought from India by missionary monks or pilgrims.[104] Later, when contact between Southeast Asia and Sri Lanka intensified, pilgrimages from Southeast Asian countries were recorded. What was of primary concern for monks in the later period was to obtain the rules for holding a correct and "pure" ordination.

The introduction of Buddhism cannot be regarded as something separate from the introduction of Indian culture as a whole, and because this process evolved gradually and peacefully, it is entirely possible that the presence of Buddhism escaped notice or at least was an unremarkable presence. Because Buddhism was a part of Indian civilization, which was considered a "high culture" compared with indigenous cultures that lacked writing systems, Buddhist texts originating from India and Sri Lanka were seldom translated into vernacular languages but were regarded as sacred or even magical in their original linguistic form. This could explain why we do not have any data about the first introduction of Buddhism to Southeast Asia, except for the Sri Lankan chronicles in which Suvarṇabhūmi may have been wrongly attributed to Southeast Asia. We must, therefore, rely on evidence gleaned from archaeological and epigraphic data.

It is well known that trade relations between India and Southeast Asia go back to prehistoric times. In the early protohistoric period, there is evidence of a trade in metals, such as tin and gold, precious stones, valuable timber, and spices. However, these goods do not pertain to Buddhism, except for an ivory comb found at Chansen in central Thailand. The comb, which dates from the first or second century CE, is engraved with a pair of horses, a goose with an elaborately plumed tail, and a row of Buddhist symbols.[105]

The oldest substantial archaeological evidence for Buddhism consists of Buddha images said to be in the Amarāvatī style, which flourished from the second to the fourth century in the region of Andhra Pradesh. The images were found at sites in Thailand, Vietnam, Sumatra, eastern Java, and the Celebes.[106] However, the one found in the Celebes is of Indian origin; the other images show the mixed influences of Gupta and Sri Lankan styles as well as strong local features, and date no earlier than the fifth century.[107]

Scholars overemphasize the fifth century date, and use it to argue for a later time when Buddhism was introduced. But the fact that the images bear different influences, especially the local ones, and yet still preserve the characteristics of the Amarāvatī style, indicates that contact must have occurred earlier. The prototype must have been Amarāvatī images introduced either by Indian merchants or Southeast Asian merchants who went to India, or possibly, by monks from India.

There is another artifact, a kind of sculpture that could shed light on the presence of Buddhism, and that is the *dharmacakra*, or "Wheel of Dharma" found mainly in areas where Dvāravatī culture predominated. The cult of the *dharmacakra*, which is a visual representation of the preaching of the Buddha's first sermon, extends to the time when the Buddha was not yet depicted in human form. In India, *dharmacakras* are found at Sañcī, where one is set atop a column in the vicinity of the great *stūpa.* Few remains of freestanding *dharmacakra* still exist in India, although numerous bas-reliefs depict scenes of devotees worshipping the *dharmacakra.* The tradition flourished throughout the Amarāvatī period but died out during the Gupta and subsequent eras, and in India from around the third or fourth century.[108]

Numerous *dharmacakra* are found in the Dvāravatī *maṇḍala,* and even if this style cannot be dated earlier than the Gupta, the tradition goes back to the Mauryan period.[109] It has been noted by scholars that once a tradition becomes established outside its original home, it retains some original, archaic features.[110] This seems to be true of the *dharmacakra* cult. Even when the motifs and styles change, the basic conceptual form is retained. *Dharmacakras* represent a very old tradition that was implanted in the area no later than the fourth century CE.

With regard to architectural styles, a close resemblance has been traced between religious buildings in Beikthano of the Pyu *maṇḍala* and those of

Nāgārjunakoṇḍa.[111] In Thailand there are also *stūpa*, large and small, which show features of the Amarāvatī style.[112]

As for epigraphic data, some brief inscriptions in the Brāhmī and old Pallava scripts dating from the first to third centuries CE have been found engraved on clay or carnelian seals. However, these inscriptions shed little light on the dating issue because, apparently, these seals were used mainly for business transactions with the exception of two clay seals inscribed with "Sangha Siri" in Brāhmī script that date to the second century CE.[113] The *dharmacakra* and the *ye dharmā* inscriptions that have been found all over the region are a continuation of an ancient tradition that existed in India from the first century on.[114]

In light of archaeological and epigraphic data from different regions throughout Southeast Asia, we can conclude that by the first or at least by the second century CE, Buddhism was already known in Southeast Asia. The first contacts came about by merchants who probably introduced the Buddhism of India and Sri Lanka to Southeast Asia. Here we might ask: Granting that Buddhism was the faith of these merchants, then how would the people of Southeast Asia have known that they were Buddhists, since it is unlikely that the merchants would have publicly proclaimed themselves as such? The awareness of Buddhism as a distinct religion could only have come from the monks because teaching was a function of the monastic missions. Missionaries and pilgrims maintained close connections with their homelands, traveling back and forth, thereby keeping the Buddhism of the region abreast of developments in India and Sri Lanka.

The introduction of Buddhism should be seen not only as an introduction but also as the spread and development of Buddhism in Southeast Asia. With the help of the three factors of trade, missions, and pilgrimage, Buddhism was introduced, reintroduced, expanded, and developed throughout Southeast Asia from around the first to the second century CE. These factors were essential in giving shape to the form that Buddhism took in Southeast Asia for centuries. With the introduction of Buddhism by merchants, monks, and pilgrims, the religion remained eclectic in nature. But it was through the work of missionary-monks that Buddhism developed a scholarly tradition and formed an elite. Missions and pilgrimages, which were facilitated by trade relations, provided the Buddhism of Southeast Asia with information about Indian Buddhism. However, once Buddhism was firmly implanted, new waves of development were introduced and added without discarding any of the old tradition. Buddhism in different regions of Southeast Asia developed its own unique local character due to different social and historical circumstances.

We cannot point to one specific area in Southeast Asia that was the first to receive Buddhism due, in part, to the shifting of trade and trade routes over such a vast and diverse an area as Southeast Asia. Since the introduction of Buddhism was a gradual process that stretched across many areas and centers while exposed to Indian influences at the same time, it is futile to try to pinpoint a specific area. Similar reasoning applies to the areas from which Buddhism was introduced. It is likely that Buddhism came from different parts of India as well as from Sri Lanka. Archaeological and epigraphic data indicate that South India and Sri Lanka were two of the original areas from which Buddhism became known and practiced in Southeast Asia, but the Deccan and northern regions of India also played a role.

Many factors helped to introduce, nourish, and spread Buddhism in the region. This was a long process that evolved at its own pace and in different streams over an immense area, and because this process was not recorded, we cannot determine the exact date when Buddhism was first introduced. The question is not *when* Buddhism was first introduced, but rather, when did the people of Southeast Asia *recognize* this religion as Buddhism. The questions that naturally flow from this perspective are: What kind of Buddhism was introduced to Southeast Asia, and what was its content?

4

Features of Southeast Asian Buddhism Prior to the Eleventh Century

Due to the paucity of sources, it is impossible to provide a chronological account of the history of Buddhism beginning with its introduction in the region. What is possible is to reconstruct its features from epigraphic and archaeological data, supplemented by Chinese records and local legends. However, a picture reconstructed solely from Southeast Asian data would be incomplete without using source materials from India and Sri Lanka. As was demonstrated earlier, Buddhism in Southeast Asia was constantly exposed to and influenced by changes and developments from India and Sri Lanka.

With regard to epigraphic data, most of the Dvāravatī inscriptions are not widely known because they have been, for the most part, translated only into Thai. The Pyu inscriptions from Burma are more accessible and will be incorporated for a more complete picture of Buddhism in Southeast Asia. New archaeological discoveries will also be examined, as will studies conducted in areas like Thailand where previously such information was unavailable.

These sources should help uncover some of the features of Southeast Asian Buddhism from its beginnings until the eleventh century when Theravāda Buddhism is said to have emerged as the dominant religion on mainland Southeast Asia. From its features, countries of origin, and prevailing trends, the way it evolved should become clear, as should the place that Buddhism assumes within the religious structure of Southeast Asia.

EPIGRAPHIC SOURCES

Most of the inscriptions found in Southeast Asia are religious in nature, to the regret of some historians who long for more data describing secular events. However, due to the lack of specific dates, proper names, or names of particular schools of Buddhism, the inscriptions yield little information that can be used for the study of the history of Buddhism. The majority of the quotations from canonical texts in the inscriptions are ones common to all sects, although the language used can, in some instances, help to identify the sects or schools to which they belong. However, the situation is not so straightforward as to automatically ascribe all Pāli inscriptions to the Theravāda tradition, or all Sanskrit inscriptions to the Sarvāstivāda or the Mahāyāna traditions.

Inscriptions other than the so-called "quotation inscriptions" can mostly be categorized as "eulogy inscriptions," which often serve as prefaces to "donation" or "royal inscriptions." These two types of inscriptions are records of a king's political exploits or his meritorious deeds. Eulogy inscriptions and royal inscriptions can be composed in either Pāli or Sanskrit. Donation inscriptions that belong to people other than royalty or nobility are few in number. Nearly all of them are found in the Dvāravatī tradition, written in a vernacular tongue.

Grouped according to language, there are three linguistic categories of inscriptions: Pāli, Sanskrit, and the vernacular. Four categories by subject matter can be discussed: quotation, eulogy, royal, and donation. These categories are provisional ones used only for the sake of research, for there is no absolute distinction among them. For example, quotations taken from texts might be used as eulogizing stanzas prefacing a royal inscription, in which case, three categories would appear in the same inscription.

The inscriptions are dated in paleographic terms from the fifth to the eleventh century CE. The scripts used closely resemble the so-called "Pallava" script, but sometimes resemble the Sri Lankan style of Pallava.[1] Over time, from around the eighth and ninth centuries, the Southeast Asian "Pallava" script evolved into distinctive local or regional scripts.[2] Pre-Devanāgarī and Devanāgarī scripts were also used, but they appear less frequently.[3]

All the inscriptions will be examined as a group, and even though the scripts may change, the texts used remain constant in the same tradition. For centuries, the quotation inscriptions primarily cited the same passage, but this does not mean that no development in the selection or presentation of quotations occurred. It just means that there is no real distinction between the two sets of data.

Problems concerning language, paleography, and the relationship between epigraphic and archaeological data will be set aside temporarily. Even if the data ultimately cannot be distinguished by means of categorization of subject matter, for the sake of convenience, it will be presented in that manner.

QUOTATION INSCRIPTIONS

The inscriptions in this category come from quotations found in texts, both canonical and extra-canonical. They can be written either in Pāli or Sanskrit, but with different provenances. Quotation inscriptions in Pāli are mainly found in the Pyu and Dvāravatī *maṇḍalas*,[4] while quotation inscriptions in

Sanskrit come primarily from the *maṇḍala*s of Śrīvijaya and central Java.[5] However, this does not mean that no Sanskrit inscriptions appear in the areas where Pāli inscriptions are found.

In paleographic terms, the Pāli inscriptions of the Pyu and Dvāravatī traditions date from the fifth century on.[6] Sanskrit inscriptions found in the peninsula and the archipelago may be as old as the Pāli inscriptions, but those found in the Pyu *maṇḍala* date from around the seventh century.[7] No quotation inscription in Sanskrit has ever been found in a Dvāravatī *maṇḍala*.[8] In the Khmer *maṇḍala*, quotation inscriptions in Pāli are of a later date, and none have been found in Sanskrit,[9] although non-quotation inscriptions in Sanskrit are numerous. The texts found are inscribed on stone, on gold or copper plates, on *stūpa*s, on the base of Buddha images, and on the walls of caves.

Quotation inscriptions contain material drawn from canonical texts and, to a lesser extent, non-canonical ones as well. They usually consist of a short stanza that summarizes the doctrine. Sometimes the citation is excerpted and arranged in accordance with the type and shape of the inscribed object, as in the case of the *dharmacakra* inscriptions.

Ye Dhammā/ *Ye Dharmā* Inscriptions

This is by far the most common quotation inscription. Textual sources for this stanza include the *Mahāvagga* of the *Vinayapiṭaka* from the Pāli canon and the Buddhist Sanskrit text the *Mahāvastu* of the Lokottaravādin Mahāsaṃghikas. The Pāli version from the *Mahāvagga* (*Vinaya*, Part I, 40) is as follows:

ye dhammā hetuppabhavā
yesaṃ hetuṃ tathāgato āha
tesañ ca yo nirodho
evaṃvādī mahāsamaṇo ti.

In most cases, the Pāli inscriptions agree with the *Mahāvagga*, except when *tesaṃ* is sometimes inscribed as *yesaṃ*. The Sanskrit version differs slightly from the *Mahāvastu* and could have come from another text which is now lost.[10] A Sanskrit version found in Southeast Asia reads as follows:

ye dharmmāḥ hetuprabhavāḥ
hetun teṣan tathāgato hy avadat
teṣañca yo nirodho hy– [var. yo nirodha evaṃvādī/yo nirodho evaṃvādī]
evaṃvādī mahāśramaṇaḥ.

A third type is written mainly in Pāli but with the addition of one or two words in Sanskrit. These inscriptions cannot be described as being Buddhist Sanskrit ones, because they could be the result of scribal errors or slips due to a familiarity with Sanskrit. One such inscription found in Cambodia, and in paleographic terms dated to the seventh century, uses the Sanskrit word "*hetuprabhavā*" in place of the Pāli word "*hetuppabhavā*," but otherwise, the declension and euphonic rules follow Pāli grammar.[11] In an inscription from Sārnāth in India dated to the second century, the Sanskrit forms, *hetuprabhavā* and *mahāśramaṇa,* replace the Pāli forms of *hetuppabhavā* and *mahāsamaṇo,* although the declension remains Pāli throughout.[12]

Inscriptions of this third type are found in abundance in the Pyu and Dvāravatī *maṇḍalas*. In the Pyu *maṇḍala*, a Sanskrit version was also found, but in the Dvāravatī *maṇḍala*, no Sanskrit version has been found with the possible exception of some votive tablets, which could have originated elsewhere. There are, however, other Sanskrit inscriptions in the Dvāravatī tradition, but they are not Buddhist in nature.[13] Sanskrit *ye dharmā* inscriptions were found in West Borneo[14] and on gold plates from central Java. In the latter, the *ye dharmā* is accompanied by other stanzas reproduced here from de Casparis's reading:

Plate i

A. 1. ājñānāc=cīyate karma janmanaḥ karma kāraṇaṃ
   2. jñānā<n> na cīyate karma karmmābhāvān=na jāyate
   3. ye dharmmā hetuprabhavāḥ hetun=teṣāṃ
   4. tathāgato avadat teṣāñ=ca yo
B. 1. nirodha <e>vaṃvādī mahāśramaṇaḥ kuśalaṃ
   2. sarvapāpasya kāraṇaṃ kuśalasyopasaṃ-
   3. padā //

Plate j

A. 1. ajñānāc=cīyate karmma janmanaḥ karma kāraṇaḥ jñānān=na
   2. [c]cīyate karmma karmmābhāvān na jāya(n)te//
B. 1. ye dharmmā hetuprabhavā hetun=teṣāṃ tathāgata uvāca teṣāñ=ca yo niro-
   2. dha evamvādī mahāśramaṇaḥ // rūpiṇas=sarvvasattvā hi sarvva santi nirātmikāḥ
   3. sarvve bhadraṃ vipaśyanti mā kaścit=pāpam=āgaman /[15]

The first stanza is known to have come from West Borneo where it is inscribed four times together with the *ye dharmā* in Sanskrit.[16] It also appears in the Mahānāvika Buddhagupta inscription.[17] Because it cannot be traced to any known source and because it always appears with other canonical quotations, it can be assumed that it, too, is a quotation. The incomplete stanza beginning with *sarvvapāpasya* is no doubt the famous *Ovādapaṭimokkha* stanza.[18] It is interesting to note that in the same set of inscriptions both the *ye dharmā* and the *ājñānāc=cīyate* contain variants. The variant readings do not appear to be scribal errors, since the change from *avadat* to *uvāca* indicates that the person who commissioned the inscription had a good knowledge of Sanskrit.

In the Pyu and Dvāravatī traditions, the inscriptions are written on bricks, stone, gold and copper plates, and votive tablets. In some instances, the inscribed bricks were used in the building of *stūpas*. Other inscribed objects were often placed inside *stūpas*,[19] or the stanza was inscribed on the outer surface of small *stūpas*.[20] Occasionally the inscription might include other stanzas or quotations. Gold plates discovered at Maunggan have the stanza incised at the beginning of each plate.[21]

These inscriptions can be classified as *dharmacetiya* in contrast to *dhātucetiya* and *upabhogacetiya* or objects used by the Buddha.[22] It is clear that such inscriptions were considered sacred, since they contained the doctrine in summary form. We cannot assume that all of the patrons who sponsored these inscriptions were able to read Pāli, but at least we can say that they must have known the essential import of the stanza. So far as the context shows, the tradition appears to be closely connected to *stūpa* construction and the cult of relics.

Paṭiccasamuppāda Inscriptions

The *paṭiccasamuppāda* formula is found throughout the *Tripiṭaka*. The following version from Hmawza in the central Irrawaddy River valley in Burma is inscribed on a gold plate. The text runs as follows:

> avijjāpaccayā saṅkhārā saṅkhārapaccayā viññāṇa . . . [and so forth.][23]

In the Dvāravatī *maṇḍala*, the formula is found inscribed on the Wheel of the Dharma. Since all of the surviving wheels are broken, the text is incomplete, but judging from the remaining fragments, it appears that the text probably agrees with the Burmese inscription.[24]

A Sanskrit version found in Java dates from the seventh or eighth century CE. It is a lengthy text with a commentary, which the inscription calls *Vibhaṅga,* and it was edited and studied by de Casparis in *Prasasti Indonesia II.*[25] De Casparis identifies the text as Sarvāstivādin, however, the commentary contains no Sarvāstivādin tenets, such as *avijñaptirūpa* or *viprayuktasaṃskāra* when it glosses the terms *rūpa* and *saṃskāra.* Further research must be conducted before we can reach any conclusion about which school is associated with this inscription.

Ariyasacca Inscriptions

The next group of inscriptions provides the essential part of the *Dhammacakkappavattanasutta*: the exposition of the Four Noble Truths and the knowledge of these truths. The subject matter of these inscriptions may be found together with the *ye dhammā* stanza, as seen in an inscription from Si Thep, which begins with the *ye dhammā* and then is followed by a stanza on *ariyasacca* (Noble Truths) with excerpts from the *Udāna* and the *Dhammapada.* There is also a unique example of texts connected with the four truths inscribed on a Wheel of Dharma (c. seventh or eighth century), which can be seen as follows:

Inscriptions on the outer rim of the wheel

I, IV, IX, XII	saccañāṇaṃ
II, V, VII, X, XIII	kiccañāṇaṃ
III, VI, (VIII), XI, XIV	katañāṇaṃ

Inscriptions on the spokes

1. dukkhasaccaṃ
2. dukkhasaccaṃ pariññeyyaṃ
3. dukkhasaccaṃ pariññātaṃ
4. samudayasaccaṃ
5. samudayasaccaṃ pahātavvaṃ
6. samudayasaccaṃ pahīnaṃ
7. nirodhasaccaṃ
8. nirodhasaccaṃ sacchikātavvaṃ
9. nirodhasaccaṃ sacchikataṃ
10. maggasaccaṃ
11. maggasaccaṃ bhāvetavvaṃ
12. maggasaccaṃ bhāvitaṃ

13.–14. niyyānikahetudassanādhipatteyyabhāvena maggasacce
15. niyyādhikahetudassanādhipatteyabhāvena maggasacce

Inscriptions on the middle ring

a. tiparivattaṃ. b. dvādasākāram. c. dhammacakkaṃ
d. pavattitaṃ e. bhagavatā.

Inscriptions on the inner ring

A. saccakiccakatañānaṃ B. catudhā catudhā kataṃ
C. tivattaṃ dvādasākāram D. dhammacakkaṃ mahesino.[26]

The texts given in the inscription are not actual excerpts from the canon, although an account of the Four Noble Truths with its corresponding knowledges can be found in the *Mahāvagga* of the *Vinayapiṭaka* and in the *Dhammacakkappavattanasutta.* In the above inscription, the connection between the knowledges listed on the outer rim is shown in relation to the Four Noble Truths on the spokes. In addition to the four truths, the inscription gives the duties required for each truth, which are found in fifth-century texts, such as the *Paṭisambhidāmagga* and the *Visuddhimagga* of Buddhaghosa, as well as Dhammapāla's commentary on the latter.[27]

The final part of the inscription consists of a summary stanza of the Four Noble Truths and their knowledges, which is found elsewhere either inscribed singly or with other quotations. The source of the stanza has not been determined, but it is quoted in the *Sāratthasamuccaya* and the *Paṭhamasambodhikathā,* both works that date later than the inscriptions.[28] All that can be said with certainty is that the inscriptions and these texts quote from a common source, which is now lost. The stanza was recorded in inscriptions only in the Dvāravatī culture, and it has a close connection to the cult of the *dharmacakra.*

There is another inscribed wheel of which only two spokes survive. The inscription reads: *udapādi vijjā uda* (*pādi*).[29] This is from the latter part of the *Dhammacakkappavattanasutta.* The selection and arrangement of texts must have differed from the complete wheel mentioned above. Nevertheless, it belongs to the same tradition of the Four Noble Truths and the Wheel of Dharma.

Udāna, Suttanipāta, and *Dharmapada* Inscriptions

Quotations from the *Udāna, Suttanipāta,* and *Dharmapada* texts are found with the *ye dhammā* stanza, which serves as a preface. They are found only in inscriptions from the Dvāravatī tradition. An inscription dated in paleographic terms to the sixth century consists of the *ye dhammā*, a summary stanza of the Four Noble Truths, and stanzas from the *Udāna* and the *Dhammapada*, as follows:

The *ye dhammā*

Summary stanza of the Four Noble Truths

From the *Udāna*

yadā have pātubhavanti dhammā
ātāpino jhāyato brahmanassa
athassa kankhā vapayanti sabbā
yato pajānāti sahetudhammaṃ
yadā have pātubhavanti dhammā
ātāpino jhāyato brahmanassa
athassa kankhā vapayanti sabbā
yato khayaṃ paccāyanaṃ avedi.
yadā have pātubhavanti dhammā
ātāpino jhāyato brahmanassa
vidhūpanaṃ titthati mārasenaṃ
suro va obhāsanaṃ antalikkhan ti

From the *Dhammapada*

anekajātisamsāraṃ
gahakāraṃ gavesanto
gahakāraka diṭṭho'si
sabbā te phāsukā bhaggā
visaṅkhāragataṃ cittaṃ

sandhāvisam anibbisaṃ
dukkhājāti punappunaṃ
punagehaṃ na kāhasi
gahakūṭaṃ visaṅkhataṃ
taṇhāṇaṃ khayam ajjhagā ti[30]

Another inscription dated later in the seventh or eighth century has only two stanzas, one each from the *Suttanipāta* and the *Udāna*:

Suttanipāta, verse 558

abhiññeyyaṃ abhiññātaṃ
pahātabbam pahīnaṃ me

bhāve(tabbañ ca bhāvitaṃ)
tasmā buddho' smi brāhmana.

Udāna

yadā have pātubhavanti dhammā
ātāpino jhāyato brāhmanassa

athassa kankhā vapayanti sabbā
yato pajānāti sahetudhammam.[31]

The inscription is badly damaged, and it is possible that the illegible part included further stanzas from the *Udāna,* as did the previous inscription. The first inscription is engraved on an octagonal pillar with quotations from four different texts. The design may be intentional, since the number eight could refer to the Eightfold Noble Path, and the number four suggests the Four Noble Truths. Most monolithic inscriptions from the Dvāravatī tradition, are found on octagonal pillars.

Gold Plate Inscriptions from Hmawza and Maunggan

A set of gold plates inscribed with excerpts from the Pāli *Tripiṭaka* was found at Hmawza in the Pyu *maṇḍala.* The passages do not correspond exactly with their counterparts in the *Tripiṭaka* except for the *pratītyasamutpāda* formula and a passage from the *Paṭisambhidāmagga.* The excerpts vary in content. One passage describes the Buddha's entry into Rājagṛha with the three former matted-hair ascetics (*jaṭila*):

siddhaṃ danto dantehi sahapuraṇajaṭilehi [sic] vippamuttehi siṃginikasavaṇṇo rājagahaṃ pavasi bhagavā. mutto muttehi sahapurāṇajaṭilehi siginikasavaṇṇo [sic] rājagahaṃ pavasi bhagavā. tiṇṇo tiṇṇehi sahapurāṇajaṭilehi vippamuttehi siginikavaṇṇo[sic] rājagahaṃ pavisi bhagavā. dasabale dasav[ā]so dasadhammacupeto so dasasata [ṃ] parivāro rājagahaṃ pavasi bhagavā.[32]

The episode can be traced to the *Mahāvagga* of the *Vinayapiṭaka,* and the *Nidānakathā* of the *Jātaka* commentary.[33]

Other passages are from the *Suttantapiṭaka*, but they are simply lists of dharmas that appear in several *sutta*s, and for that reason cannot be identified with specific *sutta*s. For example, the passage on the Tathāgata's *vesārajjañāṇa* beginning with "cattārimāni bhikkhave tathāgatassa vesārajjāni yehi vesārajjehi samannāgato tathāgato ābhāsanthānaṃ paṭijānāti parisāsu sihanādaṃ nadati," and so forth, is found, although not verbatim, in the *Mahāsīhanādasutta* and in the *Catukkanipāta* of the *Aṅguttaranikāya.* The list of the *bojjhaṅga* is also found in several places.[34]

There is, however, one passage that can be said with certainty to be a quotation from the *Paṭisambhidāmagga* of the *Khuddakanikāya*:

katamehi bhagavā cuddasehi budhañāṇehi samannāgato tathāgato. duk[khe] ñāṇaṃ buddhāñāṇaṃ dukkhasamudaye ñāṇaṃ buddhañāṇaṃ dukkhanirodhe ñāṇaṃ buddhañāṇaṃ dukkhanirodhagāminīpaṭipade ñāṇaṃ buddhañāṇa [*sic*] atthapaṭisaṃbhide ñāṇaṃ buddhañāṇaṃ dhammapaṭisambhide ñāṇaṃ buddhañāṇaṃ niruttipaṭisambhide ñāṇaṃ buddhañāṇaṃ paṭibhānapaṭisa[m]bhide ñāṇaṃ buddhañāṇaṃ yamakapaṭihāre ñāṇaṃ buddhañāṇaṃ [ma]hākārunasamāpattiyā ñāṇaṃ buddhañāṇaṃ sabba[ññu]tañāṇaṃ buddhañāṇaṃ anāvarañāṇaṃ buddhañāṇaṃ imehi bhagavā cuddasehi buddhañāṇehi samannāgato ti ti [*sic*][35]

There is also a list of seven *vipassanāñāṇa* (insight knowledge) whose provenance cannot be identified, in contrast to the eight *vipassanāñāṇa* of the *Visuddhimagga* and the ten *vipassanāñāṇa* of the *Abhidhammatthasaṅgaha*. There are also stanzas from the *Dhammapada* and the *Vinayapiṭaka*.

The plates found at Maunggan are more varied. Apart from the *ye dharmā* and the stock formula phrase praising the Buddha (*iti pi so bhagavā*), there are passages from the *Vibhaṅga* of the *Abhidhammapiṭaka*, as in the following example:

samphusanā samphusitattaṃ vedanakhandho saññākhandho sankhārakkhandho

ditthivipphanditaṃ ditthi anaṃ vuccati chalāyatanaṃpaccayā phasso tattha kataṃ[a] phassapaccaya vedananaṃ ceta[s]i[kaṃ]

saññojanaṃ gah[o] paṭilaho paṭiggaho abhiniveso paramaso mummago . . .[36]

An important feature of the gold plate inscriptions is that they are in the form of palm-leaf manuscripts. This suggests that Buddhist manuscripts existed in the Pyu region at that time. The excerpt from the Pāli *Abhidhamma* affirms that the inscriptions belong to the Theravāda tradition. Even though they do not agree exactly with the present versions of the *Tripiṭaka*, there can be no doubt that they were quoted from manuscripts that carried a slightly different version.

Sāgaramatipariprcchā Inscriptions

A stone inscribed with three stanzas, dated in paleographic terms to around the sixth century CE, was found in Kedah (present day Malaysia) in a ruined *stūpa*. The verses were identified by Lin Li-Kouang as a quotation from the *Sāgaramatipariprcchā*, a Mahāyāna text preserved only in Chinese and Tibetan translations and cited in the *Śikūāsamuccaya*. The stanzas read as follows:

balāni daśa catvāri vāiśaradyāni yāni ca
aṣṭādaśa ca Buddhānāṃ dharmmā āveṇikā hi ye
ye pratītyasamutpannā na te kecit svabhāvataḥ
ye" svabhāvan na vidyante teūāṃ sambhāvataḥ kvacit
jānīte ya imāṃ kotīṃ akotīṃ jagatas samam
tasya kotīṃ gataṃ jñānaṃ sarvvadharmmeṣu varttate.[37]

In the *Sāgaramatiparipṛcchā*, the three stanzas are arranged in a different order. The first stanza gives the common enumeration of the qualities of the Buddha, and the last two present ideas common to the Mahāyāna philosophical schools of Mādhyamaka and Yogācāra.[38]

The first two types of quotation inscriptions are found in both the Pyu and the Dvāravatī traditions. The *ye dharmā* verses in Sanskrit are found in the Pyu areas, in West Borneo, and in Java, but do not appear in the Dvāravatī tradition. The script shows strong influence from the Pallava script of the fifth century on. Later the script increasingly assumed a more local style, but the *ye dhammā* remains the favored quotation. In the Dvāravatī tradition the *paṭiccasamuppāda* and the *ariyasacca* quotations were inscribed on *dharmacakras*, which merits further investigation. The fourth type is found only in the Dvāravatī tradition, the fifth only in the Pyu tradition, and the sixth quotation only in the south of the peninsula.

EULOGY INSCRIPTIONS

This type of inscription occurs both as an independent eulogy and as a benediction preceding the body of an inscription. A eulogy inscription consists of verses praising the Buddha, the Dharma, and the Sangha. The inscriptions can be roughly divided into two groups: quotations that cite a text, either canonical or extra-canonical, and original writings.

Canonical eulogies have been found in the Pyu regions of Maunggan and Hmawza, and are dated in paleographic terms to the fifth or sixth century. The texts, all written in Pāli, are formulas eulogizing the Buddha and the Dharma. The following eulogy appears in the Pāli *Suttantapiṭaka*:

iti pi so bhagavā arahaṃ sammāsambuddho bhagavā vijjācaranasampanno sugato lokavidū anuttaro purisadamasārathi satthā devamanussānaṃ buddho bhagavā ti . . .

svākkhyāto bhagavatā dhammo sandiṭṭhiko akāliko ehipassiko opanāyiko paccataṃ veditabbo viññūhiti, . . .

The formula praising the Sangha is missing, but since the praises of the *Triratna* (Three Jewels) are normally recited together, one can infer that one for the Sangha was there as well.[39]

A eulogy inscription that cites an extra-canonical text was found east of Bangkok near the Cambodian border. The two-part inscription, which bears a date equivalent to 761 CE, is written in the late Pallava script.[40] The first part has three Pāli verses eulogizing the Three Jewels; the second part is written in Khmer and mentions the name of Kamaraten[41] Buddhasira, who gave cows to the temple and made a wish.

In the first part considered here, the verses are written in a highly ornate language in the *Vasāntatilakā* meter. The text has long been regarded as the earliest example of Pāli literature composed in Thailand. However, identical verses occur at the beginning of the *Telakaṭāhagāthā,* a text composed in Sri Lanka that was edited by Edmund R. Goonaratne and published in 1884 in the *Journal of the Pali Text Society.* Goonaratne describes the verses as follows:

> This is a small poem in ninety-eight Pāli stanzas, in which are embodied some of the fundamental doctrines of Buddhism. The verses are pathetic, and are written in elaborate language. The author is unknown . . .The verses are supposed to represent the religious meditations and exhortations of a great Thera who was condemned to be cast into a caldron of boiling oil, on suspicion of his having been accessory to an intrigue with the Queen-Consort of King Kelani Tissa. Reference to the story is made in the Mahāvaṃsa, the Rasavāhiṇī, and the Sinhalese work, the Saddhammālaṅkāra, which is a compilation from the Rasavāhiṇī. The incident happened in the reign of King Kelaṇi Tissa, B.C. 306–207.[42]

The stanzas in question are the second, third, and fourth verses of the *Telakaṭāhagāthā.* Here is a comparison of the two versions:

Inscription, verse 1
yo sabbalokamohito karuṇādhivāso
mokkhāṃ karo (nirama)laṃ varapuṇacaṇḍo,
ñeyyo da(mo na)vikulaṃ sakalaṃ vivuddho
lokuttaro namatthi taṃ sirasā munendaṃ.

Telakaṭāhagāthā, verse 2
yo sabbalokamahito karuṇādhivāso
mokkhākaro ravikulalambarapuṇṇacando,

ñeyyodadhiṃ suvipulaṃ sakalaṃ vibuddho
lokuttamaṃ namatha taṃ sirasā munindam.

Inscription, verse 2
sopānamālam amalaṃ tiraṇālayassa
saṃsārasāgarasamuttaraṇāya setuṃ,
samvvādhatīrāyyapi cajjattakhemama(ggaṃ)
dhammaṃ namassa ta sadā mūṇiṇā pasatthaṃ.

Telakaṭāhagāthā, verse 3
sopānamālam amalaṃ tidasālayassa
saṃsārasāgarasamuttaranāya setuṃ,
sabbāgatībhayavivajjitakhemamaggaṃ
dhammaṃ namassatha sadā muninā paṇītaṃ.

Inscription, verse 3
deyyaṃ dadāpyamapiyāttapasannacittā
dātvā narā phalamūlaṃ ratta(naṃ) sarānti,
taṃ savvadā dasavalena pi suppasatthaṃ
sanghaṃ namassa ta sadā mitapuññakhettaṃ.

Telakaṭāhagāthā, verse 4
deyyaṃ tad appam api yattha pasannacittā
datvā narā phalaṃ uöārataram labhante,
taṃ sabbadā dasabalen'api suppasatthaṃ
saṅghaṃ namassatha sadāmitapuññakhettaṃ.[43]

Because the *Telakaṭāhagāthā* is a complete work, and its version of the text can be used for clarification in those places where the readings of the inscription are obscure, it is possible that the inscription is based on the *Telakaṭāhagāthā*, and that the differences are due to scribal errors or memory lapse. The fact that the second part of the inscription is written in Khmer also suggests that the Pāli quotation comes from another source.

B. C. Law has dated the *Telakaṭāhagāthā* to the tenth or eleventh century.[44] If the reading of the date of the inscription is correct, then the work must have been written prior to the eighth century to allow for the passage of time until it reached Southeast Asia. However, the date given for the inscription was put in parentheses by the scholar who deciphered it. Uraisri Varasarin has suggested that the script belongs to the later Angkorian period, which began around the ninth century.[45] In any case, the inscription cannot be dated later than the ninth century.

This discovery forces a reconsideration of the theory that Sinhalese or Sri Lankan Theravāda Buddhism did not come to the region until the tenth or eleventh century.[46] The quotation from this small work shows that well before that time scholars, at least the author of this inscription, was knowledgeable about Sinhalese Buddhism. The fact that this is a small work confirms that they knew Sinhalese Buddhism, not just by name, but its literature as well, and, in this case, a short, non-canonical work.[47] Further, this suggests that relations between Southeast Asia and Sri Lanka were well established.

From the Dvāravatī tradition, there is a simply written Pāli eulogy to the *Triratna*:

namo buddhassa namo dhammassa namo saṅghassa.[48]

Eulogistic inscriptions in Sanskrit belong either to the Khmer *maṇḍala* or the peninsular and insular areas of Southeast Asia. In the Khmer *maṇḍala*, Buddhism is mentioned along with Hinduism, especially Śaivism. Sometimes Buddhism appears to be less prominent than Hinduism.[49] However, most of the inscriptions have a royal provenance, and with Hinduism playing a more important role as a political instrument, it is not uncommon to find inscriptions eulogizing Hindu gods, Buddhas, as well as bodhisattvas.[50] Inscriptions that are purely Buddhist definitely belong to the Mahāyānistic or Tantric tradition. Some inscriptions show a profound understanding of Mahāyāna doctrine, as does this inscription of which Face A dates to 1036 CE and Face B to 1046 CE:

Face A

namo vuddhāya saṃsāra samamadhyusthitāya yah
ādvyopi catuṣkāyaś caturmmārabhayād iva.

[The inscription continues in Khmer about the merit made by a king.]

Face B

tasmai śivāya (na)mo namasya pādāmvujojasravajādibhirryah
ekasvabhāvo khilabhā(vayukto)ranekabhāvopyapi śūnyabhāva[51]

[The inscription continues in Sanskrit giving an account of and eulogizing a king named Śrī Sūryavarman.]

An interesting point to note here is the mention of the *catuṣkāya* (four bodies) of the Buddha. The most common form of doctrine or speculation regarding the body (*kāya*) of the Buddha is the one of the three bodies (*trikāya*), not four bodies. But the *catuṣkāya* is not without textual reference, since the *sambhogakāya* (enjoyment body) is sometimes divided into two types.[52]

The doctrine espoused on Face B appears to be the *svabhāva* theory, which is one of the main tenets of the Vijñānavāda school. Even though the term *śūnyabhāva* also occurs, the passage cannot be ascribed to the Mādhyamaka school.

Later in the twelfth century, the *Trikāya* doctrine is found in the so-called "hospital inscriptions" of Jayavarman VII.[53] Here, too, the content seems to be *Vijñānavādin.* In the following stanza, the Buddha is eulogized together with the Bhaiūyaguru Buddha and the two bodhisattvas, Sūryavairocana and Candravairocana, who accompany him:

namo vuddhāya nirmmāṇadharmmasāmbhogamūrttaye
bhāvābhāvadvayātīto['] dvayātmā yo nirātmakaḥ
bhaiṣyaguruvaidūryyaprabharājajinanname
kṣemārogyāni janyante yena nāmāpi śṛṇvantām
śrīsūryyavairocanacandarociḥ śrīcandravairocanarohiṇīśaḥ
rujāndhakārāpaharau prajānāṃ munindrameror jayatām upānte.

In the Khmer *maṇḍala* and the *maṇḍala*s in the peninsula and insular regions, there are also eulogy inscriptions of mixed type, with both Hindu and Buddhist elements, as for instance in Java:

namaś śivāya namo buddhāya.[54]

In both these examples, Hindu gods are placed before the Buddha, but there is no indication that Buddhism was regarded as inferior to the Hindu gods. This type of inscription has not been found in either the Pyu or the Dvāravatī traditions. In fact, Sanskrit inscriptions, whether Hindu or Buddhist, are rare occurrences in those *maṇḍala*s.

Another type of eulogy inscription is one with stanzas that honor a king or a noble, using Buddhist terminology to praise the royal's qualities and deeds. These inscriptions often offer insight into how Buddhism was regarded at that time. An inscription dated to the tenth century CE from the Khmer *maṇḍala* concerns a nobleman who restores the Buddhist faith after the religion lapsed into a state of obscurity. It reads:

> Thanks to the efforts of Kīrtipaṇḍita, the Buddhadharma has reappeared from the storm just as, in autumn, the moon emerges from the clouds of the rainy season. In his person, the doctrines of *śūnyatā,* of the *cittamātra,* etc., which have been eclipsed by the night which is the wrong teaching, reappear like the rising sun . . . He illuminates the flame of the True Dharma, the *Madhyavibhāgaśāstra* and others, which extinguish the suffering caused by the defilements. He draws from the foreign country, to expand the studies of Buddhism, multitudes of philosophical treatises and texts such as the *Tattvasaṃgrahaṭikā.*[55]

This inscription confirms my assumption that the Yogācāra school of the Mahāyāna was prominent in the Khmer tradition.

DONATION AND ROYAL INSCRIPTIONS

Inscriptions of this type are found in Pāli, Sanskrit, and local languages, which often form the second part of the inscription. In the Dvāravatī *maṇḍala,* there are examples of donation inscriptions of common people, unique to this tradition. In other areas, most of the inscriptions, which are usually of a later date, relate to kings, the royal family, or high officials. The historical content of the inscriptions mainly concerns royal deeds and biographies or lineages of kings. Buddhist concepts are used in the eulogizing stanzas.

The donation inscriptions of the Dvāravatī *maṇḍala* provide a great deal of information regarding how Buddhist merit was made in those days and with what intentions and goals. The inscriptions, dated from the sixth to the eighth century, are written in ancient Mon, the oldest form of the Mon language, which differs from the medieval form of the Mon language found in Burma.[56]

The meritorious acts recorded in these inscriptions are typically Buddhist and ones that are common to India, Sri Lanka, and even present-day Buddhist countries. They include the casting of Buddha images, repairing damaged images, applying fresh paint or gold leaf to images, building *stūpa*s and *vihāra*s, donating gifts to monasteries, and freeing caged animals.

The donors came from all walks of life: commoners, dancers, *rishi*s, brahmans, shamans, kings, and nobles.[57] In one inscription, a king joins his people in making merit: “This merit is made by the king together with his friends who are common people.”[58] In another instance, a nobleman joins his entourage: “Kundarījana who founded Anurādhapura had the Chief Sināyadha act as representative together with the people of the city to arrange singing and dancing for the commemoration of this sanctuary."[59]

The inscriptions show that during the sixth century CE there were close ties between a ruler and his subjects, and close ties between Sri Lanka and central Thailand, if the name, "Anurādhapura," mentioned in the inscription is the same Anurādhapura in Sri Lanka. The donors express the wish to transfer merit to the living and to the dead as well as to themselves. They also aspire to see the Buddha Maitreya or to become a Buddha. Some donors wish for the well-being of all living beings.

While the language used is ancient Mon, there are also some Pāli and Sanskrit loaner words such as *puñña* and *puṇya.* They often appear in both Pāli and Sanskrit forms, sometimes within the same inscription. Some terms cannot be said to be either Pāli or Sanskrit, but rather, seem to be a hybrid as, for example, *upājhāya* (P. *upajjhāya,* S. *upādhyāya*) and *Meyatrīyyā* (P. *Metteyya,* S. *Māitreya*).

There are donor inscriptions from other traditions as well, and this type of inscription became prolific in Burma in the twelfth century, at a time when Sinhalese Theravāda Buddhism had already attained supremacy. In the Khmer *maṇḍala,* some interesting inscriptions have been found in northeast Thailand that refer to the building of a monastery and the setting up of boundary stones, which are prevalent in that area.[60] Stone lintels carved with scenes from the *Jātaka,* the *Avadāna,* and the life of the Buddha also have been found. They belong to the Dvāravatī tradition but exhibit considerable influence from both local and Khmer artistic sources. In other inscriptions from the Khmer tradition, there is mention of the casting of images, both Hindu and Buddhist.[61]

It is inscriptions found in the Khmer *maṇḍala* that reveal the clearest tendency of a synthesis between Hinduism and Buddhism. Images belonging to both religions are usually mentioned in the same inscription. There is evidence that Hindu gods, the Buddha, and other Buddhist images were cast by the same patrons.[62] One inscription states that a brahman studied both Buddhist and Hindu philosophy, and that Buddhism adopted some of the rituals of Hinduism.[63]

The primary patrons who sponsored the inscriptions were, for the most part, kings or members of the nobility, and the inscriptions provide some details of the special relationship between religion and ruler. One important inscription mentions Sūryavarman, an overlord of the Angkorian *maṇḍala,* who probably at one time ruled over the central part of Thailand, an area formerly under Dvāravatī influence. The text records one of the *Phra niyama* or royal regulations of Sūryavarman:

> Śaka 944 [1023 A.D.] . . . His Majesty King Sūryavarman [Phra pāda Karaten kaṃrateṅ kamtuan añ Śrī Sūryavarmadeva] issued this royal regulation for people to observe as *samācāra*, a rule to be followed. In the residence of the *tāpasvin* or the monks ordained as Mahāyāna or Sthavira, let them be ordained with true mind, offering the *tapas* to His Majesty King Śrī Sūryavarmadeva. If anyone invades and does bad deeds in these Tapovanāvāsa, disturbing these ascetics who are performing the *yogadharma*, and thereby preventing them from praying in order to offer the *tapas* to His Majesty the King. . . . Let him be apprehended and brought to court so that he can be judged most severely.[64]

This is the only inscription in which the sectarian names, Mahāyāna and Sthavira appear. The king apparently supported them both on the condition that they pray for him. The later part of the inscription is illegible, but it is likely to be additional *Phra niyama* concerning religious matters.

Another aspect of Khmer inscriptions is the curse that will befall those who plunder the offerings hidden inside religious monuments. An inscription of a *rājabhikṣu*, most likely a prince who became a monk, says:

Face I

1. āsīt śrīrājabhikṣuḥ pravaranaraśirā--sa
2. dājuṣṭpādāṃbhojāḥ kurvvīta sīmāḥ pravara
3. maniśilā varddha śobhāḥ catasraḥ vīsarjja
4. d bhūṣitāṅgān sugatatnuyutān kṣetradā
5. sādiyuktān vīharān sānghikānanāṃ
6. daśa ca sakathine cīvare dve sacaityaḥ//
7. sarvvānāṃ jagatāṃ hitāya divase kurvvīta dānaṃ sadā
8. vastraṃ cīvaradanam annam aśanaṃ pānaṃ satāmvūlakam
9. ārāmaṃ vividhāvaropitatarupuṣpaiḥ phalaiḥ nna-kaṃ
10. śrīmatsaṅghaniṣevitas surataruḥ śrīrājabhikṣur yy---
11. caturjjāyai- dattaṃ me calayanti durātmaka- (āḥ)
12. narakaviṅśan te śeṣaṃ santānair yyanti saptabhi- (ḥ)

Face II

1. -- trikonā naraka sughorāḥ
2. - ṇyacatūkonakṛtā sugāḍhāḥ

3. pañcaśaśsaptadaśaṣṭakonāḥ
4. pāpiṣṭhvāsāya pare pare syuḥ
5. - - - sāyantrasamanatasaṇgatāḥ
6. - - - - - - - - māṅsamedhakāḥ
7. - - - - - - - ḥ jīvitihiṅsakīdhamāḥ
8. savisphuriṣṭhā narakāḥ pare kva cit.[65]

[The remaining part is a list of donations. The numerals correspond to each line of the inscription.]

The inclusion of a warning curse is quite a common practice in Khmer inscriptions, but such curses were also found in Burmese inscriptions within the Theravāda tradition some centuries later. In the above lines, the threat of a curse is usually followed by the blessings that will accrue to those who refrain from stealing or damaging the gifts donated to the monks.

Inscriptions from the Śrīvijaya *maṇḍala* that date to around the seventh or eighth century provide important information on how monasteries and *stūpas* were built, what gifts were given to monks and brahmans, and the casting of images of bodhisattvas such as Padmapāṇī and Vajrapāṇī.[66] In one inscription that dates to around the seventh to ninth century, the distribution of materials for the copying of manuscripts is mentioned together with the devotion given to Prajñāpāramitā and Agastya:

> . . . the *caṅkrama,* the refectory, together with the Uposatha hall, food for the community (*sāṅghikapaudgalaṃ*) and for individual monks daily . . . The adoration of the [*Prajñā*?] *pāramitā,* the writing [copying?] together with notepad and ink, the food for the group of brahmans who belong to the deserve-to-be-revered Mahātman Agastya (*ijyāgastimahātmano dvijagaṇasya-ānnañ ca*). Sermons which do not lack gifts such as incense, lamps, garlands, canopies, yak-tail whisks (*cāmara*), [and] Chinese [silk] flags. Other meritorious deeds according to the Doctrine, the unceasing observance according to the Dharma, protecting the people, equanimity towards the desirable and the undesirable, the overcoming of the senses [sensual pleasure]. . . By him who has become rich by [his valor] . . . Arnāya by name.[67]

This inscription reveals that a mixed religious situation existed in the peninsula of Thailand between Buddhism, most likely Mahāyāna, and Hinduism.

Thus far, Buddhist inscriptions in Southeast Asia can be divided into two main parts. Pāli inscriptions are found in the Pyu *maṇḍala* in the middle

Irrawaddy River valley in Burma and in the Dvāravatī *maṇḍala* in the central, upper central, and northeastern parts of Thailand. The majority of them are quotations from canonical texts with the exception of a few royal inscriptions in Pāli from northern Thailand. Sanskrit inscriptions and those with Mahāyānistic elements belong to the Khmer and the Śrīvijaya *maṇḍalas*, but are also found in Java and West Borneo. Those inscriptions that quote from texts appear to be of the same date as those of the Pyu and the Dvāravatī *maṇḍalas*.

In the Pyu *maṇḍala*, both Pāli and Sanskrit inscriptions of the quotation type are found, but those exclusively in Sanskrit are rare and of a later date. In the Dvāravatī area, Sanskrit inscriptions of this type are yet to be found. Donation inscriptions that record the aspirations of the donor and the transfer of merit are written solely in vernacular languages and are found only in the Dvāravatī tradition.

The *ye dharmā* stanza is the most frequently used one. The popularity of the stanza is not limited to India, Sri Lanka, or Southeast Asia; it is found also in Yunnan Province of southern China. The stanza occurs in inscriptions with Mahāyāna and Tantric texts, and in this case is associated with those traditions as well.[68] Otherwise, when the stanza is found alone, either in Pāli or Sanskrit, it cannot simply be identified as either Theravāda or Mahāyāna. A language similar to Pāli was evidently used in the inscriptions of sects other than the Theravāda in South India,[69] and the Mahāyāna school was not the only one to use Sanskrit as a sacred language.[70] To further complicate the issue, Sanskrit was sometimes used as a sacred language by the Abhayagirivihāra in Sri Lanka.[71]

The inscriptions are closely related to religious buildings or religious objects. By examining the archaeological data, we shall be able to discover the nature of the context in which the inscriptions appear.

ARCHAEOLOGICAL SOURCES

Our knowledge in this field is rather inadequate. There is less archeological data from Burma than there is from Cambodia. In Thailand the situation has improved somewhat in recent years. Due to the lack of sustained and systematic excavations, the archaeological evidence available to us is like a jigsaw puzzle with missing pieces. This evidence, for the most part, has been interpreted by art historians, who even among themselves, cannot agree on dates or artistic styles.[72] Any statement made by art historians on the subject should be regarded as provisional.

There are four principal schools or periods of Indian art that influenced the art of Southeast Asia: the Amarāvatī (second to third centuries CE); the Gupta (fourth to sixth centuries CE); the Pallava (550 to 750 CE); and the Pāla (750 to 900 CE).[73] Another important influence came from Sri Lanka, especially during the Anurādhapura period (third century CE to the eighth century CE) that affected the development of Southeast Asian art no less than did India.[74]

These influences do not mean that no process of localization took place. Quite the contrary, the various Southeast Asian cultures in different regions modified these outside influences and made them their own, from as early as the fourth or fifth centuries.[75] In addition to localization, there was also sub-localization among different traditions, especially at times when a shift in political or cultural dominance occurred.[76] Sub-localization took place, for example, in the central part of Thailand and in the peninsula, as well as in the insular areas of Southeast Asia. Mixed styles developed in areas where the boundaries of different cultures overlapped. Styles developed unevenly, inconsistently, and influences from India and Sri Lanka were not the same in all areas. Furthermore, in some areas a certain style persevered, while in others new styles replaced previous ones.

Since it is not possible to present here the full extent of archaeological data pertinent to our discussion, we shall try to summarize it under topics related to the type of archeological find.

ARCHITECTURAL STRUCTURES

Only a few ancient buildings have survived intact, and not one is free from reconstruction, repairs, or additions. This is partly explained by the fact that Buddhism continues to be a living faith in Southeast Asia. In addition, not only did various schools of Buddhism flourish in different periods, but also Hinduism was always present on the scene. Sometimes the different religions were on equal footing, but at other times one or the other predominated. This can be seen in buildings that were originally Buddhist, but later were "converted" for Hindu cultic use, and vice versa.

Most of the Buddhist buildings in the Pyu and Dvāravatī *maṇḍala*s were either *stūpa*s or *vihāra*s. The *stūpa*s show influence from the Andhra area, especially Amarāvatī.[77] Originally the *stūpa*s were hemispherical mounds, but later a square or rectangular base, sometimes very elaborate, was added. W. M. Sirisena has studied the architectural styles and the site plans at Pong Tuk in the Dvāravatī *maṇḍala,* and he has come to the conclusion that they are similar to those of the Anurādhapura style in Sri Lanka.[78] The area probably had early contacts with Anurādhapura because an inscription mentions the name of that city.[79]

Dvāravatī *stūpas* were decorated with bas-reliefs in terracotta or stucco depicting episodes taken from the *Jātakas* and *Avadānas*.[80] In most cases, how the specific location of these *stūpas* relates to an overall city plan is unknown. Fortunately, aerial photography is a very useful tool,[81] but in some countries like Burma, due to government regulations, photographic data is not available.

In the Dvāravatī region, most cities were built in an oval or round shape encircled by moats. The main *stūpa*, usually the city's largest, was located in the center of the city, although large sanctuaries and *stūpas* can also be found outside the city. For example, Nakhon Pathom, known in the local chronicles as Nagara Jayaśri, the largest of the ancient cities of Southeast Asia, has the Chula Pathon (P. Cūla Padona) *cetiya* located in the center of the city and outside the city, the Pra Pathom *cetiya* (a building that combines *stūpa* and shrine attributes). It is logical to assume that the *stūpa* in the center of the city served as the center of religious activities for the townspeople, while the *stūpa* outside the city served the forest monks.

The construction of the *stūpa* as a memorial mound or tumulus over the remains of the deceased predates Buddhism. From canonical references, we know that it is not essential for a *stūpa* to be built in a monastery compound; it can stand alone as a single monument but this does not mean that *stūpas* were never built within monastery precincts. The important point to note is that the main *stūpa* of a city or pilgrimage center did not belong to any one school of Buddhism. In Andhra Pradesh in India, for example, we know from inscriptions and records that numerous monks of various schools lived harmoniously together beside the great *stūpas* of Amarāvatī and Nāgārjunikoṇḍa.[82] In this respect, ancient Southeast Asia seems to have followed the pattern found in India, where most of the ruins of monasteries were found to be located near a *stūpa*, although not necessarily within the same delineated boundary.[83] Even today in Burma, the monastic residence (*saṅghāvāsa*) and the temple for the Buddha (*buddhāvāsa*) are built in separate areas. The same is true of Thailand, but even where it is not observed, it is still evident from the original plan of the monastery that two separate areas existed, one for monks (*saṅghāvāsa*) and one for the Buddha (*buddhāvāsa*).

The *stūpa* has symbolic significance on several levels.[84] It is not simply a symbol of the Buddha's attainment of *nirvana* but also a symbol of the Buddha himself, especially when it houses his physical relics (*śarīradhātu*). In areas with Sanskrit inscriptions and strong Mahāyāna characteristics, we find architectural structures built to house images, in contrast to the *stūpas*, which are solid and cannot be entered. These structures are often very complex, as is the Bayon at Angkor Thom in Cambodia and perhaps on the grandest scale of all, the magnificent Mahāyāna *stūpa* of Barabudur in Java.[85]

IMAGES: BUDDHAS AND BODHISATTVAS

The earliest style of Buddha images found in Southeast Asia is that labeled as "Amarāvatī." In actuality, these images should be called "à la Amarāvatī," because, with the exception of the one found in the Celebes, they are the work of local artists and of a later date. Pierre Dupont in his detailed study of the subject concludes that all of the images show a strong influence from the art of Anurādhapura in Sri Lanka.[86] Mirella Levi D'Ancona adds a slightly different interpretation by proposing that those found in Champa, Java, and the Celebes were imported. According to D'Ancona, the image from Champa belongs to the Amarāvatī style and should be dated around the fourth century CE; the other two were imported from Sri Lanka and date to the sixth century.[87] The two scholars do agree on one point: the images found in Khorat, Pong Tuk, and Java all show influences from Sri Lanka and are in the Gupta style.

These Buddha images are in the standing or upright posture, with hands in the *vitarka* or *abhaya mudrā,* a style that prevailed in Andhra Pradesh and in Anurādhapura at approximately the same time. Later, the favorite *mudrā* for the standing Buddha in the Gupta style was the *varada* or *abhaya mudrā,* and for the seated Buddha, the *dharmacakra mudrā.*[88]

In addition to the standing posture, there are three seated styles: *vīrāsana, vajrāsana,* and the so-called "European" style (seated on a throne with the legs down). Buddha images in the southern Indian style, including those from Sri Lanka, are always in the *vīrāsana* style and usually display the *vitarka* or *abhaya mudrā.* Sri Lankan artists favor the *dhyāna mudrā.* Images in the northern Indian Gupta and Pāla styles are seated in the *vajrāsana* style and display the *dharmacakra* or *bhūmisparśa mudrā.* Boisselier has summarized the preferences for the various *āsanas* and *mudrās* in Southeast Asian art, noting that the whole of Southeast Asia had succumbed to the influence of South India and probably Sri Lanka too, prior to the seventh century CE:

> The whole area, with the exception of Burma and Indonesia, was to retain a constant fidelity to the representations of figures seated in the *vīrāsana* posture (the right leg bent and positioned over the left leg and not in the *vajrāsana* posture in which the legs are tightly crossed in such a way as to render the soles of

> both feet visible) and an equally constant aversion to the *dharmacakra mudrā,* the *vitarka mudrā* being employed exclusively. The school of Dvāravatī (c. 7th–9th century), whose widespread and lasting influence was felt over most of the central and east of Indo-China, was responsible for developing and disseminating a special form of the *vitarka mudrā,* executed with both hands positioned symmetrically . . . During its earliest centuries, Khmer Buddhist art faithfully followed the example of Dvāravatī, but it tended to neglect the art of Dvāravatī during the Angkorian period, when its artists found themselves serving a country almost all of whose habitants were by then of the Mahāyāna Buddhist persuasion. Those artists produced very few images representing figures in the attitudes other than the *samādhi* position, and they usually chose to depict the figures sitting on the coils of the nāga-king, Mucalinda . . . To begin with Indonesian art responded to the same trends as the rest of South-east Asia; from the middle of the 8th century onwards, it moved intentionally towards the esoteric Mahāyāna Buddhism and was receptive to influences from the art of west Bengal . . . If we consider its purely iconographic aspect, Indonesian art emerges as the art that was most obviously influenced by the traditions of north-east India.[89]

The Dvāravatī tradition tended to preserve the styles of South India and Sri Lanka, even when influenced by the Gupta style at a later date. There are examples of Buddhas seated in the European style in Dvāravatī and Java, but the Dvāravatī images preserve the *vitarka mudrā,* whereas the Javanese images adhere very closely to their Gupta prototypes and display the *dharmacakra mudrā.*[90] Still later, when Pāla influence reached the region, the Burmese of Pagan, and to some extent the Lanna Thai of northern Thailand, adopted the *vajrāsana* and the *bhūmisparśa mudrā.* While Pāla influence was evident, it does not mean that the iconography is identified as belonging to Mahāyāna or Tantra; it remains strictly within the Theravāda tradition.

The iconography of Buddha images cannot be used to identify a specific sectarian tradition. However, bodhisattva images, particularly Avalokiteśvara or Mañjuśrī, most definitely belong to the Mahāyāna tradition. Avalokiteśvara images have been found in the Khmer *maṇḍala,* the south of Thailand, Indonesia, and less frequently in the Pyu and Dvāravatī areas.[91] Those images from the Dvāravatī areas were found in regions that came under the influence of the Angkorian *maṇḍala,* which naturally exhibit Khmer stylistic influences.

Tantric images were produced only during the later period, primarily in the Khmer *maṇḍala.* Some images in the Angkorian *maṇḍala* are said to be Prajñāpāramitā, Vajrasattva, or Hevajra, and date to the eleventh century.[92]

The cult of Prajñāpāramitā is mentioned in inscriptions concerning the casting of images. In Southeast Asia, the area most influenced by Tantric Buddhism was Java, where numerous images have been found. The great *stūpa* of Barabudur has frequently been interpreted as a *maṇḍala*.[93]

BUDDHIST SYMBOLS

Buddhist symbols in Southeast Asian art are numerous and used mostly as motifs in decorating a building or monument. For the sake of brevity, only three important types will be discussed: the Wheel of Dharma (*dharmacakra*), boundary stones (*sīmā*), and votive tablets. The first and the second seem to be limited to Dvāravatī culture, while the third is pan-Buddhist.

The symbol of the wheel (*cakra*) atop a post has its roots in Vedic culture. It is reasonable to assume that the wheel stands for the sun, as seen in this description of the Vājapeya sacrifice:

> A wheel-shaped cake of grain is placed on the top of the post, to which an animal victim is tied; a ladder is brought; the sacrificer mounts upon it saying to his wife: "Come, let us mount to the sun!" He then mounts and seizes the wheel, saying, "We have attained the sun, O gods."[94]

The symbol of the wheel also conveys a sense of time and order (*ṛta*). With the sun considered to be the source of life and power, the *cakra* also stands for power, hence the concept of the *cakravartin* or universal monarch. The cyclical progression of the sun might have contributed in some way to the concept of *saṃsāra*, described in Buddhism as the "Wheel of Life" or "Wheel of Existence" (*bhavacakra*) and in Hinduism as the "Wheel of Transmigration" (*saṃsāracakra*).[95]

Buddhism first appropriated and then modified the ancient concept of *cakra*. Even if the cult of *cakra* was common to all Indic religions, it appears that Buddhist artists were the first to give it a material form. It is usually set upon a post or pillar—a symbol of stability and power—and placed in the vicinity of a *stūpa*. The tradition of erecting pillars as symbols of sovereignty is probably pre-Aśokan, but the pillar surmounted by a *cakra* appears to have originated in the Aśokan era in the third century BCE.[96] Very few *cakra*s have survived in India proper, however, there are inscriptions that mention the erection of this type of pillar in the Andhra region.

In Southeast Asia, the tradition was transmitted and preserved in the Dvāravatī culture where thirty-three *dharmacakra* were found. At first, scholars were uncertain how to interpret them. Some suggested that they belonged to the chariot of Sūrya, the sun god; others maintained that they represented royal power, and, hence, the concept of the *cakravartin.* With the presence of one or two deer, we have a scene of the First Sermon, the *Dharmacakrapravartanasūtra* (P. *Dhammacakkappavattanasutta*) that took place in a deer park, and since there are two with Buddhist inscriptions in Pāli, one would have to conclude that they are Buddhist religious symbols.[97]

Other examples of symbols found include the so-called "Gajalakṣmī" motif or other unidentified figures. The *dharmacakra,* the symbol of the first sermon, together with the Gajalakṣmī figure, which represents the birth of the Buddha, when placed upon a post before a *stūpa,* comprise, more or less, the most important episodes in the life of the Buddha: his birth, his first sermon, and his *nirvāṇa.*[98]

The second Buddhist symbol found in Southeast Asia is the *sīmā* or boundary stone, usually four or six in number, to delineate the area in which the Sangha performs its monastic rites (*saṅghakarma*) according to the Vinaya rules. These boundary stones are an absolute necessity for a Buddhist monastery. References to them are found in inscriptions in northeastern Thailand, where scenes from the life of the Buddha, the *Jātaka,* and perhaps the *Avadāna* were elaborately carved on stone slabs that were used as *sīmā* stones. The practice could be connected to a Neolithic cult present in the area, in which large stones were used to mark the boundary of a tomb or some other sacred precinct.[99] What is important to note is that these stones provide definitive evidence that monasteries existed here whose monks observed the Vinaya rules in some strict sense.

Votive tablets, the third type of symbol, are pan-Buddhist. Some scholars have even described them as the Buddhist symbol *par excellence,* since they have never been found in connection with Hinduism. They have been discovered over vast areas, from India to Central Asia to southern China, Vietnam, and throughout the Malay peninsula.[100]

Alfred C. A. Foucher links their origin to the four great pilgrimage sites, proposing that votive tablets were made as souvenirs for faithful pilgrims who visited these holy places. Votive tablets were an easy and less expensive way to make merit.[101] They are usually inscribed with the *ye dharmā* stanza either on the top rim, the lower part, or on the reverse side, and in some cases, accompanied by the name of the donor or the person to whom the merit acquired by making the tablet was dedicated.[102]

In addition to these three main types of symbols, representations of the Buddha's footprint are also to be found, suggesting that Buddhism had spread throughout the area, especially in the central part of Thailand by the fifth century at the latest.

BAS-RELIEFS

On mainland Southeast Asia, some of the bas-reliefs from the Dvāravatī tradition have survived. These bas-reliefs decorate the bases of *stūpa*s, and others are carved on cave walls or engraved on *sīmā* stones. Bas-reliefs do not always belong to the Pāli tradition, as represented by the quotation inscriptions found in the same area. For example, in the archipelago, the famous bas-reliefs of Barabudur have been studied thoroughly by scholars and identified as mainly of Mahāyāna inspiration.[103]

The early bas-reliefs found in the Dvāravatī area can be dated from around the seventh century CE. None of those in Burma has been reported to be older than the eleventh century. At the Cula Pathon in Nakhon Pathom, stucco bas-reliefs depicting Buddhist tales have been identified by Piriya Krairiksh as having been inspired by Sanskrit sources, especially the *Avadāna*s of the Sarvāstivādins.[104] While most of the stories depicted in bas-reliefs are to be found in the Pāli *Jātaka*s, one story of the tortoise and the merchants, for example, is not, and it is only known from Sanskrit sources. Thus, some bas-reliefs are obviously from non-Pāli or non-Theravādin sources.

After drawing connections between the stories of bas-reliefs and the *Avadāna*s, such as the *Divyāvadāna* and the *Avadānaśataka*, which Krairiksh believes to be works of the Sarvāstivādins, as well as the *Mahāvastu* of the Lokottaravādins, he concludes that the Buddhism of Dvāravatī was not Pāli Theravāda Buddhism, but rather, "Sanskrit Hīnayāna Buddhism." He summarizes his position as follows:

> The earliest representations of Buddhist folk tales found in Thailand probably are the terra-cotta and stucco reliefs discovered at Chula Pathon Cedi, near the town of Nakhon Pathom . . . The reliefs are thought to illustrate the *Jātaka* stories . . . These stories were compiled, together with their commentaries, in Sri Lanka in the fifth century A.D., and are known as the *Jātaka-aṭṭhakathā*. As this work is included in the Pāli canonical literature of the Theravāda school of Buddhism, it is inferred that the Buddhism practised in Dvāravatī belonged to this school . . . However, it will be shown by the identification of some of the Chula Pathon reliefs and through the comparisons of the existing texts that, contrary to the expectation, the majority of the scenes illustrated do not derive from the *Jātaka-aṭṭhakathā*, or from other Pāli sources, but from the Sanskrit

> *Avadāna* tales. These were the creations of the Sarvāstivāda, the Hīnayāna school of Buddhism that used Sanskrit . . . This finding suggests that Sanskrit Hīnayāna Buddhism may have flourished in *Dvāravatī* during the sixth and the seventh centuries A.D., a hypothesis that is affirmed by the existence of two silver medals inscribed with the Sanskrit word *śrīdvāravatīśvarapuṇya* . . . both of which were dated by palæographical method to the seventh century A.D.[105]

I agree with Krairiksh that there was Hīnayāna Sanskrit Buddhism in Dvāravatī, which can also be supported by other bas-reliefs that depict the Buddha together with three Hindu gods and a *rishi.* This particular scene high on the walls of a cave could have derived from the *Mahāvastu* or may even have been inspired by the *Kāraṇḍavyūha,* a Mahāyāna *sūtra.*[106] However, this bas-relief cannot be used as evidence to rule out the existence of Theravāda Buddhism in the Dvāravatī culture since there is strong support from the Pāli inscriptions.

Moreover, the bas-reliefs should be not be regarded as belonging exclusively to the Sarvāstivādins. The *Avadāna* and *Jātaka* stories were not the sole domain of that school; they are also found in most of the Buddhist Sanskrit traditions, including the Mahāyāna. Examples include the Mahāsaṅghika's *Mahavastu-avadāna,* the *Jātakastava,* the *Jātakamālā,* and so forth.[107] *Avadāna* literature exists even in the Pāli canon, *pace* Krairiksh's statement that "[t]he *Avadānas* are tales of glorious and heroic deeds performed by the Buddha and some of his followers in their previous existences, and hence they hold the same relation to the Sarvāstivada school as did the *Jātaka* to the Theravāda school."[108] This seems to suggest that there is no *Avadāna* literature in Pāli, but to ascribe all *Avadāna* literature solely to the Sarvāstivādins requires solid proof.[109] None of the identifications of the Dvāravatī bas-reliefs are, as Krairiksh himself admits, conclusive.[110] The texts to which he traces the tales are not exclusively Sarvāstivādin; they include the *Mahāvastu,* the *Jātakamāla,* the *Sūtrālaṅkāra,* and also the *Jātaka* of the Theravādins. Therefore, one can agree with Krairiksh insofar as there was Sanskrit Hīnayāna Buddhism in Dvāravatī, but to identify this form of Sanskrit Hīnayāna as Sarvāstivādin goes beyond the evidence. Here the phrase, "Sanskrit Hīnayāna" must be taken to refer to several schools of Hīnayāna, not just the Sarvāstivādins. Moreover, one cannot rule out the Mahāyāna school either. That is, if one uses the existence of a story in a text as the sole evidence to identify the specific school of the story, it follows that since some of the bas-reliefs are traceable to Mahāyāna texts, then the Mahāyāna must have been present. On the other hand, neither can we claim that the Theravādins were not actively engaged in Dvāravatī at that time.

These folk tales are the common heritage of all schools of Buddhism. The compilers of the *Jātaka* stories may not have included all of them at the time that the commentary was written, but this does not suggest that the stories were unknown in the Pāli tradition. The collection that we now have is no older than the fifth century, and probably was not finalized until much later, given the fact that the order and number or even the titles of the tales do not absolutely agree even among the Theravāda collections of Sri Lanka, Burma, and Thailand.[111]

Furthermore, a *stūpa* such as the Chula Pathon does not belong exclusively to one particular school of Buddhism. The bas-reliefs seem to reflect various sources from different schools.[112] The *stūpa* served as the central monument of the city, accessible to any and all Buddhists. Most likely, Theravādins had no objection to the depiction of stories drawn from other Buddhist sources, even for a *stūpa* within their own monastery precincts. After all, texts such as the *Paññāsajātaka*[113] or the *Tamnān Mūlasāsanā* include stories from non-Pāli traditions. The fact that stories from non-Pāli sources, even though they do not show any definitive Mahāyāna influence, are depicted on the base of a *stūpa* does not rule out the possibility of the prominence of Theravāda Buddhism nor the existence of Mahāyāna Buddhism in Dvāravatī culture.

The fact that Sanskrit was used on the medals mentioned by Krairiksh has no bearing upon the question of the school(s) of Dvāravatī Buddhism, because Sanskrit was the royal or official language throughout Southeast Asia, and it was the brahmans, not the monks, who advised the king on administrative matters. Even after Burma was "converted" to Theravāda Buddhism, Aniruddha's donative inscriptions were still written in a kind of quasi-Sanskrit.

RELATIONSHIP BETWEEN EPIGRAPHIC AND ARCHAEOLOGICAL DATA

It is evident that inscriptions, especially those of the quotation type, were not selected at random, but rather were consciously chosen for a particular edifice like a *stūpa*. These quotation inscriptions serve a different function from royal or donation ones. They must be considered as texts, or even manuscripts, since they are copied from scriptural sources.

Among the texts quoted, the *ye dharmā* stanza is the one most frequently used. It appears in both Pāli and Sanskrit forms, as well as southern Indian and northern Indian scripts. The tradition of inscribing this stanza persisted until at least the late ninth century. Other texts that are closely connected to the stanza are the *pratītyasamutpāda* and the *āryasatya*. The *ye dharmā* stanza can be considered the shortest form of the *pratītyasamutpāda*. The first two lines refer to the cause of all dharmas (*samudayavāra*), and the third line to their cessation (*nirodhavāra*). In the same sense, the Four Noble Truths are a form of the *pratītyasamutpāda,* with the first two truths comprising the arising of the world, and the last two its cessation. Hence, there is a close relationship among all three quotations, which are the most frequently cited. The *ajñānāc=cīyate* stanza also carries the same import as the *pratītyasamutpāda.*

Primarily, these stanzas are associated with *stūpas*. The *ye dharmā* stanza is inscribed on bricks or gold plates and found in several locations: buried inside a *stūpa*; inscribed on the outside of a *stūpa* or on the bricks used for building a *stūpa*; and inscribed on the base of an image or on a votive tablet. When the text is found on a *stūpa*, it is probably regarded as a relic but not as one of the traditional three kinds of relics. The stanza has been designated as *dharmadhātu,* and a *stūpa*—or indeed, any object on which it is inscribed—then becomes a *dharmacetiya.* Some scholars go so far as to identify it with the *dharmakāya* of the Mahāyāna concept of "three bodies" (*trikāya*).[114]

The practice of enshrining a text within a *stūpa* is not foreign to either the Indian or the Sri Lankan tradition. S. Paranavitana, followed by Diran K. Dohanian, reasons that the practice was introduced to Sri Lanka by Mahāyānists, basing his theory on the plaques inscribed with Sanskrit texts that were found in Indikutasāya and Vijirārāma, and dated later than the eighth century.[115] The original idea of enshrining texts could well have originated with the Mahāyāna, as Paranavitana asserts, especially since there is evidence that the Mahāyānists were actively engaged in the copying of texts and repeatedly emphasized its importance.[116] However, this practice was not totally absent from the Theravāda of Sri Lanka or other sects on the Indian subcontinent. And the practice seems to have been popular well before the eighth century, the earliest date for evidence of this practice in Sri Lanka.[117] In India, a *ye dharmā* inscription in Pāli with some traces of Sanskrit (that is, in the two words *prabhavā* and *mahāśramaṇa*) was found in the ruins of a *stūpa* at Sārnāth, and dated epigraphically to the second century CE.[118] Another example from Cambodia, but one engraved on the back of a standing Buddha image, dated to around the seventh century, exhibits similar characteristics, with the Sanskrit word, *prabhavā.* In Southeast Asia the practice of inscribing texts in both Pāli and Sanskrit and enshrining them is evident at the latest by the fourth or fifth century CE.

A major dispute erupted in Sri Lanka in the ranks of the Sangha over the relative importance of textual study vis-à-vis practice, with textual studies finally being accorded priority.[119] Thus, texts were considered to be very important even by monks who had no Mahāyānist leanings. The texts that were placed within a *stūpa* were not exclusively Sanskrit or Mahāyāna texts; rather, the texts used were often ones common to all sects. In view of the rarity of physical relics, the Dharma itself was a more widely available sacred "object" with which to consecrate a *stūpa*.

Paranavitana seems to suggest that since the *dharmakāya* is superior to the *nirmāṇakāya,* the enshrining of texts would be preferred over bodily relics. Texts would not, however, replace or be superior to bodily relics. If bodily relics could be acquired, they were always preferred; this also holds true in Mahāyāna practice. In some cases, bodily relics and textual relics were found together.[120]

As for Paranavitana's interpretation of a *stūpa* containing a text as the *dharmakāya,* a cosmic form of the Buddha, this seems at odds with Theravādin tradition. In fact, the term *dharmakāya* is used in the canon in a doctrinal sense or, in an extended sense, as the text itself. This usage persists in the Mahāyāna tradition as well, for instance, in the opening stanza of the *Bodhicāryāvatāra* and in the content of the *Dharmaśarīrasūtra.*[121] Moreover, the concept of *dharmadhātu* is not foreign to the Pāli canon. As the basic principle of all dharmas, *pratītyasamutpāda* is called *dhammaṭhiti, dhammadhātu, dhammaniyāma,* and so on.[122] It is not surprising that the shortest form of the *pratītyasamutpāda,* the *ye dharmā* stanza, emerged as the most popular text to be interred in a *stūpa.*[123]

In the Theravādin tradition, a *stūpa* or a material object bearing an inscription quoted from scripture is simply a *dharmacetiya* in the ordinary sense, and not the "cosmic body" of the Buddha. The reference to the introduction of the text known as *Dharmadhātu,* which has been labeled as Mahāyānistic, does not mention the relation between this text and the practice of enshrining a text in a *stūpa.* What was rejected by the orthodox monks in Sri Lanka was not the practice of enshrining texts per se, but enshrining the texts of the Mahāyānists. The practice is not, therefore, unique to the Mahāyānists nor does it have to originate from the Mahāyāna tradition. And it is certainly incorrect to assert, as Paranavitana has, that " . . . the extension of the veneration at first paid to bodily relics of the Buddha to the metal fragments on which words attributed to him were written was due to the influence of the Mahāyāna conception of the three bodies."[124] Although the concept of the three bodies was in use among the Mahāyānists in Sri Lanka, it does not follow that this doctrine had any direct correlation to the cult of enshrining texts in *stūpa*s. Even the author of the *Saddharmmaratnākāra* draws no such connection between the practice and the doctrine of the three bodies.

The other object inscribed with texts is the *dharmacakra*. As noted earlier, the *cakra* is an ancient Indian symbol that was appropriated by Buddhists. Two texts have been found inscribed on the *cakra:* the Four Noble Truths and the *pratītyasamutpāda*. In the first, the wheel becomes the symbol for the First Sermon, the *Dharmacakrapravartanasūtra*, or in short, the *dharmacakra*. In the second, the wheel stands for the *bhavacakra*, the "Wheel of Life."

All of these material objects of worship—*stūpa*, images and motifs, votive tablets, and *dharmacakra*—are closely interrelated, having been found in the same location. Buddhist images were often placed in the alcoves at the base of a *stūpa*. Votive tablets were usually interred in *stūpa*s together with quotation inscriptions. *Dharmacakra*s were set atop pillars erected in front of a *stūpa*. Taken as a group, these material objects formed a complex symbol system in Southeast Asian Buddhism.

PATTERNS AND DEVELOPMENT OF SOUTHEAST ASIAN BUDDHISM

It is common practice for scholars to label the Buddhism of Southeast Asia as Theravāda or Mahāyāna on the basis of the language of inscriptions or of archaeological remains identified by art historians as either Theravāda or Mahāyāna. This, however, is an oversimplification.

In the case of language, any document using Pāli is usually labeled as belonging to the Theravādins, or occasionally narrowed further to the Theravādins of Sri Lanka. Sanskrit inscriptions that do not show any overt influence of the Mahāyānists have been assigned to the Sarvāstivādins.[125]

Because Pāli is used only in the Theravāda tradition, the first conclusion seems more secure.[126] However, the language used in inscriptions of other sects found in the Andhra Pradesh area of India and dated to around the third to fourth century is very similar to Pāli. The differences may stem from the orthographic or epigraphic conventions of the time, as, for instance, the absence of double consonants or long vowels. But these conventions do not appear in the Pāli inscriptions of Southeast Asia, which are written in what is known as "standard" Pāli. This would seem to indicate that the Pāli used in the region does indeed belong to the Theravāda and most probably the

Theravādins of Sri Lanka as well. However, it is worth noting that there is evidence that Pāli was still in use in India during the Pāla period. A Pāla-style votive tablet was found in a *stūpa* in Thailand, but it was evidently imported from India and inscribed with the *ye dharmā* stanza in Pāli.[127]

Sanskrit, which became the *lingua franca* of India, was more widely used than Pāli for that reason, and its use was by no means limited to the Sarvāstivādins. Sanskrit made its impact felt in Buddhism rather early, as seen in the progressive trend towards a Sanskritized Prakrit language. The languages used in Buddhist texts become more and more Sanskritic over time, and even Pāli did not escape this trend.[128] The *Mahāvastu* of the Mahāsaṅghika-Lokottaravādins is written in Buddhist Sanskrit, and Mahāyāna texts are written either in Buddhist Sanskrit or in more or less standard Sanskrit.

Therefore we cannot agree with Nihar Ranjan Ray, who in his study *Sanskrit Buddhism in Burma*, cites the Sanskrit *ye dharmā* inscriptions to assert that Sanskrit Buddhism in Burma is Sarvāstivādin. The Sarvāstivādins were not the only ones to use Sanskrit. The *ye dharmā* in Sanskrit was widely used and adopted by the Mahāyāna tradition, but the evidence is inconclusive to pinpoint the sect to which the *ye dharmā* inscriptions belong. The issue is further complicated by the Theravādins of the Abhayagirivihāra in Anurādhapura, who are said to have used Sanskrit alongside Pāli and whose monastery served as a center for the Mahāyānists as well as the Theravādins.[129] It is reasonable to conclude that the Sanskrit texts found in Southeast Asia could have come from Sri Lanka. In this case, the term "Theravāda" only adds to the confusion, since the Abhayagirivihāravāsins, even if they were open-minded toward the Mahāyāna doctrines, were still regarded as belonging to the Theravādins of Sri Lanka. Thus, an inscription that cited a stanza from a Buddhist text in Sanskrit could belong to any one of at least three schools: Sarvāstivādins, Mahāyānists, or the Abhayagirivihāravāsins of the Theravādin of Sri Lanka.

Another point needs to be made concerning art objects and artistic styles. Scholars tend to interpret art objects in the northern Indian style as Mahāyāna and those in the southern style as Hīnayāna or even Theravāda.[130] This facile interpretation is very misleading, for style does not necessarily cleave so tenaciously to sectarian divisions. If one identifies every Buddha image in the *vajrāsana* as belonging to the Mahāyāna, then nearly every Burmese image would be identified as Mahāyāna, even though it is self-evident that those images are products of Theravādin inspiration.

Even when images, especially those of the Buddha, are found in a place known to be a Mahāyānist sanctuary, one cannot claim that the images are exclusively of Mahāyāna inspiration, for the Mahāyānists never rejected the iconographical tradition of Hīnayāna Buddhism. Most sanctuaries have undergone extensive renovations and alterations according to a particular style or preferences of the time, at one time Hīnayāna, then later Mahāyāna, or even Hindu. No one image or motif can be an absolute indicator in identifying a sanctuary as Theravādin or Mahāyānist. Not only was it common to find objects belonging to both traditions in the same area, it was also possible for Hindu images to be found there as well. It is likely that a sanctuary could be Hindu and Buddhist at the same time.[131] To define the differences just among the Buddhists themselves is an even more difficult enterprise.

Regarding *stūpas*, some scholars try to link the cult of building large *stūpas* to the Caityaka school.[132] However, this cult is not limited solely to the Caityakas. For example, more than one sect resided in the vicinity of the great *stūpas*, such as Amarāvatī or Nāgājunikoṇḍa. At Bodhgayā, monasteries of various sects from different countries were built to accommodate pilgrims, which is a clear indication that large scale *stūpa* sites were public monuments and not the specific domain of any one sect. The same holds true for the *stūpa* sites in Southeast Asia, and may explain the apparent discrepancies between epigraphic and archaeological data, as can be seen in the case of the Chula Pathon Cedi where stories from non-Pāli sources adorn its base. A *stūpa* is a public treasure, and any sect could participate in its decoration and veneration. From archeological ruins, the sites suggest that other Hīnayāna sects or even the Mahāyāna ones were active there, but such activity does not preclude the presence of the Theravādins in the area.

It is imperative that these sources and data be analyzed very carefully. One cannot use a few lines of inscription in Pāli or Sanskrit to say that the Buddhism of a particular area was Theravāda, Sarvāstivāda, or Mahāyāna, unless supported by other evidence.[133] Remains of buildings or *stūpas* yielding data such as images that cannot clearly be connected to a specific sect should not be designated as belonging to a particular sect.

From epigraphic data it appears that in the Pyu and the Dvāravatī regions, Buddhism—in particular, one that used Pāli and was presumably Theravādin—was predominant. In the Khmer region and Indonesia, inscriptions from the sixth to seventh century CE, even though written in Sanskrit, do not show the particular features of Mahāyāna Buddhism. From the eighth century on, strong waves of Mahāyāna influence came to the archipelago and the Khmer *maṇḍala*, and subsequently, to central Thailand, which at the time was under the sway of Dvāravatī culture. Even so, the Theravādins held their own against the Mahāyānists and coexisted with them.[134]

The Mon area of southern Burma, traditionally regarded as the place where the mission sent by the Third Buddhist Council first landed, has yielded scant evidence of Buddhism. Only one Buddha image in the Gupta style has been reported from Thaton.[135] The rest of the archaeological finds are Brahmanical in nature.[136] In the area north of the Pyu *maṇḍala,* the religion there seems to have been a *nāga* cult, followed later by Tantric Buddhism from the northeast of India that came via the land route.[137]

While it is uncertain exactly when Tantric Buddhism arrived in Burma, we have evidence that it was flourishing by the tenth and eleventh centuries CE, predating the adoption of Theravāda Buddhism by Aniruddha of Pagan. The Tantric cult was called "Ari" in Burma. Some of its practices are similar to a kind of Buddhism found in Cambodia and recorded by Zhou Daguan (Chou Ta Koun, Chou Ta-Kuan) who traveled to that country in the thirteenth century.[138]

What we can say is that in terms of Buddhism, Theravāda was the main sect in the Pyu and Dvāravatī cultures, and that Mahāyāna was dominant in the Khmer areas and the archipelago. However, this does not rule out the presence of other Hīnayāna sects or Mahāyānists in the Pyu and the Dvāravatī traditions, nor does it mean that there was no Theravāda or Hīnayāna presence in the Khmer *maṇḍala* and the archipelago.

When available evidence indicates that Buddhism and Brahmanism coexisted, the question arises: how important was sectarian affiliation in the Southeast Asian context? Objects of art were shared among various Buddhist sects, as well as those of Hinduism. The same was probably true in India and Sri Lanka. Our received picture can be easily distorted by an overemphasis on texts dealing with the formation of the different sects, a subject of focused study by Western scholars.

The evidence from epigraphic and archaeological data does not suggest any substantial separation or gulf between the sects. Hīnayānists and Mahāyānists appear to have lived in the same area or even in the same monastery.[139] In the Buddhist universities of Nālandā and Vikramaśīla, monks of different sects must have resided together. Lay support was not limited to one particular sect, for inscriptions have been found of a king who supported at least two sects at the same time.[140] The situation in Southeast Asia was similar with ample support from the inscriptions quoted in this chapter.

Information about the Buddhist sects in Southeast Asia may be gleaned from the diary records of Chinese pilgrims, and such eyewitness accounts have been used to determine which schools were active in particular regions. However, these sources do not always provide accurate first-hand information, and we should be wary in using them. Information about the sites that the pilgrims actually visited is a more reliable source than hearsay evidence. Reporting on the religious situation of Southeast Asia, Yi Jing (I-Tsing, I-Ching) writes:

> At the (eastern) extremity there is the so-called "Great Black" Mountain, which is, I think, on the southern boundary of Tu-fan (Tibet). This mountain is said to be on the south-west of Shu-Chuan (Ssu-Chuan), from which one can reach this mountain after a journey of a month or so. Southward from this, and close to the sea-coast there is a country called Śrīkshatra [*sic*] (Prome); on the south-east of this is Laṅkasu (probably Kāmalaṅkā); on the east of this is Dvā(ra)pati (Dvāravatī, Ayudhya); at the extreme east, Lin–i (Champa). The inhabitants of all these countries greatly reverence the Three Jewels (Ratnatraya). There are many who hold firmly to the precepts and perform the begging dhūta which constitutes a custom in these countries. Such (persons) exist in the West (India) as I have witnessed, who are indeed different from men of ordinary character . . . In the islands of the Southern Sea—consisting of more than ten countries—the Mūlasarvāstivādanikāya has been almost universally adopted (lit. "there is almost only one"), though occasionally some have devoted themselves to the Sammitinikāya; and recently a few followers of the other two schools have also been found. . . . Setting out from Kwan–chou . . . and proceeding still southwards one arrives at Champa, i.e. Lin–I . . . In this country Buddhists generally belong to the Çryasammitinikāya, and there are also a few followers of the Sarvāstivādanikāya. . . . Setting out south-westwards, one reaches (on foot) within a month, Poh–nan (Kuo), formerly called Fu–nan. Of old it was a country, the inhabitants of which lived naked; the people were mostly worshippers of heaven (the gods or devas), and later on, Buddhism flourished there, but a wicked king has now expelled and exterminated them all, and there are no members of the Buddhist brotherhood at all, while adherents of other religions (or heretics) live intermingled. The region is the south corner of Jambudvīpa (India), and is not one of the islands of the sea.[141]

From Yi Jing's account very little is learned about the schools of Buddhism on the mainland, but one thing is clear: Yi Jing does not mention any specific school when he describes the Buddhism of the mainland apart from coastal Champa. If the Buddhism he encountered was mainly Sarvāstivāda or Sammatīya, he would not have failed to mention it. Thus, the assertion that Buddhism in the Pyu and Dvāravatī regions was Sarvāstivādin finds no support either from inscriptions or Chinese records.

Furthermore, Yi Jing was wrong in the case of Funan and the Khmer regions, since other epigraphic data from around the time his record was written tell us that Buddhism was flourishing side-by-side with Hinduism.[142] It is possible that his account of the archipelago is more accurate, but there is insufficient epigraphic or archaeological data to verify whether or not the main sect in the insular region was, in fact, the Sarvāstivādins. The quotation inscriptions in Sanskrit from the region do not show any specific Mahāyānistic features, but given the cautions mentioned earlier, these inscriptions cannot be assigned without reservation to the Sarvāstivādins. Yi Jing is probably right that the Mahāyāna school had not yet attained its apogee in the seventh century CE; the real evidence for Mahāyāna in this area begins only in the eighth century.[143]

According to the evidence thus provided, the Theravāda sect remained the main creed in the Pyu and Dvāravatī regions, that is, in central Burma and most of present-day Thailand. The oldest evidence are inscriptions in Pāli dating from around the fourth century CE at the earliest. Inscriptions in Pāli were continuously in use in this region, especially in Burma and Thailand, until the nineteenth century.

For a long time, the Buddhism of the Pyu and Dvāravatī traditions has been labeled as Hīnayāna, but not as Pāli Buddhism. Its origin, even when it used Pāli in its canonical texts, is said to be South Indian, not Sri Lankan, which would not have emerged until the twelfth century. These long-held misconceptions probably began with the scholar, C. O. Blagden, who thought that the Pyu people primarily professed Hinduism, with some elements of Sarvāstivāda Buddhism mixed in.[144] The misconception was perpetuated by Finot and to some extent by N. R. Ray. Even works such as Michael Aung-Thwin's *Pagan: The Origins of Modern Burma* and Emmanuel Guillon's article, "Jalons pour une histoire du bouddhisme en Asie du Sud-Est," doggedly supported these ideas, noting that Buddhism in the Pyu and Dvāravatī region was Sarvāstivādin.[145] But this position has been challenged by other scholars and proved wrong, in my estimation, by both epigraphic and archaeological evidence.

Ray regards the original home of Pāli Buddhism of the Pyu *maṇḍala* to be South India, although he does not specify the region as "South India" as such, a term which could refer to a variety of places within a specific region. Some scholars use the term to encompass the whole area south of central India, while others use it in a narrower sense for the area not further than thirteen degrees north latitude. This narrow designation comprises the area where the Pallava, Pāṇḍya, and Coḷa became the chief powers in succession.

From the quote below, it is apparent that Ray uses the word in the narrow sense:

> The source from where this Buddhism was fed and nourished was evidently the Andhra-Kuntala-Pallava region of Deccan and South India, from such centres as Amarāvatī, Nāgārjunikoṇḍa, Kāñcīpuram, Kāvaripaṭṭanam and Uragapuram where Theravāda Buddhism during these centuries had established famous and flourishing strongholds. . . . It is, therefore, reasonable to assume that Theravāda Buddhism which in Burma today is of the Sinhalese form was originally introduced not from Ceylon but from the Deccan and South India, where in the time of the celebrated pilgrim I-ching (671–95) "all followed the Sthavira nikāya though there existed a few adherents of other nikāyas also." . . . In fact it seems that it was not till the middle of the twelfth century that Ceylon came to play any important rôle in the history of Buddhism in Burma."[146]

Ray's interest is only with Theravāda Buddhism in Burma. If we accept that the situation was more or less the same in Dvāravatī, then Ray's assumption, if valid, should apply to both regions. We agree with his point that Theravāda Buddhism, and indeed other sects as well, should have come to Southeast Asia from the Deccan plain in India. But it cannot be determined with certainty that it came only from South India, and Ray's assertion that Sri Lanka played no role until the twelfth century is groundless on several accounts.

First, Theravāda Buddhism was flourishing both in Sri Lanka and in the Andhra region at the same time. South India does not yield any data on Buddhism until later. The only literary source for Buddhism in South India is the *Maṇimekhalai,* which appears to be dated no earlier than the fifth century CE, due to the fact that the author knew the works of Dharmakīrti, the famous fifth-century Buddhist logician.[147] Epigraphically, the so-called "Pallava" scripts used in the Pāli inscriptions of Southeast Asia have features in common with the Pallava script used in Sri Lanka. Archaeologically, the images said to belong to the Amarāvatī school reveal influences of the Anurādhapura style as well as the Gupta style. Second, the Chinese pilgrims record that the Sthaviranikāya was dominant in Sri Lanka. Third, Sri Lanka maintained close relations with Andhra Pradesh and South India. Examples of Theravādin inscriptions from the vicinity of Nāgārjunikoṇḍa, which date to the third and fourth centuries, are:

> Success! Adoration to the Lord Buddha . . . For the benefit of the . . . Therīyas of the fraternities [of monks] of Taṃbapaṃṇa [Ceylon] who have converted Kashmir, Gandhāra, Chīna, Chilāta, Tosali, Avaraṃta, Vaṅga, Vanavāsi, Yavana, Damila, Pulara and the Isle of Taṃbapaṃṇi . . .[148]

> Let there be success! The pair of feet of the Lord [Buddha] has been installed, with a prayer for the welfare and happiness of all beings, in the monastery of the teachers, the Therīyas [i.e., Theravādins] Vibhajjavāda, who cause delight to [convert to the Buddhist doctrine] [the people of] Kaśmīra, Gandhāra, Yavana, Vanavāsa, and Tambapaṃnidīpa, who reside in the Great Monastery [of the Mahāvihāravāsins], and who are expert in determining the meaning and the words of the nine classes of the teachings of the Buddha and who uphold the tradition of the noble lineage.[149]

Not only do these inscriptions show that Sri Lankan Theravāda Buddhism was present there, but also that the faith was propagated all over India, if the inscriptions accurately portray what happened. Although political relations between Sri Lanka and South India were not always close, this point has been overemphasized, and new evidence provides a different picture. At least we can say that the Sanghas of the two areas were closely related.[150] Monks from South India came to study in Sri Lanka, among them the famous Dhammapāla. Both Buddhaghosa and Dhammapāla felt compelled to go to Sri Lanka because the Buddhist texts there were numerous and more complete than in India. At times, monks from Sri Lanka, especially the Mahāvihāravāsins, escaped sectarian persecution and sought refuge in South India.

Moreover, the Sri Lankan Sangha maintained close relations with the mainstream Buddhists in North India.[151] Such Theravādin tenets as the *bhavaṅgacitta* are recorded in the *Karmasiddhiprakaraṇa* and other northern texts.[152] From the fourth and fifth centuries on, Sri Lanka was an important center of Buddhist studies, and not just of the Theravāda, but also of Mahāyāna and Tantra, a fact supported by epigraphic, archaeological, and Chinese records.[153] Buddhists in Sri Lanka were constantly aware of the religious and political situation in India. Even the war with the Tamils in the second century did not terminate relations with India, as suggested by Bareau, who thinks that the Theravāda school of Sri Lanka preserved its ancient characteristics precisely because of this disruption.[154] The evidence shows that Sri Lanka was constantly affected by the situation in India, but it did not alter its principal contribution of propagating Buddhism in India and abroad.

Ray goes on to remark that there is no mention of the old kingdoms of Burma in the Sri Lankan Pāli chronicles or in the commentaries written around the fifth, sixth, and seventh centuries.[155] But neither is there any reference to Southeast Asian kingdoms in the literature of India. Even Dvāravatī with its rich Pāli heritage is not mentioned in Indian or Sri Lankan literature. Mention of specific Southeast Asian countries is, in fact, quite rare, or if it is mentioned at all, it is usually in the form of an unspecified generic name, like Suvarṇadvīpa, Dvīpāntara, or Suvarṇabhūmi.

And finally, Ray's last point is at odds with his assertion that Buddhaghosa was a native of Burma.[156] If Budddhaghosa wrote most of the commentaries referred to above, how could he have failed to mention its name?

The most conclusive evidence to prove that Sri Lankan Buddhism played an important role in the history of Buddhism in Southeast Asia is epigraphic: a sixth century inscription that mentions Anurādhapura and a later citation (eighth or ninth century?) from the *Telakaṭāhagāthā,* a text indisputably composed in Sri Lanka. Therefore, Sri Lanka must be included whenever the sources of the Buddhism of Southeast Asia are studied. We cannot deny that it may have come from the Deccan, but neither can we negate the possibility of it coming from Sri Lanka. What is untenable is the statement that Sri Lanka played no role until the twelfth century.

On the basis of epigraphic and archaeological data, North India must also be considered as a source for Southeast Asian Buddhism. The tradition of the *ye dharmā* inscriptions appears to have originated there. The ones found in India do not follow the same epigraphic tradition of omitting double consonants and long vowels, but they do follow perfect standard Pāli and Sanskrit. Epigraphy and manuscripts belong to separate traditions. This trend was followed in creating such inscriptions in Southeast Asia, which are all written in standard orthography.

It may be asserted that the script used is always the so-called "Pallava" script, which is of southern Indian origin, however, its use does not exclude contact with the Buddhism of northern India. In general, the southern script was used to record Sanskrit, and the northern script to record Pāli.[157] We find that in the archipelago, as well as in the mainland, though to a lesser degree, the proto-Devanāgarī and Nāgarī languages were also used in inscriptions.[158]

This fact, together with the influence in iconography of the Gupta, Pāla, and the Anurādhapura styles, suggests that Ray has overemphasized the role played by South India as the sole source for Southeast Asian Buddhism, especially the Theravāda school. He assumes that the Theravāda lost its hold in North India at a very early time.[159] This assumption contradicts both epigraphic and archaeological evidence, since in northern India inscriptions in Pāli were found as late as the Pāla period.

Regarding so-called "Sanskrit Buddhism," which was apparently present in every region of Southeast Asia, Ray identifies it as Sarvāstivādin. However, there is no hard evidence to support his claim. While Chinese records are vague about mainland sects, they are on firmer ground for the archipelago. It is premature to state that Sanskrit Buddhism in Southeast Asia was Sarvāstivādin solely on the basis of *ye dharmā* inscriptions being written in Sanskrit. The inscriptions could belong to other Hīnayāna sects, which also used Sanskrit, or even to the Mahāyāna. Around that same time period, the Mahāsaṅghikas, who also used Sanskrit, were flourishing in Magadha, an area which Ray claims as the origin of the Sarvāstivādins of Burma.

In summary, what can we say about the religious situation of Southeast Asia? Canonical texts were quoted in inscriptions, which leads us to the assumption that the Pāli canon existed in some form in the Pyu and Dvāravatī regions by the fifth century CE at the latest. The inscriptions were compiled consciously from several texts in such a way as to show a mastery of diverse sources. There is also some evidence for the presence of other Hīnayāna sects, but due to the paucity of data, they cannot be identified with any certainty.

Beginning with the eighth century CE, traces of Mahāyāna Buddhism were found mainly in the Khmer, Śailendra, and Śrīvijaya sites. Even though Mahāyāna Buddhism influenced Dvāravatī culture, the older, local traditions continued to flourish. The school of Mahāyāna in the aforementioned regions appears to be that of the Yogācāra. In time, Tantric Buddhism also reached Southeast Asia, but its influence seems to have been limited mainly to Cambodia and Central Java.

The region north of the Pyu *maṇḍala* that was to become the center of the Pagan kingdom adhered to the local religion, but later on it came under the influence of a form of Tantra called "Ari" in Burmese, until the Theravāda asserted its control through the patronage of the famous king Aniruddha. Data from the region to the south reveals that the most prominent religion was Hinduism, most likely, Vaiṣṇava. This area, which is reported by Mon and Burmese sources as the seat from which Aniruddha introduced

Theravāda to Pagan, appears to bear some Buddhist influence from the Dvāravatī tradition.

Epigraphic data, especially from the Dvāravatī tradition, reveals that Buddhism was primarily a religion of the masses, but other monastic elites also were present, since the specificity of the texts selected and the unique design of the monuments could only have been the work of scholar-monks. The idea of inscribing essential doctrines like the Four Noble Truths and the *pratītyasamutpāda* formula on *dharmacakras* also points to the academic study of Buddhism in the Dvāravatī culture.

It must be remembered that the cult of inscribing texts to be enshrined in *stūpas* should be treated separately from a strict study of the texts. It is quite possible that the common people, in addition to the elites, participated in this cult. The bas-reliefs around the bases of *stūpas* depicting the life of Buddha, stories from the *Jātaka,* and the *Avadāna* may have had a didactic function of teaching both devotees and pilgrims. Popular practices seem to have been similar to those described by Chinese pilgrims in India, ones common to all Buddhist communities: building *stūpas* and *vihāras*, making offerings to the monks, the casting of Buddha images, venerating images and the footprint of the Buddha, and so on. These practices, however, cannot be labeled strictly as Theravāda or Mahāyāna. Furthermore, religious diversity was the rule in every part of Southeast Asia, and wherever Buddhism was present, Hinduism was there also. The two religions usually coexisted in harmony or even, as was the case in Cambodia, in synthesis rather than discord.

The same claim can be made for all schools of Buddhism: Theravāda, other Hīnayāna schools, Mahāyāna, and Tantra—all were present in Southeast Asia. The Theravāda school may have been the strongest, especially in the western part of the region in the Pyu and Dvāravatī areas where it dominated, with Mahāyāna being the strongest in Cambodia and in the peninsula and the archipelago. What factors permitted this peaceful coexistence among the various religions and schools? The questions to be considered next are why and how these religions and schools arrived at this regional distribution, to what extent was synthesis achieved, and how did this distribution and synthesis transform Buddhism in Southeast Asia?

5

Perceptions Toward Religion in Southeast Asia

Whenever the religious situation in Southeast Asia is studied, a perennial problem arises concerning indigenous beliefs and how they relate to the new religions coming from India. In chapter 2, we focused on indigenous beliefs and in chapter 4, the relations among the Indian religions in Southeast Asia. According to epigraphic and archaeological data, a line appears to be drawn between the western and the eastern regions of Southeast Asia vis-à-vis Indian religions. In the western area, Buddhism, especially the Pāli tradition (presumably Theravāda), predominated, and in the eastern area a strong impact from Brahmanism and Mahāyāna Buddhism was felt.

However, this general division does not tell the whole picture since there is evidence that other schools of Buddhism existed in both areas. What kind of ideology was present that allowed this situation to develop? The favorable climate for the coexistence of different creeds was undoubtedly due to outside factors. It could have been connected to a shift in trade or changes in the sea routes in the eighth century. Likewise, local factors, including indigenous beliefs generated from within Southeast Asian culture, facilitated the coexistence of various religious traditions and how the peoples of this region perceived religion.

INDIGENOUS BELIEFS

The problem posed by trying to determine the nature of indigenous belief systems has intrigued such great scholars as George Cœdès, Paul Mus, and H. G. Quaritch Wales. Their work focused on the search for the substrata underlying Southeast Asian cultures, extracting information from "cultural fossils" hidden under the Indian religions. Reexamining these older studies can help to recapture some of the important concepts in indigenous beliefs.

In Cœdès's book *The Indianized States of Southeast Asia*, indigenous beliefs are mentioned, but only in the broadest sense. In summing up the studies of P. Mus, A. M. Hocart, and J. Przyluski, Cœdès notes that with regard to indigenous religions, there was "belief in animism, the worship of ancestors and of the god of the soil, the building of shrines in high places, [and] burial of the dead in jars or dolmens." With regard to mythology, a cosmological dualism existed "in which are opposed the mountain and the sea, the winged race and the aquatic race, the men of the heights and those of the coast . . ."'[1]

Cœdès does not explain how these beliefs and concepts evolved, nor does he offer any explanation of how they relate to Indian beliefs. Neither does he explain what he means by "animism" nor the concepts of "power" and "empowerment" discussed in chapter 2 of his book.

Paul Mus attempted to describe the religiosity of the region in the era before the coming of the great religions of India in his article "Cultes indiens et indigènes au Champa,"[2] which could well be the first attempt to assess the contributions of indigenous cultures to the process of Indianization in Southeast Asia. In this seminal work, Mus gives his account of indigenous beliefs, focusing his research on the area where the Cham culture once flourished in the period directly preceding the arrival of Indian culture. Nevertheless, his exposition covers a vast area that embraces India, China, and Southeast Asia, an area that could be accurately described as a pan-Asian culture. Comparing the circumstances to those of the Mediterranean civilization, Mus writes:

> A hundred, two hundred or a thousand kilometers of land, divided by mountains, forests and hostile tribes, like the Indo-Chinese peninsula or the Deccan in the ancient times. Wherever sea lanes establish communication, it is reasonable to expect a cultural unity, and it makes more sense to speak of a religion of the monsoon zone of Asia than to speak of Indian religion, or Chinese religion, prior to the civilizations which were later to give meaning to these words.[3]

Mus sums up the situation by using the term "animism," after warning that the word has been overused.[4] He describes the animism of the inhabitants of ancient India, Indochina, and southern China as beliefs "in spirits, present in all things and in all places—disembodied human souls, spirits of waters and woods," and also notes that these inhabitants "credited certain men with the magic power of conjuring them up or warding them off."[5] A point worth stressing is that for Mus spirits of inanimate things, for example, in mountains or trees, are not separate or external entities possessed by a spirit, but instead, the spirit is the vital essence of the thing itself. Mus emphasizes the relations between these spirits and the people:

> But the omnipresence of the spirits is only one side of the religion we are studying: the other is the conviction that through suitable procedures it is possible to summon them, to propitiate them or to ward them off. The two aspects go together, and I believe that it is the activities of sorcerers—their techniques of conjuring up—which, more than anything else, has peopled the sphere of communal human life with various spirits: in fact the spirits are seen not at all in isolation but always in relationship with man, embodying in some fashion something that he desires if not something that he fears. Everywhere they are conceived of in terms of humanity.[6]

Among these spirits, Mus accords primacy to the spirit of the soil. He proposes that the cult of the lord of the soil best characterizes the form of religion that he believes took hold in monsoon Asia. Following E. Chavannes, who quotes from the Chinese *Book of Rites,* Mus defines the lord of the soil as the divinization of the energies in the soil. The concept is, therefore, that of an impersonal amorphous entity, which according to Mus is not quite a genie and is not a superhuman being either; rather, it is a being to be abstracted from man—invisible, but made in his image. Most importantly, "its basis is rather in events than in the human person."[7]

Mus admits that the concept has its limitations. On the one hand, there is an impersonal, impalpable god, and on the other hand, a human group by reference to which this god assumes a position of god. The question is how to make the god aware of the needs and the desires of the people? To resolve this dilemma, sacrifice becomes an important means of communication between god(s) and humans. In the sacrificial process, the god is transformed into a tangible entity like a tree or a stone in which the god is located or is made manifest. This does not mean that the god resides *inside* the tree or stone, but, rather, that the entity is conceived as the god itself, consubstantially. In the lord of the soil, we have a concentrated or intensified form of the god.[8]

It is Mus's contention that religion of this type should be understood in three ways: the divine, the human, and the ritual point of view.

Mus links the concept of sacral kingship to that of the cult of the soil. He regards the chief of a social group to be the medium for the divine. The expression of the energies of the earth is common to both the god and the chief. With this understanding, the social group is assured of the soil's fertility and the well-being of the group, which is seen as residing in the chief. Thus:

> The stone corresponds to the divinization of the energies of the soil. Over against it stands a human group. Between the two is to be interposed a link in touch with man on the one hand and the god on the other. This link is the temporary personification of the divinity. Sometimes a victim that has been sacrificed concentrates the abstract entity in it for the duration of the rite, and furnishes it with its eyes and ears. Sometimes, more conveniently, the group delegates a priest, and pre-eminently its chief, to receive the deity into himself and to represent it.[9]

Following this same line of reasoning, Mus proposes further that the delegated chief is represented also by his ancestors, who, when they passed away, were buried in the earth. By the burial act, a close relationship between the soil god and the ancestors is established. Mus cites examples of the Chinese cult of the soil as supporting evidence.[10]

The next question is how does this concept of "lord of the soil" relate to the great religions of India and the great civilizations that were later established in the region, namely, the Indian and the Chinese. In Chinese civilization, the cult of the soil constitutes the principal religious concept, but in Indian civilization, this indigenous concept came into contact with the influx of Aryan culture introduced from the West. This hybrid culture, Mus thinks, was infused with or localized by pre-Aryan religious concepts that resulted in the cult of *Yakṣa*s, which is the cult of tutelary divinities, and the cult of Śiva, which is represented by the simple image of the Śivaliṅga, who is regarded as a concentrated form of the soil or earth's potency.[11]

In the cult of tutelary divinities, Mus sees the gods of Indo-Aryan origin as undergoing the process of fixation or localization in the soil.[12] Maintaining a good relationship with a local soil god confirms the cohesiveness of the community. From this we may venture to say that at the village level a bond is established between the local god and the head of the village, who as chief functions in a sense as the symbol for all the people in that community. Village gods would be subsumed under regional gods, which, in turn, would be subsumed under a "national" god, which would be connected to the king. Therefore, the phenomenon is hierarchical, from the village god to the "national" god or the god of the dynasty.[13] For Mus, the same applies to the cult of Śiva:

> For a linga worshipped in the capital of a kingdom, great or small, or even in a mere village, is not an allegorical representation of the God, reigning in his

> distant heaven. It is not Śiva, it is 'a Śiva', the 'Śiva of the country': the prosperity of the people or of the dynasty depends on it. In a word it is the equivalent of the well-known stone or mound of the earth genie worshipped by the Vietnamese and the Chinese.[14]

As in pre-Aryan religion, the mediator is said to be the Vedic chief whose position enables him to unite the ruled with the rulers. For Mus, Hinduism is a religion of the chief, which remains, in his opinion, preeminently a religion of royalty. Buddhism also is mentioned as bearing "the heavy imprint of the royal ritual," and this ritual, to Mus's way of thinking, is more Indian than Indo-European.[15]

The interaction of local and Indian cultures that occurred when the latter was introduced to Southeast Asia is seen as comparable to that of local and Aryan cultures in India. Local gods were identified with different forms of Aryan gods. The cult of the soil represented by a concentrated form in, for example, a stone, remained the basis, although its expression could be transferred into a *liṅga* or images of Hindu gods fixed or localized into indigenous tutelary divinities. The hierarchical scheme functioned in the same way: the village gods would be inferior to those of the cities, and those of the cities inferior to the ones in the capital.

Thus, Mus holds that the assimilation of Indo-European or Indo-Aryan religion into the pre-Aryan monsoon religion, which would evolve into what we call Indian religion, occurred in India long before Indian culture was known in Southeast Asia. The religions that originated in India must be considered as a synthesis of Indo-Aryan and indigenous forms, common to the entire monsoon region. Consequently, Southeast Asians did not perceive Indian religious concepts as radically different. Furthermore, Mus proposes that the religious beliefs that became rooted in Southeast Asia were a diffusion of ancient Asiatic concepts mixed with the cult of the soil. He suggests that the ideas "were instantly recognized, understood and endorsed by peoples who perhaps were not always aware of wholly changing their religion in adopting those of India."[16]

Mus maintains that the process of Indianization of the Cham people, for instance, came in three stages: first, indigenous religion; second, applying and assimilating Hinduism; and last, a reversion to the indigenous.[17] This tripartite paradigm was adopted by Wales, who applied it extensively to his work on the religiosity of Southeast Asia.

Wales wrote three principal books on the religions of Southeast Asia: *The Making of Greater India* (1951), in which he proposes the concept of "local genius;" *The Mountain of God* (1953), in which Mus's ideas about the cult of soil are expanded and identified with the cult of the "Mountain of God" that originated in Mesopotamian civilization; and *Prehistory and Religion in Southeast Asia* (1957), which summarizes his mature ideas on Southeast Asian religions. In these works, especially the last, Wales reconstructs the religious situation of Southeast Asia in prehistoric times, using a twofold method borrowed from the disciplines of archaeology and anthropology. For the latter, he uses data from the surviving primitive societies in Southeast Asia.

Wales proposes that in the Paleolithic Age the religion that was called the "Lord of Beasts" and later the "Sky God" came into existence because at that time a nomadic society of hunter-gatherers constantly on the move were unattached to the land.[18] In the Neolithic Age, agriculture gradually begins to develop and as a result the earth or soil assumes a greater importance. The earth joins with the deity of the former religion of the Paleolithic period to form a divine couple: Father Sky and Mother Earth.[19] In this period, the Megalithic culture appears which, according to Wales, was a major component of the Old Asiatic religion.[20] For example, he writes:

> I should now like to proceed with the new evidence I have obtained as to the association of what I have called the "Old Asiatic religion" with the Older Megalithic, both in the west and in the east, because this closeness of association adds to the probability that it was the Older Megalithic that brought the Old Asiatic religion from the West. But I realize that the reader will need to know what I mean by the Old Asiatic religion, and the way in which it transformed the character of the Older Megalithic until in later ages through loss of culture the primitive beliefs returned.[21]

On first reading, it seems that Wales thinks that it was the Older Megalithic culture that brought the religion. But later on, he appears to reverse his position. In any case, Wales identifies this religion with a sacred mountain cult in which the mysterious potency of the earth was concentrated.

Concerning the earth god, Wales follows the theories given in Mus's article, "Cultes indiens et indigènes au Champa." For Mus the concept is built around the idea that earth or soil constituted the central cult of the age, which Mus calls "the monsoon religion" and Wales calls "Old Asiatic religion."[22] Wales modifies the concept in two ways. First, he thinks that the cult of the soil should be seen as a form of the "Mountain of God," which he believes to have originated in Mesopotamia. Second, he sets Mus's idea into a time frame by arguing that the cult belonged to the Neolithic period.[23]

Wales's account connects the evolution of different types of beliefs and cults with the nomadic movement of various ethnic groups, especially in the Neolithic era. Following Robert von Heine-Geldern, Wales proposes:

> With the full Neolithic . . . was the Quadrangular Adze culture, which probably came into South-east Asia and North-east India from the north between 2500 and 1500 B.C., for it must have been established in the latter area well before the coming of the Aryans. It seems to have come in several waves and is associated with the peoples speaking Malayo-Polynesian (Austronesian) languages. It pushed right through to Indonesia and beyond, but in Further India it mixed with and influenced another Neolithic culture, the Shouldered Adze, which was associated with the peoples speaking Môn-Khmer (Austro-asiatic) languages. One of the features of the Quadrangular Adze culture was the erecting of megalithics, and a complex of religious beliefs associated with them.[24]

For this "complex of religious beliefs," Wales quotes Heine-Geldern's description of their present-day form:

> [T]he megaliths are connected with special notions concerning life after death; that the majority are erected in the course of rites destined to protect the soul from the dangers believed to threaten it in the underworld or on its way there, and to assure the eternal life either to the persons who erect the monuments as their own memorials while alive, or to those to whom they are erected after their death; that at the same time the megaliths are destined to serve as a link between the dead and the living and to enable the latter to participate in the wisdom of the dead; that they are thought to perpetuate the magic qualities of the persons who had erected them or to whom they had been erected, thereby furthering the fertility of men, livestock and crops and promoting the wealth of future generations.[25]

Wales qualifies this description as being an "anthropological not a historic one." Trying to trace the beliefs back in time, he reasons that:

> When the anthropologists' accounts are examined closely, and certain known parallel developments are taken into consideration, surviving features are

> discovered which cannot be explained in terms of this fertility cult. They point rather to the former existence of more complex religious concepts. These oblige us to form the opinion that what we have before us today represents essentially a return to primitive animism and ancestor worship, as a result of a loss of culture after the advanced influences had been ceased to operate.[26]

Wales holds that the Older Megalithic culture in Southeast Asia—which according to Heine-Geldern had spread from the Mediterranean region to Southeast Asia around the third millennium BCE—was influenced by the higher religions that developed in the urban centers of Mesopotamia. Wales thus considers that the Old Megalithic culture emanated from Mesopotamian cities.[27]

In the protohistorical period, Wales believes that the "Bronze religion" (his term) was shamanism. His theory is based largely on the interpretation given to the bronze drums found scattered throughout Southeast Asia.[28] Wales describes shamanism as primarily an ancient religion that survives among some of the Turco-Tatar and Mongol tribes of Central Asia and Siberia, though it is continually being diminished by the spread of higher religions from the south. Wales goes on to note that the term has been abused by the majority of writers who use it to include all kinds of "prophets, soothsayers and medicine-men." For Wales:

> Shamanism proper is the magico-religious complex most fully developed among the nomads of Central and Northern Asia, and is essentially an ecstatic experience put at the service of society. That is its first mark of distinction from the activities of miscellaneous healers and prophets who are to be found everywhere. Secondly, in strict shamanism the shaman calls to his aid certain spirits whom he controls, and is never "possessed" by them. It is with their help that his soul leaves his body in an ecstatic state induced by music and the dance, and travels, usually to the celestial regions, sometimes to the underworld. There is no "possession" either by gods or by ancestors, although there may be an admixture of such mediumship where there has been influence from, or co-existence with, cultures in which that type of practice thrives.[29]

The source of shamanism in Southeast Asia, according to Wales, is clear: it is best known from its survivals in Central Asia and Siberia. Nomads from the north and west would have brought it into Yunnan and northern Indochina, and from there it spread throughout Southeast Asia, both mainland

and maritime.[30] Wales's theory of the advent and development of shamanism in Southeast Asia is best summarized as follows:

> The religion of these nomads was shamanism, with the worship of celestial deities. This religion, though doubtless already influenced by Babylonian and Assyrian cosmology, was then free from the influence of the great world religions, as well as the ancestor worship of the settled agricultural Mongoloid peoples. In Yunnan and northern Indochina there took place towards the middle of the first millennium B.C. a hybridization of the nomadic bronze-using people's culture with that of the settled Neolithic Malayo-Polynesian speaking population in this region. Though democratization took place, the shamanism was at first strictly the religion of the upper class, representing the new arrivals, while the local people continued to follow an impoverished form of the religion belonging to the Older Megalithic. This was largely a cult of chthonic force, in which the ancestor element did not yet predominate. As the influence of this hybrid culture spread down the coast of Annam and through Indonesia, probably not later than the middle of the first millennium B.C., it gradually lost strength, so that in the Lesser Sunda Islands the Older Megalithic maintained itself or at least ultimately succeeded in regaining much of its old position.[31]

Wales's description of religiosity in the Neolithic and Bronze Ages of Southeast Asia at this point is strongly influenced by the concept of diffusion. Theories on the migrations of different races are still a matter of debate. Some scholars advocate a directional migration of north to south, while others favor south to north.[32] Above all, we have no evidence to substantiate that there was any contact between prehistoric Mediterranean cultures and prehistoric northern Indian cultures, or prehistoric Southeast Asia. Nor is there any evidence that nomads from Central Asia and Siberia migrated into Southeast Asia.

If our aim is to prove that shamanism existed in Southeast Asia, then a search for "fossils" must be conducted in our modern societies. Of course, there are still traces of shamanism everywhere, but not in the strict sense proposed by Wales. And it is unacceptable to maintain that in each evolutionary period the religious situation must be this or that "ism" in its pure form. Wales recognizes this problem later in his rather contradictory exposition by using the term, "hybridization."[33] His claim that the shamanism of the Dongson cultures was related to the celestial gods seems to contradict his earlier definition of shamanism, when a shaman communicated not only with the sky but also the underworld. In this case, the contrast between the chthonic cult of the Older Megalithic and the celestially oriented shamanism of the Bronze Age seems to bear no relevance to the religious situation of Southeast Asia.

An important notion that Wales derives from Mus is that indigenous religions would finally reemerge once the influence of the "great religions" of India had waned.[34] His hypothesis is that the "local genius" (of the Older Megalithic culture and the Dongson culture) "reacted" to the Indian religions in different ways.[35] This accounts for the variations in the religious situation in the Khmer, Cham, and Indonesian cultures. In the case of Khmer religion, it was the Older Megalithic cult, and for the Cham, it was the Dongson culture. In the development of Indo-Javanese religion, both the Older Megalithic and the Dongson cultures were responsible; the former is the more ancient and did not reappear until the last period of Indo-Javanese history before the coming of Islam. Wales also thinks that because of the celestial character of the Dongson culture, Mahāyāna Buddhism was more acceptable to the Cham and Indo-Javanese societies than to the Khmer, whose indigenous culture was the Older Megalithic.[36]

This theory of "local genius" is based on the idea that the indigenous tradition reasserts itself and shares equally or fundamentally in the process of Indianization. Wales gives credit to the indigenous culture for originating the process and regards Indian civilization simply as its instigator. For Wales, the great monuments of Angkor Wat and Barabudur are the achievements of local genius. In the case of the Khmer, the pyramidal temple—an architectural style interpreted by Wales as chthonic or megalithic by nature—suggests that the "local genius" behind the style is the Older Megalithic culture. In the case of the Javanese, Barabudur was fashioned to resemble steps leading toward the sky, and, hence, is an expression of Dongson culture.

Wales limits his account to the Khmer, Cham, and Javanese traditions. He proposes that Southeast Asia be divided into two distinct areas: a western zone that includes Burma, Thailand, and possibly, Sri Lanka, and an eastern zone that embraces the areas mentioned above. He ignores the western zone, Sri Lanka included, because he thinks that "local genius" was never much in evidence there. In his opinion, the acculturation in the western zone was so complete that the phenomenon of "local genius" never emerged.[37]

To the contrary, evidence in the Pyu and Dvāravatī *maṇḍala*s, precisely those areas disparaged by Wales, shows strong localization of Indian culture. This occurred very early, and may well be the earliest sites among all cultures of Southeast Asia.[38] Indeed, it is the Khmer and Javanese cultures that show much stronger influence from India, and for that reason, one would assume that those sites would be less localized than any others in the region. The absence of any religious buildings on a grand scale does not mean that localization never occurred. Moreover, the belief in an earth god, or a god of the soil, or shamanism was evident among other regional cultures, not just the Khmer or Javanese.[39]

Wales cites archaeological data to support his hypothesis of radically different indigenous cultures. However, if his evidence is examined closely, there is little, if any, significant difference between the Khmer tower or *prasat,* claimed by Wales to have been inspired by Old Megalithic religion, and the Cham tower, which Wales says represents Dongsonian culture.

An evaluation of the points that Mus and Wales raise is in order. First, Mus suggests that what occurred can be called, "macrosystemism." He views religious development in Southeast Asia as a general extension of monsoon religion, but this does not mean that the process remained uninfluenced by outside forces. In India, the Aryans intervened by bringing with them the Indo-European (Indo-Aryan) religion, and in Southeast Asia, Indian religions were present as early as the beginning of the Common Era. Mus sees these two phenomena as parallel ones, suggesting that the indigenous beliefs of Southeast Asia would be similar to the indigenous beliefs of India, that is, the monsoon religion with its primary cult being one of the earth or soil, with connections to ancestor worship.

Mus used the same model to describe the religiosity of both India and Southeast Asia. However, in the case of Southeast Asia, he sometimes overemphasizes the cult of the soil. Remnants of this cult persist, especially in the concept of kingship. In Southeast Asia, it is common for the king to be called the "Lord of the Land," as well as other epithets such as the "Lord of Life" or the "Great Warrior," which suggest beliefs other than the cult of the soil.[40] Because the line of kingly succession has always been very flexible, this seems to point to beliefs other than the cult of the soil, which, because of its close relationship with the cult of ancestors, would promote a very strict line of succession, as was the case in China.

In Southeast Asia, the belief in spirits, gods, and the vital force that resides in all things, which did not originate in India, usually persisted. The names attached to the beliefs remained in the vernacular, except in instances of status raising, in which case the name might be translated into Sanskrit or Pāli. For example, the spirit of the land becomes Bhūmidevatā.[41] Even if Indian deities are added to the pantheon, they do not dethrone the old gods. In some cases, the nature of the local and Indian gods and spirits coincided, but this should cause no surprise, since Mus has pointed out that the concepts originated from essentially the same set of circumstances.

Studies confirm that, in general, Southeast Asian society has remained agricultural in character.[42] The lives of the people are still bound up with spirits germane to the agricultural cycle,[43] which the people believe allows them to survive. These spirits could be rain gods or spirits that govern the growing of rice, for example. The main feature of Southeast Asian religion before its contact with Hinduism and Buddhism was a kind of animism, one that entailed propitiation, worship, and interaction with nature spirits or ancestors.[44] As it was in the case of the concept of kingship, it is uncertain if a belief in the spirit of the soil was the most important one due to lack of data to support Mus's assertion. Recent studies suggest that these spirits fulfill different functions according to the needs of the people, as can be seen in the cult of *neak ta* in Cambodia, *chao* or *phii* (*phī*) in Thailand, and the *nat* cult in Burma. In Thailand there is also a belief in the *khwan*, which is a central component in the vital forces of all life.[45] The question remains: how was it possible for this belief system to assert itself and, at the same time, react to new systems imported from the outside?

When an indigenous ideology confronts a new belief system—in the case of India, it was the Indo-European, and in the case of Southeast Asia, it was the great religions of India—Mus's idea that the chief or king served as a mediator proves convincing, but his theory of localization seems to have functioned in another way. The Indian deities were not identified with, nor did they become local gods, even though Hindu and Buddhist deities, including the Buddha, were worshipped in the same manner as local gods. These deities assumed the character of local gods and sometimes became identified with a specific locality, yet they retained their Indian names. It is common to find expressions such as the Śiva or a Viṣṇu of such and such a town or the Buddha of such and such a place.[46] Indian gods were usually accorded a higher status over the local gods.[47]

Indigenous beliefs and spirit cults, thus, appear to have existed alongside Indian religions rather than being replaced by them.[48] There is no evidence to suggest that all the spirits of the local religions were eliminated by Indian successors. And if it was the case in India that the Indo-European gods were localized, then the same could be applied to Southeast Asia. However, there is no evidence to suggest that local deities became identified with the Indian gods. Their characteristics and names may be analogous, but their essential character remained distinct.

Therefore, when Mus proposes that the course of religious development in Southeast Asia was "indigenous-Indianized," followed by the reassertion or revival of the indigenous belief system, he seems to contradict himself. In the case of India, he does not describe the outcome of the synthesis between the indigenous and the Indo-European cultures as "Indo-Europeanized" followed by a "reappearing of the indigenous." The evidence Mus cites to support his idea, with regard to the Cham, is the leader, the king, who expresses himself by using thoroughly Indian religious concepts.[49] But this only shows how the elites became Indianized; it provides no information about the beliefs and practices of the people, of common society, so therefore, a picture of Cham religious life cannot be drawn. Mus's example does not explain how local gods became identified with Hindu ones, nor is it clear whether the local gods were subservient to Indian ones. Both could exist side by side. In Mus's model, indigenous beliefs do not "reappear," but, rather, they continue to be present.

As for Wales, his theory could be characterized as one of "continuity." It is not clear exactly what he means when he uses the terms, "Old Asiatic" or "Older Megalithic," terms that appear to have been introduced from elsewhere. He asserts that they are the result of the actions of "local genius." While Wales uses Mus's paradigm, he does so not as an evolutionary scheme for the cultures of Southeast Asia, but rather, to prove his concept of "local genius." Wales holds that if the Thai had not conquered the Khmer, who as a result adopted Theravāda Buddhism, then the Older Megalithic would have reappeared in Cambodia, just as the cult of the soil reappeared among the Cham.

Wales's concept of "Older Megalithic" is now considered to be outdated. Megalithic remains cannot be dated with any certainty since Megalithic culture is still a living culture in many parts of Southeast Asia. Moreover, there is no overall uniformity in the scattered regional megaliths that would justify the use of the concepts "pan-cultural" or "pan-regional."[50] When one considers the inadequacy of the available data, any such broad conclusions are merely conjectural, which makes Wales's assertions on the evolution of religious systems in Southeast Asia unsustainable.

Both Mus and Wales are still trapped in this seminal point. Even when Mus tries to avoid this pitfall, he still falls into the trap. By constructing a sequence or series of phases in the evolution of religious society and culture in Southeast Asia, which he describes as "indigenous," "Indianized," and "the reappearing of indigenous culture," Mus draws quite a well defined contrast between Indian and indigenous religion. When Wales divides Southeast Asia into eastern and western zones, he uses the degree of influence of Indian culture or religion as his yardstick of measurement. Yet the interest of the two pioneers in indigenous beliefs has had the effect of leading other scholars to take this issue into consideration in their own studies of the religious situation in Southeast Asia.

Recent emphasis on indigenous beliefs as an important component of the religiosity of Southeast Asia has led to another set of problems. It entails not only the difficulty of defining indigenous beliefs vis-à-vis Indian religions, but also of selecting appropriate methodologies. These two problems are related. Sometimes the chosen definition leads to the selection of the methodology, and at other times the chosen methodology dictates the definition.

A common understanding would be that any religion originating in India should be called an Indian religion. But what are these religions? How should Hinduism be defined? Can Buddhism to be treated as something entirely separate from Hinduism? How did these two main traditions interact? Had the so-called "syncretization" of Hinduism and Buddhism already taken place in India?

Many scholars, among them sociologists and anthropologists, have sought to answer these questions first by using the concepts of the "Great Tradition" and the "Little Tradition."[51] These terms express a dichotomy based on observed differences by researchers between what might be called a textual or scriptural religion and religion as it is actually practiced.[52] In the case of India, religion as prescribed in official, normative (usually Sanskrit) texts is defined as the "Great Tradition," whereas one that is practiced by the masses, especially in villages, is defined as the "Little Tradition."[53] In the context of Southeast Asia, religious traditions from India are seen as the "Great Tradition," and ones from indigenous cultures as the "Little Tradition."

Variations in the interpretation of these two terms are present, but the basic thrust remains the same: to see the religiosity of India or Southeast Asia as a phenomena consisting of conflicts and tensions between these two poles. When this model is imposed, the questions concerning religiosity in India and Southeast Asia are formed accordingly. Instead of trying to understand religion from the point of view of the indigenous population, scholars often superimpose their own concepts of religion and methodology to deal with the supposed conflict, a notion that may never have occurred to those who profess these creeds.

As a result of this way of thinking, what the masses actually practice is constructed as a debased version of what is written in the canonical texts. Furthermore, the analysis may use terms such as "primitive," "local," "animistic," "supernatural," or more positively, "indigenous beliefs." If one examines what scholars have used as the standard or normative texts in Hinduism, we find that works such as the *Mahābhārata* and the *Purāṇa* are, in fact, collections of popular religious beliefs that in principle belong to the "Little Tradition." In this case, the use of the Sanskrit tradition to support the "Great Tradition" fails.

It is true that Robert Redfield, over half a century ago, cautioned us to regard the two traditions as an integrated entity, as "two currents of thought and action, distinguishable, yet ever flowing into and out of one another."[54] This concept, however, is vague on the details. If the two traditions are not to be seen separately, then why separate them? Which principle determines whether or not a certain tradition should be termed "great" and which "little" if they are passing back and forth between each other?

Redfield proposed a related categorization (examined by Terence Day some thirty years later), which suggests that the two types of civilization be divided into primary and secondary ones. The former is found in India and China where civilization is indigenous, with each having evolved from the pre-civilized people of its own culture. An example of the secondary type is found in the peasant societies of Latin America where recorded events have been overlaid with a strong imprint of another civilization whose armies invaded the Americas from abroad. Needless to say, the civilization of Southeast Asia easily reflects the second category.[55]

Any historian of Indian civilization will find Redfield's categorization difficult to accept. Yet it is possible to categorize Indian civilization as primary because it influenced other civilizations, but to argue that it evolved solely from a pre-civilized people of its own culture is not valid.

Redfield's approach is insufficient to lead one to a better understanding of Hinduism. When his argument is applied to Buddhism, it seems more plausible. This could be because Buddhist scriptures are more cohesive and more discernible with regard to popular and canonical aspects than those of Hinduism. The dichotomy thus becomes more striking. Buddhism, especially in its Theravāda form, has been dissected into parts according to the specific application of a particular academic discipline. For example, terms such as "normative" versus "non-normative," "popular" versus "elite," "court" versus "peasant" Buddhism, and so forth, begin to emerge. The various types of Buddhism proposed by scholars can be classified by specific disciplines.

According to the discipline of philosophy, Buddhism is divided into early, Hīnayāna, Mahāyāna, and Tantric phases. Sociological and anthropological approaches usually distinguish "court Buddhism" from "Buddhism of the masses." Buddhism is also viewed according to the specific region in which it is found, such as Sinhalese, Burmese, Thai, Lao, or Khmer. When discussing indigenous beliefs, however, the word "religion" is often preferred over "Buddhism." This results when concepts like structuralism, functionalism, and regionalism are applied to the data.

The philosophical approach is usually labeled as diachronic, and the sociological and anthropological ones labeled as synchronic. At a certain point when scholars realized the lack of historicity of the last two approaches, they tried to incorporate a historical view into their studies. As a result, we now have hybrid approaches such as "sociohistorical," for example.

Yet in all these approaches, the dichotomy persists, and in most cases, the approaches overlap. It is possible to say that Mahāyāna Buddhism arose out of the tension between monastic and secular tendencies and in reaction to the Abhidharmic or scholastic trends found in early Buddhism. Hīnayāna Buddhism is seen as the result of tension between ecclesiasticism and scholasticism, with Tantric Buddhism developing as a resurgence of indigenous ritual practices, or as some claim, a triumph of the mystical aspects of Mahāyāna Buddhism.[56]

In addition, a linear historical model was adopted, which viewed the history of Indian Buddhism as an evolution from a "primitive" form of Buddhism to a Tantric one. However, a careful study of the sources reveals that the model of a strictly linear evolution does not hold. Hīnayāna was never supplanted by Mahāyāna, and neither was Mahāyāna supplanted by Tantrayāna. Studies based solely upon literary works that outline the doctrines and practices of different types of Buddhism, which may have been active in different periods, can be misleading. By no means do they prove the exclusive prevalence of the schools that actively produced a body of literature. In the seventh century, the Chinese pilgrim, Xuan Zang (Hsuan-Tsang), divided the monks in India into eight categories. The first and most common category was the "undeclared" monks who did not belong to any one school. In general, according to Xuan Zang, Hīnayāna monks and monasteries outnumbered those of Mahāyāna.[57]

It must be said that the evolutionistic model is not totally wrong. In any religion, a certain amount of development is natural and unavoidable. It probably began as soon as the Buddha preached his first sermon. Because his followers and subsequent converts came from many different backgrounds, different interpretations came into being, creating a need for commentarial literature that appeared very early in Buddhism.[58] But to see this development as following a strictly linear pattern of evolution from early or "primitive" to a more advanced "scholastic" Buddhism, or from "monastic" to "secular," without taking into account the sociocultural factors, seems unwise.[59] A religion can develop in various ways depending on many factors and conditions.

In the case of Buddhism in India, one often forgets that Buddhism was one of many Indian religious movements, and was in every sense "Indian." Any convenient compartmentalization of Indian religions into Hinduism, Buddhism, or Jainism, is without a doubt a misrepresentation of the real situation. It may be that the Buddhists and the Jains had a more conscious sense of their religious identity, but they were still a part of the worldview of Indian ethics and ideologies. These religious expressions still resembled each other, whether they were Hindu, Buddhist, or Jain. Even so, it is probably easier to identify the Buddhists and the Jains rather than the Hindus, since the term, "Hinduism," is a purely academic construction that is used to denote a wide variety of Indian beliefs. In fact, what is called "Indian religions" should be viewed as one unitary development. They are essentially "Indian," and as such should not be studied as this "ism" or that "ism." It is commonplace for scholars to regard the Brahmanical tradition as the only genuine orthodox Indian religion with Jainism, Buddhism, and the other Śramaṇic movements as heterodox.[60] This scholarly designation reveals the superimposition of Western concepts onto the religious situation of India and Asia in general, creating a false comparison when Christian theology is made the norm. By using a Western, Christian model everything outside the norm is labeled as heretical or heterodox.

Can one be entirely certain that these Śramaṇic movements were heretical or heterodox in the Indian context? If we look back to that time period, both Brahmanic and Śramaṇic movements seem to have shared not only the same concepts and ideologies, but also enjoyed support from the same social groups, even the same kings and ministers. For example, one cannot claim that King Ajātaśatru, who appears in the *Upaniṣads* in Buddhism and in Jainism, belonged exclusively to the Buddhists.[61] Textually, the three traditions were interwoven to the extent that verses and passages from the *Suttanipāta* and the *Dharmapada* have parallels in the *Upaniṣads*, the *Rāmāyaṇa*, the *Mahābhārata* as well as Jaina texts.[62] If texts from other Śramaṇic schools were available, further parallels might be found.

While differences do exist, they would not have been emphasized until a later period when the Buddhist and the Jaina canons were being systematized and becoming more distinctive. In contrast, the *Upaniṣads*, which remained essentially unedited, bear all the hallmarks of a collection of confusing and often naive views of what has been called philosophical doctrines or arguments. These so-called "primitive" or early doctrines reveal trends that were also present in Buddhist texts. One reason for Buddhism's rapid spread after the third century BCE could be due to the fact that it was among the first groups to attempt to systematize its scriptures and monastic organization.[63]

At around that same time, what is now called Brahmanism, Buddhism, and Jainism, were beginning to emerge as separate entities in the Indian mind. For that reason, they shared many of the same ideas.[64] Only later did they become gradually more distinctive, and still later when they began to differentiate themselves from each other.[65] From this point of view, the dichotomy between "orthodoxy" and "heterodoxy" does not apply. The Śramaṇic tradition should not be seen as something emerging in opposition to the Brahmanic tradition, but, rather, as an internal movement and an integral part of Indian religion as a whole. The reaction to blind ritualism and the consequent attempt to reinterpret and internalize the ritual agenda was common to both the Upaniṣadic and Buddhist traditions, and should be viewed only as a trend that existed in India starting from about the seventh century BCE.[66]

It is futile to try to reconstruct a pure, a primitive, or an early Buddhism. If we disregard the scholastic and philosophical differences, then all religions in India seem to share three main features and practices: yoga, Tantra, and *bhakti*. By yoga, we mean meditation; by Tantra, ritual and ceremony; and by *bhakti*, devotion and worship. Further, to study the religious situation in India by using the dichotomy between the "Great Tradition" and the "Little Tradition" tends to complicate the issue rather than clarify it.

In the case of Southeast Asia, the situation becomes even more complicated when one considers the need to include practices and beliefs that developed in reaction to and interacted with the new religions from India. How did this occur and in what manner? Were there any perceptual changes? If the situation in India as described above is accurate, then how much more unrealistic is it to study or write a separate history of either Buddhism or Brahmanism in Southeast Asia? How many more misinterpretations will arise if they continue to be treated separately?

Religion may well have been the means by which Southeast Asia received material culture, that is, its artistic forms, images, and written scripts. It cannot be assumed that Hinduism and Buddhism arrived separately in the region. As we have shown above, these religions must be viewed essentially as Indian and not intrinsically different in terms of culture. Moreover, as Mus points out, there were similarities in beliefs between these two religions. But this does not mean that these Indian beliefs arrived intact and were the same throughout all regions of Southeast Asia. Some regions may have expressed themselves more as Buddhist, while others as Hindu due, in part, to differing political, economic, and social situations in various areas.

In the case of Southeast Asian religion, it seems inappropriate to label certain popular practices as either indigenous or Indian. When people act or express themselves in a religious way, it is unlikely that they do so from a specifically Indian (or otherwise) religious conceptualization. Today if one asks Southeast Asians who profess to be Buddhist or Muslim whether they consider themselves to be Buddhist or Muslim, they will answer accordingly. But to make such a profession does not mean that they do not also propitiate spirits or follow other practices considered to be non-Buddhist or not strictly Islamic from a normative viewpoint.

The problem is clear when studying Buddhism in Southeast Asia. It is viewed either as a higher religion set against a primitive or animistic belief system, or as a total system, a Buddhism that has integrated practices and features of local religions. In the latter case, the totality of the religion has to be explained by dissecting it, and as a result we have different types of Buddhism. Thus, processes such as assimilation, synthesis, syncretism, and subjugation have been introduced in order to elucidate the polylithic character of religious practice in India and Southeast Asia.

However, much of our data does not really reflect these processes. For the most part, the terms are used without a specific definition. The most frequently used term is "syncretism," a term suggesting the combination of or the effort to reconcile or integrate different belief systems. Consequently, syncretism must be regarded as a conscious and intentional act. There is no evidence that an intentional effort ever existed to reconcile these beliefs. Can we say that the *ye dharmā* stanza, which is definitely Buddhist, was inscribed on the base of a Śivaliṅga with the conscious intention of synthesizing or syncretizing Hinduism and Buddhism?[67] It may simply be that the stanza was regarded as one of the most suitable verses to inscribe on a sacred object, or that it was believed to confer sacredness on the object inscribed with no conscious knowledge that it belonged to another religion. In inscribing the object, the sponsor or artisan had no intention of reconciling the two faiths, and most likely was unaware of any differences between them.

A study on Cambodia notes that the Khmer had many gods that resided in various places: mountain tops, huge old trees, caves, and so forth. The names of these local gods, while possibly similar to Hindu gods, bore no characteristics of universality. The study notes that this is not unlike the situation in Bali where offerings were often first made to the local gods. Moreover, the local gods were the deified founders of the village communities that bore names that sounded like Sanskrit. As Nidhi Aeusrivongse asserts:

> It is very difficult to distinguish the indigenous and Indian elements in the religious beliefs of the Khmers. The meaning of the Indian elements is limited to what can be found in Sanskrit texts, and the difficulty remains formidable because most of the evidence we have was made to bear the appearance of Sanskritic culture. However, there is no question that religious beliefs, as well as other social institutions in Angkor, were the result of a syncretism that took place perhaps from the beginning of contact between the two cultures. Some vestiges of the syncretic nature of Angkorean belief have been pointed out by Bhattacharya in his study of iconography, as for example, the association of the Viṣṇu at Prasat Kravan with a crocodile or lizard or the Naṭarājā of Bantay Samre with two Asuras embracing his legs (seemingly inspired by autochthonous mythology). We are on a more solid ground when we confront the transformation of the *nāga* Ananta to a dragon, or again, the presence of the rhino as *vāhana* of Agni.
>
> The origins of these specific gods, beneath the names of the Hindu pantheon, were deities of local communities. They had been revered by local people before classical Indian culture arrived in Cambodia. Their names and, to a large extent, their forms were transformed in the process of Sanskritization. Even in the Angkorean period, the transformation of names was not complete, as some gods were still mentioned in the inscriptions under Khmer names. . . . It is thus possible to imagine that in the process of "Indianization," a number of local gods with Khmer names were "merged" with gods holding Hindu names, their figures (if they had any recognizable figure) being transformed to a *liṅga* or even an image.[68]

The same situation has been reported in Thailand, Burma, and in Malay areas where there were efforts to set these local gods into a Brahmanical framework as well. In the Khmer tradition, we find not only is there an effort to identify the gods of Buddhism with those of Brahmanic origin, but also local ones with the Indian. In the first case, it was done intentionally by scholars who wrote the inscription:

I. vītarāgam ahaṃ vande yo'nvarthām abhidhān dadhat/
saṃsārasāravairāgyañ cakāra jñānasampadā//
II. bhāti vuddhāgahemādrau cīvarāruṇamaṇḍalaṃ/
māramātsaryyatamasāṃ saṃhṛtāv iva bhāskaraḥ//
III. caturbhujadharaṃ vande lokeśvaram iveśvaram/
darśayantaṃ svaviṣṇutvañ caturyyugadhare kalau// [69]

This passage could also be interpreted as an example of how different creeds could coexist peacefully together in Khmer society. Filliozat points out that a concept such as *vītarāga*, that is, to be free from desire, and the donning of the yellow robe would not be foreign to a Śaivite. The identification of Avalokiteśvara with Śiva is not unique to the Khmer tradition; it is also found in Java. Both received the concept from India.[70] Perhaps even in India these gods were considered as more or less the same, that is to say, as deities deserving of trust and to be eulogized.

Synthesis, if the word can be used, is not so evident in the other cultures of Southeast Asia. The following description of what occurred in the Thai cultural context, which may, more or less, be representative of the situation in other countries in Southeast Asia, is one that justifies our reluctance to use the terms "syncretism" and "synthesis" when discussing the relationship between indigenous beliefs and Indian religions:

> The belief in supernatural beings is innate in man. The Thai people as a race call such supernatural beings by the generic word "*phii,*" which includes both gods and devils. The *phii,* like man in a general sense, are of two classes, the good *phii* and the bad *phii.* When the Thai came in contact with the highly Hinduized Khmer or Cambodians in Central Siam in the 12th century A.D. and had become a ruling race in that region, they adopted most of the Khmer Hinduized cultures, especially the ruling class. Throughout subsequent centuries the Thai and the Khmer mixed racially and culturally to an appreciable degree. By this time the Thai were gradually becoming known as the Siamese and the old Thai word *phii* like its owners had also undergone a change in meaning. In the famous stone inscription of the great Siamese king Ramkhamhaeng dated 1283 A.D. reference was made to the king of Khmer of that time as "*phii fa*" which literally meant the heavenly *phii.* Actually *phii fa* meant a divine king, a cult which had been adopted by Siamese kings of the later periods. Instead of referring to a divine king as *phii fa* as hitherto, it has now changed into "*thep*" or "*thevada*" from the Sanskrit "*deva*" and "*devatā*" which mean a god, or literally,

> a shining one. It followed that all the good *phii* of the Thai had by now become *thevada* or gods in their popular use of the language.[71]

While the examples given in this quote belong to different periods, they seem to describe a similar tendency. If syntheses can be detected in Angkorian society more so than in the Thai, can we say that it was a real synthesis or an example of syncretism? If one considers the case of "the association of the Viṣṇu at Prasat Kravan with a crocodile or lizard" as cited in an earlier quote, the introduction of animals may have nothing to do with religious concepts. It only shows that the artisan had localized or infused his tradition in making these statues, most likely, unconsciously.[72]

In all these examples of the "merging" of local gods into Hindu ones, the fact remains that the concept of local gods has been altered. There is another possible interpretation. Since efforts toward "merging" were initiated by kings, they could have sprung from political considerations. The king, who was regarded by the people as being endowed with both spiritual and political prowess, appropriated the local gods and tried to unite them under his faith, the state religion.

In Khmer culture, fertility and ancestral cults appear to have remained conceptually the same, even after contact with Indian religions. We may say that the indigenous cults were dressed in Indian attire.[73] If concept and intention were not involved in this process, then the words, "synthesis" and "syncretism" should not be applied.

All of these conceptual approaches should be used together conjointly, but with great caution. The evolutionary approach is useful in enabling us to see how religions developed. However, religion is more than simply a set of events, and it may not develop according to the theory of evolution. For example, religious development in Southeast Asia did not evolve on its own, but was strongly influenced by religions from India. But this does not mean that religions from India effaced local practices and beliefs. The process is profoundly complicated, involving numerous factors—political, economic, and social—and most crucial of all is the perception toward religion of the populace. If this factor is overlooked, then the processes of syncretism and so on would exist only in the minds of scholars, and these processes would be inaccurate when wrongly applied to or used for describing, explaining, or stating that the religious phenomena in Southeast Asia had evolved in a particular way.

The flaw in applying such Western approaches lies in resorting to categories like Hinduism or Buddhism as prepackaged preconceptions before making an effort to understand the unique practices and belief systems of the people. This flaw may be due to the influence of methodologies applied in the study of Judeo-Christian religion, in which the importance of religious texts is so central. When European scholars began to study Eastern religions, it was natural for them to look first at the canonical texts, and from that study construct a conceptual model of these religions. As a result, Hinduism, for example, was defined as what was found prescribed in the Veda and other Sanskrit texts, whereas Buddhism was seen as a philosophical movement.[74] Later on, when sociologists and anthropologists began to study actual practice, they found phenomena that lay beyond the textual record. If the phenomena were viewed as alien, or if observations contradicted a text, then they were labeled the "Great Tradition."

Sociological and anthropological studies deal with the lived tradition, but these studies often omit a crucial point. Traditions receive their vitality from the people who practice them, who express themselves through them, and who live in them. Without the people, a tradition is not a living one. If a conceptual system does not match the empirical evidence, then it cannot be said to reflect the true situation. Western scholarship often runs the risk of imposing such normative terms as Hinduism and Buddhism on local beliefs in total disregard of the real situation as lived by the indigenous people.

We can conclude that the religious situation in Southeast Asia is multidimensional, consisting of different creeds, which seem to coexist peacefully. Only the most favorable circumstances would allow this phenomenon to occur, circumstances that reflect a particular Southeast Asian attitude towards religion.

SOUTHEAST ASIAN CONCEPTS OF RELIGION

Certain problems can be cleared up if we try to understand how the people of Southeast Asia perceived religion. Any superimposition of concepts from a monolithic religion derived from the Judeo-Christian tradition only generates a distorted image of religion in Southeast Asia, and, by extension, in the East as a whole. Patterns and paradigms that are used in the West are not really applicable to Southeast Asia.[75] When investigating the attitudes of the people of Southeast Asia towards religion, we turn again to inscriptions and archaeological finds supplemented by local legends.

In the previous chapter, we found that inscriptions express Southeast Asian religiosity in a variety of ways. In the Dvāravatī tradition, it is not only kings who are donors, but also common people, who might include *rishi*s, shamans, and dancers. They expressed themselves religiously through the Buddhist faith without being identified with a specific school. In the Khmer tradition, the recorded donors were mainly the elites: kings and nobles. It was common for Hinduism and Buddhism to be honored alongside each other, but at other times specific aspects might be intentionally syncretized as it was in the case of Avalokiteśvara and Śiva. However, this phenomenon is not unique to Southeast Asians or the Khmer, since it also occurred earlier in India in a process of mutual development and influence.[76]

It is worth noting that there is no direct reference to indigenous beliefs in these inscriptions, except for those found in the Dvāravatī region, but this does not mean that they were not present. The fact that later inscriptions and present-day practices embody these indigenous beliefs indicates that they were long established. The evidence for local beliefs appears, quite surprisingly, in the period in which scholars believe that Sinhalese Theravāda Buddhism came to dominate the area.

In Burma, the kings still supported the *nat* cult. In Thailand, it was necessary to correctly propitiate the "Pra Khaphung Phii," which is the lord of all the *phii* in this realm, in order to ensure that the kingdom would prosper.[77] In an inscription on the base of an image of Śiva, known to the Thai by another of his epithets, Īśvara, the three faiths are listed together more or less on equal terms:

> In sakarājā 1432, a year of the horse, on Sunday the fourteenth day of the waxing moon of the sixth month (when the moon had) attained the ṛkṣa of hasta, at two nālikā after dawn, Cau Brañā Śrī Dharmāśokarājā founded this (statue of the) Lord Īśavra to protect the four-footed and two-footed creatures in Möaṅ Kāṃbèṅ Bejra, and to help exalt the religions (*śāsanā*)—the Buddha's religion, the Brahmanical religion, and the Devakarma—so that they will not lose their lustre. May they function harmoniously together.[78]

The translators explain that the Sanskrit word *devakarma* (*debakarrma* in the inscription), meaning "religious act or rite," or "worship of the gods," refers here to "the cult of ancestral and tutelary divinities." They quote related inscriptions to support their interpretation.[79]

What can we learn from these local legends? They were originally preserved primarily as an oral tradition and written down only after Sinhalese Theravāda Buddhism became dominant. Even though their characteristics are strongly Theravāda, nevertheless, they still show traces of local concepts in, for instance, legends of the Buddha's relics, which were usually guarded by local gods. In Burma and Thailand, these legends generally begin with a visit paid by the Buddha to some local site such as a forest or a river. The Buddha then predicts that in the future this site will become either a great city or the site of a *stūpa* where his relics will be enshrined. Following the prediction, the local *devatā* or a particular animal or bird will guard the site, waiting for the day when the king or other nobles will come to fulfill the prediction. The legends are Buddhist in content, but in spirit they reflect local tutelary beliefs.[80] This type of legend was also typical in India. Fa Xian, for example, describes numerous pilgrimage sites as having been predicted by the Buddha himself. In both India and Southeast Asia, the building of a *stūpa* must be instigated by a god. It is Indra in Indian contexts, and local gods in Southeast Asian contexts.[81]

Among these chronicles and legends is the story of a princess named Cāmadevī in which the establishment of the city-states in northern Thailand is described. The chronicles tell us that four *rishi*s founded the city of Haripuñjaya. In their search for a ruler for the new city, they find Princess Cāmadevī of Lavapura (Lopburi) in central Thailand to be a suitable candidate and invite her to be their ruler. The princess moves to the new capital and brings with her the Buddhist canon and Sangha together with artisans and craftsmen. In such a way, she brings civilization to the local "uncivilized" people, who presumably become Buddhists.

Princess Cāmadevī came from Lopburi in central Thailand, which is considered to be the heartland of the Dvāravatī Buddhist tradition. The city was founded by four *rishi*s, which seems to point to the centrality of local beliefs and ancestor worship, or to a Brahmanical tradition. *Rishi*s also play a role in Burmese inscriptions.[82]

What we have here is a picture of the people of Southeast Asia who express themselves through different beliefs or local practices. From all appearances, both the introduced culture and the indigenous one seem to have existed together harmoniously as a "symbiosis," rather than either as a syncretism or a synthesis. This picture accords well with the conclusion drawn by J. Frits Staal who states:

> The concept of religion is a Western concept, and though its origin is Roman, it has been colored by its age-long associations with the monotheisms of the West. Western religion is pervaded by the notion of exclusive truth, and it

claims a monopoly on truth. It is professed by "People of the Book," in the apt phrase the Koran uses to refer to the Jews, Christians and Muslims. Scholars and laymen persist in searching for such religions in Asia. In order to identify them, they seize upon labels from indigenous categories, rent from their original contexts. Thus there arises the host of religions: Vedic, Brahmanical, Hindu, Buddhist, Bonpo, Tantric, Taoist, Confucian, Shinto, etc. In Asia such groupings are not only uninteresting but uninformative and tinged with the unreal. What counts instead are ancestors and teachers—hence lineages, traditions, affiliation, cults, eligibility, initiation, and iṇjunction concepts with ritual rather than truth-functional overtones. These notions do not pertain to the question of the truth, but to the practical question: What should the followers of a tradition do? (AGNI II, xiv).

If the so-called religions of Asia are not really religions, and are characterized by the fact that practice and ritual are more important than truth, belief, or doctrine, we can immediately draw some interesting conclusions. It is not possible to believe in different truths, unless they happen to be consistent with each other, but it is easy to adhere to different practices, without much restriction. If we try to do the first we are in trouble, unless we tolerate contradictions as easily as the Muslim philosopher Averroes (Ibn Rushd), who accepted for example, that the world was infinite on the account of reason (viz., Aristotle) and at the same time was created because of faith (viz., the Koran) (see e.g., Gauthier 1948). However, there is no difficulty in celebrating Passover and attending mass—the only *caveat* being that both should not occur at the same time. In Asia, it is therefore possible for a person to adhere to two 'religions.'[83]

In Southeast Asia, not only is it possible for people to profess, or rather, express themselves through two or more religions at the same time, but also it is possible for the symbols of those religions to be represented in the same place. It is not surprising to find Śivaliṅgas lying on the ground in monasteries in Thailand.[84] Neither is it surprising to know that the Supreme Patriarch of this Theravādin country distributed images of Guanyin, the Chinese equivalent of Avalokiteśvara, to Theravādin followers. He did not manufacture the images himself, but the fact that he agreed to distribute them as objects of veneration with no hesitation whatsoever shows how liberal is the attitude toward religion or sects. It would seem that any belief in which the people—elites or the laity, king or commoner—can put their trust has the capacity to serve the ends of religion. We might even say that for Southeast Asians, religious acts seem to be more prudential in nature rather than religious, in the sense understood from the viewpoint of monotheistic religions. This does not prevent different practices or rituals from having different functions.

INFLUENCE OF INDIAN RELIGIONS ON INDIGENOUS BELIEFS

When considering material culture, it appears that Southeast Asians have only a very vague understanding of the concept of icons. There are no examples of images of deities connected with local cults or religions before the arrival of Indian civilization. This does not, however, mean that images fashioned in an Indian style were always recognized as Hindu gods. For the most part, they were recognized as local gods and worshipped in a local way. However, in most cases, Hindu or Buddhist images were regarded as unique and did not become integrated with the local gods.[85] It would take centuries before Southeast Asians fashioned local deities in human form. There are in Southeast Asia special images of the Buddha whose sacredness is believed to be more powerful than other ordinary images of the Buddha. Such a belief could have originated out of this process of localization.

Indian conceptual systems, especially Buddhist ones, introduced a multilevel cosmology. The Three Realms—*kāmabhūmi, rūpabhūmi,* and *ārūpyabhūmi*—appear in mural paintings. However, on a popular level and in the minds of most Buddhists of Southeast Asia, the Three Realms are hell, the human world, and heaven or the divine realm. This is expressed through the Buddhist concept of merit making, which emphasizes the making of merit so that one can be reborn in the heavenly realm and thus avoid hell.

In Southeast Asia, the concepts of "making merit" and "the transference of merit" figure mainly in Buddhist inscriptions, where we find examples of a shaman or *rishi* making merit through Buddhist means. Good deeds can be transferred not only to living or deceased relatives, but also to various kinds of spirits such as the *nat, devatā,* or *phii.* The following is a typical example from Burma of an inscription that tells of the donor's motives:

> May my ancestors before me and descendants after me, as well as my other relatives, the monks and all other men, abundantly reap the benefits of my good deed. May my two former husbands, Sinbyubin and Mingaung, partake of our merit equally to us. May every creature inhabit every region, from the highest abode of *nats* to the lowest Avīci hell, be benefited by this good deed.

> May our guardian *nats* also, and the guardian *nats* of the Religion, the earth, the trees, and all other *nats* of the universe, have their share of the merit . . .[86]

It would seem, then, that the concept of making and sharing merit is derived from Buddhism. The benefit accrued from merit making is accorded to both kinsmen and others. (This too is evidence against the broadly held categorization of Hīnayāna as being only a benefit for oneself and of Mahāyāna as being a benefit for all beings.) Even today, making merit is connected exclusively to Buddhism. People turn to Brahmanical cults and spirit cults for blessings and assurance rather than for merit. In Southeast Asia, at present, we may assume that Buddhism established a moral hierarchy. People accept Buddhist norms as the highest religious authority, and even the spirits seem to have become Buddhist in Buddhist inscriptions.

By way of contrast, Brahmanism functioned largely within a ritual hierarchy. Among the spirits, *phii, nat,* or *naek ta,* the ones believed to be better and more powerful are those derived from Brahmanical or Buddhist traditions.[87] Later, when Brahmanical influence from India declined, Buddhism gained ascendancy in terms of ritual.[88] This may be due to an emphasis on the sacredness of the monks, who are considered morally superior to the brahmans. In any given Buddhist ceremony in Thailand, it is possible to find all three religious actors present in the same ritual: Buddhist monks may be chanting the *paritta,* while lay people offer food to the monks for the purpose of making merit; brahmans may be performing rituals to bless and bring prosperity to the sponsoring family or community; and spirits of all kinds are propitiated to ward off bad luck. In such a ritual example, the three components would follow in succession. Normally the Buddhist rites would be first, but sometimes spirit cults, the simplest in form of ritual expression, might open the ceremonies.

There is no rigid or distinctive function among these creeds. The Buddha or a Buddha image can be propitiated in the same way as a Brahmanical god or a local deity. For example, people seek help from monks in the form of magical spells or diagrams, or to heal themselves from illness. It is not uncommon for someone in Thailand to ask a boon from a Buddha image.

It should be noted here that inscriptions whose content is Brahmanical or Mahāyānist usually lack any reference to merit making or the transfer of merit, and if mentioned, it is usually incidental.[89] The temples and the donations of wealth, animate and inanimate, seem to function primarily for administrative and economic purposes. Of course, the temples are also religious sanctuaries, but for practical purposes, they seem to serve political and economic interests.

So far the attitude of Southeast Asian peoples toward religion allows for a multidimensional situation to exist. We find different creeds coexisting. The situation can be described neither as "syncretic" nor "multilayered." Yet we do find a prominent creed that has been accorded a higher status than others, suggesting that there are additional factors influencing the direction of the development of religions. Apart from geographical factors, the concept of kingship is the most important.

RELATIONSHIP BETWEEN KINGSHIP AND RELIGION

A leader or ruler stands as the bridge between politics and religion. Heinz Bechert sums up the concepts embedded in Southeast Asian kingship, noting that kingship has been described according to four "ways of action."

> First, the king is "cakravartin," i.e., a universal monarch as described in canonical Buddhist texts; second, he is a "bodhisattva," a Buddha-to-be, an identification developed under the impact of Mahāyāna Buddhism; third, he is a promoter and protector of orthodox Theravāda like Aśoka; and fourth, he is a "devarājā," a god-king in the Hindu tradition. Each of these elements could be defined as ways of action: the "cakravartin" is the emperor of universal peace, the "bodhisattva" leads all beings on their way to final salvation, the "new Aśoka" protects the Sangha and the holy traditions, and the "devarājā" is bound to the rājadharma, i.e., the moral precepts of kingship as described in the Hindu sacred books, the *Purāṇas* and *Dharmaśāstras*, and reflected in the "dasa rājadhamma" of Buddhist Jātaka tales. These ideas were essential for the building of state and society in Indian Buddhist tradition, and they were very useful for the justification of state power and for the charismatic appeal of the ruler, though not for practical politics.[90]

In all probability Bechert's summary accurately reflects the situation. However, if it is the case that these concepts "were essential for the building of the state and society," as he contends, then, we must examine the evidence, not only from the viewpoint of the ruler or king, but also from that of the ruled. Bechert misses a vital point in describing these concepts as purely "Indian" or "Buddhist." The people naturally regard their king as sacred, but it is uncertain if they regard him as a "*cakravartin*" or a "bodhisattva." Such imported or imposed concepts could not have assumed such importance if the concept of sacred kingship had not already existed in Southeast Asia.

The much-discussed concept of *devarājā*, which is said to have developed in Khmer tradition, does not have to be attributed to the Indian tradition either. The term seems to be either a translation of the Khmer title *kamrateṅ añ jagat ta raja* into the Indian word "*devarājā*," or vice versa. The word is found in a Khmer inscription that includes a reference to a Śaivaite ritual performed by a chief advisor (*purohita*) of Jayavarman II (805–850 CE). Presumably the ritual was performed to elevate the king to the status of a god, and thus, the translation, *devarājā* or god-king. It has long been an established fact that this is the origin of the concept of the god-king that later influenced the concept of Thai kingship. A careful reading of the inscription, however, tells us otherwise. The word does not refer to King Jayavarman II, who at that time claimed to be a *cakravartin*, but instead to an object of worship, either an image or a Śivaliṅga created and consecrated as the king of god(s) in the nation, or as a national god. The function of this national god was to protect the king and his descendants. What we have here might be interpreted as the internalization of the king in the form of a national god. The dichotomy between the mortal and the immortal aspects is evident. Politically speaking, the god worshipped by a *cakravartin*, who reigns over all kings, had sovereignty to rule as the chief among the gods. However, we cannot accept that the *devarājā* mentioned in this inscription was the origin of the concept of the god-king in Southeast Asia, since the word signifies a national god, not a god-king. Therefore, it should not be used to describe "a king who claims to be a Hindu god." When a king embraces the Buddhist creed, he does not become a *buddharājā*, an error by the same analogy used for the word "*devarājā*," which does not have an inscription to support its use. "Sacred kingship" is a concept that still prevails throughout all Southeast Asian cultures, and perhaps by extension to any culture that has a monarch.

Studies have revealed that the concept is not Indian in origin. In India *devarājā* was never used specifically to mean a sacred king, but rather, a king of the gods—either Indra, Śiva, Viṣṇu, or as a name for a specific Buddha—otherwise, it just means a king in general.[91] There is no evidence for how this concept came to be used to legitimize the authority of a king. It was a common practice for a king to take epithets of Hindu gods as his name, implying that he thought of himself as a god and was revered as such by his subjects.

On the Buddhist side, a king is regarded not only as a "bodhisattva" but also a Buddha. Judging from the names of kings like Paramatrailokanātha and

Sarvajña, the emphasis seems to be on the qualities of a Buddha rather than a bodhisattva. And the concept need not be traced specifically to Mahāyāna influence; it is a pan-Buddhist concept. The tradition, however, is found only in Sri Lanka and Southeast Asia, which adhere to the Theravāda school. It is not found in the Mahāyāna countries of China or Japan. There are some instances in which the emperors of China claimed to be a bodhisattva, including Maitreya, but there is no example that an emperor claimed to be a Buddha.

The adoption of Aśoka as a royal paradigm should not be confined solely to the Theravādin Buddhist tradition, as any king who professed or supported Buddhism would be so regarded, whether Theravādin or Mahāyānist. In Thailand, the concept of kingship is linked to the epic of *Rāmakirti* (*Rāmāyaṇa*), rather than to the legend of Aśoka.[92] Neither should the word "*dharmarājā*" be limited to the Buddhist sense, as a concept used in contrast to "*devarājā*." When the concept is used in Buddhist scriptures, *dharmarājā* does refer to the Buddha, but other creeds of India also used it as a title for any just king. When the concept is used in Southeast Asia for a king, the title is linked to other qualities that cannot be delineated as either Buddhist or Brahmanical. In a sense, the epithet is more connected to Yama, the Lord of Justice, than the Buddha.

In the evolution of the concept of kingship in Southeast Asia, indigenous concepts were enhanced by Indian concepts. When royalty referred to Indian religions to legitimize themselves, it was the ritual, rather than the concept, that really mattered. In royal names or titles, qualities figuring in Brahmanical, Buddhist, and local traditions are equally significant. However, it was rare for the people to refer to or address the king by his real name; out of deference and respect, they would refer to the king by his title. These titles differ from culture to culture, but all tended to reflect a similar meaning. A king is seen as the "Lord of Life," "Lord of the Land," and as the "Protector of the Nation."[93]

The "ways of action" proposed by Bechert may be a valid scholarly approach. From the viewpoint of the people, the king is perceived as a god (most of the time) without any attempt to identify which god. The ways of action are, in effect, expressions of the same attitude through different beliefs. The king is seen as the center of every constitution and every institution of a nation or a tribe. This leads to the rather dubious notion that the king employs concepts from religion to legitimize his claim to power, and that the religion in question becomes the state religion. However, the definition of "state religion" as a religion used to legitimize political power may not apply in the context of Southeast Asia polity. It was, or still is, common for a monarch to endow himself with all the qualities inspired by both Buddhism and Brahmanism. This tendency is evident throughout the history of Southeast Asia. The effort to become more Buddhist is evident in Thailand, but this has been the case only since the nineteenth century.

The relationship between the king and the three traditions found in Southeast Asian religion can be described as follows: as a Buddhist, he is foremost among laymen and he is the protector of the faith; as a supporter of Brahmanism, he presides over ceremonies for the welfare of the nation and the people; within the context of indigenous beliefs, he propitiates the spirits for the welfare and prosperity of the country. The king's preferred faith symbolically becomes the dominant creed, subsuming all others. It should also be noted that there exists a close relation between the king and the people. He acts as their spiritual leader and guardian. In fact, almost everything concerning kingship may be called spiritual or symbolic, even the king's claim to be the owner of all the land. In this manner, the king influences his people by his personal beliefs, yet without imposing his personal creed. One may say that these two components of the concept of kingship—that a king is both a political and a spiritual leader—are not separated in the minds of Southeast Asians. Consequently, what the king believes or practices is always acceptable to the people, since what he believes and practices is always regarded as the most superior creed. The king, as noted above, does not strictly adhere to a particular creed and does not impose a particular creed on his subjects, giving them instead the freedom to adopt any creed that is not directly hostile to the king.

Apart from being a major factor in the adoption of a religion, a king's decision to apply different creeds to different needs also affects the structural distribution of religions in Southeast Asia. As discussed in chapter 3, this phenomenon was partly due to a shift in the trade routes beginning in the seventh century. However, the crucial factor was probably that the Khmer, Cham, and Javanese kings appropriated the social and political concepts of Mahāyāna Buddhism and Brahmanism, which should not be considered separately—both should be regarded as fundamentally Indian. Where Mahāyāna Buddhism was present, there was also a strong influence of Brahmanism, and often the two appeared in the same context in the same inscription or temple sanctuary.

Given all the available evidence, an attempt to reconstruct Buddhism will be made by setting it against historical fact. It is generally accepted that the Khmers, the Chams, and the Javanese were more politically unified and formed what scholars call the "great *maṇḍalas*." In creating these political unities, the kings made extensive use of Brahmanism and Mahāyāna Buddhism.

Kenneth R. Hall and other scholars have studied these great *maṇḍalas* and how they evolved.[94] Hall regards their evolution basically as an economic development. The temples built by the Khmer kings served as economic units, and through them the king achieved a unified administrative hold over the land. Hall, using evidence from Khmer and Javanese inscriptions, develops a model for the functioning of the Khmer and Javanese temple hierarchies and discusses the temple's role in the political and economic development and integration of the Khmer state. He proposes that there was a three-tier hierarchy of temples: central, regional, and local. The central shrine was directly associated with the king himself, and the king's creed was the central creed under which the regional temples of different deities were subsumed. The regional temples may have functioned as shrines for deities worshipped by lesser kings who had become vassals under Khmer sovereignty. The regional community was connected to local agricultural communities by village temples. In such a way the Khmer kings integrated their empire. The idea of hierarchy among deities of different ranks is not so different from the one proposed by Mus and it accords with the establishment of a *devarājā* as god of the nation. The political and economic aspects have been summarized by David Welch:

> Southeast Asian leaders legitimized their rule primarily through spiritual prowess, guaranteeing the prosperity of the society. These leaders saw the construction and endowment of temples as the foremost means of ensuring such prosperity. The provisioning of temples with endowments of land, labour, and resources made possible the development of an economic system centered on these temples. Temples became local storage and redistribution centres and provided a sanctioned means by which resources and capital could be accumulated and labour mobilized, permitting the development of underutilized lands. Elite families cemented political alliances and helped legitimize the subordination of one local area to another centre by sharing in the giving of gifts. Regional elites expanded their power by consolidating land management under the authority of regional temples.[95]

Even if there is no direct evidence that temples functioned as political or economic units in the Dvāravatī or Pyu zones, we can surmise that their monasteries could have served this purpose as well. At the very least, they stood at the center of a town or a city. Apparently, the monasteries were never considered a part of the elaborate administrative network; centers in the two zones were loosely connected by a common culture rather than by a political organizational structure. Srisakra Vallibhotama claims that it was not until the Khmer culture, and consequently, Brahmanic and Mahāyānist cultures, penetrated into the Dvāravatī area that the cities there were brought into close contact.[96]

The reason the Khmer and the Javanese traditions made use of Brahmanism and Mahāyāna Buddhism was that at around the eighth century the two religions were at their most prominent. Java lay along the main sea routes and always maintained close contact with the Khmer and the Cham. In fact, Jayavarman II, who established the great Khmer *maṇḍala*, was reported to have spent time in Java.[97] The archipelago was always exposed to changing tides from outside. The impact of Mahāyāna and the revival of Brahmanism was felt first in this area, which then spread along the sea routes to Champa and Cambodia. The same pattern was repeated when Islam began to spread eastward from India. The Cham, who had close connections with Java, also became Muslim.[98] Since the thirteenth century, Cambodia's links with Thailand became ever stronger, and from that time on Cambodia came more under the influence of the religious culture in Thailand than the one in Java.

What is crucial here is not which religion was chosen, but rather, how a religion was applied in accordance with the king's purpose. From this point of view, the much-debated issue of whether this or that king was Brahmanical or Buddhist should be dropped. Kings usually supported both creeds, and in all likelihood saw little difference between them, since both appear side-by-side in inscriptions. In some inscriptions, a king might express himself in Buddhist terms, but in Brahmanical terms in others. The application of a certain religion was dictated more by political and economic goals than doctrinal ones.

The fact that the Khmer Empire became so highly organized and expanded over such a vast area that included Dvāravatī and perhaps reaching as far as the Pyu circle affected the history of Buddhism in Southeast Asia. Even though Khmer sovereignty was short lived and constantly waxed and waned, nevertheless, it made a strong cultural impact. Yet there is evidence that Buddhism in Dvāravatī, especially the Sthavira school, persisted together with other creeds, as seen from Sūryavarman's inscription in chapter 4.

Historically, it is possible to say that Mahāyāna Buddhism became a national or state religion, that is, it became a creed preferred by a king over Hīnayāna Buddhism. Mahāyāna Buddhism left more substantial evidence in the heavily studied area of Indochina, leading some scholars to set forth a theory of the sequential development of religions, beginning with various schools of Hīnayāna (usually excluding Pāli Buddhism), followed by the flowering of Brahmanism and Mahāyāna, and culminating in the introduction of Theravāda Buddhism from Sri Lanka.[99]

Yet as has been shown, Theravāda, most likely emanating from Sri Lanka, was active in the area as early as any other school and, in fact, left more material evidence in the form of scriptural citations than all others combined. However, its influence seems to have been strong only in the areas that now comprise lower Burma and central Thailand. Mahāyāna Buddhism seems to have reached these areas from the east with the expansion of the Khmer culture, although there is no doubt that some influences came directly from India or Sri Lanka. In any case, Mahāyāna Buddhism and Brahmanism never became as prominent in these areas, although it is evident that Brahmanism was used politically in the Dvāravatī and Pyu cultures. This may be because both the sciences of governance and of ritual observance were far more complex and sophisticated in Brahmanism than in Theravāda Buddhism or Buddhism in general.[100]

This, then, is the general view of religiosity as it developed in Southeast Asia. People perceived religion as the institution in which to place their trust, with all religions being regarded as auspicious, and which could be applied to different situations in everyday life. Religion in Southeast Asia can be regarded as a compound phenomenon that is interwoven with political concepts such as kingship and other societal ones.

Given this view of religion, the religious culture of Southeast Asia can be described as polylithic from the beginning. Scholars should not be reluctant to say that religious society in Southeast Asia is composed of many religions, whose practices in most cases reveal strong influences of indigenous beliefs, especially animism. The idea that one professes to belong to a single religion is foreign to the Southeast Asian mind, which sees no need to synthesize multiple beliefs into one exclusive belief. Different beliefs and practices were not relegated to distinct functions in society. They are seen as hierarchical, but according a higher status to one belief by no means debases the others. Similarly, in the Buddhist society of Southeast Asia today, Buddhist monks generally ignore practices that are not in strict accordance with Buddhist doctrine, but they make no sustained effort to prevent people from performing them. Southeast Asian religion can be likened to a piece of cloth woven from gold and silver threads and embellished with jewels. Even though the materials remain separate, yet it is still the same piece of cloth. The word that best describes the relations among beliefs is "symbiosis" rather than "synthesis" or "syncretism," both of which involve a conscious effort to reconcile different beliefs.[101]

The evolution of these beliefs did not occur at random, but rather as a response to a variety of dynamics or factors that include concepts of kingship, and political, economic, and social circumstances all of which helped unite different cultural tendencies to form what became known as the religiosity of Southeast Asia.

The concept of kingship as the symbol of the nation and its peoples provides the framework in which rituals and ethics of different beliefs can function together. Political, economic, and social circumstances differentiated the zones within which the various religions from India created different impacts. In the western part of Southeast Asia, people identified themselves as Buddhists, but without any clear understanding of the different schools of Buddhism. Of course, it is possible that a king or some learned monks may have noted discrepancies in minor practices and tried to standardize them, but this was a question of ethical or ritual lapses being observed, not a question of different philosophical forms of Buddhism. The purification of the *sāsanā* was motivated not by doctrinal but by practical considerations. If one were to ask a Southeast Asian Buddhist what his *sāsanā* is, in all probability, the answer would be "*Buddha-sāsanā.*" But if one probes further and asks whether he or she is a Theravādin or a Mahāyānist, most likely, no answer would be forthcoming, because the question makes no sense to them. This leads to a serious question: In these circumstances can these so-called "Theravāda Buddhist countries" be called Theravāda Buddhist at all?

6

"Theravāda" Buddhism in Southeast Asia

Buddhism in Southeast Asia has long been part of a complex system of beliefs and practices that also included Brahmanism and indigenous beliefs. The eclectic nature of the numerous elements of this religiously diverse situation was generally accepted on equal terms by Southeast Asian peoples, albeit in most instances unconsciously, and used to fulfill their various needs.

Before examining the history of Theravāda Buddhism proper, historical issues raised in the preceding chapters about Theravāda Buddhism prior to the eleventh century should be addressed, for the reason that after the eleventh century, countries in mainland Southeast Asia were labeled as "Theravāda Buddhist states" by modern scholars. How was Theravāda Buddhism "introduced" into these countries?

Our picture of Theravāda Buddhism would be incomplete if we do not take into account additional research done on Theravāda Buddhism. Even though these are mainly studies of more contemporary Southeast Asian Theravāda Buddhism, they include useful historical background and doctrinal points. The question is whether or not the historical data and the doctrinal material have been sufficiently scrutinized and understood before being used. In many cases, what we have are received versions of the history of Theravāda Buddhism or else distorted views of Buddhism used without proper verification.

CHARACTERISTICS

The first issue that needs clarification is the confusion between Theravāda Buddhism as it is now known and what some scholars label as early or "primitive" Buddhism. Theravāda Buddhism may be the most conservative form of Buddhism preserved today. Thus, modern scholars regard it as the purest form of Buddhism because it is devoid of all irrational accretions. This view is the result of focusing on sacred texts and normative literature to the exclusion or neglect of the actual lived tradition existing in Theravāda Buddhist countries.[1]

Beliefs and practices in Theravāda Buddhist countries derive from both indigenous and Indian cultures. In the Southeast Asian context, every issue having so-called popular overtones cannot be ascribed to the influence of Mahāyāna Buddhism. Neither can Brahmanism be treated separately from other beliefs that came from India. All channels of religious expression regardless of origin should be considered as being coexistent.

A typical misunderstanding about the lived tradition in Theravāda Buddhist countries that is still sometimes apparent today is exemplified by the scholar Melvin Spiro, who wrote:

> Normative Buddhism, as is well known, is currently expressed in two major forms: Mahāyāna and Theravāda . . . With its numerous saints and saviors, its masses for the dead, its elaborate and ornate rituals, Mahāyāna Buddhism—the Buddhism of the Greater Vehicle—is related to Theravāda Buddhism—the Buddhism of the Elders—much as Catholicism is related to Protestantism. Lacking saints and saviors, and possessing a few simple rituals, the latter form of Buddhism is found primarily in Southeast Asia. . . . In his discussion of the Buddhist creed, J. H. Bateson (1911) summarizes the teachings of Buddhism in the following five concepts: materialism, atheism, pessimism, nihilism, and egoism. To this conceptual set, I would add one more concept, viz., world-renunciation, the attitudinal and behavioral consequence of subscribing to the above set. Even a brief discussion of these doctrines will indicate how unusual they are when taken as the defining doctrines of a religious tradition.[2]

The points made by Spiro, following and elaborating on J. H. Bateson, deviate from what is described in the Buddhist texts. Spiro's account is inaccurate with regard to both doctrinal and historical developments.[3] First, what is the point of Spiro comparing Mahāyāna and Theravāda Buddhism to Catholicism and Protestantism?[4] Moreover, in Buddhism, "man" is not "an aggregate of five material factors," as Spiro mentions later in his discussion (see note 2 of this chapter). Does Spiro mean the five elements—earth, water, fire, wind, and atmosphere—or the five *skandhas*—form, feelings, perception, volitional factors, and consciousness? In Buddhist texts, whether Theravāda or Mahāyāna, "man" is described as an aggregate of the five *skandhas*. Of these five *skandhas*, only one is "material," that is, derived from one of the five basic elements. The other four are mental or psychological states. The Buddha did not teach that these aggregates would disappear completely after death. If that were true, then there could be no transmigration or, for that matter, no reason would exist for renunciation or salvation.

However, neither is renunciation a complete negation of the world and society. Credit can be given to the Buddhist monastic system for reintroducing the *śramaṇa* (recluse) back into society.[5] Buddhist monks, especially those of the Theravādin tradition, usually live near or in towns and cities. We can see by examining the Vinaya rules how much the Sangha relies upon and cares about its position and image in society.[6] It is incorrect to equate Buddhism as a religion with otherworldly asceticism and to suggest that by renouncing the world Buddhists aspire to detachment from persons, material possessions, and even themselves. It is true that Buddhism teaches that people should be detached from the defilements, but this detachment does not entail a negation or a rejection of society. Monks still live together as a community, and in Theravāda Buddhist societies, monasteries serve as centers for an entire community. The monastery's role in town or village activities could be compared to that of a town hall or other institutions that play a social service role in a community.[7] To "renounce the world" means to free the self from impediments like excessive material possessions or overly burdensome family affairs, so that one is free to pursue the goal. It is totally inaccurate to say that Buddhists are forced to renounce the world.

Spiro accepted these points and used them as his basis to examine a Theravāda Buddhist society, namely Burma. When he looked at the real situation in the country, Spiro detected some discrepancies, and sometimes he even contradicted himself. His definition of the normative and non-normative is, for example, muddled in the statement: ". . . and having discovered in my Burmese research that the doctrines of normative Buddhism only rarely constitute the Buddhism of the faithful, I also discovered that the latter have acquired other additional forms of Buddhism which for them are equally, or nearly equally, normative."[8] Sprio concluded that supernaturalism in Burma, as well as supernaturalism in other Theravāda Buddhist countries of Southeast Asia, is a system separate from the Buddhism of Southeast Asia. It survived, in Spiro's view, because Buddhism, especially in its Theravāda form, lacked this supernatural aspect, which is crucial to meeting the simple needs of the common folk. For Spiro, anything supernatural by definition *is not* Theravāda Buddhism. He regarded the presence of supernaturalism as something that is absent in Buddhism:

> Agreeing that Burmese animism and Buddhism are separate systems, an earlier generation of Western scholars concluded, as we have seen, that the former was

> the "true" religion of the Burmese. It is primarily because Buddhism, at least in its Great Tradition aspects, abdicates almost all concern for worldly goals, that they mistakenly (in my opinion) perceived Buddhism to be nothing but a veneer. Scott, for example, had no doubt but that this was the case because, he observed, "when a Burman wants to build a house, launch a boat, plough or sow his fields, start on a journey, make a purchase, marry a wife himself, or marry his daughter to another, bury a relation, or even endow a religious foundation, it is the spirits he propitiates, it is the nats whom he consults" (Scott 1921:390). Although Scott's generalization is true, his conclusion is false. For the Burman consults the nats, not in defiance of Buddhism, but in default of Buddhism. Orthodox Buddhism, neither as a philosophy nor as religion, has anything to say about these mundane matters. Since the world and its affairs have nothing to do with salvation, Buddhism, as a salvation religion, has nothing to do with them.[9]

In fact, supernaturalism is quite a common feature in Theravāda Buddhism, both in the texts and in popular practice. It is not regarded as something foreign or unacceptable to what scholars call "normative" Buddhism. For instances of supernaturalism in canonical texts, the best examples are found in the *Mahāsamayasutta,* the *Ratanasutta,* and the *Āṭānāṭiyasutta.* The first text contains nothing doctrinal whatsoever, but instead gives in verse form lists of gods, goddesses, and demons.[10] The second text comprises verses taught to the monks so that they could help pacify an epidemic in Vesālī.[11] The last *sutta* addresses the problems experienced by the disciples of the Buddha, who while living in the forest, were haunted by evil spirits. In order to help the disciples, a protective spell was recited to the Buddha by Vessavaṇa (Kubera), one of the four Great Kings and the protector of the northern region, so that the Buddha could transmit the spell to the monks.[12] In Buddhist ceremonies, it is this *sutta* that is frequently recited by monks to dispel evil spirits. Therefore, if what is meant by supernaturalism includes any reference to ghosts, spirits, or sorcerers, then, it can be found scattered throughout the Buddhist canon, as shown in the work of Joseph Masson.[13]

The situation in Thailand is similar to the one in Burma. But in neither case should we conclude that it is a fault in Buddhism that allows supernaturalism to persist, as Melford Spiro argued.[14] Rather, supernatural beliefs remain because they form an important part of the belief system of Southeast Asian people. Supernatural beliefs offer the people a comforting assurance, an auspiciousness, and a protection against life's problems. People would not hesitate to invite monks to chant the *paritta* before performing a spirit possession ceremony or a bloody sacrifice. Naturally, the monks depart before the actual spirit ceremony or sacrifice begins. When the monks are asked about who is doing the protecting, they answer that it is the power of the Buddha's words in the chant that protects the people from being harmed by evil spirits. It is common in any *paritta* ritual for monks to invite spirits and gods to come and listen to the recitation.[15] It is, therefore, not surprising to find in fifth-century inscriptions that shamans, sorcerers, or *rishi*s are present at a ceremony for the casting of a Buddha image. Neither is it surprising that brahmans in Thailand invite monks to chant *paritta* before the beginning of Brahmanical ceremonies.

People who identify themselves as Buddhists have no qualms about propitiating the Buddha or special images of the Buddha revered as a god who has the power to grant boons and ward off ill omens. In Thailand, there is a tradition of seeking out and paying homage to monks who are believed to have achieved extraordinary spiritual attainment. Such an achievement is considered to be an act of great merit. However, instead of seeking advice on moral practice or meditation techniques, most people visit revered monks just to be in their presence or to receive blessings and amulets from them, in the belief that this, too, is a source of great merit. Sometimes an important Buddha image or a holy monk is entreated to heal the sick, although this practice is prohibited in the Vinaya rules.

A similar situation is found in Sri Lanka, considered by many to be the cradle of the most orthodox form of Theravāda Buddhism. In the following quote, Bechert describes the problems caused when terms such as "folk religion" or "popular cults" are used:

> Some of the cults of the gods in Sinhalese tradition were definitely not "popular" cults, but formed part of the established system of state ceremonies and state ritual of the Sinhalese kingdom. This does not contradict the fact that Buddhism was the state religion, because . . . such rituals, though considered essential for the prosperity of king, state and nation, could not be performed by bhikkhus because of the "supra-mundane" function of the *sāsanā*.[16]

In monastic Buddhism—in principle, the purest form—popular beliefs can be easily detected. After all, monks are not separate from the society of which they are a part. They ordain not always to attain *nirvāṇa* but to gain merit, receive an education, make a living, or raise their status in society.[17]

Some monks are also involved in supernatural activities, which has always been true, not only in Southeast Asia today, but also during the Buddha's lifetime in India.

What is recorded in the sacred texts forms a part of Buddhism to be sure, but Buddhism is not to be found in texts alone. A living religion cannot be said to be truly "alive" if we neglect the actual situation in which it is found, or said another way, until it is brought to life by those who profess it. And we cannot say that this aspect of Buddhism is not normative. Popular practices are no less a part of Buddhism in comparison to the texts, which at times has been either under or overemphasized. It is more accurate to say that the lived tradition is a better representation of Buddhism in Southeast Asia than what is called "normative" Buddhism.

While Spiro classified Buddhism into four types—nibbanic, kammatic, apotropic, and esoteric—how should these classifications of Buddhisms, which are practiced by commoners, elites, and kings alike, be understood?[18] One who pursues nibbanic Buddhism can very well use or apply Buddhism kammatically, apotropically, or even esoterically. However, one who pursues kammatic Buddhism cannot ignore the nibbanic aspect. The final goal would be *nirvāṇa*, although it could be postponed if devotees regarded their personal store of merit as still insufficient.

The approaches of Bechert and Tambiah were an improvement over Spiro's, but again, the dichotomies raised represent pseudo-problems. Tambiah, by trying to establish a principle for the study of Theravāda in Southeast Asia, especially in Thailand, adopted, what at the time was a new, sociohistorical approach. Tambiah, nevertheless, did make a contribution to the methodology of the study of Buddhism in Southeast Asia in his use of both synchronic and diachronic approaches. In *Buddhism and the Spirit Cults in North-east Thailand*, Tambiah described the relationship between Buddhist and non-Buddhist traditions as "reciprocity."[19] He also described the dynamics involved in the belief system in a Buddhist village society. To interpret the relationships between these beliefs, he applied synchronic categories of opposition, complementarity, linkage, and hierarchy. And to the development of these beliefs together, he applied diachronic categories of continuity and transformation. But in the end, he was unable to truly divorce himself from the old dichotomy of the "Great" and "Little" traditions." In chapter 14, Tambiah set out to explain how the brahman and the Buddhist monk can coexist, giving a typically misleading presentation of the case:

> The term for the *sukhwan* officiant, *paahm*, etymologically derives from *brahman*; alternatively he is called *maukhwan* (expert in *khwan* rites). It is the first term that acts as a cue beckoning us to investigate further. . . . The *brahman* and the *bhikkhu* were in their country of origin, India, unaccommodating antagonists; the *brahman* did in time virtually eliminate the Buddhist monk while incorporating in his religion some of the ethical achievements of Buddhism. The questions that therefore spring to mind are: How is it that the *brahman* and the *bhikkhu* can co-exist peacefully in Thai society? What different circumstances experienced by the *brahman* and *bhikkhu* in further India have made possible this co-existence? Finally, what is the connection between the classical *brahman* priest and the contemporary village *paahm* or *maukhwan*?[20]

Tambiah's explanation seems sound, but his theory depended upon identifying the *paahm* as a brahman. He was correct to say that etymologically *paahm* derives from an Indian word, but there is no evidence to prove that it derives from Brahmanism. The word *paahm* may simply be an elite form of *maukhwan*, an expert in *khwan* rites, from which it evolved.

The concept of *khwan* is not an Indian one. It is the vital force in the human body, but it is not the same as *vijñāna* (consciousness) of the Indian philosophical tradition. When the Thai embraced Buddhism, they also adopted the concept of *vijñāna*. Tambiah described the meaning of both terms in the Thai context as follows:

> The concepts of *khwan* and *winjan*, both expressing the notion of spiritual essences connected with the human body, are difficult to define and describe. Taking *khwan* first: some writers have rendered it as 'life soul'; others as 'benevolent guardian spirit of an extremely ephemeral essence'. The villagers' characterization of *khwan* subsumes a number of ideas: the *khwan* resides in the human body; it is attached to the body and yet can leave it. The causes and consequences of the *khwan*'s departure are formulated in a circular manner: The *khwan* takes flight and leaves its owner's body (*cao khong*) when he is frightened, sick or in trouble, or *caj bau dee* (mind not good). The very act of its fleeing the body in turn exposes the owner to suffering, illness and misfortune. . . . The *khwan* must be understood in relation to *winjan*. The *winjan* is also a spiritual essence and also resides in the body. But it is different from *khwan*. The *khwan* can leave the body temporarily, thereby causing illness, but it can be recalled and mental and physical health thereby restored. At death the

khwan leaves the body for good, followed by the *winjan*. The *winjan* leaves the body only with death. In fact, death is described as the escape of *winjan* from the body. After death, people are not concerned with the *khwan*, only with the fate of *winjan* and its subsequent transformation.[21]

Tambiah conceded that: "It is apparent that there is complementarity and opposition implied by this pair of concepts."[22] Thai people might agree with him on the first point, but it is doubtful if they ever thought of *khwan* and *winjan* as opposing forces. In fact, Tambiah finally admitted that:

> The Thai villager thus conceptually distinguished two spiritual essences. This duality does not fit into simple 'body/soul' dichotomy; if we are to fit the Thai notions we can say that two aspects of the 'soul' are distinguished. While the villager makes the conceptual distinction, he becomes highly inarticulate and vague if the anthropologist strives to make him verbalize their respective properties . . .[23]

The situation could not be otherwise, since a Thai would not formulate such questions about these two concepts. Thais regard them as belonging to entirely different fields. Tambiah's account of the departure of the *khwan* at death is rather presumptuous. Thais do not think of the *khwan* in connection with birth or death. This is an obvious point, since *khwan* can exist in inanimate objects like a house or a car. When the term is applied to animate objects, then the concept of *khwan* pertains to this life, and the concept of *winjan* pertains to the transmigration process. Once again, Thais are less concerned with any apparent dichotomy or in an analysis of beliefs; they simply accept the concepts in a traditional way, rather than in how the concepts function.

In the Thai case, the term in general use is *maukhwan* rather than *paahm*. It seems obvious to me that Tambiah was trying to raise questions out of what I call a "pseudo-situation," when he emphasized the word, *paahm*, over the more common word, *maukhwan*. The important point does not concern whether or not any antagonism or reciprocity existed between brahman and *bhikkhu*, but, rather, what was the nature of the relations that existed between indigenous and Buddhist traditions.

Regarding what constitutes Buddhist traditions, it is difficult to discern systematically what part can be labeled as indigenous and what part is Buddhist. The evidence suggests that it is incorrect to say that tension exists between them. Even Tambiah knows that there is no antagonism between *maukhwan* and *bhikkhu*, who belong to the same society. The *maukhwan* were educated in Buddhist monastic schools and were, in most cases, former monks. How can one separate the two practices if this close relationship has existed for ages? Could we claim that the *maukhwan* consciously assumes his role, or, because he has grown up in this environment, he performs what he regards as fitting and auspicious for the occasion? How, then, would questions arising from the context of the antagonism between brahman and *bhikkhu* of India be compared historically or socially in the case of Buddhism in Thailand? It is best to examine how the people perceive religion, rather than trying to impose a dichotomy or a structure on their religious beliefs.

Bechert also divided Buddhism into different types.[24] The categories he used, which included "court Buddhism," "popular Buddhism," and "elite Buddhism," do not accurately reflect the actual situation in either Southeast Asia or India, for that matter. No Buddhist in Thailand would say that the Buddhism they practice is essentially different from the one practiced by the king, nor would the king think that his Buddhism differs from that of the people. Buddhist rites performed by the king to gain merit and to ensure the prosperity of the kingdom are not conceptually or materially different from those performed by the people. The contrasting concepts of "elite" and "popular" are a useful tool of analysis, but while Buddhism has always nurtured both monastic and lay elites, it does not follow that they behaved or expressed themselves religiously in a way fundamentally different from ordinary people. Schopen has shown that even in India what we regard as "popular Buddhism" was the same Buddhism as the monks practiced.[25] Such categories should be considered only as tools for the study of Buddhism, not as any final or absolute distinction. The methodology is acceptable if it is used for descriptive purposes only, but not as a conclusive characterization of Theravāda Buddhism in Southeast Asia.

With a variety of scholarly viewpoints to consider, studies on Theravādin Buddhist practice could be termed confusing or inconclusive. B. J. Terwiel at one time summed up the situation in this way:

> A survey of the literature on the practice of religion in Theravāda Buddhist countries reveals what may be a unique situation in the study of religions. Many authors state unequivocally that Theravāda Buddhists adhere to more than one religious tradition. Apart from "otherworldly" Buddhism, these Southeast Asia peoples adhere to other strands of religion, generally classed under rubrics such as "non-Buddhistic beliefs," "folk religion," "animism," or "supernaturalism."

> Yet, though virtually all authors recognize this situation, there is no consensus in their views on how the different subsystems are interrelated.
>
> Some authors, while differentiating between Buddhist and non-Buddhist practices and beliefs, maintain that these different types of religion have in the course of centuries become so intermingled that at present it is impossible to draw a distinction between them. They cannot state where Buddhism ends and religion of [a] different type begins. Such views are expressed unequivocally by some and implicitly by others; these authors appear to have decided that religion in Theravāda Buddhist countries is a blend of two traditions. Others maintain that the undistinguishable mixture is made up of three different types of creeds.
>
> Some authors, however, consider that the distinction between Buddhism and non-Buddhism can be clearly drawn; these scholars tend to see Buddhism and non-Buddhism as complimentary subtypes of religion, with each subtype fulfilling a distinct function in society. From these perspectives, Buddhism is concerned with future lives and otherworldly goals, whilst local religious beliefs deal with the magical side of everyday life. One author recognizes two religious orientations but, instead of giving them complementary status, deems them to be incompatible and opposed. Yet other researchers distinguish between Buddhism on the one hand and animism on the other, but do not appear to rely on functionalist explanations of this phenomenon (curiously enough mainly local scholars). And then there are more complex analyses in which more than two sub-religions are distinguished.[26]

Terwiel went on to state: "Suffice it to note that there is a general agreement amongst them only with regard to the opinion that, next to Buddhist faith, there can be found in Theravāda Buddhist countries one or more layers of non-Buddhist religion."[27] Thus, much of the scholarly literature can be grouped under two rubrics: those that explain the situation as an example of syncretism, and those who argue for distinctiveness, separateness, or opposition, proposing modes of interaction or differing functions between different layers of creeds.

The problem may lie in the label "Theravāda Buddhism" itself. The word "Theravāda" is sometimes used in order to avoid using the derogatory term "Hīnayāna." But this usage causes its own confusion, since Theravāda represents only one of many schools that are grouped under Hīnayāna.[28]

Historically, Theravāda Buddhism is found mainly in Sri Lanka and Southeast Asia. This again leads to confusion since, according to the chronicles, the Theravāda school of Southeast Asia was entirely inspired and derived from

Sri Lanka. Contemporary studies on the history of Buddhism in Southeast Asia trace everything connected with Buddhism, at least the Theravādins, to Sri Lanka, including the misconception that Theravāda did not arrive in Southeast Asia until the establishment of close relations between the region and Sri Lanka. This is inaccurate because it fails to take into account the roles played by South India and Andhra Pradesh. Furthermore, in later centuries religious relations between Sri Lanka and Southeast Asia were marked by mutual interaction and mutual influence.[29] Buddhism, or at least the ordination lineage and the sacred texts, were reintroduced to Sri Lanka from Southeast Asian countries on several occasions. Even the term "Theravāda" became conflated with Sinhalese Buddhism, which, in turn, was regarded as orthodox Theravāda. Some scholars saw orthodox Theravāda in the most narrow sense as the Theravāda Buddhism that was purified and unified in favor of the Mahāvihāra sect by King Parākramabāhu (r. 1158–1186).[30] Cœdès rightly cautioned us on using the term "Sinhalese Buddhism" as a school of Buddhism that used Pāli, but this too produced further confusion. Some scholars use "Theravāda" to signify only this post-reform Buddhism, but this is too narrow a meaning, since the word had been used for over one thousand years, long before Parākramabāhu's so-called "reunification."[31]

Can Theravāda Buddhism be defined? Should these countries be called Theravāda Buddhist at all? The tensions, layers, and substrata exposed in the course of many studies suggest that we may have been misled by imposing the name "Theravāda Buddhist" on these countries. For in these studies, the practice is always to apply the term "Theravāda Buddhism" to the countries of Southeast Asia, and never just Buddhist or Southeast Asian religion in general. In fact, the only basis for labeling these countries as Theravāda Buddhist—or preferably, simply Buddhist—is that Buddhist beliefs have been the most respected and have supremacy over other beliefs, whether Brahmanic or indigenous.

HISTORICAL ISSUES

Evidence, both epigraphic and archaeological, shows that Sri Lanka cannot be excluded as an early source for Buddhism in Southeast Asia. It seems to have been the only source of Theravāda Buddhism, because there is no evidence to connect it to other parts of the Indian subcontinent. It is uncertain whether or not the Aśokan mission was sent; or if it was sent, for lack of evidence, it cannot be said that the mission represented the Theravāda school.

Theravāda Buddhism with its use of the Pāli canon reached the area as early as other schools of Buddhism and Brahmanism. Had scholars carefully examined the quotation inscriptions discussed in chapter 4, this would have been obvious for a long time. Instead we find, as late as 1985, Aung-Thwin asserting that:

> The archaeological remains of this pre-Pagan urbanized culture show that it is uniform to a significant degree. Mongmai, Hanlaṅ, Binnaka, in the central dry zone, and Śri Kṣetra, Beikthano, and Winka, south of it, were related in several ways. They apparently used the same Tibeto-Burman language (Pyu) and wrote in Devanagari, Kadamba, and the Pallava script of Andhra. . . . Their belief system included Sarvāstivādin Buddhism (an early branch of the Hīnayāna whose doctrines were similar to those of the later Theravāda and who wrote their texts in Sanskrit), elements of Hinduism, and a rather wide-spread Southeast Asian practice of urn burial. More important, some of their material and ideological culture show continuity with the Pagan period. Their ideology of salvation, for example, was closely related to the doctrine of the future Buddha (Metteya) and the four Buddhas of this kappa (the present cosmic age) . . .[32]

Aung-Thwin raises a problem when he identifies Buddhism in that area of Burma as including Sarvāstivādin beliefs without providing any substantive evidence. Applying definitive names to the various schools in Buddhism should be done with great care, since the names originated for different reasons: sometimes geographical, sometimes doctrinal, or because of different interpretations of the Vinaya rules.[33] The names, Theravāda or Mahāsaṅghika, should not be treated on a par with Sarvāstivāda or Sautrāntika. The first pair of names does not convey any doctrinal value, whereas the second pair does. From this standpoint, if one claims that the Sarvāstivāda flourished in such-and-such an area, then one must provide evidence of Sarvāstivādin tenets. A mere stanza of Sanskrit verse such as the *ye dharmā* is insufficient evidence to confirm Sarvāstivādin presence to the exclusion of other schools. The facile criterion that any Buddhist Sanskrit text which cannot be identified positively as Mahāyāna is therefore Sarvāstivādin should be dropped. However, one cannot deny the possibility of a Sarvāstivādin presence if evidence were supplied.[34]

Emmanuel Guillon adds another scholarly contribution to the discussion of the history of Buddhism in Southeast Asia.[35] However, he relied on earlier scholarship and did not utilize newly discovered evidence. Not only is his account misleading regarding the origin of Buddhism in Southeast Asia, but also, it is confusing in its use of terms. The spread of Mahāvihāravāsin Buddhism was not the work of Mahāvihāra monks as such, but the work of monks from Southeast Asia who traveled and trained at the Mahāvihāra in Sri Lanka. Again, caution should be used when using terms like "Mahāvihāra." Even though Parākramabāhu favored the Mahāvihāra, he was successful in unifying all of the sects. From this point of view, only one form of Buddhism existed in Sri Lanka following the unification of the sects.[36]

To study the history of Buddhism in Southeast Asia with any accuracy, both India and Sri Lanka must be considered, and most importantly, the religious context in Southeast Asia as a region. How and why was Buddhism alone able to survive as a national religion in mainland Southeast Asia? Here again, Buddhism must be understood as a system of practices and beliefs infused with other Indian and Southeast Asian elements.

It is common for scholars to assert that Theravāda Buddhism, especially as it formed in Sri Lanka, did not reach Southeast Asia until the tenth or eleventh century. Some further claim that Mahāyāna and Tantric Buddhism preceded the Theravāda. For example, the Sinhalese scholar-monk, Hammalawa Saddhātissa once wrote:

> Although Buddhism was soon well established in Ceylon, there are very few historical references to Buddhist contact with mainland South-East Asia. In fact it was the Mahāyāna form of Buddhism that first penetrated the mainland kingdoms direct from India. However, the first contact with the Theravāda was made before 1000 A.C. [*sic*]. The powerful Burmese dominion of Anuruddha had been converted to the Theravāda through contacts with Ceylon and, as a result, northern Thailand, which formed part of his kingdom, was similarly influenced.[37]

Saddhātissa's description is somewhat misleading. In chapter 4 of this volume, the point was made that Theravāda—or at least a school of Buddhism using Pāli—flourished in the Pyu and Dvāravatī areas. Wherever there are quotations from the Pāli *Abhidhamma*, one can conclude that the Theravāda school was active. The evidence thus far shows that the Theravāda arrived earlier than other forms of Buddhism. If influences from India reached Burma by land routes, then this would mean that it was only in northern Burma, and that the influence there was not the earliest one.[38]

Misunderstandings arise from the incomplete and fragmentary nature of data for the early period. After reviewing the languages used in inscriptions from Burma, Blagden, for instance, found that most of the loaner words came from Sanskrit rather than Pāli, which led him to conclude that the Mahāyāna came to the area before the Theravāda.[39] Blagden's line of reasoning, however, is faulty. We have already noted that Sanskrit was not used exclusively by the Mahāyānists. Furthermore, it is evident that brahmans advised the Burmese court.[40] As the brahmans were well versed in Sanskrit, they may have chosen to write these inscriptions in Sanskrit because that form was more familiar to them. Blagden also downplays the presence of Pāli and hybrid words appearing in the same inscriptions. The inscribers were apparently versed in both languages, and any preference for Sanskrit may have been a matter of prosody, of what sounded pleasant to the ear. Such data cannot be cited as evidence for how the religions in Southeast Asia evolved.

Another source of misunderstanding comes from heavily studied Cambodia, where the data found is overwhelmingly in Sanskrit. Here again, the same restraint should be applied, since the use of Sanskrit does not exclude the presence of other kinds of Buddhism, nor can it be used to support the theory that Mahāyāna arrived in the area before Theravāda. Again, we have seen that in the Dvāravatī tradition Pāli was dominant, and the region does not show a strong Mahāyāna influence.

Saddhātissa's remarks about the famous king of Pagan, Aniruddha, are also misleading. First, Aniruddha was not converted to Theravāda via contact with Ceylon, but instead, through the Pyu or Mon cultures of lower Burma. Second, northern Thailand was not a part of Aniruddha's kingdom. The northern kingdom of Lanna received Sinhalese Theravāda from the kingdom of Sukhothai to its south.[41]

Theravāda Buddhism has been strongly represented in Southeast Asia, particularly in the western zone, since at least the third or fourth century. Even though there is evidence for its continuity down to the present, it is incorrect to assert that only Theravāda Buddhism was there in its "pure" form, or that it came only from South India or Sri Lanka, since both epigraphic and archaeological data are equivocal. Only in the case of quotation inscriptions from the Pāli *Abhidharma* are we able to pinpoint the presence of Theravāda. But considering local and regional attitudes towards religion, a polylithic nature was inevitable. In all probability, people regarded these different creeds as undifferentiated, on the whole, although some may have preferred one creed to another. The central power, when and where there was one, did not force people to follow only one creed. In fact, there was no need to subscribe to one particular religion. Insofar as religions had something beneficial to offer,

Southeast Asians might think, "the more, the better." In the later period, if Christianity had not been so insistent on one God and one faith, it too, might have been accepted more readily into Southeast Asian religious life.

From the examples given above, it is not surprising to find that the received version was that Theravāda Buddhism as a movement began around the eleventh century CE,[42] the generally accepted date by scholars of religion in Southeast Asia. It has been presumed that the form of Theravāda Buddhism from Sri Lanka was felt in Burma and Thailand only from this time onward. This development is considered of great importance because it coincided with the emergence of the classical states of Southeast Asia, which corresponds broadly to the present political boundaries.[43] Therefore, the history of Theravāda Buddhism is seen as having close connections with the formation of the Burmese and the Thai states.

Cœdès's work, among others, gives the impression that the people of Southeast Asia were introduced to a new religion at this time.[44] If that were true, then was Buddhism new to them or not? If Buddhism was new to them, what form did it take? How did this early contact influence them? Was a remnant of Mahāyāna Buddhism received through China and northern India? Most of the time, it has been assumed that Mahāyāna and Tantric Buddhism preceded Theravāda Buddhism.

ASCENDANCY: THE RECEIVED VERSION

We shall now focus on the religious history of two peoples, the Burmese and the Thai, to further examine why the ascent of Theravāda Buddhism has long been assumed to have occurred in the eleventh to thirteenth centuries. Beginning in the tenth century, the political configuration of Southeast Asia began to take the shape it has today. The states that formed in this period until the era of Western colonization are usually called the "classical states of Southeast Asia." Prior to this, the areas of central and lower Burma were initially Pyu centers, and later on, Mon centers. Most of what is now Thailand was occupied by Dvāravatī cultures, presumably belonging to the Mon.

The Burmese and the Thai peoples are thought to have migrated from the north. After the destruction of the Pyu centers by the armies of the Nanchao, the Burmese filled the gap by settling at the Pyu village of Pagan, from which they expanded southward. They finally conquered the Mon and in the process absorbed Mon arts, Mon culture, and most important, according to modern historians, Theravāda Buddhism.

In the case of the Thai people, the theory of their southward migration is still an issue of debate. Cœdès believed that the southward movement of the Thai was an early and gradual process, and not a sudden influx due to the Mongol conquest of Yunnan.[45] Luce, however, disagreed.[46] Other scholars have proposed that the Thai never migrated from the north, because they were indigenous to Southeast Asia.[47] We are not in a position to make a judgment here, since any traces of the supposed migration have long been lost, rendering any theory mere speculation. Local chronicles relate how Thai chiefs of the north sent their sons out to build cities of their own that were located mainly to the south. Yet, in other chronicles, kingdoms as far south as Nakhon Si Thammarat were said to be Thai.[48] In those days, northern Thailand was sparsely populated, so it was a logical area for Thai expansion and the establishment of new kingdoms. At the same time, the area also experienced shifting populations of Mon and Khmer moving from south to north.

According to the *Cāmadevīvaṃsa* and the *Jinakālamālinī,* this shifting population established its kingdom in Haripuñjaya and neighboring cities as early as the seventh century.[49] They brought Buddhism with them as well as artistic styles and a written script. Even if one rejects the notion that the Khmer never dominated the northern region of Thailand politically, traces of Khmer culture have been found as far north as Sukhothai. Historically at that time, conditions in the north of Thailand were favorable to change. The movement of the Thai people into the area, whether gradual or abrupt, was bound to have an effect. At least as early as the eleventh century, the Thai were already recognized as a separate people in inscriptions from as distant as the Cham kingdom.[50]

Regarding Burma's religious history, Aniruddha is considered as the first Burmese king to embrace Theravāda Buddhism. Ray described the event as follows:

> The scene of history now shifts from the peninsular country to the upper regions of the Irrawaddy, and centres round Pagan, the seat of the Anawrahta dynasty. . . . Ridden with primitive heathenism and a very base sort of what has been identified as Mahāyānist Tantrikism, imported from Tibet, Bengal and Assam, Pagan found in the Theravāda, the new religion introduced from the land of the Talaings [i.e., the Mons of south Burma], a purer and simpler faith, a religion with a more direct appeal and a fresh message of deliverance. With Shin Arahan at the head of the Saṃgha and the support of the throne and the state at its back, the new faith soon secured a solid ground and spread far on

> all sides. Even during the reign of Anawrahta the fame of Pagan as a centre of the Theravāda faith was so well established that she exchanged religious gifts with Ceylon, and, what is more, established direct religious relations with that island where Pāli Buddhism had built up its new home after a long period of cruel Cọla persecution and its eventual banishment from South India.[51]

As for Aniruddha's so-called "conversion," let us turn to the source drawn upon by almost every scholar: the *Sāsanavaṃsa*, which gives at least three different accounts. Unfortunately most scholars cite only the concluding portion of the *Sāsanavaṃsa* and disregard any discrepant versions related earlier in the book. Curiously, none of the accounts mentions the term "Theravāda" nor does any version link the new form of Buddhism embraced by the king to Sri Lanka.

Since these accounts are crucial to our study, we quote directly from the *Sāsanavaṃsa*:

> In the city of Arimaddana in the Tambadīpa country in our Maramma circle, there reigned a ruler, King Sammuti by name. From that time on until King Anuruddha in the country called Samati, the Samaṇakuttakas, thirty thousand in number, traveled about instructing their followers, sixty thousand in number. The doctrine of these Samaṇakuttakas was as follows: "If one kills a living being, he can be freed from this sin by reciting such-and-such a *paritta*. Even if one has committed patricide and matricide, he can be freed from this karma which yields immediate results (*ānantariyakamma*) by reciting such-and-such a *paritta*. If one desires to arrange a marriage for one's son or daughter, he must first hand over (one of them) to the *ācariya* before giving them to be married. Whoever fails to do so will entail great demerit."[52]

After describing the tenets held by the Samaṇakuttakas, the author continues with an account of Shin Arahan, the *arahant* who converts King Aniruddha. Three accounts of the story are given, one each from the *Rājavaṃsa,* the *Parittanidāna*, and the *Sāsanapaveṇī*. Each one begins with the story of the *arahant*'s birth.

In the *Rājavaṃsa* version, the elders of the Sangha in the Burmese region are concerned that the *śāsana* in Burma was not very firmly established, so they ask Indra for help. Indra sends a male deity (*devaputta*) to be reborn in the womb of a brahman woman. A boy is born and is put under the protection of a monk, the Elder Sīlabuddhi. When the boy comes of age, he enters the monkhood. He studies and becomes well versed in the *Tripiṭaka*, and as is customary in Burma, becomes known by the title, "Arahanta." He then proceeds to Arimaddana city (Pagan). Indra arranges for a hunter to meet Arahanta (no given name is provided) while he sits in a forest near the town. The hunter thinks to himself: "If this person is a not a human being, then he must be a *yakkha* [S. *yakṣa*] (a type of nature-spirit); however, if he is human, then he must be a *milakkha* (barbarian)." The hunter then takes Arahanta to see the king. The scene of Arahanta's meeting with Aniruddha is modeled on the one between Nigrodha and Emperor Aśoka. The king invites the Elder to sit down wherever befits his status, so Arahanta ascends the throne and sits down. After answering polite preliminary questions about his birth and family, Arahanta preaches the *Appamāda-vagga* to the king. The king is most pleased and builds a monastery for him. As a result of the king's conversion, the Samaṇakuttakas lose their royal support and become impoverished. They are ordered to don white garments and serve the king as armed soldiers.[53]

In the *Parittanidāna* version, Arahanta appears to be a native of Vijjavāsī in Sri Lanka. First, he goes to Upadvārāvatī and then to Sudhamma to study the sacred texts. There he learns that previously a text was hidden in a Patali tree in Sirikhetta (Śrīkṣetra). Arahanta decides to go there in search of the text. There he meets a hunter, who also wonders who Arahanta is. The hunter brings the Elder Arahanta to the king. The following conversation occurs between them:

> Then the King asked the Elder: "Who, then, are you?" The Elder replied: "I, Great King, am a disciple of Gotama." The King asked further: "What are the Three Jewels?" The Elder said: "Great King, the Buddha should be seen as Mahosadhapaṇḍita, the Dharma as Ummagga [lit., tunnel, another name of the Mahosadhajātaka is Ummaggajātaka], the Sangha as the army of Videha." Since the answers were given in metaphors, the King [did not understand] and asked: "Are these the disciples of Gotama?" [The Elder answered:] "Great King, they are not disciples of Gotama: on the contrary, they are the Samaṇakuttakas, different from us." When this had been said, [the King] abandoned the Samaṇakuttakas from that time onward. They were not considered worthy even as grass. The king also destroyed on that spot the book obtained from the trunk of the Patali tree . . .[54]

The king, being well pleased with the Elder, brings him to Pagan from Śrīkṣetra. However, there is another account of the text hidden inside a tree trunk. This version must have been well known, because, even though it contradicts the other one, the author still includes it. In the second version, it is said that the text was compiled by the Samaṇakuttakas in order to show the king that they, too, adhered to the right doctrine. They hid the text in a Patali tree trunk in Śrīkṣetra, and then they spread the rumor that they had learned about the text in a dream, in which the king goes to Śrīkṣetra and finds the text. Because the doctrine appears to correspond to the Good Dharma, the king bestows great gifts on the Samaṇakuttakas. After his meeting with the Elder Arahanta, the king orders that the text be destroyed.[55]

The third account of Arahanta's life comes from the *Sāsanapaveṇī.* It consists solely of a lineage of teachers in Sudhamma from Anomadassī down to Arahanta and his chief disciple and Ariyavaṃsa. There is no mention of the meeting between Aniruddha and the Elder.[56] The author then gives his final opinion:

> Thus although there appear a variety of opinions of various teachers, yet the fact that the Elder Arahanta came to the city of Arimaddana and established the religion there alone is sufficient here. It should not be overlooked.
>
> For even in the opinion of all the teachers, the meaning truly intended is this: When the Elder Arahanta came to the city of Arimaddana, he founded the religion. And it should be understood that the Elder Arahanta was well-known by his original name, Dhammadassī, that he was a resident of the city of Sudhamma, and was a disciple of the Elder Sīlabuddhi.
>
> And that even before being ordained, he was trained in the four Vedas. Having taken ordination, mastered the Three Piṭakas with their commentaries, and gone to the other shore [attained Arahantship], he became famous everywhere. People brought him to the city of Sokkataya and honored him. He stayed there for ten years and then went back to Sudhamma where he adopted the life of a forest monk.
>
> After that in the year one thousand five hundred and sixty one of the Conqueror of the Wheel [the Buddha] . . . King Aniruddha ascended the throne. At that time in Arimaddana, the Samaṇakuttakas declared of themselves: "We are the disciples of Gotama." . . . And when the king heard about the Brahmacaryā suitable for household life, he took faith in it. As the same thing was also handed down by tradition, he did not discard it. But after he met the Elder Arahant, he stopped the regular practices of the Samaṇakuttakas, and took faith in the Sāsanā.[57]

There are many interesting points in these accounts and in the conclusion by the author of the *Sāsanavaṃsa.* In the first account there is enmity between the Samaṇakuttakas and the new school brought from the south. In the second account, several details are noteworthy. First, there are references to different places: Sri Lanka, Upadvārāvatī [*sic*], and Sudhamma. Sudhamma has always been identified as being in the vicinity of Thaton in southern Burma, but Upadvāravatī remains unidentified. Further on in the *Sāsanavaṃsa,* in the account of the establishment of the *śāsanā* in Jeyyavaddhana (Taung-u), the town of Dvāravatī is mentioned. This has been identified by scholars as the Dvāravatī of central Thailand. Upadvārāvatī could be a town near Dvāravatī, since Buddhism was evidently flourishing in that region.[58] Second, the account is less hostile towards the Samaṇakuttakas, except for the episode when the text is burned. This account also contains an additional passage, in which the text is said to be perfectly in accordance with "our" doctrine (i.e., the *sakavāda*). The hiding of texts in trees could refer to a practice followed in Śrīkṣetra, where numerous Pāli quotation inscriptions drawn from the Pāli canon were found. Third, the *Ummagga Jātaka* is still a highly regarded text by the Burmese, whereas, in Thailand, that honor is accorded to the *Vessantara Jātaka.* The last account is simply a lineage of teachers, and tells us nothing about the conversion of the king.

In these accounts, the term "Theravāda" never appears; instead, the word *sakavādī* is used. Sri Lanka is mentioned only in the second account, which suggests that the authors did not connect their *śāsanā* directly to Sri Lanka, but rather, to the lineage of Soṇa-Uttara and the Aśokan mission.[59]

All accounts link the Elder Arahanta with Sudhamma, who is regarded either as a native of the town or as a longtime resident. Overall, the Elder Arahanta's biography is a rather thin one. Even his given name is not known. "Arahanta" is a title, an epithet given to him because he was believed to have attained arahantship. Neither does the author of the *Sāsanavaṃsa* give the source for the name Dhammadassī. In sum, the Elder Arahanta appears to be more of a legendary or mythical person than a historical one. Similarly, the account of the conversion of King Aniruddha also has more of a mythical air than a historical one. One can say, however, that the first version of the story is modeled on the well-known account of the conversion of Aśoka.[60]

Scholars have long identified the Samaṇakuttakas with practitioners of Tantric Buddhism. Even if later accounts try to persuade us to believe that they were persecuted and suppressed by Aniruddha, the evidence proves otherwise. At least in the *Sāsanavaṃsa,* the author finally concludes that they were not disregarded by the king. This conclusion is supported by archaeological evidence reported by Duroiselle.[61]

In connection with the conversion stories, there is another account of how the *Tripiṭaka* was obtained from the Mon. The king, persuaded by the Elder Arahanta, sends gifts to King Manuha, the king of the Mon, and asks him for the *Tripiṭaka.* When the latter refuses, Aniruddha attacks the Mon kingdom, seizes all the sacred texts and artisans, and takes them to Pagan.[62] This account is contrary to the one given earlier in the *Sāsanavaṃsa.* Here the status of Buddhism in the Mon territory is reported in the following manner:

> Thereafter in the year one thousand and six hundred, the Rāmañña country, the place where the religion had come into existence for the three reasons already mentioned, was disturbed by three kinds of fear, namely, fear from village-plundering thieves, fear from a kind of burning fever, and fear from adversaries of the religion. And at that time the religion became very weak there. Even the monks there could not comply with [the Buddha's] teaching. In the time of King Manohāri (Manuha) . . . the religion became extremely weak. In the year one hundred [thousand] and sixty-one of the Conqueror of the Wheel [the Buddha] . . . the king named Aniruddha of the city of Arimaddana brought the Sangha from there together with the Piṭakas . . .[63]

It seems odd that the king would seek to obtain Buddhism from a region where the religion was reported to be very weak. Also the Pyu kingdom of Śrīkṣetra seems to have possessed the *Piṭaka*s, at least in sufficient numbers for the Samaṇakuttakas, if that tradition is accurate, to compile a book according to the *sakavāda.* There is evidence that Aniruddha made a search for texts and images in the Pyu areas, and brought back a number of them, leaving behind inscriptions in the *stūpa*s indicating which objects had been removed.

All that we may conclude from these various accounts is that Aniruddha, in expanding his territory to the south, realized that the people in that area followed Buddhism, presumably that of the Pāli tradition. His aim was to accommodate to the faith as it was practiced there and utilize it for his own administrative purposes. The chronicles try to connect Aniruddha's efforts to the Mon area, since it was believed that this area was where the Aśokan mission landed. The chronicles also try to establish or connect the lineage of the Sangha in Burma to that of Soṇa-Uttara. If the epigraphic and archaeological data is examined, the place where Buddhism flourished seems to have been Śrīkṣetra, rather than the Mon area. The reason for the attack on the Mon was politically rather than religiously motivated.

In Thailand, the situation seems to parallel that of Burma, in that the conversion is connected also to a great king, who in the Thai case is King Ramkhamhaeng of Sukhothai. This story has even fewer details than the Burmese one. The evidence used to substantiate how the Thai became Theravādin comes from an inscription of this king.[64] The inscription has been interpreted to mean that the king embraced the new religion of Theravāda Buddhism,[65] but when the inscription is closely scrutinized, this conclusion proves unfounded. First, the connection with the Theravāda school is only deduced, since the word does not appear anywhere in the inscription and, in fact, it rarely appears in any religious text in Southeast Asian countries. Nevertheless, many of the details indicate that Buddhism at the time of King Ramkhamhaeng was not that much different from present-day Buddhism. The use of the word "*araññika*"[66] suggests the existence of a religious link between Sukhothai and Sri Lanka. Even so, this is insufficient evidence to say that King Ramkhamhaeng was converted to Theravāda Buddhism. All that the evidence shows is that Buddhism had already been practiced long before the date of the inscription. The Sangha had been formed and the king had appointed a Sangharājā as its head. Relations between political and spiritual powers were firmly established. The cults of *stūpa* and relics seem to have been long in place as well. These are all signs of an established faith, not a newly adopted one.

At this time there was no evidence of any strong influx of Buddhism from Sri Lanka. That influence came during the reign of Ramkhamhaeng's grandson a half century later.[67] The same was true of Burma. King Aniruddha did not embrace the Sinhalese form of Theravāda, although there may have been some contact between the Theravāda of the Pyu and Mon areas and their counterparts in Sri Lanka.

Some scholars take it for granted that Buddhism in King Ramkhamhaeng's reign came from Sri Lanka, and then raise the question of which of the three schools of Sri Lanka was involved. In Thailand, Prathip Chumphon has claimed that Sukhothai Buddhism came from Nakhon Si Thammarat, not from the Pāli tradition of the Mahāvihāra, but the Abhayagirivihāra. Prathip bases his argument on the fact that all known inscriptions are in Sanskrit, and no Pāli inscriptions have been found in Nakhon.[68]

While this seems like a reasonable conclusion, it ignores the fact that in Sri Lanka itself few inscriptions in Pāli have been found. Most are either in Sanskrit or Sinhalese.[69] Therefore, the argument that no Pāli inscriptions were found in Nakhon Si Thammarat cannot be used to support Prathip's thesis.

The Sanskrit inscriptions found there show no connection or any reference to the *Abhayagirivihāra.* However, a close relationship between Nakhom Si Thammarat and Sri Lanka did exist, because a copy of the same Sanskrit inscription has been found in both places.[70]

At around the same time in the thirteenth century, King Parākramabāhu had already united the three schools in Sri Lanka. If Sukhothai Buddhism was inspired by that of Nakhon Si Thammarat, which, in turn, had adopted it from Sri Lanka, it could have only been the unified form of Buddhism accomplished by King Parākramabāhu. The question of any distinctions between the Mahāvihāra and Abhayagiri simply do not apply in this instance. Moreover, Ramkhamhaeng's inscription does not tell us that Nakhon Si Thammarat was the source of Sukhothai Buddhism, which certainly did not commence with the arrival of the Sangharājā from Nakhon Si Thammarat.

In contrast, Bizot has argued that the Sri Lankan Buddhism adopted by the Burmese in the twelfth century and the Thai in the fifteenth century was not the Mahāvihāra school.[71] Bizot first questions why the Buddhism as practiced in Southeast Asia was so different from the one described in the canon. He argues that canonical Buddhism is identified with the Mahāvihāra school of the Sinhalese Theravāda:

> The hypothesis is that the Mahāvihāra, introduced from the beginning of the second millennium, had been contaminated by the Brahmanism and the Mahāyāna of the first millennium. But this hypothesis does not seem to be acceptable. The Mahāvihāra school was not truly implanted and spread in Southeast Asia until it was able to remain intact, that is to say, much later, in the 19th century. The Sihalapakkha or "Sinhalese branch" represented and transmitted their [the Mahāvihāra] ideas from the 12th century in Burma and from the 15th in Thailand, but they were not affiliated to the Mahāvihāra as generally believed.[72]

Bizot next identified the Mahāvihāra and non-Mahāvihāra traditions in Southeast Asia by citing five ways in which they differ: the formula used for the ordination ceremony, the enunciation of the Three Refuges, how the robe is folded when worn, the list of items comprising a set of robes, and the style of the robe.[73]

The problem here is that these formulae and customs concerning the robe were being transmitted constantly back and forth between Sri Lanka and Southeast Asia. At least at the present time, the Mahāvihāravāsins use the formula Bizot describes as being composed by the non-Mahāvihāravāsins. The arrangement of the robe designated as Mahāvihārin by Bizot actually comes from the Mon tradition, which was adopted by Rāmā IV when, as a prince-monk, he established the Dhammayuttika Nikāya. Bizot seems to confuse the Mahāvihāra with the Dhammayuttika.[74] The Mahāvihāravāsin ordination formula that Bizot uses was composed by the Supreme Patriarch of Thailand (Sangharājā Sa of Wat Rājapratiṣṭha) who was ordained in the Dhammayuttika order, the order which helped to reestablish the Sangha in Sri Lanka in the nineteenth century.[75] Most important, the division of Sri Lankan Buddhism into three schools had already disappeared by the time that the Sihalapakkha, according to Bizot, reached Southeast Asia. It is hard to know what Bizot means when he says that "The Sihalapakkha or 'Sinhalese branch' represented and transmitted their [the Mahāvihāra] ideas from the 12th century in Burma and from the 15th in Thailand, but they were not affiliated to the Mahāvihāra as generally believed."[76] After all, if Buddhism in Southeast Asia came directly and only from Sri Lanka, then the Mahāvihāra, which was the most powerful among all the schools, would have had the best opportunity to spread to Southeast Asia.

The source for Buddhism in Sukhothai probably came from the Dvāravatī tradition as well as from southern China. The source of Buddhism in Pagan was the Pyu and the Mon and its own tradition of Tantric Buddhism. There are still traces of eclectic practices from the Yunnan area that persist even today. In the *Paññāsajātaka*, there are stories of Sudhana and Manoharā that do not appear in the Pāli literature of Sri Lanka, but are found in the *Mahāvastu* of the Lokottaravādin Mahāsaṅghikas,[77] and in other sources such as the Vinaya of the Mūlasarvāstivādins. The *Tamnān Mūlasāsanā* contains a version of the *Vyāghrī (Mahāsattva) Jātaka* in which the bodhisattva Brahmaṛṣi jumps off a cliff to feed a starving tiger.[78] On birthday celebrations, monks are invited to chant the *Uṇhīsavijaya*. This practice reflects the influence of the *Uṣṇīsavijayadhāraṇī*, popular in Mahāyāna societies, including Yunnan.[79] In Thailand, the recitation or chanting of *suttas* is commonly called "reciting the *mantra*," rather than "reciting the *paritta*" as in other Theravādin traditions. Traces of other types of Buddhism in Burma, especially in Pagan and areas adjacent to India, are in abundance and well preserved.[80]

In both Burma and Thailand, scholars have conflated the history of a nation with the history of religion. Since Burma and Thailand began to emerge as nations in the eleventh century, they have taken narratives of religion as the starting point for the adoption of a new faith.

We can conclude that the adoption of Theravāda Buddhism by King Aniruddha and King Ramkhamhaeng was neither an introduction nor a conversion to a new and hitherto unknown form of Buddhism. It was not a turning point in religious history, but rather, a new strategy by the two kings to apply or use religion in a political sense. The kings chose to patronize the Buddhism they found in the conquered lands. Had it been otherwise, the two kings might have persecuted all other creeds, but this did not happen. The form of Buddhism that the kings encountered in the areas in question was Theravāda, or at least a form of Theravāda that used Pāli as its sacred language.

With the data interpreted historically, what happened in terms of religious practices? Was there any difference in the character of Southeast Asian religiosity before or after this so-called "conversion" to Theravāda Buddhism?

Epigraphic and archeological data scarcely differ. The ways through which people acquired merit are similar. They sponsored the casting of images of the Buddha, transferring the merit to their kin, living or deceased, and in most cases, to all living beings.

The epigraphic data falls into the same categories as those outlined in chapter 4—quotation, eulogy, and donation and royal inscriptions—but with minor but interesting differences. Quotation inscriptions from canonical texts become fewer; the *ye dharmā* stanza appears less frequently, but still appears in conjunction with other texts. There are longer quotations from canonical or extra-canonical texts, including a passage from the *Mahāpaṭṭhāna* (of the *Abhidhammapiṭaka*)—which, since it deals with conditions, may be said to be another form of *pratītyasamutpāda*—encircled by the *mātikā* quoted from the *Dhammasaṅgaṇi.*[81] Another inscription lists the heavens of the Realms of Form (*rūpa*) from the lowest (at the bottom of the inscription) to the highest, ending with the word "*nibbāna.*"[82]

The Four Noble Truths are retained, but the truths are presented differently. The text quoted is extra-canonical, and has a hint of a mystical or magical incantation. One inscription gives the characteristics of the Noble Truths by citing only the initial syllable of each truth as seen in this example:

> The first single syllable represents the individual nature [of each truth, i.e., Du for *dukkha,* Sa for *samudaya,* and so on]. (Scholars) having deleted the first should analyze the meaning (or characteristic) of the Four Noble Truths as Sa (*samudaya*) Ma (*magga*) Nī (*nirodha*) Dū (*dukkha*); Ni, Mā; Sa, Ma, Dū; Sa, Ni, Dū; because [these initial syllables] explain the second characteristic and the following.[83]

The manuscript entitled, "Explanation of the Heart of the Four Noble Truths," explains these sets of letters. Each truth contains the characteristics of the other three. In the first truth, *dukkha,* has Sa, Ma, Ni, which equals *samudaya, magga,* and *nirodha*; the second truth, *samudaya,* has Du, Ni, Ma which equals *dukkha, nirodha,* and *magga,* and so on. We can only conclude that the people who were able to compose such stanzas without any help would have to be learned scholars. To ordinary people, these texts would be simply sacred texts, which, presumably, were thought to possess magical powers. Another inscription gives the *ye dhammā* stanza, the normal version of the Noble Truths, and a set of initials that have yet to be deciphered. Still another inscription describes the *dharmakāya,* which in this case, equates parts of the Buddha's body with spiritual states (*dhamma*). For example, the Buddha's head is equated with *sarvajñāna* (omniscience), his hair with *nirvāṇa,* his forehead with the four *dhyānas,* and so forth. At the end of the inscription, it says that one who seeks to attain Buddhahood should repeatedly recollect this *dharmakāya.*[84]

In addition, some fairly lengthy texts include a relic manual and a list of the auspicious marks in the Buddha's footprint. All of these, including the acronymic texts, must come either from manuscripts or oral tradition. Because some manuscripts on these subjects are still extant, we can conclude that the inscriptions belonged to a manuscript tradition. In Burma and elsewhere, the *ye dharmā* stanza is less frequently used as more inscriptions begin to appear on the life of the Buddha, especially regarding the events that occurred during the seven weeks after his enlightenment.

The eulogy inscriptions follow the same pattern found in the early period discussed in previous chapters. Most inscriptions of this type were composed for a specific occasion, rather than being textual citations. Two examples will illustrate this point:

> buddhaṃ pathamakaṃ vande
> dhammaṃ vande dutiyakaṃ
> saṅghaṃ tatiyakaṃ vande
> ācariyañ ca catutthakaṃ
> ratanattayaṃ namassitvā
> sirasā jānuyuggale
> antarāyam pi ghāṭatthaṃ
> sabbasatrū.[86]

namatthu namo me sabbabuddhānaṃ
namo me sabbadhammānaṃ
namo me sabbasaṅghānaṃ ratanattayaṃ vandāmi ham.[87]

The donation inscriptions take a longer form, but they do not reflect the orthodox view associated with the Theravāda school. Instead, these inscriptions commemorate events such as the restoration of *stūpas*, the casting of Buddha images, or the building of monasteries. The donor's aims and aspirations can be classified as worldly, religious, or the transfer of merit.

Worldly wishes can be summarized by two words: health and wealth. They are considered the foremost aims for oneself and others. Other popular aspirations might include being reborn with great intelligence, being reborn into a good family, or being reborn as a beautiful person. One might also aspire to avoid bad luck. Often included is a wish that whatever the donor has built will last for five thousand years, which means, symbolically, for as long as the religion endures.[88]

Among religious aims, the most frequent is to become a Buddha,[89] or to be reborn in the time of the future Buddha, Maitreya.[90] A third religious aim is the wish to attain *nirvāṇa*.[91] One would think that in a Theravādin country attaining *nirvāṇa* would be the most popular wish, but, in fact, the aspiration to become a Buddha is more popular.[92]

Worldly wishes are mentioned as wishes for others beginning with one's parents, then extending to other family members, and finally including all beings.[93] This is an example of how merit is transferred to others. The following inscription composed for a queen by a royal scholar (*rājāpaṇḍita*) is an example of such a wish:

> By this act of merit may my parents, my husband King Mahādharmaadhirājā, [his mother] Śrīdharmarājamātā, relations and non-relations, all be happy, without suffering, without any danger. May they all by the power of my merit be reborn in the six heavens and enjoy their pleasures as they desire. May I by the power of my merit be reborn as a male and be able to hear the supreme teaching of the Buddha Maitreya. May I have the chance to acquire merit of three kinds (*dāna, sīla, samādhi*), and may I be praised by Maitreya in the midst of the assembly. May no one equal me in merit, in beauty, in fame, in longevity or in wealth. In every birth if I don't permit, let no one take them from me. Let all my wealth be beneficial to the poor. May I, who

> am sinking in the cold ocean [of transmigration], deep, with no shores, attain the enlightenment of the Lord of Sages (*muninda*). May the future, lofty, righteous famous kings who will rule this country all praise my meritorious acts. May the objects of worship [in this monastery] flourish through my delight in meritorious deeds.[94]

If this inscription is compared with the results of fieldwork carried out in Thailand in the 1980s by Carlo Caldarola, there is little difference between the practices from the past and those today. Caldarola reports:

> A sample of 79 family heads of a northeastern Thai village were requested to rank the eight types of religious acts they felt most meritorious. While there was no complete agreement among the villagers, the distribution of the answers showed a remarkable pattern, and the majority of the respondents agreed by and large on the hierarchical position of each category of action in relation to the rest. The final ranking of merit-making acts was as follows:
>
> 1. Completely financing the building of a *wat* (i.e., a monastery) (this was considered to be a most meritorious act).
> 2. Either becoming a monk oneself or having a son become a monk.
> 3. Contributing money to the repair of a *wat* or giving *kathin* (post-lent festival) gifts.
> 4. Giving food daily to monks.
> 5. Observing the Buddhist Sabbath.
> 6. Strictly observing the five precepts.[95]

Strictly speaking, this hierarchy is contrary to what was recommended by the Buddha or by the monks. Observing the five precepts should have been given the highest priority, since it is the *paṭipattipūjā* or worshipping the Buddha by practicing the Dharma that comes before all others. However, this list reflects not only the present situation but also what was true in India during the Buddha's lifetime: people prefer to make merit by making material contributions rather than by practicing the Dharma.

There is little difference between the Buddhism that was practiced in the region before or after the eleventh century. There are fewer quotation inscriptions and more cryptic inscriptions in the form of magical spells or as *aides-mémoire*. Ones that were found in Thailand could be a result of exposure to the Tantric Buddhism of the Khmer, or reflect a remnant of the Buddhism practiced in Yunnan. The question of origins remains to be clarified. The one thing that is known for certain from the epigraphic data is that the Pāli tradition has always been present in this area of Burma and Thailand.

In addition to epigraphic data, there are chronicles composed in imitation of Sinhalese prototypes such as the *Mahāvaṃsa* and the *Dīpavaṃsa,* as well as legends or annals about relics or important images of the Buddha, and in Burma we have the *Kalyāṇī Sīmā* inscriptions. The chronicles usually relate the history of the Sangha and the relations between Sri Lanka and Southeast Asia. They portray royal support for Buddhism and the establishment or the purification of the Sangha. They scarcely mention the word "Theravāda," but are more likely to be concerned with the correct rituals for monastic ordination in order to establish a Sangha correctly organized according to the Vinaya rules.

What, then, can be called Theravāda Buddhism in Southeast Asia? For those who profess to be Theravāda Buddhists, it is simply, Buddhism. They do not scrutinize the sacred texts nor do they try to distinguish "foreign" influences which are non-Theravādin. Even the label "Theravāda Buddhism" is a Western or, at least, modern construct. Distinguishing between different schools such as Sarvāstivāda, Mahāsaṅghika, or Mahāyāna does not enter the mind of a typical Southeast Asian.

This Buddhism that we are trying to understand is a complex system of beliefs and practices, however, it is still regarded as one integral system, a type made possible through the concept of moral hierarchy. The concept of internalization, as suggested by Spiro, and the concepts of synthesis and syncretism are not evident, as illustrated in the last chapter. The word that best describes how Southeast Asian Buddhism developed is "symbiosis" or coexistence, not "internalization" or "syncretization."

What most Southeast Asian Buddhists know about Buddhism can be summed up in terms of the Three Jewels: the Buddha, Dharma, and Sangha. The Buddha, foremost among humans and gods, is often seen as a great god who grants favors and helps human beings escape from suffering. He is not, however, an almighty God or the creator of the universe. Buddhists understand that his power and wisdom arose from the merit he accumulated over a long period of time. His authority comes from the recognition of his great store of merit, rather than his authority alone.

The Dharma is what the Buddha taught and it is the duty of monks to preserve it. Lay devotees follow the teaching and observe the precepts according to their ability. We might be astonished to find that very few Buddhists know what the Four Noble Truths are or what they mean. The most commonly known teachings are *dukkha, anicca, puñña, karma* (P. *kamma*), *nibbāna,* and *pārami,* words that also are used in everyday speech. However, this does not mean that everyday use of these terms strictly corresponds to the scholastic definitions found in the texts. *Dukkha* and *anicca* mean essentially what they do in the texts, but without the depth of interpretation. *Puñña* means both the making of merit as well as the good result of past *karma.* The word "*karma*" usually means *vipāka,* especially bad *vipāka* (result). *Nibbāna* is understood in different ways according to one's educational level. Some understand it as an eternal city, or as *amatanagara,* in the cosmological texts. *Pāramī* in Thai culture means an accumulation of good deeds, and is basically the same as good *karma.* The doctrine of *karma* is simply understood in the sense that one will always experience the result of one's actions. Bad deeds, if condoned, can affect the whole community. Since the word *karma* is used to stand for bad deeds (*pāpakarma*), the word has assumed a negative moral connotation similar to the concept of sin (*pāpa*).

In common practice, making merit, or what Spiro calls "kammatic Buddhism," is the most popular. Inseparable from the making of merit is the transfer of merit, *puññānumodanā* or *pattidāna.* Bechert believes that this aspect of Theravāda Buddhism was incorporated later:

> In addition to this responsibility for education, the Sangha had to offer religious benefits for the lay people, e.g., the protective power of recitation of the so-called *paritta* texts. Here I should mention that Theravāda Buddhism has incorporated some non-canonical beliefs which were of great importance for this development, e.g., the theorem of the transmission of religious merit to the deceased (*puññānumodanā* and *pattidāna*). On the basis of this concept, the monks participated in funerals, and religious gifts in commemoration of the ancestors were donated to the Sangha. This too helped to develop the Sangha into a factor of social life.[96]

While it is true to say that the Sangha or individual monks interact with society mainly through the concept of the transmission of merit, it is incorrect to say that this concept is "non-canonical." There are numerous examples of merit transfer in the *Suttantapiṭaka.* The story of Bimbisāra and the hungry spirit (*preta*) in the *Tirokuḍḍasutta* is another obvious example.[97] It is a misunderstanding to say that this concept originated in the Mahāyāna school, especially when the meritorious act is dedicated to "all beings."

The Sangha is perceived by the masses primarily through the institution of the monastery. The monks are considered to be exemplary in behavior and leaders of the community, and the monastery functions like a town hall or communal meeting place. In an earlier period, the monastery served as an administrative unit. It also functions as a school, providing basic education for boys and girls. Male students who wanted to acquire a higher education could either be ordained or become a novice, depending upon their age.

These three components—Buddha, Dharma, and Sangha—form what Southeast Asian Buddhists call the *Buddhasāsanā*. In Buddhist countries of Southeast Asia, what is called a nation in the Western world can be expressed by three words: palace (= the king), monastery (= the monks), and household (= the family). The king bridges the two worlds by his leadership in both secular and ecclesiastical affairs.

In what sense, then, can these countries be labeled as Theravāda Buddhist states? All the various spirits and gods, whether indigenous or Brahmanical in origin, became Buddhicized, in that all spirits yield to the Buddha's supremacy. In essence then, the Buddha becomes the greatest spirit among all spirits. In parallel fashion, the king attains power by supporting all beliefs, but he himself remains the protector of the Buddhists.

The study of Buddhism in Southeast Asia cannot be fruitful if doctrinal differences are overemphasized. Neither can its development be understood by imposing the dichotomy of "Great" and "Little" traditions, nor by positing tensions between "higher" and "lower" levels of belief or practice. These dichotomies do not accurately reflect the actual beliefs of the people, who do not see any division or tension. Their attitude fosters a polylithic explanation, in which there is no need to gather together these diverse beliefs into one faith alone, as in Christianity, wherein one must profess a belief in only one god.

If we drop the label "Theravāda Buddhist countries," the picture becomes clearer. Southeast Asian Buddhism embraces a number of cults and practices: relics, images, votive tablets, amulets, recitations, mantras, and Maitreya, the future Buddha. All of these existed before the eleventh century, as evidenced by votive tablets, *stūpas*, and images of the Buddha found as early as the fourth century CE. They did not belong to any one school or sect. In the chronicles it is not the school that is important but the purity of the ordination lineage.[98]

EVOLVING DYNAMICS

Even amid the confusion between terminology and actual practice, there is no doubt that Theravāda Buddhism has become the most prominent creed in mainland Southeast Asia. Its ascendancy developed as a result of a prolonged process, a process that is still evolving. Today in Burma and Thailand, there are new movements that foster not only a better understanding of Buddhism, but also new forms of interpretation of both texts and practice. Thailand and Burma did not become Buddhist countries because a new faith was introduced under the patronage of kings like Aniruddha or Ramkhamhaeng. The peoples of both areas also contributed to the process, as did Buddhism as an institution. Above all, political and social circumstances both inside and outside the region also helped shape the present state of Buddhism in Southeast Asia.

Three main dynamics contributed to the ascendancy of Theravāda Buddhism: Buddhism itself; internal dynamics originating from within Southeast Asia; and external dynamics.

Buddhism, with its organized Sangha and emphasis on ethical codes rather than on a caste-based social code, was in all likelihood the first universal religious movement to arise in India. By creating a sense of nationhood, Aśoka used Buddhism as a way to overcome the divisiveness of tribal barriers. When Indian Buddhism came to Southeast Asia, it was regarded on equal footing with Brahmanism, even though there were differences between them. Buddhism was linked to moral codes and the making of merit, whereas Brahmanism was linked to its ritualistic functions, primarily at court.[98] Epigraphic data show that Brahmanism and local beliefs were not concerned with the making or transfer of merit. There is occasional evidence of hostility between Brahmanism and Buddhism in Southeast Asia. For example, in Cambodia in the early thirteenth century, there was a controversy concerning the so-called "conversion" of Buddha images into Hindu gods and vice versa. Tambiah is correct in saying that relations between brahmans and kings in the Southeast Asian context were the reverse of the situation that existed in India:

> In terms of the social order, *dharma* corresponds to the *brahman* priest, *artha* or temporal power to the king or Kshatriya, and *kāma* to the rest of society's ranks. It is my thesis, which I cannot substantiate here but hope to establish elsewhere, that the relation between priest and king that prevailed in India was reversed, and that this transformed relation between a divinized king and the *brahman* priest can best be seen in the royal cult of Devaraja in Cambodia. The same relation, or perhaps an even greater elaboration of it, was the hallmark of the Buddhist polities of Burma and Siam where the king, the focal entity in the society, united in his person both Indra and *bodhisattva*, god and Buddha-to-be. Thus in Siam, for instance, the king was divinized by a small number of *brahmans*, who were employed as court ritualists but who did not represent

> the superior values of *dharma* (morality) in relation to *artha* (force and power) of the king. Kingship appropriated both these values, and also became the protector of Buddhism as the state religion.[99]

Even if there is disagreement with Tambiah on some points—such as his total neglect of the indigenous components of kingship—his point that brahmans were not the models or teachers of moral behavior does seem accurate to me. The duty of moral teaching has been long accorded to Buddhism. The king as mediator between the spiritual and the secular worlds embodies the Buddhist moral code in a living form, as one who leads the people morally as well as politically.

Through the institution of the Sangha, Buddhism remains distinctive while at the same time closer to the people. The Brahmanic gods were placed on the same level as the indigenous gods, but the Buddha and the *arhat*s were never considered in that way. We thus can assert that it is the qualities within Buddhism itself that helped to sustain its ability to flourish in mainland Southeast Asia.

The second dynamic to contribute to Buddhism's ascendancy is internal to the region itself, emerging from the efforts of both elites and the general populace to promote the creed. For the early period, there is no evidence that the region's kings used Buddhism politically as the Khmer used Brahmanism and Mahāyāna Buddhism. There is, however, some indication that the king or the chief participated in merit-making activities along with the common people. It is logical to assume that *stūpa*s and monasteries served as communal meeting places where everyone gathered for both religious and secular purposes.

In Thailand, at least by the thirteenth century, we know from the famous inscription of King Ramkhamhaeng that the king had already assigned administrative ranks to the Sangha and appointed a Sangharājā. There is no evidence that it occurred earlier, but judging from the use of the term "Sangharājā," with no explanation, a Sangha hierarchy must have been in place before the time of King Ramkhamhaeng.

In Burma, kings beginning with Aniruddha also made use of Buddhism for political and economic purposes. By organizing the administrative structure of the Sangha, the kings of both lands attempted to control the monks. In both cases, the political application of Buddhism was a device used by the kings to govern a loosely federated nation, perhaps because the Sangha as a hierarchical organization could be more easily manipulated. Moreover, political authority enhanced by spiritual prestige was usually preferred in the region.

By maintaining his status as god—Brahmanistically or indigenously—the king set himself above and apart from the people. Yet, at the same time, by embracing Buddhism, the king identified with the majority due to the close ties that existed among the Sangha, the king, and the populace. If there was to be a purification of the Sangha, it was usually initiated by the king, and not by the Sangha.

Not all kings were so generous in their support of Buddhism. In one Burmese chronicle a complaint is noted that King Saw Lu "lived only for worldly enjoyment" and was too attached to the spirit cults, and not to the teaching of the Buddha.[100] In Thailand during the Ayutthaya period, Brahmanical rituals ranked very high and were performed in nearly all royal ceremonies, but in subsequent periods, as the kings became more and more Buddhist, Buddhist chanting was prefixed to all other rituals. It was not until the nineteenth century that Theravāda Buddhism emerged as the state religion in Thailand, and it was not until the early twentieth century that Rāma VI issued the Palace Law that the king of Thailand must be a Buddhist. Rāma VI may have been influenced more by his education in England, where the reigning monarch must be an Anglican.

The external dynamic was the political situation in India. From the eleventh century on, India was invaded by Islamic armies. As a result, Buddhism, deprived of its social and political support, declined, never to recover in the land of its birth. Only in Sri Lanka did it remain a source of a living Buddhist tradition. Coincidentally, the reformation of the *śāsanā* occurred continuously during the eleventh and twelfth centuries in Sri Lanka.

The received version of the history of Buddhism in Southeast Asia has been affected by the way in which scholars have understood Theravāda Buddhism, its characteristics, and its history within the region. Some scholars have confused the character of Theravāda Buddhism with "primitive" or early Buddhism, Sinhalese Buddhism, or orthodox Buddhism. As a result, the general agreement has been that Theravāda had little impact on Southeast Asia before the eleventh century, since Brahmanism and Mahāyāna Buddhism preceded it. This understanding has affected the way in which the history of Buddhism in Southeast Asia as a whole has been written, which, in general, has been confined to the eleventh century on. The earlier period has been neglected, or mentioned only briefly by scholars. When the introduction of Buddhism is discussed, the main focus usually is not Buddhism per se, but rather, the location of Suvarṇabhūmi. The writing of the history of the region has been left to historians, who, while they could not ignore religious data, paid only secondary attention to Buddhism. Their main task was to write a history of a nation or of a region. By ignoring the pre-eleventh century evidence, they have erroneously interpreted the records of Aniruddha and Ramkhamhaeng as signifying a "conversion" to a new faith that coincided with the emergence of a new state.

7

Conclusion

Studies by scholars, primarily from the West but also from Asia, have profoundly affected how Theravāda Buddhism is presented to the world. By and large, historians of Southeast Asia have overlooked epigraphic data. This neglect may have been due to language barriers, for not only are the inscriptions themselves in different languages, Indic and vernacular, but they have been published in various languages, including French, Thai, and Burmese. Moreover, historians find little of interest in the content of these inscriptions, in that they record religious acts or ideals but offer little "hard" historical information. Archaeological data has proved to be problematical as well because its interpretation has been mainly in the hands of art historians who cannot agree on the dating of the materials. In addition, the criteria applied in assigning sectarian or religious affiliation to archaeological finds are rather facile.

The data, even primary source material, provides few details of the religious life of the people, and does not form a complete record of how Buddhism evolved in Southeast Asia. To supplement this deficiency, this volume has examined the present state of Buddhism, using, for the most part, its Thai expression. Popular attitudes towards perceptions of religion have been taken into account in an attempt to explain and reconstruct the religious situation of the times. The region, despite its label of "Theravāda," was religiously rich with non-Buddhist beliefs and practices, some of which blended with Buddhist beliefs and continue to be active today. This hybrid religious scene has proved to be perplexing for many scholars, leading them to explain the situation in different ways, yet instead of clarifying the issues they seem to have become further entangled.

As has been noted, the early religions that came from India seem to have settled into two zones: the Theravāda Buddhist zone comprised of the Pyu, Mon, and Dvāravatī regions that lie in the western half of mainland Southeast Asia; and the Brahmanic-Mahāyānistic zone comprised of the Khmer and Cham areas and the archipelago. The Hīnayāna schools spread into the region somewhat earlier than Mahāyāna ones. The Brahmanism of that time, while felt, was largely limited to court rituals and secular uses.

Reasons for this particular pattern of distribution include trade relations and the religious situation in India. In the early centuries of the Common Era, Buddhism spread in India and to Sri Lanka where it was disseminated along the trade routes from South India and Sri Lanka to Southeast Asia. During this early period, trade reached Southeast Asia via both coastal and trans-peninsular routes. Southeast Asia became a destination, not just a way station en route to China. Trade was not one way but mutual, since cities located along coastal and land routes also participated in trade with India and other regions, establishing a network between centers or nascent cities already existing at the time. It was through these trade relations that Southeast Asia was first brought into sustained contact with Indian cultures. The exact nature of the encounter between Indian cultures, especially with regard to religion, is unknown. It is thought that traders brought Buddhism with them, but the data does not provide any firm evidence. We cannot determine exactly how the local people first encountered the new faith. We can only speculate that they did not consciously discriminate or sense substantial differences between their own belief system and the ones imported from India.

Later, when the trade routes shifted toward the south to the insular and archipelago areas, the Mahāyāna, coincidently, began to exert its influence and what became known as Hinduism began to form. The religious impulse of Brahmanism and Mahāyāna Buddhism both affected and took root in these and closely related areas like Champa and Cambodia. In general, Brahmanism was considered as more dominant in the region than Mahāyāna Buddhism, although in some periods the latter flourished as a result of royal patronage, usually short-lived. Frequently, both religions are mentioned together in inscriptions. The important point is not which belief was *chosen*, but rather, how beliefs were *used*. The evidence shows that both religions were employed politically and economically, legitimizing the ruler with spiritual power, who consolidated his administration through networks of religious establishments.

Many artifacts and inscriptions belonging to the two religions have been found in Cambodia, Champa, and Indonesia. Apart from eulogies to gods and kings, the inscriptions list inventories of donations, both animate and inanimate, regarding religious establishments, strictures on land use, and revenue collection. They reveal economic and administrative concerns, rather than purely religious ones. However, some include curses against those who would steal donated objects, but interestingly, they omit any mention of the donors' wishes, the donors' aspirations, or a record of the transfer of merit. By way of contrast, the Dvāravatī, and later the Mon and Burmese inscriptions usually do record the donors' wishes and the transfer of merit. In the eleventh and twelfth centuries, the Burmese also attached curses to donation inscriptions, usually followed by good wishes and blessings for those who rejoiced in the merit made.

The western or "Buddhist" zone also reflects some influence from Brahmanism and the Mahāyāna. In Dvāravatī, such influence can be attributed, in part, to the expansion of the Khmer *maṇḍala.* For Burma, influences probably came directly from India via seaports or by land trade routes as in northern Burma. But as a religion, Brahmanism was never strong in the Buddhist zone.

Two questions remain to be answered: To what school did the Buddhism of the early period belong? And from where did it come?

Regarding the first question, care must be taken when considering sects or schools of Buddhism. It is clear that in the Buddhist zone there is evidence for the long and continued use of Pāli as a sacred language in the canonical texts, including the *Abhidharma,* leading us to conclude that this is most likely a Theravādin tradition. The Pāli inscriptions far outnumber the Sanskrit ones. In the western zone, no Sanskrit inscriptions have been found whose contents are Buddhist apart from the *ye dharmā* stanza. Early Buddhist inscriptions in Sanskrit have been found in the insular and the archipelagic regions, but they contain no indicators of any specific sectarian affiliation.

Other schools must have been present, as some scholars suggest that the Sarvāstivādins flourished in Burma and Thailand in the early period, but the evidence given is inconclusive. The *ye dharmā* stanza in Sanskrit alone cannot be used to substantiate the thesis. Similarly, the bas-reliefs that depict *Jātaka*s not found in the Pāli canon cannot override other evidence clearly inspired by Pāli sources.

As to the question of the source for Buddhism in Southeast Asia, R. N. Ray rejects Sri Lanka and instead proposes that it came to Burma from Andhra Pradesh and South India. Yet Sri Lanka has always been the center of Pāli Buddhism, maintaining close ties to South India, and indeed with India as a whole. It appears in a list of seaports in the *Niddesa* and the *Milindapañha* that Ray uses to support his thesis of how Buddhism came to Burma. We do not deny Ray's thesis, except insofar as he ignores Sri Lanka's role. Evidence found in the Dvāravatī region leaves no doubt that Sri Lanka was closely tied to the area, and is one of the sources of early Theravāda in Southeast Asia. One inscription mentions the city of Anurādhapura; another quotes three stanzas from the *Telakaṭāhagāthā,* a short poem composed by a Sri Lankan Thera but relatively unknown in Sri Lanka. Archeological finds also support our assertion. There are early images of the Buddha in the Amarāvatī style with strong influence from Sri Lanka, and close resemblances between the architectural styles of Dvāravatī and Anurādhapura.

This early form of Theravāda Buddhism survived the vicissitudes of history as well as the political and ethnic developments occurring over the centuries. By the twelfth century, it had spread westward to Cambodia and Laos, and north to upper Burma and northern Thailand.

New problems arise when we examine the characteristics of Buddhism or, more specifically Theravāda Buddhism, many of which originate from a Western scholarly approach. The task is to define the "isms" that are found in Buddhism, Hinduism, and Brahmanism within an Asian frame of reference, rather than a Western or Judeo-Christian one. Certain scholars in this field are concerned with questions such as: What is your "holy" text? What is your creation myth? Such researchers may at times assume that someone who professes to be a Buddhist must be a Buddhist as exclusively prescribed by the holy texts. Another trend is to see "primitive" Buddhism as an embodiment of rationalism and scientific thought, and to maintain that this is true "Theravāda Buddhism."

While the names of different schools do appear in Buddhist texts, we should not assume that the concept of "schools" in early India or in Southeast Asia has remained unchanged today, or that the schools once resembled Christian sects. Varying principles were used in assigning names to the schools, and if we are not careful in our choice of analytical principles, we run the risk of confusing a historical term for a conceptual one, or a philosophical term for a doctrinal one.

Can we even use the term "Theravāda Buddhism," which has been so misunderstood and misapplied in both conceptual and historical contexts? The term rarely appears in the Pāli texts, and there is only a brief mention of it in the *Mahāvaṃsa* and the *Dīpavaṃsa.* In the local chronicles of Southeast Asia, to which we so far have had access, it has yet to be found.

The problem stems, in part, from the scholarly work done by German and British Indologists and Buddhologists in the nineteenth and early twentieth centuries. They believed that Theravāda Buddhism was closest to the early or primitive Buddhism taught by the Buddha himself. However, if we examine the early Indian context, there is no "pure" or "primitive" aspect of any of the religions, and certainly no "ism" existed. Since all religions in India emerged from the same social background, they can be said to be Indian. The same moral, philosophical, and intellectual foundation pertains to all Indian religions. In the rush to differentiate these religions, scholars used the tool of "isms." However, if by religion we mean what is actually practiced by the masses, then these differences were scarcely felt by the people.

Later, anthropologists entered the discussion and found elements and practices that they labeled as non-Buddhist. In an effort to explain the non-Buddhist elements, they devised new theories, which incorporated such concepts as "syncretism," "synthesis," and "internalization." The issue arising from the attitude of Southeast Asian peoples towards religion—if we may use the term—is different from that fostered by monotheistic traditions. Southeast Asians see no problem in holding more than one belief or practice at the same time. The conflicts seen by Western scholars—and Asian scholars trained in the West—are, for the most part, quite foreign to the average Thai or Burmese. Tambiah and Terwiel both observed this lack of conflict, but neither fully examined or understood it.

In chapters 4, 5, and 6 of this volume, examples were given of how Southeast Asians express themselves religiously. In terms of religious activity, there is little difference between Brahmanical and Buddhist practices, or even between Indian and indigenous religions. People donate material goods, cast images, build sanctuaries, and so on. The activities remain the same, but they are expressed religiously in different ways. The only concept that can be said to be particular to Buddhist practice in Southeast Asia, past or present, is that of merit making and the transfer of merit.

Within the context of Southeast Asia, Theravāda Buddhism must be understood as the Buddhism practiced by the societies of the region. When the term "Theravāda Buddhist countries of Southeast Asia" is used, it only means Buddhist countries of Southeast Asia. As we have demonstrated, this is because we cannot label the religious beliefs and practices of the region as pure or original Buddhism, or pure Theravāda Buddhism, or orthodox Theravāda Buddhism.

The term "Theravāda Buddhist countries of Southeast Asia" has been used by scholars primarily to denote countries that practice one kind of Buddhism in contrast to other parts of Asia that follow Mahāyāna traditions. It is, therefore, a broad, geographic term for religion found in a certain region, rather than as a religious category per se.

It may be possible to use the term "Theravādin," but only in reference to the purity of ordination lineages. Yet even here, this simply means a monastic tradition that follows the authorized version of the ordination ceremony as sanctified by the Sangha of Sri Lanka. In that case, the word "Theravādin" should be used only in conjunction with the history of the Buddhist Sangha, and not the history of Buddhism in Southeast Asia as a whole.

There is no denying that in Burma, Cambodia, Laos, and Thailand, Buddhism, especially the forms of Buddhism that use Pāli as its sacred language, prevails. Moreover, the vast majority of people from those countries profess to be Buddhist, because they follow or accept the norms recommended by the Buddhist Sangha. Those facts cannot be overlooked in studying how religion is practiced in the region. It is not enough to say that Theravāda Buddhism was introduced into the area from the eleventh century on, since this fails to explain why it alone among other religions was chosen and accepted by the kings and the peoples of Southeast Asia. I would propose that its supremacy stems from the fact that it has always been present in the western zone of mainland Southeast Asia from the beginning of contact between that area and India. It is very likely that Buddhism of the Theravāda school was the prevailing religion among the common people. The ascension of Theravāda Buddhism to its present status has been a continuing process due to royal patronage, regional trade patterns, political conditions in Southeast Asia as well as in India and Sri Lanka, and the attitude of the populace towards religion. This process still pertains in Thailand and Burma where Buddhism is very much a lived tradition.

From a historical point of view, Buddhism and its evolution has been classified by scholars as occurring in two phases. In the period before the eleventh century CE, Buddhism was described as a mixture of Hīnayāna and then Mahāyāna schools. Scholars of Southeast Asian origin assert that their "national" Buddhism descended in a direct line from the Buddha, or at least from the Sangha of the Third Council in Aśoka's reign. We have shown that there is insufficient evidence to support such assertions.

In the study of the history of Southeast Asian Buddhism, it is common to speak of its "introduction" to the region. An earlier generation of historians concluded that with scant primary documentation available, only a vague and uncertain picture emerged of how, when, and what kind of Buddhism was introduced. This was due to their conception of history as a succession of events. In fact, there are more primary materials pertaining to religion than anything else. These are not records of historical events, but, rather, records of religious practice, which were regarded as having no historical value. Inscriptions, especially quotation inscriptions, were rarely published, and thus had little impact upon the writing of religious history.

The second phase of the history of Southeast Asian Buddhism is said to have taken place from the eleventh century on. This phase has been linked to the expansion of power of two great kings, Aniruddha of Pagan and Ramkhamhaeng of Sukhothai. Western scholars have maintained that in this period the dominant creed changed to Theravādin Buddhism. In fact, Burmese and Thai sources do not use the word "Theravāda" in this context, because for them the Buddhism they had always known was continuous. All the evidence shows that there was no such "introduction" or "conversion." The expansionist policies of the two kings did not figure as a crucial factor in the evolution of Theravāda Buddhism in the areas they had conquered. In the case of King Aniruddha, he had to conform to the prevailing creed, and in the case of King Ramkhamhaeng, Buddhism had already been present long before his reign began. In both cases, Buddhism had been well established in those areas ruled by the kings.

In the *Sāsanavaṃsa* and in King Ramkhamhaeng's inscription both the context and terminology show that the kings were already familiar with Buddhism. In Burma, the Samaṇakuttakas were portrayed negatively in contrast to the new monks coming from the south of Burma. If we read the chronicle carefully, we find that the kings of Pagan supported the Samaṇakuttakas. This does not rule out the possibility of the existence of other Sanghas in Pagan, but neither can one say that the people of Pagan belonged to the Samaṇakuttaka tradition.

For King Ramkhamhaeng, there is no mention of any other religious tradition being present. Buddhism seems to have been established in Sukhothai long before his reign. Neighboring cities to the north such as Haripuñjaya and Lampang as well as the Dvāravatī sites in the central Chao Phraya valley had become Buddhist long before the twelfth century. Local chronicles relate that there were intermarriages between princes and princesses of these kingdoms, so we can surmise that Buddhism also spread through this means. In the Ramkhamhaeng inscription, the state was already involved in the administration of the Sangha. The development of the *araññika* (forest monk) tradition did not mean the suppression of any former Sangha, for together all lineages constituted one Sangha patronized by the king. The type of Buddhism as deduced from the inscription is regarded as Theravāda, but the inscription is not specific on this point. The Sangharājā is said to have come from Nakhon Si Thammarat, a city that maintained close connections with Sri Lanka, so it was assumed that the Buddhism of the Sangharājā was that of Sri Lanka. By that time, the various Sri Lankan Sanghas had been unified by King Parākkamabāhu. The result of this unification became known in academic circles as "Sinhalese Theravāda Buddhism."

The crucial point for the understanding of the situation is that there was no introduction as such, but rather, a continuation. It is no longer possible to overlook the evidence of the Pāli tradition that was present from the earliest known period in Burma and Thailand without any interruption, or to say that the history of Southeast Asian Buddhism begins only from the eleventh century, or by maintaining that the early history of Buddhism was unknown, uncertain, or unimportant, and its impact was not felt until the time of Aniruddha.

Further confusion arises when scholars attempt to find the so-called "original place" of this Buddhism. While Western scholars regard Sri Lanka as the source of Theravāda Buddhism of Southeast Asia, Asian scholars trace its origin to the time of the Buddha, or at least to Aśoka, since to them Buddhism is the *Buddhasāsanā,* the teaching of the Buddha, without the label "Theravāda." Certainly, these scholars recognize Sri Lanka as the source in the later period, but a thorough examination will reveal that Sri Lanka was the source for the purification of the Sangha, not of Buddhism as a whole. In most cases, the old Sangha persisted after new groups from Sri Lanka were established. Religious relations between Sri Lanka, Burma, and Thailand revolve around the issue of introducing and reintroducing the pure lineage of the Sangha with the new lineages, but the important point is that all lineages were considered as "*Buddhasāsana,*" and not as separate schools of Buddhism. In Thailand, for example, different sects formed and continue to form, but there is only one Sangha under the Supreme Patriarch appointed by the king.

The only region where the word "introduction" might be appropriate is Cambodia, where Brahmanism and Mahāyāna Buddhism both flourished before the thirteenth century when it became Theravāda Buddhist. Pāli was used instead of Sanskrit for royal inscriptions and even in loan words, in contrast to Burma and Thailand where Sanskrit forms were usually preferred. This resulted from the collapse of the administrative system of the Khmer Empire on the one hand, and the influence of Buddhism from Thailand from the thirteenth century onwards on the other.

In view of the evidence accumulated in the course of this research, the two prevailing theories—one formed primarily by Western scholars and the other primarily by Asian scholars—should be reconsidered. The first theory is that the Hīnayāna, excluding Theravāda, was the first to reach Southeast Asia, followed by the Mahāyāna, and culminating with the advent of Theravāda Buddhism in the eleventh century. The second, proposed by Asian scholars, is that Theravāda was first introduced from India in the reign of Aśoka, followed by Mahāyāna and Brahmanism, and then, finally, the return of Theravāda. The two paradigms do not accord with the data. The first paradigm may apply to Cambodia but nowhere else. In central Burma and central Thailand, Theravāda Buddhism was already flourishing as early as the fourth century, and possibly before, and this tradition, which used Pāli as its sacred language, shows every sign of continuity as the prevailing creed in those areas up to the present time. Our conclusion thus runs opposite to those of Western scholars such as Luce and Asian scholars such as Saddhātissa.

Nevertheless, the attempt to identify any one school as dominant seems pointless, since both epigraphic and archaeological data reveal that in actual practice different beliefs were held at the same time. To think in terms of the rise or fall of this or that school is outmoded. In Burma, the Samaṇakuttakas were presented as flourishing before they were replaced by what Nihar Ranjan Ray calls the "new and simpler faith," i.e., the Theravāda. In Thailand, Brahmanism and Mahāyāna Buddhism are claimed to have been superseded by Sinhalese Theravāda Buddhism. In fact, all these faiths, including the indigenous ones, should be accorded equal respect, rather than relegating some to the periphery out of a preconceived notion that the region is "Theravāda Buddhist." Even today with Buddhism declared as the state religion, other practices and belief systems coexist together. They may not be as highly organized as Buddhism, but it cannot be denied that they play crucial or even equal roles in the everyday religious life of the peoples of the so-called "Theravādin countries" of Southeast Asia.

One may go further to conclude that inasmuch as we cannot describe Japan or China as Mahāyāna countries, so also we cannot describe Burma, Cambodia, Laos, or Thailand as Theravādin ones. To assign labels narrows our view of the religious life of the peoples of Southeast Asia. A broader perspective is needed to help us understand the situation both past and present.

There are still numerous gaps to fill in regarding the historical evolution of Buddhism in the region. It has been impossible to identify the sectarian affiliation of Sanskrit inscriptions due to a paucity of indicative detail. All evidence—epigraphic, archaeological, as well as chronicles and legends—should be used with utmost caution. Using different scripts or artistic styles to identify the original site where Buddhism arose is inadequate. For example, it is presumptuous to identify a Buddha image in the Gupta style as Mahāyāna, solely on the notion that Mahāyāna was flourishing in North India at the time. Specific religious conditions in Southeast Asia should not be identified simply by the faith of the reigning king or dynasty, as is frequently the case in studies of Khmer culture, in which scholars try to determine whether this or that king was a Śaivite, a Vaiṣṇava, or a Buddhist. When data about common people are available, it should be incorporated, as we have tried to do in this research, since it gives a more complete picture of religious activity and expression.

It is possible that future comparative studies of quotation inscriptions found in the Pyu and Dvāravatī regions may yet yield details on different readings of the *Tripiṭaka.* These lithic records are probably the earliest extant manuscripts in Pāli. Since no scholarly work has yet been done on this subject in a European language, this present research should be seen as preparatory and preliminary, as a step towards an understanding of the particular religious conditions in ancient Southeast Asia that have generally been neglected by scholars. The conclusive dating and interpretation of inscriptions and archaeological finds remain to be determined. And no doubt new evidence awaits discovery.

Notes

Source Materials

1. The term "Southeast Asia" will be used throughout this study except in quotations and references where "South East Asia," "South-East Asia," and other variations are used.

2. SEAMEO's Project for Archaeology and Fine Arts (SPAFA) is hosted by the government of Thailand and works under the aegis of the Southeast Asian Ministers of Education Organization.

3. An example of the misrepresentation of the religious situation in Southeast Asia, particularly with regard to Theravāda Buddhism, can be drawn from Charles Keyes's *Golden Peninsula* (p. 79):

> Although Theravāda doctrines were probably transmitted orally in Pāli from the time of Aśoka, they were not written down until the first century B.C. In the fifth century A.D., the Theravāda Buddhist tradition was interpreted by the famous monk Buddhaghosa, and his interpretations have remained the orthodox interpretations for Theravāda Buddhists to this day . . . Orthodox Theravāda Buddhism, the Buddhism that used the Pāli texts and followed the interpretations of Buddhaghosa, did not flourish in either Ceylon or Southeast Asia until many centuries after Buddhaghosa's death. Although Buddhism was an important element in the syncretic traditions of the classic civilizations in Southeast Asia, such Buddhism was most usually that of a school other than Theravādin. Moreover, it was often found as one among Indianized traditions as can be clearly seen, for example, in the case of Angkor. Indeed at times, Theravāda Buddhism all but disappeared; however, a few centers in southern India, Ceylon, and lower Burma and perhaps central Thailand continued to preserve the tradition despite the vicissitudes to which it was subjected.

This passage reveals a number of fundamental and, unfortunately, all-too-typical misunderstandings, which will be discussed over the course of this study concerning the relation between Pāli and Aśokan Buddhism, and the status of Theravāda Buddhism in ancient Southeast Asia—misunderstandings that are further aggravated by an overemphasis on the doctrinal aspects of Theravāda Buddhism.

4. In this study, the word "Brahmanism" will be preferred to "Hinduism" in most cases, because it is traditionally known in Southeast Asia as the "religion of Brahma."

Chapter 1

1. Luce, *Old Burma-Early Pagan*, vol. 1, 13–14.

2. Benda, *Continuity and Change*, 122–23.

3. This term appears in the *Suvarṇaprabhāsottamasūtra* and the *Mahāvyutpatti*, the latter of which is a glossary of Buddhist terms.

4. This term appears in the *Saddharmapuṇḍarīka.*

5. For a study of Hīnayāna schools, see Bareau, *Les sectes bouddhiques du Petit Véhicule*; and Lamotte, *Histoire du bouddhisme indien*, 571ff.

6. See, e.g., Vogel, "Prakrit Inscriptions."

7. See, e.g., N. R. Ray, *Theravāda Buddhism in Burma*, 45:

> In fact it seems that it was not till the middle of the twelfth century that Ceylon came to play any important rôle in the history of Buddhism in Burma. It was in 1167 that Panthagu, the then Primate of the Burmese kingdom, chose Ceylon as his refuge, and in 1180 Uttarajāva, the Primate who had succeeded Panthagu, returned from a pilgrimage to Ceylon as the 'First Pilgrim of Ceylon.' In 1190, Capata, Uttarajāva's disciple, earned the title of the 'Second Pilgrim of Ceylon.' On his return he tried to convert the whole realm to the Sinhalese form. These missions coupled with Capata's attempts to Sinhalese Burmese Buddhism led to the gradual predominance of Sinhalese Buddhism in Burma and the wiping out of even the memory of the original source.

What Ray means by "original source" is the eastern Deccan and the far South of India. Ray is entitled to his opinion here, but we cannot accept that Buddhism in Sri Lanka did not have any impact on early Buddhism in Burma whatsoever. Ray seems to have been obsessed by the history of the Sinhalese Sangha, rather than Sinhalese Buddhism per se. While there are no records of visits to Sri Lanka earlier than those of the Theras in question, neither are there any records of Theras going to the eastern Deccan and the far south of India. For a discussion of areas other than Burma, see Saddhātissa, "Pāli Literature of Thailand;" and Keyes, *Golden Peninsula.*

8. See Higham, *Archaeology of Mainland Southeast Asia.*

9. This timeline is based on the chronological table in Ibid., xv–xvi.

10. 1500 B.C. here may be a misprint.

11. Metallurgy is discussed in Part I of Smith and Watson, *Early South East Asia*; and in Topic II of *Research Conference on Early Southeast Asia, Bangkok and Nakhon Pathom*, April 8–13, 1985.

12. See, e.g., Bayard, "Roots of Indo-Chinese Civilization," 89–114.

13. Ng, "Historical Settlement in Mainland South East Asia," 262–72.

14. See the introduction to Part I of Smith and Watson, *Early South East Asia.*

15. Ibid., 14; See also Groslier, "La cité hydraulique angkorienne," 161–202; Vickery, "Early State Formation in Cambodia," 95–115; and Higham, *Archaeology of Mainland Southeast Asia*, 255ff.

16. Smith and Watson, *Early South East Asia*, 4–5, 78, 98, 137.

17. Wolters, *History, Culture and Region*, 12ff.

18. Porée-Maspéro, *Étude sur les rites agraires.*

19. Williams, *Southeast Asia: A History*, 25.

20. de Jong, "Early Buddhism," 432.

21. Cœdès says:

> Contrairement à l'occidentale, celle de l'Inde, dans laquelle la manière de vivre est conforme à une certaine doctrine philosophico-religieuse, forme un tout dans lequel le spirituel et le matériel sont indissociables: l'adoptation de l'hinduisme entraînait celle

> de l'état social indien, et l'adoption du genre de vie des Indiens entraînait la pratique de l'hinduisme . . . On a la preuve épigraphique qu'au Cambodge existaient des catégories d'individus portant le même nom (*varṇa*) que la caste indienne et correspondant à des activités déterminées.

See Cœdès, "Le substrat autochtone et la superstructure indienne au Cambodge et à Java," 373. However in his later work *The Indianized States of Southeast Asia*, Cœdès admits that his description holds only for "élites," and states that: "La structure générale de la société, le genre de vie et les croyances du peuple, les conditions économiques appartiennent à un autre monde qui est encoure fort mal connu." Be that as it may, he is still very persistent in the matter of caste, saying, "Au Cambodge par exemple, la division ancienne de la population en classes spécialisées héréditairement dans tel travail déterminé, et désignées par le même mot (*varṇa*) que les castes indiennes, l'encadrement de la population par une bureaucratie dont les fonctions sont désignées par les mots indiens, ont grandement facilité l'intégration de la société khmère dans la société indienne." It seems that this was only a case of adopting the terms, not the concept.

22. See, e.g., Srisakra Vallibhotama, *Boranakhadi Thai nai thotsawat thi phan ma*, 68ff.

23. See Manit Vallibhotama, *Suvarnabhûmi yu thi nai*, 92, who also notes that studies of skeletons of Mon and Thai people reveal that they are so similar that one cannot make any substantive distinction between them (p. 96).

24. For parallel usages in southern Indian inscriptions, see Sastri, *History of South India*, 14.

25. Higham, *Archaeology of Mainland Southeast Asia*, 242.

26. See D. G. E. Hall, *History of South-East Asia*, 19ff., for a discussion of this issue.

27. The theory of mass migration is now considered obsolete. See Ibid. Some scholars, such as H. B. Sarkar still use the terms, "Indian migration," and "early migrant community."

28. Sarkar, *Cultural Relations between India and Southeast Asian Countries*, 68ff.

29. Sastri, *History of South India*, 26. We find no references to Vedic rituals in Southeast Asia in the evidence available to us. For a detailed study of Brahmanism in Cambodia, see Bhattacharya, "Les religions brahmaniques."

30. See D. G. E. Hall, *History of South-East Asia*, 19ff.

31. See Cœdès, *Indianized States*, 276nn.11–16.

32. de Jong, "Early Buddhism," 426.

33. For a discussion of this point, see D. G. E. Hall, *History of South-East Asia*, 19ff; and Bayard, "Roots of Indo-Chinese Civilization."

34. D. G. E. Hall, *History of South-East Asia*, 21.

35. Ibid., 13, 20–21.

36. See Dani, *Indian Palaeography*, 227–50.

37. Cœdès, *Indianized States*, xvii.

38. Ibid., 218ff.

39. Ibid., 76, 82; *Charuek nai Prathet Thai*, vol. 1, 95–97, 126–28. Some scholars suggest that Śrīvijaya does not refer to a state but to a king.

40. For discussions of these names and their locations, see Pelliot, "Deux itinéraires de Chine en Inde;" Wheatley, *Golden Khersonese*; and Jacques, "'Funan', 'Zhenla'."

41. For the Sanskritization of place names, see Duroiselle, "Place-Names in Burma," 173–74.

42. See Wolters, *History, Culture and Region*; and Jacques, "'Funan', 'Zhenla'."

43. See Wolters, *History, Culture and Region.*

44. Cœdès, "Le substrat autochtone," 371; and Briggs, "Hinduized States."

45. Wolters, *History, Culture and Region*; and Higham, *Archaeology of Mainland Southeast Asia*, 239ff.

46. Higham, *Archaeology of Mainland Southeast Asia*, 239.

47. Ibid.

48. See Mabbett, "Kingship in Angkor." In *World Conqueror and World Renouncer*, Tambiah translates the term as "galactic." For further discussions of the term, see Wolters, *History, Culture and Region*, chap. 3; and Higham, *Archaeology of Mainland Southeast Asia*, 239ff. The concept has its origin in the Arthaśāstra. See Modelski, "Kautilya," 549–60.

49. Higham, *Archeology of Mainland Southeast Asia*, 240.

50. Some scholars suggest that Indian concepts should be considered on an equal basis with other dynamics involved in the development of Southeast Asian society. Their ideas are discussed in Higham, *Archaeology of Mainland Southeast Asia*, 240.

51. Dates given here are those assigned by Higham. For regions not treated in Higham, the dates given by Cœdès are used.

52. For the names of these centers, see Jacques, "'Funan', 'Zenla'."

53. For a discussion of the debates on the center or capital of Śrivijaya, see D. G. E. Hall, *History of South-East Asia*, 44ff.; and Rajani, *Towards a History of Laem Tong.*

54. For a discussion of the Khmer system of irrigation, see Groslier, "La cité hydraulique angkorienne."

55. Higham, *Archaeology of Mainland Southeast Asia*, 269.

56. Ibid., 240.

57. See Mabbett, "The 'Indianization' of Southeast Asia."

Chapter 2

1. Studies on the indigenous beliefs of Southeast Asian peoples have improved steadily. Research primarily in the fields of archaeology, ethnology, and folklore provide new information about Southeast Asian beliefs before the advent of Indic religions. Yet the picture is still far from complete. Deriving religious ideas from these various fields of study is conjectural due to incomplete data. For an archaeological study of mainland Southeast Asia, see Higham, *Archaeology of Mainland Southeast Asia.* For Burma, see Stargardt, *Ancient Pyu of Burma*; *Études birmanes en hommage à Denise Bernot*, Études thématiques 9; and articles in *Myanmar Historical Research Journal.* For Cambodia, see *Recherches nouvelles sur le Cambodge*, Études thématiques 1; and Higham, *Civilization of Angkor.* For Thailand, see Higham and Thosarat, *Prehistoric Thailand*; *Thailand: Culture and Society* (in Thai with abstracts in English); and reports from the Department of Fine Arts (primarily in Thai). For Laos, there is little other than the work of G. Condominas, *Le bouddhisme au village.* For ethnology and folklore in Burma, see Htin Aung, *Folk Elements in Burmese Buddhism*; Brac de La Perriere, *Les rituels de possession en Birmanie*; and Rodrique, *Nat-Pwe.* In Cambodia, see *Recherchers nouvelles sur le Cambodge*, Études thématiques 1; for the cult of Naek Ta, see Forest, *Le culte des génies protecteurs au Cambodge.* In Thailand, *Thailand: Culture and Society* (in Thai with English abstracts); Siraporn Nathalang, ed., *Thai Folklore: Insight into Thai Culture*; articles in *Tai Culture* and *Asian*

Review; O'Connor, "Agricultural Change and Ethnic Succession;" and Tambiah, *Buddhism and Spirit Cults in North-east Thailand.* For research conducted on the Mon, see Halliday, *Mons of Burma and Thailand;* and Guillon, *Mons: A Civilization of Southeast Asia.*

2. The word "culture" is used here in the broadest sense of the term, avoiding any theorized definition or interpretation. The people of Southeast Asia, especially those who call themselves Buddhists and, to some extent, those of other creeds who were born into a religion and a belief system, rather than those who profess or declare to be a faithful member of a religion, turn to religion and beliefs to meet their spiritual or material needs. Religion is a part of their lives but it is not the only part. For a study on the theoretical aspects of religion, see Pals, *Seven Theories of Religion.*

3. See Spiro, *Burmese Supernatrualism;* and *Cambridge History of Southeast Asia,* vol. 1, 276ff.

4. For a discussion of the term "Southeast Asia" as a geographical unit, see Schwartzberg, "Introduction to Southeast Asian Cartography." For a discussion of cultural aspects, see Chihara, *Hindu-Buddhist Architecture.*

5. An excellent study of ethnicity and culture as well as the migratory pattern of people across mainland Southeast Asia can be found in O'Conner, "Agricultural Change and Ethnic Succession in Southeast Asian States," 968–96.

6. See Higham and Thosarat, *Prehistoric Thailand,* 26ff. This work provides a wide range of archaeological data but is almost totally void of interpretation on religion and beliefs. For a brief discussion on prehistoric Southeast Asia, see *Cambridge History of Southeast Asia,* vol. 1, 136. For archeological studies on the prehistory of Burma, see Ba Maw, "First Discovery in the Evolution of Anyathian Cultures," 97–106; and Stargardt, *Ancient Pyu of Burma.* For Cambodia, see *Recherches nouvelles sur le Cambodge,* 143–95; Higham, *Civilization of Angkor,* 13–22. It is possible that high humidity, high temperatures, and seasonal flooding could be factors for the scarcity of human remains in Burma and Cambodia.

7. Higham and Thosarat, *Prehistoric Thailand,* 63.

8. Stargardt, *Ancient Pyu of Burma,* 15.

9. Higham and Thosarat, *Prehistoric Thailand,* 50, 55–56. Their description of one of the earliest sites illustrates the common features of the graves:

> The earliest deaths at Khok Phanom Di saw the corpse interred in a shallow grave cut into the ashy remains of pottery firing, or the accumulating middens of shellfish. There was, nevertheless, some pattern to this behaviour, for in most cases the body was positioned with its head to the east, and one person was buried with some shell beads. . . . [T]he pattern of inhuming the dead with the head pointing to the east continued, but we find many more burials, with individuals set out in clusters. . . . A notable amount of energy was also expended on mortuary rites. Bodies were wrapped in fabric shroud, sprinkled with red ochre and laid on a wooden bier in individual graves.

10. Ibid., 53. The occupants of Nong Nor buried their dead in an upright position, whereas at Khok Phanom Di, the corpses were found laid out on their backs.

11. See *Encyclopedia of Buddhism,* vol. 11, 520. In the Pamirs and the Aral Sea area as well as among the Sauromatians the deceased were colored red or red paint was placed in the grave.

12. Ibid., 152.

13. Higham and Thosarat, *Prehistoric Thailand*, 56, 78. The majority of burial offerings at Khok Phanom Di are pottery vessels. The mortuary ritual during the Paleolithic period, despite some modifications, remained basically the same. Graves in close proximity were found with a similar orientation, with males and females placed in different directions.

14. *Encyclopedia of Buddhism*, vol. 11, 156.

15. In Chinese society, this practice has been observed since time immemorial. In the first stratum of the practice, living beings, including humans, were buried alive, a practice that later was changed when live beings were replaced by statues. See de Groot, *The Religious System of China*, vol. 2, book 1, 382–417.

16. See *Encyclopedia of Buddhism*, vol. 13, s.v. "Keyes, Charles F.," 516.

17. See Ibid., vol. 9, 336ff. For studies of these so-called "*sīmā*" stones, see *Muang Boran* 1, no. 2.

18. Stargardt, *Ancient Pyu of Burma*, 30, 32.

19. Kempers and Johan, *Kettledrums of Southeast Asia*, 132; Pham Huy Thông, *Dong Son Drums in Vietnam*, 262ff. For a discussion of the feathered men, see the "Rock Art of Thailand" in Higham and Thosarat, *Prehistoric Thailand*. The houses in the figured scenes have either a convex roof or a concave one. They appear to be similar to ones found in Indonesia and Polynesia, but dissimilar to ones in Vietnam. See also Waterson, *The Living House*, especially noting the color plates and the first chapter that describes houses of similar types in Indonesia and Polynesia.

20. For reference to Schärer's unpublished thesis, see Schwartzberg, "Cosmography in Southeast Asia," 702–10.

21. In rock art or cave painting, human figures are often depicted with large heads or decorated with feathered headgear. They could represent individuals in a ritual dance wearing masks.

22. Higham and Thosarat, *Prehistoric Thailand*, 141.

23. The science of geomancy is highly developed in China. See de Groot, *The Religious System of China*, vol. 2, book 1.

24. The belief in a sun god is common among ancient peoples, especially the Indo-Europeans. See *Encyclopedia of Buddhism*, vol. 14, 132–43; Macdonell, *Vedic Mythology*; and Pandey, *Sun-Worship in Ancient India*.

25. Siraporn Nathalang "Tai Creation Myths," and "Conflict and Compromise," 81–98 and 99–120, respectively. See also Siraporn Nathalang, "An Analysis of the Creation Myths," 88–115; and Pichet Suypan, "Nam Tao Pung," 116–36.

26. Siraporn Nathalang, "Tai Creation Myths," 90.

27. Thaen is perhaps related to the Chinese word "*tian*," meaning heaven or sky.

28. For detailed studies on *phii*, see Anuman Rajadhon, *Popular Buddhism*, 99–126; Anuman Rajadhon, *Essays on Thai Folklore*, 151–66; and Tambiah, *Buddhism and the Spirit Cults in North-east Thailand.*, 263ff.

29. See Pranee Wongthet, "Ancestor Worship among the Khamu," 137–48.

30. Anan Ganjanapan, "Wai Pii Muang and the State's Power in Lanna," 149–61.

31. See Anuman Rajadhon, *Popular Buddhism*, 127–33.

32. Wolters, *History, Culture and Region*, rev. ed., 18ff.

33. For studies on the *nat* cult, see Htin Aung, *Folk Elements in Burmese Buddhism*; Rodrique, *Nat-Pwe*; and Bekker, "Transformations of the *Nats*," 40–45.

34. See Wales, *Divination in Thailand*; and Klausner, *Reflections on Thai Culture*.

35. A more detailed discussion of these particular beliefs is beyond the scope of this present study. Those interested in early belief systems in Southeast Asia should consult the works of C. Keyes, B. J. Terweil, S. J. Tambiah, Anuman Rajadhon, Melford Spiro, and François Bizot, among others.

Chapter 3

1. There is not a large corpus of scholarship on the history of Buddhism in Southeast Asia. Two works by N. R. Ray, *Sanskrit Buddhism* and *Theravāda Buddhism in Burma*, deal only with Burma and not Southeast Asia as a whole. Other works belong to the disciplines of sociology and anthropology, which, for the most part, use and interpret only contemporary data. Since the region is considered to be exclusively Theravādin, Buddhism in these works refers only to Theravāda Buddhism.

2. See, e.g., Htin Aung "Burmese Buddhist Historiography," 1123–36. Htin Aung uses Burmese chronicles to claim that a group of monks visited Burma in 508 BCE, reasoning as follows:

> The chronicles claimed that the Buddha visited both lower and upper Burma. Many countries in Southeast Asia and Ceylon also made the same claim. Because of the distance, the sea, the terrain, those countries explained that the Buddha came flying, using His supernatural powers. With regard to one visit, the Burmese chronicles mentioned that He came in a more prosaic way, by ship. In addition, they were precise as to the date for the particular visit; it was in the 20th year of the Buddhist ministry. From this the modern historian could conclude that in B.C. 508 a group of adventurous monks penetrated Burma, bringing with them the new religion.

However, Htin Aung gives no evidence beyond the chronicles to substantiate his assertion, so the date cannot be verified. In fact, there is no such datable evidence even in the *Tripiṭaka*. Htin Aung later concludes that Buddhism was introduced by the mission sent during Aśoka's reign:

> The "official" introduction of Buddhism into Burma took place in B.C.. 247 when Asoka's mission of monks reached Suvannabhumi, "the golden land." There had been unnecessary controversy among modern scholars as to the exact location of Suvannabhumi, some arguing that it was not in Lower Burma but either in the valley of the Menam Chao Phya or the northern part of the Malay peninsula. All these three regions at the time belonged to the Mons who were then the dominant race in the western half of mainland Southeast Asia. Their land was the land of gold and its great port and the capital was Thaton in Lower Burma. Ships from India and Ceylon did not yet dare to go round the Malay peninsular and they discharged their cargoes at Thaton, from where the precious goods were carried further east overland along the portage routes . . . Thus Asoka's mission landed at Thaton and Buddhism became the official and national religion of the Mons.

Htin Aung's work provides an example of how Buddhism's arrival in Southeast Asia is bound up with nationalist pride.

3. This is true only if we unquestioningly believe that Suvarṇabhūmi is located in Southeast Asia.

4. See D. G. E. Hall, *History of South-East Asia*, 18–19; and Cœdès, *Indianized States*, 21ff.

5. Relations between trade and the monastic system are examined in H. P. Ray, *Monastery and Guild*. For contacts between China and India using the land route, see Xinru Liu, *Ancient India and Ancient China*.

6. This is best depicted in Wheatley, *Golden Khersonese*, xviii–xx. He traces the role the peninsula played from prehistoric times when it served as "a gigantic causeway over which a succession of cultures had diffused imperceptibly from the mainland of Asia towards the Archipelago, the South-West Pacific and Australasia." However, during the first fifteen hundred years of the historical period, the peninsula also played the role of a barrier because it is situated almost exactly halfway between India and China. Another barrier to trade was the seasonal monsoons whose winds change direction during the course of the year. This meant that all sailing had to follow the wind direction of the prevailing monsoon.

7. In some of the *Jātakas*, a ship sails originally from Southeast Asia. See, e.g., *Jātaka* no. 463 and *Jātakamāla* no. 14; see also Majumdar, *Ancient Indian Colonies*, 35ff.

8. For the protohistorical period, see Glover in *Research Conference on Early Southeast Asia*, 333–64; for the historical period, see H. P. Ray, "Early Maritime Contacts," 42–54. For issues about intra-regional trade, see articles by Bennett Bronson, Jan Wisseman Christie, Phasook Indrawooth, and Mayuree Veraprasert under the topic of trade and communications within Southeast Asia in *Research Conference on Early Southeast Asia*.

9. Information on the sea routes used by merchants and pilgrims as well as the traveling conditions can be found primarily in diaries kept by Chinese pilgrims such as Fa Xian. Paul Wheatley has studied these routes. See his *Golden Khersonese*, especially, part one. For a scientific study of wind systems, see Grimes, "Journey of Fa-Hsien." For routes used by other Buddhist missions, see Pachow, "Voyage of Buddhist Missions."

10. The routes described in Indian literature are usually mythical ones. In the *Jātaka*, none of the protagonists actually reaches Suvarṇabhūmi. For a short summary of the literature in which the names of Suvarṇabhūmi and Suvarṇadvīpa appear, see Wheatley, *Golden Khersonese*, chap. 18 and the appendix entitled, "Notes on Indian Texts," 204ff.

11. *Jātaka*, nos. 39, 360, and 463.

12. *Niddesa I*, 154–155.

13. *Milindapañha*, 331, 359.

14. *Mahākarmavibhaṅga*, 50–55.

15. For discussions and opinions on the date of these texts, see Lévi, "Ptolémée," 51; and Majumdar, *Suvarṇadvīpa*, 58. Majumdar believes that the list of *Niddesa* was probably drawn up between the end of the first and the beginning of the third century CE. N. R. Ray challenges Majumdar's date, claiming that the Pāli canon was compiled by the sixth or fifth century BCE. See N. R. Ray, *Theravāda Buddhism in Burma*, 2–5.

16. In "The Role of Pāli in Early Sinhalese Buddhism," 29, K. R. Norman seems to suggest that early relations between India and Sri Lanka flourished along the western rather than the eastern coast of India:

> Tradition has it that Vijaya and his followers arrived in Ceylon on the day that the Buddha died (Mhvs 6.47). Vijaya came from N. India, from the kingdom of Lāḷa (*Mhvs* 6.36). Although the *Mhvs* (6.5) implies that Lāḷa lay between Vanga (Bengal) and Magadha, it is identified by some with Ptolemy's modern Gujarat (*DPPN* s.v.), and this would agree with the statement that on the way to Ceylon Vijaya landed at Suppāraka, i.e. modern Sopāra (*Mhvs* 6.46), or Bharukacchu, i.e. modern Broach (*Dpvs* 9.26).

17. For details of inland towns, see Higham, *Archaeology of Mainland Southeast Asia*, 270–79.

18. Ibid., 242–44. Higham gives the approximate date of contact between Southeast Asia and India as between 300 BCE and 300 CE. He provides no solid evidence, but states:

> If the Indian merchant guilds prospered on the western trade route, why not also in an easterly direction? The seasonal wind pattern across the Bay of Bengal reflects the regular rise and ebb of the monsoon, and maritime technology was well equipped to cope with the necessary distances . . . The fact is that Indian merchant venturers did sail eastward in growing numbers, and their exploits were incorporated into Hindu epic literature. The fabled land beyond the sunrise is referred to in the Indian literature as *Suvarṇabhūmi*, or *Suvarṇadvīpa*, which meant "land of gold." Gold was to be found there, but the voyages were, according to the *Rāmāyana*, beset by storms and other perils.

Higham reasons that trade was then motivated by the prohibition of exporting gold coinage from the Roman Empire during the reign of Vespasian in 69 CE. He goes on to describe the Indian merchants who traded with Southeast Asia as being "from a country with a sophisticated and mature tradition of statehood. They were familiar with the notion of a supreme monarch, and inherited the established role of the brāhman in both ritual and state administration." It is unclear what Higham uses as his source of information for "the fabled land beyond the sunrise," which would definitely place Suvarṇabhūmi (Suvarṇadvīpa) to the east of India. However, to date, we cannot find any text that would provide specific information about Suvarṇabhūmi's location. Moreover, it is doubtful that any mature political concepts existed at that time. Of course, the concept of a supreme monarch did exist, and such monarchs figure prominently in both Buddhist and Hindu texts, but more from an ideal state point of view, rather than in actual fact. Merchants could not and, in the Indian context, should not inherit the established role of the brahman, either in rituals or administrative positions.

19. For a discussion of *dharmacakras* found in Thailand, see Dhanit Yupho, *Dharmacakra*. See also the section "Archaeological Data" in chap. 4 of this volume.

20. For the location of these seaports, see Wheatley, *Golden Khersonese*, 9, 34, 40, 44, 53, 64ff.

21. For detailed studies, see Chhabra, *Expansion of Indo-Aryan Culture*; and de Casparis, "Palaeography as an Auxiliary Discipline," 382ff.

22. Lists in the *Niddesa*, the *Milindapañha*, and the *Mahākarmavibhaṅga* refer to Sri Lanka either as Tambapaṇṇi or Siṃhaladvīpa, and mention it after Suvarṇabhūmi. See, e.g., *Niddesa* I, 155: "Suvaṇṇakūṭaṃ gacchati, Suvaṇkabhūmiṃ gacchati, Tambapaṇṇiṃ gacchati, Suppāraṃ gacchati;" and *Mahākarmavibhaṅga*, 53: "Suvarṇabhūmiṃ Siṃhaladvīpaṃ ca prabhṛtāni ca dvīpāntarāṇi paśyanti." See also Wheatley, *Golden Khersonese*, 42ff.; Norman, "The Role of Pāli," 29ff.; and also Norman, *Pāli Literature*, 66ff, who discusses the original home of Pāli and gives some evidence that Sri Lanka was a popular port at the time.

23. N. R. Ray, *Theravāda Buddhism in Burma*, 29ff.

24. See Vogel, "Prakrit Inscriptions," 22. See also chap. 4 of this volume.

25. See Wheatley, *Golden Khersonese*, especially part 4 for a discussion of "The Isthmian Age."

26. For the trans-peninsular routes, see Klin Khongmuaenphet, "From West to East," 51–58; and Rajani, *Towards a History of Laem Thong*, iii.

27. Jean Boisselier argues that the center of Funan culture was in central Thailand rather than in the Mekong delta. See "U Thong" (1966) and "Nouvelles données sur l'histoire ancienne de la Thaïlande" (1966). Apparently, Boisselier later rejected this idea. In 1980, in *Oriental Art*, ed. Jeannine Auboyer, et al., 229, Boisselier wrote:

> There existed in the south of the peninsula [in this case, the southern part of Vietnam], in the very earliest centuries of the Christian era, an Indianized kingdom . . . mentioned in Chinese texts. Almost nothing is known about the art of this kingdom to which a mere handful of objects (seals, some gems) found at Oc-èo can be attributed with certainty. For a while it was thought possible that another, larger group of objects might be from [there as well], but this theory has been disproved by the most recent excavations in Thailand (especially by those at U Thong), which show that the objects in question cannot have been made earlier than the 7th or 8th century.

However, the similarity between the objects found in central Thailand and those of Oc-èo cannot be denied. Even if the center of Funan culture was not in Thailand, the two areas certainly had some cultural contact in the early period. For a detailed study of Oc-èo, see Malleret, *L'Archéologie du delta du Mékong*. For a discussion of pre-Dvāravatī culture in Thailand, see Higham, *Archaeology of Mainland Southeast Asia*, 269ff.; and Mayuree Veraprasert and Srisakra Vallibhotama in *Research Conference on Early Southeast Asia*, 168–69 and 247–58, respectively.

28. See Dhida Saraya in *Research Conference on Early Southeast Asia*, 259–82.

29. Ibid. See also *Charuek Boran Run Raek phob thi Lopburi lae klai khiang*, 99ff.

30. For detailed studies of these sources, see Lévi, "Ptolémée;" Majumdar, *Ancient Indian Colonies*; Wheatley, *Golden Khersonese*; Dhanit Yupho, *Suvarnabhûmi*; Rajani, *Towards a History of Laem Thong*; and K. Hall, *Maritime Trade*.

31. See Sastri, "Dvīpāntara," 1–4.

32. The English translation is mine. See *Niddesa* I, 154–155 (the primary readings are taken from the Thai script edition):

> Athavā kāmataṇhāya abhibhūto pariyādinnacitto bhoge pariyesanto nāvāya mahāsamuddaṃ pakkhandati . . . Gumbaṃ [v.l. Tigumbaṃ] gacchati, Takkolaṃ gacchati, Takkasīlaṃ gacchati, Kālamukhaṃ gacchati, Maraṇapāraṃ gacchati, Vesuṅgaṃ

gacchati, Verāpathaṃ gacchati, Javaṃ gacchati, Tamaliṃ [v.l. Tāmaliṃ] gacchati, Vaṅgaṃ gacchati, Eḷavaddanaṃ [v.l. Eḷabandhanaṃ] gacchati, Suvaṇṇakūṭaṃ gacchati, Suvaṇṇabhūmiṃ gacchati, Tambapaṇṇiṃ gacchati, Suppāraṃ gacchati, Bharukacchaṃ gacchati, Suraṭṭhaṃ gacchati, Aṅgaṇekaṃ gacchati, Gaṅgaṇaṃ gacchati, Paramagaṅgaṇaṃ gacchati, Yonaṃ gacchati, Paramayonaṃ gacchati, Allasandaṃ gacchati

33. Lévi, "Ptolémée," 1–55.

34. Ibid., 29. Lévi comments on the names, Suvaṇṇakūṭaṃ and Suvaṇṇabhūmi as follows:

> Les deux noms suivants, *Suvaṇṇakūṭa* et *Suvaṇṇabhūmi*, doivent être traités ensemble. L'un d'eux, Suvaṇṇabhūmi "la terre d'or" est une appellation classique bien connue, qui correspond à la Chrysê des Grecs et des Latins. Il serait dangereux d'en préciser à l'excès de valeur, c'est plutôt une direction, comme nous disons, les Indes Orientales, les Indes Occidentales. Suvaṇṇabhūmi, c'est en gros les pays situés à l'est du golfe du Bengale, ce que Ptolémée appelle l'Inde Outre-Gange . . .

He speculates further on Suvarṇakūṭya and provides references from Sanskrit literature on the products of the region. For Suvarṇakūṭya, there is a reference that locates the site to the east of India, but the reference is filled with mythical elements:

> Le Saddharma smṛtyupasthāna sūtra . . . place à l'Est de Jambudvīpa, dans la mer de Joyeux, 'une île appellée Muraille d'Or; elle est toute recouverte d'un sol d'or; elle est habitée par des démons effroyables d'aspect de grande puissance.

35. B. C. Law, *Chronicles of Ceylon*, 62–63. In connection with the list of missions sent to different lands after the Third Council, Law writes: "As regards Suvaṇṇabhūmi, it is suggested that probably the original place-name was Suvaṇṇagiri, which was the seat of southern viceroyalty in Aśoka's time in view of the fact that the *Dīpavaṃsa* description differs materially from that in the *Mahāvaṃsa*." In a footnote, Law quotes the two texts mentioned, adding "Cf. *Samantapāsādikā* I, pp. 68ff., where both descriptions are given without any comment." The earlier chronicle (*Dīpavaṃsa*) does not place the country on the seashore; instead it associates it with the Piśācas.

36. For Sanskrit and Pāli place names, see Duroiselle, "Place-Names in Burma," 173–74. His description concerns only Burma, but could apply to other regions of Southeast Asia:

> A large number of districts, towns and even villages in Burma possess two names and sometimes more. Of these, only one is thoroughly Burmese and generally known among people, the other or others being either imported from India through the medium of the sacred books of Buddhism and their commentaries, or coined on the model of those existing in India. The former type of name may be called classical and the latter type, pseudo-classical. The origin of this practice of renaming already existing towns is not far to seek, and may be referred, in the first instance, to the desire of a people freshly converted to a new faith (Buddhism in this case), to sanctify, so to say, their own land, and to identify it as closely as possible with the land in which the new cult originated. Thus they made Buddha come over to Burma on many missions, or the locus of some of his births in previous existences was placed in Burma . . . Secondly, it may be attributed

> to the pride of the Burmese race, and to its endeavour to affiliate the Burmese dynasties not only to the great dynasties of India, such as the Solar and Lunar, but above all to show the direct descent of Burmese kings from the clan of the Sakyas, of which the Buddha was a member . . .

As to their age, Duroiselle thinks that

> . . . some of these, such as Mweyin on the upper Irrawaddy, Sriksetra or Old Prome and Hamsavati (Pegu) go back to soon after the beginning of the Christian era, while others, mostly in the Deltaic Provinces, must have been transplanted after the 5th–6th century. Most of them, however, do not antedate the 11th century, when the purer form of Buddhism imported from Thaton spread rapidly all over the upper country, and when devotion and scriptural learning were intense.

The same practice was followed in Thailand, especially for place names occurring in chronicles such as *Cāmadevīvaṃsa* and *Jinakālamālinī*. In these chronicles, the Buddha is reported to have visited various places in Thailand, where he predicted that in the future such places would be sites of a particular town or a great *stūpa* that would enshrine his relics. The four great pilgrimage sites (the Buddha's birthplace, first teaching, etc.) are believed by many to be located in Thailand. Both the Thai and the Khmer affiliate their royal dynasties to the great *vaṃsas* of India. In *Theravāda Buddhism in Burma*, 32, N. R. Ray asserts that in Pāli literature, both canonical and commentarial, references to place names such as Haṃsāvatī and Sudhammavatī are sites in Burma. Such claims should be rejected; the truth of it was probably just the reverse. Pāli and Sanskrit names fall into two groups. The first group consists of names largely drawn from Pāli canonical works that in the Buddhist chronicles of Burma and Thailand refer to local sites or regions. Hence, a cultural center in Burma or Thailand that considered itself a "Magadha" would call the area to the north "Kashmir," while China would be called "Vesālī," and so on. The second group, usually in Sanskrit, consists of official names used for the royal record.

37. See quote cited in note 32.

38. See discussion in note 22.

39. Wheatley, *Golden Khersonese*, xxii–xxiii, figures 2, 3.

40. Majumdar, *Ancient Indian Colonies*, 46.

41. Ibid., 48.

42. Wheatley, *Golden Khersonese*, 123ff.

43. For a detailed discussion of this term, see N. R. Ray, *Theravāda Buddhism in Burma*, 21ff. Ray thinks that it refers to Burma. In *Golden Khersonese*, 116ff., Wheatley rejects the claim for Burma and proposes that it was the area around the Gulf of Thailand. See also Luce, "The Advent of Buddhism to Burma," 121.

44. Lévi, "Ptolémée," 36; and Wheatley, *Golden Khersonese*, 117.

45. The oldest epigraphic evidence for this name is a ninth century inscription from Nālandā in India, in which Sumatra is referred to as Suvarṇabhūmi. However, the so-called "Suvaṇṇabhūmi inscription" of Kyanzittha dated to 1098 CE does not actually use the name and, therefore, it cannot be used as evidence. The name occurs in the inscriptions of Jayavarman VII (eleventh century) and in the inscription of King Ramkhamhaeng (1292 CE); otherwise, there are no sources of any kind in Southeast Asia prior to the fifteenth century.

46. See *Epigraphia Birmanica*, vol. 2.

47. Most scholars—Majumdar probably being the first one—accept without positive verification that Thaton is Suvarṇabhūmi; this consequently became the generally received opinion.

48. The English translation is mine. See *Sāsanavaṃsa*, 10–11:

> Tesu pana navasu ìhānesu Suvaṇṇabhūmi nāma adhunā Sudhammanagaraṃeva. Kasmā pan' etaṃ viññāyatā ti ce: Maggānumānato ṭhānānumānato vā. Kathaṃ maggānumānato? Ito kira Suvaṇṇabhūmiṃ sattamattāni yojanasatāni honti. Ekena vātena gacchantā nāvā sattahi ahorattehi gacchanti. Ath' ekasmiṃ samaye evaṃ gacchantā nāvā sattāhaṃ pīnadīghāvattamacchapiṭṭhen'eva gatā ti Aṭṭhakathāyaṃ vuttena Sīhaḷadīpato Suvaṇṇabhūmiṃ gatamaggapamāṇena Sudhammapurato
>
> Sīhaḷadīpaṃ gatamaggapamāṇaṃ sameti. Sudhammapurato kira hi Sīhaḷadīpaṃ sattamattāni yojanasatāni honti. Ujuṃvāyu-āgamanakāle gacchantā vāyunāvā sattahi ahorattehi sampāpuṇāti. Evaṃ maggānumānato viññāyati. Kathaṃ ṭhānānumānato. Suvaṇṇabhūmi kira mahāsamuddasamīpe tiṭṭhati. Nānāverajjakānam pi vāṇijānaṃ upasaṃkamanaṭṭhānabhūtaṃ mahātitthaṃ hoti. Ten' eva mahājanakakumārādayo Campānagarādito saṃvohāratthāya nāvāya Suvaṇṇabhūmiṃ āgacchanti. Sudhammapuraṃ pi adhunā mahāsamuddasamīpe yeva tiṭṭhati. Evaṃ ṭhānānumānato viññāyati.

49. The English translation is mine. See Ibid., 11:

> Apare pana Suvaṇṇabhūmi nāma Haribhuñjaraṭṭham yevā ti vadanti, tattha suvaṇṇassa bāhullatā ti vadanti. Aññe pana Siyāmaraṭṭhaṃ yevā ti vadanti. Taṃ sabbaṃ vīmaṃsitabbaṃ.

Haribhuñja (Haripuñjaya) is located in present-day Lamphun in northern Thailand. It became the center of Theravāda Buddhism in the eighth century, if the chronicles are accurate. While no antiquities from the earliest period have been discovered, there are Pāli inscriptions dating from the tenth century onwards. The people of Haribhuñja reportedly abandoned the city because of a cholera epidemic, and migrated to Sudhammapura and Haṃsāvatī. The chronicle says that ". . . because they spoke the same language [presumably Mon], they became acquainted very quickly" (*ubbhinnaṃ bhāsā pi ekasadisaṃ eva vācikā pi na kiñci nānattaṃ honti, tasmā te sabbe khippaṃ vissāsikanti*). See Cœdès, "Documents sur l'histoire politique et religieuse du Laos occidental," 17.

50. Cœdès, *Recueil des Inscriptions du Siam*, part 1, 37.

51. *Inscriptions du Cambodge*, vol. 4, 64 (K. 774).

52. Majumdar, *Ancient Indian Colonies*, 47.

53. Ibid., 46–47.

54. See Cœdès, "Documents sur l'histoire politique et religieuse du Laos occidental," 148.

55. Wheatley, *Golden Khersonese*, 177ff.

56. The Mon civilization in the central and lower northern parts of Thailand has proven to be older than that of lower Burma. Luce, an authority in Burmese studies, thought that the Mon came to Burma from Thailand. In *Old Burma-Early Pagan*, 26, he writes: "Mon-Khmer speakers have everywhere been pioneers in wet rice cultivation. As a result, they suffered from chronic over-population. They started apparently from Tonking,

and spread over all the rice plains of Further India and East India. Most of the Mons of Burma came originally from Siam." If Luce is right, then the Rāmaññadesa referred to in the old texts would be in Thailand rather than in the southern part of Burma. Cœdès goes further and suggests that even the Buddhism of lower Burma came from the Mon of the Dvāravatī culture. See Cœdès, "Les Mōns de Dvāravatī," 112ff.

57. Some inscriptions left by merchants reveal that they were well acquainted with religious terms, since the inscriptions are mostly quotations from religious texts. See the section "Epigraphic Sources" in chap. 4 of this volume.

58. See *Dictionary of Pāli Proper Names*, vol. 1, 865. The Buddha declared Cittagahapati to be preeminent among laymen who preached the Buddha's doctrine. From this, it may be assumed that numerous laymen preached the doctrine.

59. See the section "Epigraphic Sources" in chap. 4 of this volume.

60. The term "mission" is a borrowed term from the Christian tradition, but when used in the Buddhist context, it does not carry the same import. The aim of Buddhist missions was not so much to convert non-Buddhists or prohibit them from practicing non-Buddhist beliefs, bur rather the primary aim was to spread the Buddha's teachings or the "Good Dharma." The nature of Buddhist missions probably evolved from the perceptions people had toward religions in India and Southeast Asia. See chap. 5 of this volume for a discussion of this point. For a general understanding of the term "mission," see *Encyclopedia of Religion*, vol. 9, 563–70. The article on "Buddhist Missions" by Erik Zürcher (pp. 570–73) is too short to supply any substantive discussion on the diffusion of Buddhism to Southeast Asia.

61. Even in the later period, Chinese pilgrims used commercial vessels. See Wheatley, *Golden Khersonese*, 38, for translated passages from Fa Xian's diary describing the hazards of the high seas.

62. Higham, *Archaeology of Mainland Southeast Asia*, 251ff. For detailed studies of beads, seals, and other early artifacts, see Malleret, *L'Archéologie du delta du Mékong*, especially vol. 3. For artifacts found in Thailand, see Mayuree Veraprasert in *Research Conference on Early Southeast Asia*, 168ff. For inscriptions on seals, see Kongkeaw Veeraprajak, "Inscriptions from South Thailand." These seals were found in peninsular Thailand, some dating from the first century CE. The inscriptions are very short, usually containing only one word. The seals may have been used in business transactions, for we find words such as *dātavyam*, meaning "to be given" and *apralasanasya*, meaning "not to be moved" or, alternatively, "belonging to Apralasana." From the sixth century on, the inscriptions show a religious inclination, with words such as *surudharmasya* (one who possesses good virtue) or *śrammana* (monks, recluses) being used.

63. The only study on this subject is Masson's *La religion populaire dans le canon bouddhique pâli* (1942). Masson unfortunately completed only one of two planned volumes on the various gods and genies that appear in the *Tripiṭaka*. The second volume was to have investigated cults, sacrifices, divination, magic, and other beliefs.

64. Phasook Indrawooth in *Research Conference on Early Southeast Asia*, 155–67.

65. Ibid. For additional references, see Phasook Indrawooth's bibliography.

66. This identification has been accepted by many scholars but without citing any textual or traditional sources. See, for example, Ibid; and Wheatley, *Golden Khersonese*, 189.

67. Dhanit Yupho, *Dharmacakra*, 27.

68. There are numerous studies on this subject. For references, see the section "Archaeological Sources" in chap. 4 of this volume.

69. See Sugimoto Takushū, "Buddha called Mahādeva and Pitāmaha."

70. For contacts between maritime Southeast Asia and the Cham and Khmer, see Mabbett, "Buddhism in Champa," 296ff.

71. *Vinaya* I, 20–21. For references in other sources, see Lamotte, *Histoire du bouddhisme indien*, 325.

72. Lamotte, *Histoire du bouddhisme indien*, 325ff.

73. Ibid.

74. See *Dīpavaṃsa* VIII, 1–13; *Mahāvaṃsa* XII, 1–55; *Samantapāsādikā* I, 63–69; see also Lamotte, *Histoire du bouddhisme indien*, 319ff. Lamotte compares sources such as the rock edicts of Aśoka, the *Mahākarmavibhaṅga*, and the Nāgārjunakoṇḍa inscriptions (p. 329).

75. See Ibid.

76. See Bhikkhu Bodhi, *Discourse on the All-Embracing Net of Views*, who translates the *sutta* and provides both a commentary and a sub-commentary.

77. Lamotte, *Histoire du bouddhisme indien*, 335.

78. Bechert and Gombrich, *World of Buddhism*, 83.

79. *See Mahākarmavibhaṅga*, 62:

> Anavataptasarasaś ca kuṅkumam ānīya Kaśmīrāyām pratiṣṭhāpitam. tac cādyāpi lokopabhuktaṃ. vihāraś ca kārito' dyāpi ca tatraiva prativasanti. yathā ārya Gavāmpatinā Suvarṇabhūmyāṃ yojanaśataṃ janapado' bhiprasāditaḥ. yathā ca Pūrvavidehā ārya-Piṇḍola Bhāradvājenābhiprasāditā . . . . yathā cārya Mahendreṇa Siṃhaladvīpe Vibhīṣaṇaprabhṛtayo rākṣasāḥ samaye sthāpitā deśaś cābhiprasāditaḥ. . . .

80. For references to Gavāmpati in Pāli and Sanskrit sources, see *Dictionary of Pāli Proper Names*, vol. 1, 756–57. The *Sāsanavaṃsa* also tells of an episode wherein the Buddha asks Gavāmpati to establish the teaching in Sudhammapura in the Rāmañña country. This shows that the story recorded in the *Mahākarmavibhaṅga* was known to the author of the *Sāsanavaṃsa* in the nineteenth century. We can surmise that the legend circulated in Burma long before that time.

81. However, if one carefully scrutinizes the *Mahākarmavibhaṅga* account, it appears rather mythical. Legendary places, such as Anavatapta and Pūrvavideha, are referred to and Siṃhaladvīpa is taken to be the Lankādvīpa of the Rāmāyaṇa, since Vibhīṣaṇa, the younger brother of Rāvaṇa, is mentioned.

82. Rock Edict XIII found in Girnar (Junāgarh, Kathiawar), Kalsi (Dehra-Dun, Uttar Pradesh), Shahbazgarhi (Peshwar, Northwest Frontier Province of Pakistan), and Manshehra (Hazara, Northwest Frontier Province of Pakistan). See Basak, *Asokan Inscriptions*, 63ff.

83. The meaning of the word "Dharma" as used in the edicts of Aśoka has long been debated among scholars. Some understand it to mean the Buddhist Dharma or teachings of the Buddha, but for others, it means the general usage of the word, which refers to norms of conduct. In the edicts in which the word appears, the context does not suggest the Buddhist Dharma. See, e.g., Basak, *Asokan Inscriptions*, xxii, who advocates that it only means the Buddhist Dharma; see also c.f. Thapar, *Ancient Indian Social History*, 33ff.

84. See Basak, *Asokan Inscriptions*, 73; and Law, *Chronicles of Ceylon*, 62.

85. This occurred rather late. The identification of Suvarṇabhūmi with the Buddhist mission is found in the famous fifteenth century Kalyāṇī inscription.

86. *Dīpavaṃsa* VIII, 1–13; *Mahāvaṃsa* XII, 1; *Samantapāsādikā* I, 37.

87. *Encyclopedia of Religion*, vol. 2, 386.

88. There are numerous works on this subject. Regrettably, many of them only list the details of each mission without mentioning the cause or effect on Buddhism in Sri Lanka or Southeast Asia. See, e.g., Sirisena, *Sri Lanka and South-East Asia*; and Hazra, *History of Theravāda Buddhism*.

89. For an excellent survey of Indian and Sri Lankan monks who propagated the doctrine in Southeast Asia and the Far East, see Pachow, "The Voyage of Buddhist Missions."

90. Ibid. See also H. P. Ray, "Early Maritime Contacts," 42ff.

91. Pachow, "The Voyage of Buddhist Missions," 1ff.

92. Ibid., 15ff.

93. Ibid., 9ff.

94. Cœdès, *Indianized States*, 58.

95. Professor Lewis Lancaster has examined the "portable" and "fixed" aspects of religious sanctity. He suggests that sanctity in Buddhism is of the portable kind, because it is able to cross cultural boundaries and spread easily to lands beyond India. Yet, the concept of "fixed sanctity" in Buddhism is also apparent, which paves the way for pilgrimage to develop. Some sacred sites, such as the birthplace of the Buddha, were "transferred," as it were, from India to their homelands by foreign Buddhists, who created or identified these sacred places in their own countries. Thus, even "fixed sanctities" in Buddhism became "portable." Lewis Lancaster, personal communication with author, September 1989.

96. *Dīghanikāya* II, 140–41.

97. Ibid., 141–43.

98. See Strong, *Legend of King Aśoka*, 109ff.

99. Ibid., 120. For detailed studies of the *stūpa*, see Tucci, *Indo-Tibetica*; and Snodgrass, *Symbolism of the Stupa*.

100. Many of these legends remain untranslated. In Thailand, they are called *Tamnān Phra That* (Legends of relics). The genre is treated briefly in Wyatt, "Chronicle Traditions in Thai Historiography," 116ff., who calls these legends "monumental" *tamnān*, which is appropriate, since they include legends about important images of the Buddha as well as relics. See also Charnvit Kasetsiri, *Rise of Ayudhya*, 1ff.

101. *Epigraphica Indica*, vol. 17 (1923–1924): 322–24.

102. Wheatley, *Golden Khersonese*, 203.

103. See Dohanian, *Mahāyāna Buddhist Sculpture of Ceylon*, 16–17, who describes the situation of Sri Lankan Buddhism at the time as "internationalism," since monks from Sri Lanka kept in close contact with India and traveled frequently to pilgrimage sites there.

104. For texts mentioned in connection with missionary monks, see Pachow, "The Voyage of Buddhist Missions," 11, 13–14. For lists of Pāli works known in the Pyu tradition, see Luce, "The Advent of Buddhism to Burma," 125ff. The list of scriptures proposed by Luce should not be followed strictly, since the inscriptions from which he compiled his

list contain passages common to many *sūtra*. See also the section "Epigraphic Sources" in chap. 4 of this volume.

105. See the illustration in Higham, *Archaeology of Mainland Southeast Asia*, 273.

106. Wheatley, *Golden Khersonese*, 189.

107. Dupont, "Les Buddha dits d'Amarāvatī en Asie du Sud-Est."

108. For additional references, see the section "Archaeological Sources" in chap. 4 of this volume. For a discussion of setting the wheel on a pillar, see Irwin, "'Asokan' Pillars," parts 1–4.

109. Irwin, "'Asokan' Pillars, Part I," 709, 720; Irwin, "'Asokan' Pillars, Part IV," 738; and Ito, "On the date and analysis of stone Dharmacakra," 1227–37.

110. Auboyer, et al., *Oriental Art*, 161, 374.

111. Ibid., 133.

112. *Tamnān Mūlasāsanā*, 109. See also Higham, *Archaeology of Mainland Southeast Asia*, which incorporates much of the data found in *Tamnān Mūlasāsanā*.

113. H. P. Ray, "Early Maritime Contacts," 52ff.

114. Lamotte, *Histoire du bouddhisme indien*, 546-49; Shizutāni, *Indo bukkyō himei mokuroku*, No. 1699; (Gupta period) Nos. 48, 58, 74, 103, 107, 109, 118, 138, 139, 153, 159, 162, 170; (Pāla period), Nos. 14, 23, 28, 29, 31, 32, 35, 36, 38, 41, 43, 53 (?), 57, 59, 63, 70, 71, 74, 76–78, 93, 95, 96, 98, 100, 101, 104, 107, 108, 113, 115, 117, 124, 127, 131–34, 138, 140, 144, 145. See also Yuyama, "'Jūni innenju' oboegaki."

Chapter 4

1. For a detailed study of the so-called "Pallava" influence on Southeast Asian scripts, see Chhabra, *Expansion of Indo-Aryan Culture*. Some of Chhabra's assertions, however, are questioned by de Casparis in "Paleography as an Auxiliary Discipline," 382–85, who writes of his own understanding of "Pallava" script in Southeast Asia:

> Apart from the Oc-Eo and Vo-canh inscriptions the other epigraphic texts in South East Asia before the middle of the eighth century are written in a script called "Pallava" on account of its general similarity with the script used in the inscriptions of the Pallavas of Kañcī. The name "Pallava" has generally been applied to the script of these South East Asian inscriptions since Vogel's masterly study of the Kutai inscriptions published in 1918. The use of the term has been strengthened by an important study by B. Ch. Chabra, *Expansion of Indo-Aryan Culture during Pallava Rule*. It has to be admitted that there is little *direct* evidence linking the Pallavas with the early inscriptions of South East Asia . . . It is curious that some of the most striking similarities between South and South East Asian "Pallava" are with some inscriptions in "Pallava" script in Ceylon.

Other scripts such as Brāhmī are also found in Southeast Asia and can be dated as early as the first century CE, but they appear primarily inscribed on small seals and thus yield little information. In Khmer studies, French scholars seem reluctant to use the term "Pallava," preferring instead the term, "pré-ankorienne" for the early inscriptions. For a comparative chart of "Pallava" scripts and the "Pallava" scripts of the inscriptions found in Thailand, see *Charuek nai Prathet Thai*, vol. 1; and also an article by Kanika Wimonkasem in *Premier Symposium Franco-Thaï*, 166ff. For early scripts used in Burma, see U Tha Myat, *Pyu Reader* (in Burmese). For the "Pallava" script of Sri Lanka, see *Epigraphia Zeylanica*, vol. 5, plate 15.

2. de Casparis, "Palaeography as an Auxiliary Discipline," 387ff. See also Dani, *Indian Paleography.*

3. See de Casparis, *Prasasti Indonesia I* and *Prasasti Indonesia II.*

4. Information on the *ye dharmā* stanza and other short inscriptions can be found in the *Annual Report of the Archaeological Survey of India and the Annual Report of the Archaeological Survey of Burma.* Unfortunately, the inscriptions are rarely published in facsimile, and therefore are not accessible to palaeographic study. One source to consult is U Tha Myat, *Pyu Reader*, even though the inscriptions are traced by hand and their provenance is unknown. See also N. R. Ray, *Theravāda Buddhism in Burma.* Inscriptions found in Thailand are published in *Charuek nai Prathet Thai*, vol. 1, with passable photographs.

5. See *JRASMB* 18, part 1 (1940), especially Wales, "Ancient Indian Colonization in Malaya," 8, 23; see also Chhabra, *Expansion of Indo-Aryan Culture*; and de Casparis, *Prasasti Indonesia I* and *Prasasti Indonesia II.*

6. The gold plate inscription found in Maunggan is dated by Finot in "Un nouveau document sur le bouddhisme birman," to around the fifth century CE. Inscriptions found in Thailand are dated to around the same time. In both the Pyu and the Dvāravatī traditions, this type of inscription continues until the tenth or eleventh century. See *Charuek nai Prathet Thai*, vol. 1, 12ff.

7. See N. R. Ray, *Sanskrit Buddhism*, 19ff. These inscriptions, including a *ye dharmā* stanza, are inscribed on the pedestal of a Buddha image found in the city of Old Prome and date from the seventh century. The first inscription is written in two languages, but, unfortunately, it gives no information that would identify it with a particular school of Buddhism. Since the *ye dharmā* stanza is common to all schools of Buddhism, it, too, cannot be identified with any one school.

8. The only two Sanskrit inscriptions found in the Dvāravatī area of central Thailand are an inscribed copper plate and a lithic inscription. On the copper plate is the story of a king and his donation to a sanctuary of Śiva. See *Boranwitthaya rueang mueang U Thong*, 21–25. The lithic inscription is so badly damaged that only two words can be read, so it yields no meaningful information. See *Charuek nai Prathet Thai*, vol. 1, 129–31. There are also two seals inscribed with "*śridvāravatīśvarapuṇya*" (meritorious deeds of the King of Dvāravatī). See *Charuek nai Prathet Thai*, vol. 1, 95–97, 126–28.

9. See Bhattacharya, "Les religions brahmaniques," 17. An inscription on the back of a Buddha image reads: "ye dhammā *hetuprabhavā* tesaṃ hetuṃ tathāgato avaca/ tesañ ca yo nirodho evaṃvādī mahasamaṇo//" (the italics are mine).

10. For this stanza, see Lamotte, *Histoire du bouddhisme indien*, 547ff. For this type of inscription found in Yunnan, see two articles by Liebenthal, "Sanskrit Inscriptions from Yunnan I;" and "Sanskrit Inscriptions from Yunnan II." The stanza is also often placed at the end of chapters or at the end of Mahāyāna *sūtras* or Tantric texts such as the *Ratnaguṇasamccayagātha* and the *Pañcakrama.* See Yuyama, ed., *Prajñā-pāramitā-ratna-guna-samcaya-gāthā.* For the stanzas found in India, see Shizutani, *Indo bukkyō himei mokuroku*; and Yuyama, "'Jūni innenju' oboegaki."

11. See Bhattarcharya, "Les religions brahmaniques," 17.

12. See Oertel, "Excavations at Sârnâth," 74. Interestingly, this inscription is found with other inscriptions that mention the name "Sarvastivādin."

13. See note 8 above.

14. See, e.g., Chhabra, *Expansion of Indo-Aryan Culture*, 23, 54; and Wales, "Ancient Indian Colonization in Malaya," 7. A fourth century date for the inscriptions may be too early.

15. de Casparis, *Prasasti Indonesia II*, 123.

16. Chhabra, *Expansion of Indo-Aryan Culture*, 54–55.

17. Ibid., 22–23.

18. *Dīghanikāya* II, 49; and *Dhammapada*, v. 183.

19. Prince Damrong Rajanubhab, *Monuments of the Buddha*, 10.

20. *Charuek nai Prathet Thai*, vol. 1, 79–82.

21. See *Epigraphia Indica*, vol. 5 (1898–1899), 101ff.; Finot, "Un nouveau document," 121ff.; N. R. Ray, *Theravāda Buddhism in Burma*, 33–34.

22. Prince Damrong Rajanubhab, *Monuments of the Buddha*, 9–10.

23. N. R. Ray, *Theravāda Buddhism in Burma*, 37ff. I have been unable to locate Ray's citation from the ARASB (1938–1939). At about this time the Burma branch of the Archaeological Survey had already stopped issuing the report.

24. *Charuek nai Prathet Thai*, vol. 1, 111.

25. de Casparis, *Prasasti Indonesia II*, 47–167, especially 68–69, where he bases his conclusion mainly on the fact that *tṛṣṇā* (craving/thirst) in the *Vibhaṅga* part of the inscription is divided into three types: *kāma* (craving for sensual pleasures), *bhava* (craving to become something), and *vibhava* (craving not to become something). He regards this division as particular to the Sarvāstivādins, whereas in the Pāli canon *tṛṣṇā* would be divided in relation to the six classes of sense objects (visual, aural, and so on). The Nālandā inscription of the *Pratītyasamutpāda* with the *Vibhaṅga* represents another tradition, supposedly Mahāyāna. In this inscription, *tṛṣṇā* is divided according to the Three Realms (*kāma, rūpa, ārūpya*). Because the inscription found in Java shows no connection to Mahāyāna but is written in Sanskrit, de Casparis (pp. 69–70) concludes that

> Among the Hīnayāna Schools writing in Sanskrit, the Sarvāstivādins were the only ones known to have possessed a real canon; in addition, they were the only ones known to have developed missionary activity outside India and it is evident that the presence of our text in Indonesia is to be attributed to such an activity. Since our *Vibhaṅga* version shows no Mahāyāna influence and, in addition, is written in correct Sanskrit, there is another argument in favour of a direct connection between our *Vibhaṅga* and the Sarvāstivādin School of Buddhism.

However, the division into *kāma, bhava*, and *vibhava* is found in the Pāli canon as well, at least in the *Dhammacakkappavattanasutta,* and thus it cannot be assigned solely to the Sarvāstivādins. While de Casparis's argument from the use of Sanskrit carries some weight, I disagree that it was the Sarvāstivādins who alone possessed a "real canon," and that other Hīnayāna schools using Sanskrit had none. There is no evidence for such a conclusion. Additional evidence is needed before we can conclude that the Sarvāstivādins among all the Sanskrit Hīnayāna schools were the only ones to undertake missionary activities. The fact that the inscription shows no sign of Mahāyāna influence and thus is not Mahāyānistic, can also be applied to de Casparis's conclusion, since the text does not contain any doctrine particular to the Sarvāstivādins.

26. See Cœdès, "Une Roue de la Loi," 221–26; and Boisselier, "Roue de la Loi Lop'buri," 225–31.

27. For reference to these works, see Cœdès, "Une Roue de la Loi," 221–26.

28. The *Sāratthasamuccaya* was published in the Hewavitarne Bequest Series (Colombo), vol. 27. It is a commentary on the *Catubhāṇavāra,* a compilation of twenty-seven extracts from the *Nikāyas,* mainly from the *Khuddhakapāṭha.* We have no definitive information on the date of these two works. See *Dictionary of Pāli Proper Names,* vol. 1, 842 and vol. 2, 1107. For the *Paṭhamasambhodhikathā,* see Cœdès, "Une vie indochinoise du Bouddha."

29. *Charuek nai Prathet Thai,* vol. 1, 125.

30. *Udāna,* 1.1–3; *Dhammapada,* v. 153–54; *Charuek nai Prathet Thai,* vol. 1, 116–22.

31. *Charuek nai Prathet Thai,* vol. 1, 237–40.

32. Luce, *Old Burma-Old Pagan.*

33. *Vinaya* I, 38; *Jātaka-aṭṭhakathā* I, 84. There are a few minor differences between the text of the inscription and the one published in the Pali Text Society edition. The inclusion of some words, such as "*pavasi*" or "*siginikasavaṇṇo,*" may be due to scribal errors. The Pali Text Society version is below (words in italics differ from the text of the inscription):

> danto dantehi saha purāṇajaṭilehi *vippamutto* vippamuttehi *siṅginikkhasuvaṇṇo* rājagahaṃ *pāvasi* bhagavā. mutto muttehi saha purāṇajaṭilehi *vippamutto* vippamuttehi *siṅginikkhasuvaṇṇo* rājagahaṃ *pāvasi* bhagavā. tiṇṇo tiṇṇehi saha purāṇajaṭilehi *vippamutto* vippamuttehi *siṅginikkhasuvaṇṇo* rājagahaṃ *pāvasi* bhagavā. *dasavāso dasabalo dasadhammavidū dasabhi* c'upeto so dasasataparivāro rājagahaṃ *pāvasi* bhagavā.

34. Luce, "The Advent of Buddhism to Burma," 125–27, assigns these excerpts to specific texts, but this is an unacceptable practice since the passages sometimes appear in more than one place. Nevertheless, his list of texts does help create a picture of the *Tripiṭaka* in Pyu times. An adaptation of Luce's list appears below with my notes enclosed in brackets.

> 1. *Vinaya, Mahāvagga* I, 23. The Buddhist Creed, *ye dharmmā hetuprabhavā,* etc., the stanza spoken by Assaji, which led to the conversion of Gotama's chief disciples, Sāriputta and Moggallāna. It is engraved in Pāli on both of the Maunggan gold plates, found seven miles south of Śrīkṣetra and now at the British Museum. Edited by U Tun Nyein in *Epigraphia Indica,* vol. 5, no. 11 (1896–1899), pp. 101–2. It is found twice in Sanskrit on stones near Sandoway in the south Arakan. See E. H. Johnston, BSOAS 11, no. 2 (1944): plate 4, fig. 2, and pp. 359, 363–64, and 383. It is found in either language, set in molds, or stamped on countless terracotta votive tablets at almost all the ancient sites in Burma. As Cœdès says in JSS 20 (1926): 5–6, it "must rapidly have acquired in the eyes of the ancient Buddhists a sort of magic virtue, . . . a quite irresistible charm for the conversion to the Faith of any who had not heard it."
>
> 2. *Vinaya, Mahāvagga* I, 1. *Paṭicca-samuppāda,* the Chain of Causation. See Excerpt 1 (leaves 1 to 5) of the Khinbagôn gold leaf manuscript. In Pāli, see U Lu Pe Win, ed., ARASB, (1939), pp. 12–22. A fuller version, starting from the beginning of the *vagga,* is

shown on a stone found at Kunzeik village on the east bank of Sittaung River, some four miles northeast of Pegu. See Aung Thaw, *Historical Sites in Burma* (1972), pp. 110–11.

3. *Vinaya, Mahāvagga* I, 22. Sakka's song in praise of Gotama entering Rājagaha. See Excerpt 7 (leaves 18–19) of Khinbagôn gold leaf manuscript.

4. *Dīgha Nikāya 2. Sāmaññaphala suttanta* 49. Dr. Jīvaka's praise of Gotama before King Ajātasattu, *iti pi so bhagavā* and so on. See Excerpt 8 (leaf 20) of Khinbagôn gold leaf manuscript. Also on the second Maunggan gold plate. Also, clear but fragmentary, on the gold leaf found at Kyundawzu village, Śrīkśetra. See Charles Duroiselle, *ARASI*, (1929): plate 51 (a), and 109.

5. *Dīgha Nikāya* 16. *Mahāparinibbāna Suttanta.* List of the thirty-seven elements of Enlightenment, concluding with the Aryan eightfold path. See Excerpt 3 (leaf 6) of the Khinbagôn gold leaf manuscript. [This passage appears more than once in the canon, and thus cannot belong solely to this *sutta*.]

6. *Majjhima Nikāya* 12. *Mahāsīhanāda Sutta* 71–72. The four *Vesārajjāni* (self-confidences of a Buddha). See Excerpt 4 (leaves 6–14) of the Khinbagôn gold leaf manuscript. [This passage also appears in numerous places in the canon.]

7. *Khuddaka Nikāya* 2. *Dhammapada gāthā* 273. The four "Bests" (*seṭṭho*). See Excerpt 5 (leaf 18) of the Khinbagôn gold leaf manuscript.

8. *Khuddaka Nikāya* 12. *Paṭisambhidāmagga.* The fourteen *buddhañāṇāni* (enlightened knowledges). See Excerpt 5 (leaves 14–17) of the Khinbagôn gold leaf manuscript.

9. The first Maunggan gold plate lists also in ascending numbers the four *iddhipādā* (bases of potency); four *sammappadhānā* (right efforts); four *satipaṭṭhānā* (earnest thoughts); four *ariyasaccāni* (noble truths); four *vesārajjani* (confidences); five *indriyāni* (senses [Luce is wrong here: as qualities, *indriyāni* is the same as *balāni,* faculties (or forces) used to attain enlightenment and not the senses.]); five *cakkūni* (eyes [of a Buddha]); six *asaddharaṇāni* (uniquenesses of a Buddha); seven *bojjhaṅgā* (elements of Buddhahood [actually, elements of enlightenment, for *arhats*, not just the Buddha]); *ariyo aṭṭhangiko maggo* (eightfold noble path); nine *lokuttarā dhammā* (supernatural [supramundane?] states); ten *balāni* (strengths); fourteen *buddhaññāṇāni* (Buddha knowledges) eighteen *buddhadhammāni* (conditions of Buddhahood). [This is probably derived from a list like the *Dasuttara Suttanta* of the *Dīghanikāya.*]

10. *Abhidhamma Vibhaṅga* (PTS 6, 144). Pāli stone fragment (three pieces) found on the second terrace of the Bawbawgyi pagoda, Śrīkṣetra. See *ARASI* (1911): plate 47 (fig. 1 and 2) and p. 89; (1912): plate 68 (fig. 1) and pp. 141–42. Edited by Finot in *JA* 20 (July–August 1912): 134–36, and (July–August 1913): 193–95. [Although Finot identifies this excerpt as being from the *Dhammasangaṇī,* Duroiselle suggests that it is from the *Vibhaṅga.* They could both be right or both wrong, since there is no exact counterpart to the inscription. We have to assume that it derives from *abhidhamma* text that is very close to these two.]

11. Buddhaghosa, *Visuddhimagga,* chapter 21 (Ñāṇamoli, *Path of Purification,* 745). List of seven of the eight *ñāṇadassanā* (contemplative knowledges) mentioned at the

beginning of the chapter. See Excerpt 3 (leaf 5) of the Khinbagôn gold leaf manuscript. [N. R. Ray calls this, *vipassanañāṇa*, and I follow Ray. With all the parallels in the Pāli canon, it is rather surprising that Luce does not conclude that these inscriptions belong to the Theravāda tradition.]

35. The text is given here according to the inscriptions, but some spellings may not agree with the received form. Emendations given in brackets belong to N. R. Ray. In the Pali Text Society's edition of the *Paṭisambhidāmagga* (p. 133), the concluding passage reads:

> Imāni cuddasa Buddhañāṇāni. Imesaṃ cuddasannaṃ Buddhañāṇānaṃ aṭṭha ñāṇāni sāvakasādhāraṇāni, cha ñāṇāni asādhāraṇāni sāvakehi.

36. See note 34, no. 10.
37. See Wales, "Ancient Indian Colonization in Malaya," 8–9. The following translation is provided: "There are ten *bala* (powers), four *vaiśāradya* (assurances, extraordinary skills), and eighteen *dharma āveṇikā* of the Buddhas. The dharmas (moments of consciousness) that arise from co-operating circumstances have in no case real existence; there can be nowhere any (dharmas) which do not exist in the state of reality. Who knows this summit of the universe to be at the same time no summit—his knowledge, having reached the summit, extends over all dharmas." The translation of the second and third stanzas is awkwardly worded. Parallel verses appear in the *Mūlamadhyamakakārikā* 1.5, 1.12, 15.6, and so on.
38. For this text see, *Bussho kaisetsu daijiten*, vol. 2, 31–32.
39. See note 34, no. 4. See also, N. R. Ray, *Theravāda Buddhism in Burma*, 33–34.
40. *Charuek nai Prathet Thai*, vol. 1, 179–86.
41. *Kamaraten* is a Khmer title for a high government official.
42. Goonaratne, ed. "*Telakaṭāhagāthā*," 49.
43. *Prachum silacharuek*, vol. 3, no. 56.
44. B. C. Law, tr. "*Telakaṭāhagāthā*," 25ff., provides an introduction to his translation in which he notes:

> The *Telakaṭāhagāthā* (verses on oil-pot) is a non-canonical Pāli poem dated the 10th or 11th century A.D. containing 98 stanzas written in chaste language. Its author is unknown. The story of this poem can be found in the *Mahāvaṃsa* (Ch. 22; narrated as briefly as possible), the *Rasavāhinī* and the Sinhalese work *Saddhammālaṅkāra*, which is a compilation from the *Rasavāhinī*. The story is somewhat differently narrated in the *Kākavaṇṇatissārāññavatthu*. It is apparent from a careful study of the poem that the author was well acquainted with the texts and commentaries of the Buddhist scriptures and that he knew Sanskrit well. Although two stanzas at the end are missing, it is no doubt a *Sataka* (a poem in 100 stanzas). . . . The poem contains the religious exhortations of a Thera named Kalyāṇiya who was condemned to be thrown into a vessel of boiling oil as he was suspected to be an aider and abettor to an intrigue with the queen of King Kalaṇitissa who reigned at Kelaniya.

45. Uraisri Varasarin, personal communication with the author, August 1989.
46. See, e.g., N. R. Ray, *Theravāda Buddhism in Burma*, 45, who claims that it was not until the middle of the twelfth century that Ceylon came to play any important role in the history of Buddhism.

47. Most scholars are very conservative on the question of whether ancient Southeast Asia possessed a complete canon. From the *Telakaṭāhagāthā* we can infer that it is likely that the region possessed at least most parts of the canon, and that may very well have been the entire Pāli canon. See note 34.

48. *Charuek nai Prathet Thai*, vol. 1, 287–91. All quoted material from *Charuek nai Prathet Thai* strictly follows the spelling provided therein.

49. See Briggs, "Syncretism of Religions," 230–49. For a better study, see Filliozat, "Sur le çivaïsme et le bouddhisme du Cambodge," 59–99.

50. *Charuek nai Prathet Thai*, vol. 3, 107.

51. Ibid., 176–80.

52. For a detailed explanation of the four bodies, see *Bukkyō daijiten*, vol. 2, 1789–1791. See also, Nagao, "Theory of the Buddha-Body," 32–33, who explains:

> The sāṃbhogika-kāya, the second body, is the same as the Reward-body described above [saṃbhoga-kāya]. Saṃbhoga means "enjoyment." . . . The Buddha's biography tells us that after he attained his enlightenment under the bodhi-tree, the Buddha spent several weeks pondering, with appreciation, over the dharma which he himself had realized. This is called "the Buddha's own enjoyment of the dharma-delight." . . . But this "for one's own enjoyment" later developed into "for the enjoyment of others." This is the sharing of one's own dharma-delight with others, i.e. the preaching of the dharma to others. Therefore, the sāṃbhogika-kāya is said to be the Buddha-body seen at an assembly for sermons—a gathering of people who wish to hear the Buddha's preaching. This is none other than a Buddha-body that is visible, in the sense that human beings can understand it intellectually (and emotionally, as well).

53. *Charuek nai Prathet Thai*, vol. 4, 189–201, 202–14.

54. Damais, "Études d'épigraphie indonésienne II," 43. See also the two works by de Casparis, *Prasasti Indonesia I* and *Prasasti Indonesia II*.

55. "Inscription de Vat Sithor (Srei Santhor)" in *Inscriptions du Cambodge*, vol. 6, 195ff.

56. Diffloth, "Reconstructing Dvāravatī-Old Mon," 117ff. This article contains a summary of Old Mon inscriptions found in Thailand. The earliest ones date to the sixth century. For a study of the vernacular languages in which Southeast Asian inscriptions are written, see Shorto, "Linguistic Protohistory," 273–80.

57. Examples of this type of inscription are published in *Charuek nai Prathet Thai*, vol. 2. The texts have been transliterated into the Thai script and are translated into Thai only.

58. The English translation is mine. The original can be found in Ibid., 81.

59. The English translation is mine. The original can be found in Ibid., 42–47. It is possible that the word *kundarījana* could be a form of the Pāli word *kuṇḍalī*, which means "one who wears an earring."

60. Ibid., vol. 1, 251–67, 280–83.

61. Ibid., vol. 3, 105–17. See, e.g.:

> Ekatra saṅgatāmūrtti ssthāpitā śambhuśārṅginoḥ/
> śrīvatsenātra pūrvvayā sāmagnā cirakālataḥ//
> munivedādriśākendre munīndrapratimā punaḥ/
> tenāpi yajvanā sthāne sthāpitā śaṅkrātprati//

bhūyaśśilāmayī devī sthāpitā sugatātprati/
nāmnā śrīśikharasvāmi dvijena varajvanā//

This roughly translates as: He [Yajñavarāha] cast images of Śiva and Brahma together with Viṣṇu [and set them] in the same place. These images had long merged into the east bank of the river. In Śaka 849 [955 C.E.], in addition to establishing an image of Śiva, he [Śikharasvāmi] also established an image of the Buddha in the same place. Moreover, this Brāhmana Śikharasvāmi, in addition to establishing the Buddha image, also established a stone image of the Devī.

See also Bhattacharya, "Les religions brahmaniques," 27, 34ff.

62. For references, see Ibid.

63. Ibid., 34ff.

64. The English translation is mine. See *Charuek nai Prathet Thai*, vol. 3, 159–63; *Inscriptions du Cambodge*, K. 410; see also Cœdès, *Prachum Silacharuek phak thi* 2, no. 19.

65. *Charuek nai Prathet Thai*, vol. 1, 254. In the cited passage, a missing syllable is marked: "-", and a full stop is marked: "/".

66. Ibid., 187–222.

67. The English translation is mine. See Ibid., 44–47; Cœdès, *Prachum silacharuek phak thi* 2, 34–36, no. 27. (The meter is *śārdūravikrīḍita* except for the last stanza in *indravajra*. A long syllable is marked: "-", and a short syllable is marked: "/").

(2) - - - / / - / - / / / - - - / - - / -
- - - ha caṅkramāśanagéhaṃ soposadhāgārakam
bhaktaṃ sāṅghikapaudgalam pratidinnaṃ.....r./ - - / -
- - - / / - / - / / / - - - / - - / -

(3) - - - / / - / - / / / - - - / - - / -
--(p)āramitārccanaṃ sahamaśīpatrārppaṇaṃ lekhanam
ijyāgastimahātmano dvijagaṇasyānnañ c. - - / -
- - - / / - / - / / / - - - / - - / -

(4) - - - / / - / - / / / - - - / - - / -
(tyā)g(e) nārahitā sadharmmakathanā dhūpapradīpānvitā
mālādāmavitānacāmaravatī cīnadhv(aj) ----
- - - / / - / - / / / - - - / - - / -

(5) - - - / / - / - / / / - - - / - - / -
(p)uṇyañ canyad api pradiṣṭam aniśaṃ dharmmaù prajapālanam
iṣṭāniṣṭasamatvam indriyajayaù khedas su. ṛ.. ṛ / -
- - - / / - / - / / / - - - / - - / -

(6) - - / - - / / - / - -
- ryyāptabhogena y / - / - -
arnnā*yanāmā g* / / - / - -
- / - - / / - / - -

68. See two articles by Liebenthal, "Sanskrit Inscriptions from Yunnan I," 1–40; and "Sanskrit Inscriptions from Yunnan II," 1–23. See also note 10 of this chapter.

69. For examples, see *Epigraphia Indica*, vol. 20 (1929–1930): 16–17, 19ff., 21ff.; *Epigraphia Indica*, vol. 35 (1963–1964): 6ff. One difference is that in the inscriptions, consonant

clusters are usually written as a single consonant. For example, *raño* is written as *raññо* and *budhasa* as *buddhassa*. Declensions like *nānadesasamanagatānaṃ* and verb forms like *parigahitam* or *hotu* are essentially the same as in Pāli. It is worth noting that the inscriptions that use a language with close affinities to Pāli are from sites in the Andhra area, such as Nāgārjunakoṇḍa and Amarāvatī. The schools mentioned include Aparaseliyas, Caityakas, Kāśyapīyas, Bhadarāyaṇīyas, and, of course, the "Theriyānaṃ Tambapaṇṇakānaṃ." Inscriptions from northern or western India usually use a language closer to Sanskrit. The language associated with a particular school probably arose out of the local dialect rather than vice versa. It is logical to assume that a regional Sangha would use the forms and sounds to which it was accustomed. The Sangīti of the Buddhists written in a northern location, for example, would probably sound closer to Sanskrit, and over time, the text becomes Sanskritized. The same would be true for the south with a language that sounds like Pāli, and after time and use, the text becomes standardized in that language. The true significance of the word, "*saṅgīti*," which we suggest may be a form of "aural editing" or "proofing by the sounds," differs from the present visual system of reading a text.

70. For example, the Sarvastivādins, the Mahāsāṅghikas, and the Dharmaguptakas also used their own versions of Sanskrit.

71. See Gunawardana, "Buddhist Nikāyas," 57.

72. See, e.g., articles in *ARASI, ARASB,* and *BEFEO*. Recent excavation reports and finds in Thailand are published by the Department of Fine Arts, usually in Thai only. For an English language source on archaeological finds in Thailand, see Higham, *Archaeology of Mainland Southeast Asia*.

73. Wheatley, *Golden Khersonese*, 193. The list comes from Wales, *Making of Greater India*.

74. See Bhattacharya, "Les religions brahmaniques," 18ff.; and Sirisena, *Sri Lanka and South-East Asia*. See also Auboyer et al., *Oriental Art*, 97ff., where Sri Lanka is included in the section on Southeast Asia. The authors note that: "It is mainly on the account of Sri Lanka's (Ceylon's) influence that the chapter devoted to that country has been placed as an introduction to the section of this book dealing with South-east Asia . . . It seems likely that Sri Lanka served as a link between India and South-east Asia during the very earliest centuries of Indian influence in that part of the world, and the development of the island's influence there has continued almost unbroken to this day."

75. See Dupont, "Les Buddha dits d'Amarāvatī;" and D'Ancona, "Amarāvati."

76. For example, art in the Dvāravatī region came under the influence of the Khmer who dominated the area early in the eleventh century, and the art of Śrīvijaya in the south was influenced by both Dvāravatī and the Khmer. The art of Dvāravatī in northeastern Thailand was highly localized, but Khmer artistic influences were also sometimes present.

77. *Borankhadi si phak*, 107ff.

78. Sirisena, *Sri Lanka and South-East Asia*.

79. See note 59 of this chapter.

80. Dupont, *L'archeologie mône de Dvārvati*; Piriya Krairiksh, *Buddhist Folk Tales*.

81. See, e.g., Srisakra Vallibhotama, *Borankhadi Thai nai thotsawat thi phan ma*.

82. The following schools figure in the inscriptions found around Amarāvatī and Nāgārjunakoṇḍa: Bahuśrutīyas, Caityakas, Pūrvaśailas, Aparamahāvanaseliyas, Aparaseliyas, Siddhārthikas, and the Tambapaṇṇakas (Theravādins).

83. Boisselier in *Boranwitthaya rueang mueang U Thong*, 161ff.

84. For studies on the concept of "*stūpa*," see Gombaz, "L'Évolution du stūpa;" and Snodgrass, *Symbolism of the Stupa.*

85. For Barabudur, see de Casparis, *Prasasti Indonesia I*; Mus, *Barabudur*; and Gomez and Woodward, *Barabudur: History and Significance.* For literary sources, see Lewis Lancaster cited in Gomez and Woodward.

86. Dupont, "Les Buddha dits d' Amarāvatī."

87. D'Ancona, "Amarāvati." See also Griswold, "Imported Images," 37–73.

88. See Auboyer, et al., *Oriental Art*, 364ff.; and for explanations of these *mudrās*, see Saunders, *Mudrā: A Study of Symbolic Gestures.*

89. In Auboyer, et al., *Oriental Art*, 374ff.

90. There are good examples of the Buddha images in Snellgrove, *Image of the Buddha.* See, e.g., the photographs on pages: 111 (Gupta style); 150 (Dvāravatī style); and 159 (central Javanese style).

91. See Aung-Thwin, *Pagan*, 36–37; Luce, *Old Burma-Early Pagan*, vol. 1, 184–200; and N. R. Ray, *Sanskrit Buddhism.*

92. Boelès, "Two Yoginis of Hevajra," 14–30.

93. See Wayman, "Theory of Barabudur as a Mandala," 139–72.

94. Horsch, "The Wheel," 63.

95. Ibid., 71.

96. See examples and pictures in Irwin, "'Asokan' Pillars."

97. For an excellent study done in Thailand, see Dhanit Yupho, *Dharmacakra.* An English translation is available in *Thai Culture, New Series*, No. 25.

98. In "'Asokan' Pillars," Irwin describes the early pillars in ancient India from pre-Aśokan times onward. He notes that they were placed directly on the ground without any foundation. For that reason, they usually collapsed quickly. One such collapse was recorded in a Buddhist legend found in the *Maitreya-avadāna* of the *Divyāvadāna*, in which the collapsed pillar was set aright by a *cakravartin.*

99. Srisakra Vallibhotama in *Premier Symposium Franco-Thaï*, 343–57.

100. Cœdès, "Tablettes votives bouddhique," 145–67.

101. Foucher, *La vie du Bouddha*, 65ff.

102. For early examples of these votive tablets, see *Charuek nai Prathet Thai*, vols. 1 and 2. For ones in Burma, see Luce, *Old Burma-Early Pagan*, vol. 1, 15–16.

103. See Fontein, "Notes on the Jātakas and Avandānas of Barabudur," 85–108.

104. Piriya Krairiksh, *Buddhist Folk Tales*, 1.

105. Ibid., 1–2. For an excellent review that adds further information, see Nandana Chutiwongs, "On the Jataka Reliefs," 133–51.

106. Jean Boisselier, personal communication with the author, September 1988.

107. The *Kacchapajātaka* depicted in the Dvāravatī bas-relief is the version that appears in the *Jātakasatava*, a work that cannot be ascribed with certainty to any one school. See Konow, "Remarks on the Khotanese Jātakastava," 255–67; and Yuyama, *Kacchapa-Jātaka.* In *Buddhist Folk Tales*, Piriya Krairiksh uses this particular bas-relief to show that the source was not the Theravādin *Jātaka*; however, neither was it in the Sarvāstivādin *Avadāna.*

108. Piriya Krairiksh, *Buddhist Folk Tales*, 1–2.

109. Strong, "The Buddhist Avadānists," 862–81. Strong has written an informative discussion of the formation of *Avadāna* literature. The end result of this formation, the *Avadānaśataka*, is a compilation that took several hundred years. Strong links this literature to Upagupta as its patron saint.

110. Piriya Krairiksh, *Buddhist Folk Tales*, 21.

111. The number, names, and the order of the *Jātaka* stories vary among the different collections in Sri Lanka, Burma, and Thailand. See Luce, "The 550 Jātakas in Old Burma," 296ff., for examples of variants by name, most of which Luce regards as scribal errors. He also gives a list of titles whose differences cannot be blamed on scribal error (see p. 301). There are also three *Jātaka*s that are not found in the Sri Lankan recension.

112. If it were possible to ascribe all the great *stūpa*s to a specific school, it would be very difficult for one like Barabudur, since its bas-reliefs are drawn from texts of several schools, such as the *Mahākarmavibhaṅga,* different sources of the *Jātaka*s and *Avadāna*s, and the Mahāyāna *Gaṇḍavyūha.*

113. See Jaini, *Paññasa-Jātaka*, vols. 1 and 2; and Norman, *Pāli Literature*, 177–79. Norman writes, "It has already been noted that the Pāli Jātaka collection is by no means complete, and stories not included in that collection can be found elsewhere in the Pāli canon and also in Buddhist Sanskrit literature. There is also a collection of 50 Jātaka stories current in South-East Asia, generally referred to as 'apocryphal' because they are not canonical."

114. Paranavitana, "Mahāyānism in Ceylon," 37ff.

115. Ibid., 44. Paranavitana states:

> The plaques at Indikutasāya and Vijiyārāma show that the Buddhists of Ceylon, especially those with Mahāyānistic leanings, had the practice of depositing, in *caityas*, metal plates on which were inscribed short extracts from the Sanskrit Buddhist writings. Their purpose is explained in a passage in the *Saddharma-ratnākara.* The 13th chapter of this work informs us that King Kassapa—which of the five who bore this name, it is not expressly stated—increased the height of the Abhayagirivihāra to 140 cubits and deposited the Dharmmadhātu therein. Later in the chapter, the author includes the *dhammacetiya* among the five different kinds of *stūpas.* By this term he evidently meant a tope built to enshrine fragments from the Dhamma (the sacred texts). The examples found in Indikatusāya and Vajirārāma are small and disconnected fragments and would bear the same relation to the whole body of the Dhamma as a small relic of the Buddha's body does to the corporeal frame. We have seen above that the Mahāyānists held that the Buddha had three bodies of which the Dharmmakāya or the body of the law was the most important; and the earthly body, the Nirmānakāya, to which belonged the relics enshrined in the early *stūpas,* was the least. To the mind of the average man the Dharmmakāya must have been represented by the written words of the Buddha, and the fragments of these would very well [be] called Dharmmadhātu and enshrined in the *stūpas* instead of bodily relics. This way of reasoning must have been particularly welcome at the time when the zeal for building the *stūpas* was unbounded while the supply of the bodily relics of the Buddha must have necessarily been limited. It is probable that this extension of the veneration at first paid to bodily relics of the Buddha to metal fragments on which words attributed to him were written was due to the influence of the Mahāyāna conception of the three bodies.

116. See Schopen, "Vajracchedikā," 147–81.

117. Dohanian, *Mahāyāna Buddhist Sculpture*, 20ff.

118. Oertel, "Excavations at Sârnâth," 74.

119. Dohanian, *Mahāyāna Buddhist Sculpture*, 3.

120. Lewis Lancaster, personal communication with the author, September 1989.

121. Part of the surviving text was published by Bongard-Levin in the *Indo-Iranian Journal* (1969): 269–80. The text appears to be a list of important works and teachings that together are regarded as the *dharmakāya*.

122. See *Dīghanikāya* II, 8; and *Saṃyuttanikāya* II, 143ff.

123. See Yuyama, "'Jūni innenju' oboegaki."

124. Paranavitana, "Mahāyānism in Ceylon," 45.

125. For this type of reasoning, see de Casparis, *Prasasti Indonesia II*, 69; N. R. Ray, *Sanskrit Buddhism*; and Piriya Krairiksh, *Buddhist Folk Tales*.

126. For the origin and development of Pāli, see Bechert, "Some Sidelights on the Early History of Pāli Lexicography;" Norman, *Pāli Literature*, 1–14; and Norman, "Pāli Language," 29–54.

127. This was inscribed on the back of a votive tablet depicting the Eight Great Episodes of the Buddha's life. The style is definitely Pāla, the language is Pāli, and the script is Devanāgarī. See *Charuek nai Prathet Thai*, vol. 5, 231–20.

128. See Norman, *Pāli Literature*; and Norman, "Pāli Language."

129. Paranavitana, "Mahāyānism in Ceylon."

130. See, e.g., Aiyappan and Srinivasan, *Story of Buddhism*, 74–75.

131. See, e.g., Filliozat, "Sur le çivaïsme et le bouddhisme," 73. The pediment of an Uposatha hall is usually decorated with Brahmanical gods like Brahma and Viṣṇu. In Thailand, it is common to see a Śivaliṅga within a monastery compound.

132. See Aiyappan and Srinivasan, *Story of Buddhism*, 59: "In view of the fact that Buddhists who migrated from North India and settled in Andhradesa built huge stūpas and called them mahachaityas and perpetuated their worship, they came to be distinguished as the Chaityakas." The authors do not cite any reference to substantiate this statement. *Stūpas* erected by other schools, as recorded in inscriptions, were also called *mahācaitya*.

133. Ray uses other scripts and Chinese sources to support his theory, but the scripts of North and South India were used equally in recording Pāli and Sanskrit. Chinese sources record the existence of the Sarvāstivādins in Magadha as well as provide information on other schools flourishing at the same time. The evidence is too sparse to come to any definitive conclusion.

134. Srisakra Vallibhotama, "Political and Cultural Continuities," 229ff. Srisakra is of the opinion that it was Mahāyāna from the Khmer tradition that brought various centers and states into close contact, perhaps because Mahāyāna Buddhism was used for administrative purposes in the Khmer tradition. The Khmer territory from the ninth century on was organized as a great *maṇḍala* with a centralized polity. Later, the Thai adopted this concept, using not Mahāyāna, but Theravāda. Yet Theravāda in Thailand was not supplanted by Mahāyāna because both schools of Buddhism were recognized by the king.

135. See Snellgrove, *Image of the Buddha*, 146ff. Snellgrove asserts the following (Boisselier could be Snellgrove's source here):

> Yet the Thaton region has yielded no indication of the existence of local workshops or of images comparable in antiquity with the vestiges found on the site of the former Prome. This absence of any genuinely ancient evidence raises a problem that has been stressed by most authors. While we are unable to suggest a possible explanation, we would at least emphasize that a bronze statue (Pl. 101), undeniably in the Gupta style, is of very special interest. Beyond all doubt imported, it suggests that, in the region where the Theravāda school was the most firmly established, iconography underwent a regeneration that is comparable to that observed in the Pyu country and due to the same influences; the newly introduced Gupta style seems at first to have existed side by side with the original school in the Āndhra tradition, and then to have gradually ousted it.

In the case of the Pyu, the Gupta style did superseded the Andhra style, but this does not apply to Thaton. First, there is no other image in the Andhra style, nor any local image that could be altered to the Gupta style. Second, due to a paucity of data, one cannot conclusively assert that Thaton, a site with little evidence of Buddhism, was "the region where the Theravada school was the most firmly established." That statement best fits the case of the Pyu, but not Thaton.

136. N. R. Ray, *Brahmanical Gods.*

137. Luce, *Old Burma-Early Pagan*, vol. 1, 18; Aung-Thwin, *Pagan*, 32; and Spiro, *Burmese Supernaturalism.*

138. See Duroiselle, "Aris of Burma," 79–93.

139. See I-Tsing, *Record of the Buddhist Religion*, 13ff. Yi Jing (I-Tsing) tells a very informative story on this matter:

> King Bimbisāra once saw in a dream that a piece of cloth was torn, and a gold stick broken, both into eighteen fragments. Being frightened, he asked the Buddha the reason. In reply the Buddha said: "More than a hundred years after my attainment of Nirvāṇa, there will arise a king, named Aśoka, who will rule over the whole of Jambudvīpa. At that time, my teaching handed down by several Bhikṣus will be split into eighteen schools, all agreeing, however, in the end, that is to say, all attaining the goal of Final Liberation (Mokṣa). The dream foretells this, O king, you need not be afraid!" Which of the four schools should be grouped with the Mahāyāna or with the Hīnayāna is not determined. In northern India and in the islands of the Southern Sea, they generally belong to the Hīnayāna, while those in China devote themselves to the Mahāyāna; in other places, some practise in accordance with one, some with the other. Now let us examine what they pursue. Both adopt one and the same discipline (Vinaya), and they have in common the prohibitions of the five skandhas ("groups of offences"), and also the practice of the Four Noble Truths. Those who worship the Bodhisattvas and read the Mahāyāna sūtras are called the Mahāyānists (the Great), while those who do not perform these are called the Hīnayānists (the Small).

It is interesting to note that the *Abhidharmadīpa*, a Sarvāstivādin work, defends the fact that members of that school also worship bodhisattvas, not just the Mahāyānists. The Theravādins would probably defend themselves in the same way.

140. See *Epigraphia Indica*, vol. 20 (1929–1930): 16–17. Compare this with pages 165–66. In the first inscription, a member of the royalty supports the Aparaseliyas, and in

the second inscription, a person who may be the grandmother of the person in the first inscription, supports the Mahīśāsakas. Both refer to a king in the Ikśvāku dynasty. In the same volume there is an inscription of the Theravādins, which also praises the king of this dynasty for his support (see pp. 22ff.).

141. I-Tsing, *Record of the Buddhist Religion*, 9ff. The identification of Dvāravatī with Ayudhya (Ayutthaya)—a much later polity in the same region—is wrong.

142. Bhattacharya, "Les religions brahmaniques," 27ff.

143. de Casparis, *Prasasti Indonesia II*, 70.

144. See Blagden, "Notes on Talaing Epigraphy."

145. Aung-Thwin, *Pagan*, 17; Guillon, "Jalon pour une histoire du bouddhisme," 123–24.

146. N. R. Ray, *Theravāda Buddhism in Burma*, 44ff.

147. See Richman, *Women, Branch Stories, and Religious Rhetoric*, 160ff., and the footnotes on pages 237–39. For Buddhism in South India see, A. Aiyappan and P. R. Srinivasan, *Story of Buddhism* (note that numerous statements in this book are not substantiated); Indrapala, "Buddhism among the Tamils;" Law, *Buddhistic Studies*; Minakshi, "Buddhism in South India;" Thani Nayagam, "Earliest Jain and Buddhist Teaching;" and Sastri, "Ancient Indian Contacts."

148. See *Epigraphia Indica*, vol. 20 (1929): 22ff. The English translation is mine. Vogel, the editor of the inscription, translates *theriyānaṃ* as "masters." Dutt thinks that the word refers to "senior nuns" (*bhikṣuṇī*). However, in the next inscription *theriyānaṃ* is qualified by *mahāvihāravāsinaṃ*. If *therī* = senior *bhikṣuṇī*, then it should be qualified by *mahāvihāravāsininām*. Vogel is correct to translate it as "masters." It could refer to the Theravādin school. The original inscription, which Masao Shizutani dates to 250–275 CE, reads as follows:

> (1.1) Sidhaṃ namo bhagavato . . . Kasmira-Gaṃdhāra-Chīna-Chilāta-Tosali-Avaraṃta-Vaṃga-Vanavāsi-Yava[na]-Da[mila-Pa]lura Taṃbapaṃṇi-dīpa-pasādakānaṃ theriyānaṃ Taṃbapa[ṃ]ṇakānaṃ suparigahe . . .

It is interesting to note that while the Chinese are said to have been converted by the Tambapaṇṇakas, Suvarṇabhūmi does not appear in the list of this inscription or the one cited in note 149 below. Also, the monastic group identifies itself as "Tambapaṇṇakas" rather than Theravādins. Vasubandhu also used the term "Tambapaṇṇakas" (and not Theravādins) to refer to the Sangha of Sri Lanka.

149. *Epigraphia Indica*, vol. 33 (1959–1960): 250. The editors, D. C. Sircar and A. N. Lahiri, date this inscription to the third century CE. Their translation of the inscription, however, could be misleading. They translate *attha* as "meaning," but *vyajana* (*vyañjana*) as "implication," and *ariyavaṃsapavenidharanaṃ* as "who know the traditions of the (four) classes of (Buddhist) recluses by heart." The English translation of the inscription is mine. The inscription reads:

1. Sidhaṃ āchariyanaṃ theriyānaṃ Vibhaja-vādānaṃ Kasmira-Gaṃdhāra-Yavana-Vanavāsa-Taṃbapaṃnidipa-pasādakanaṃ
2. Mahāvihāra-vāsinaṃ nava[ṃ]ga-Sathu-sasana-atha-vjayana-vinichhaya-visaradanaṃ ariya-va[ṃ]sa-paveni-dharanaṃ
3. vihāre Bhagavato pāda-saṃghāḍā nipatiṭhapito sava-satānaṃ hita-sukh-athanāya ti.

150. See Dohanian, *Mahāyāna Buddhist Sculpture*, 12ff.

151. Ibid., 16–17; see also Norman, *Pāli Literature*, 41, 70n, who discusses Sri Lankans' link with the Buddhism practiced in North India: "Despite the separation of the Sinhalese Buddhists from North India, it seems that literary material continued to reach Ceylon. . . . The break between North India and Ceylon was clearly not an abrupt one, or even a complete one, for Theravādins continued to reside near Bodhgayā for some centuries. The fame of the Sinhalese commentaries was sufficiently widespread in North India to attract Buddhaghosa to Ceylon."

152. See Lamotte, "Le traite de l'acte de Vasubandhu," 250: Dans les sūtra du Tāmraparṇīyanikāya, cette connaissance est nommée connaissance membre-d'existence (bhavāṅgavijñāna) . . ."

153. See Dohanian, *Mahāyāna Buddhist Sculpture*, chaps. 2–3.

154. Bareau, *Les sectes bouddhiques du Petit Véhicule*, 34.

155. N. R. Ray, *Theravāda Buddhism in Burma*, 45.

156. Ibid., 24ff.

157. For examples, see *JRASMB* (1940), plate 8. The script is southern Indian, and the language is Sanskrit. Compare it with *Charuek nai Prathet Thai*, vol. 5, 213ff., where the script is northern Indian, and indeed the inscription was probably engraved in North India, but the language is Pāli.

158. de Casparis, *Prasasti Indonesia II*.

159. See also Norman, "The Pāli Language," 70.

Chapter 5

1. Cœdès, *Indianized States*, 9.

2. Mus, *India Seen from the East*, 367–41. Originally published in French in *BEFEO*.

3. Ibid., 9.

4. Ibid. For a definition of animism and how the term developed, see *Encyclopedia of Religion*, vol. 1, 290–302.

5. Mus, *India Seen from the East*, 9.

6. Ibid., 10.

7. Ibid.

8. Ibid., 13ff.

9. Ibid., 14.

10. Ibid., 16–18.

11. Ibid., 28ff.

12. The term "localization" is used when a god becomes identified with the soil or land of a particular locale. However, it does not mean that such a localized god completely loses its original character. In studying the culture of Southeast Asia, the term is most often used to show how an indigenous culture has influenced an imported one. See generally Wolters, *History, Culture and Region*.

13. Mus, *India Seen from the East*, 19. Mus asserts that:

> Indology, preoccupied with its classical reminiscences and its Indo-European interests, has, as far as I know, almost completely neglected to use the scattered but ancient and

> specific documents which would attest, on the Indian side, very similar beliefs. In the Jātaka, the Sutta, and the Aṭṭhakathā of the Pāli tradition may be found all the elements of a government of the beyond: the family genie is responsible to the genie of the town, and he in turn to the gods presiding over the four quarters; these, finally, obey Indra, whose divine city is represented on earth by the capital of the kingdom, in a sense its material "double."

Mus's statement, quite interestingly, can be substantiated just by looking at the full official name of the city of Bangkok, which includes such phrases as "*mahindrāyudhyā, sakkadutiyavessukammaprasiddha* (*śakradvītyavaiśvakarmaprasiddha*)."

14. Ibid., 31.
15. Ibid., 35.
16. Ibid., 36.
17. Ibid., 51ff.
18. Wales, *Prehistory and Religion*, 5ff.
19. Ibid., 17.
20. Ibid., 20ff.
21. Ibid., 30.
22. Ibid., 34ff.
23. Ibid., 35ff. Wales criticizes Mus for his restricted viewpoint, which fails to recognize the importance not only of the mountain, but also that the association of the ancestor and earth god was due to a fusion of cultures. What Wales means by cultures in this context are the cultures of the Old Asiatic (the cult of the soil) and the Old Megalithic cultures.
24. Wales, *Prehistory and Religion*, 21.
25. Quoted in Ibid., 23. See also *Encyclopedia of Religion*, vol. 9, 336–46; and Smith and Watson, *Early South East Asia*, 242–54.
26. Wales, *Prehistory and Religion*, 25.
27. Ibid., 30ff.
28. Ibid., chap. 3.
29. Ibid., 61–62.
30. Ibid., 50.
31. Ibid., 107.
32. See *Encyclopedia of Religion*, vol. 13, 513ff.; and Cœdès, *Making of South East Asia.*
33. Wales, *Prehistory and Religion*, 107.
34. Ibid., 126. Cœdès also holds that the process of "Iṇdianization" was in decline by the fourteenth century. The principle by which he measures this phenomenon is the use of Sanskrit. Actually, the factors and forces of Indian culture are still active in Southeast Asia, even though they no longer come directly from India.
35. For a full explanation of his theory of "local genius," see Wales, *Making of Greater India.*
36. Wales, *Prehistory and Religion*, 109ff., especially, 125–26; 172–75.
37. Ibid., 110–11. See also Bandaranayake, *Sinhalese Monastic Architecture*, 9n1, who comments on Wales's theory of "local genius" as follows:

> Whatever might be thought of Wales' somewhat simplistic interpretation of his material in developing this hypothesis, it must be conceded that in comparison to some other approaches it is at least an attempt to investigate a fundamental historical problem by a rational method. . . . However, in the course of our analysis we make certain observations about Ceylon and the Sinhalese tradition which have some relevance to the concept of "Indianisation." This problem so far as has been dealt with mainly by scholars whose work has been concentrated on the art and architecture of the South-East Asian countries. This applies to Quaritch Wales, himself, whose observations on Ceylon are based on such apparently superficial reading that they are of little value. We [Bandaranayake], ourselves, reject Wales' division of the South and South-East Asian region into a western and an eastern zone, seen from the viewpoint of a seminal Indian source. . . .

38. See Snellgrove, *Image of the Buddha*, 139–64.

39. Mus, *India Seen from the East*, 19–21.

40. For words that refer to a king in various languages of Southeast Asia, see note 93 below.

41. See Porée-Maspero, *Études sur les rites agraire des cambodgienss*; Souyris-Rolland, "Contribution à l'étude du culte des génies tutelaires;" Anuman Rajadhon, *Essays on Thai Folklore*; and Mulder, "Concepts of Power and Moral Goodness."

42. See Ibid.

43. *Encyclopedia of Religion*, vol. 10, 352–60.

44. For Burma, see Brohm, "Buddhism and Animism in a Burmese Village;" and Spiro, *Burmese Supernaturalism*; for Thailand and Cambodia, see note 41 above as well as Porée-Maspero, *Cérémonies privées des cambodgiens.*

45. See Tambiah, "Ideology of Merit;" and Tambiah, *Buddhism and the Spirit Cults.*

46. Individual icons usually had specific names. This practice continues today in Thailand and Burma, where it is common for images of the Buddha to be given names. See *Charuek nai Prathet Thai,* vol. 2, 62, 64.

47. See Tambiah, "Ideology of Merit;" and Anuman Rajadhon, *Popular Buddhism in Siam.*

48. This coexistence is evident for both King Aniruddha of Burma and King Ramkhamhaeng of Sukhothai, neither of whom could neglect to propitiate the indigenous spirits.

49. See Mus, *India Seen from the East,* 52, who claims that Indian contributions profoundly influenced Cham culture, as evidenced by a 1050 CE inscription of an hymn by the king Śrī Parameśvara, representing, according to Mus, how a Cham thought and how he expressed himself in Sanskrit. The inscription, quoted by Mus and translated by Abel Bergaigne, reads as follows:

> Pertaining to him who is the lord of what is and what is not, having as real nature the quality of being the origin of the development of existence on earth. . . . being one with the being and the non-being that exists in the world, primordial potentiality of the being and the non-being, having as body the half of the body of Śiva who has the moon as diadem, having a beautiful body, Oh you who are part of the Lord. . . . Oh Blessed One, be as it were, by your magic power, the vanquisher of us who are prostrate before you.

However, this Cham was no ordinary Cham, but a king whose court was filled with brahmans, who probably composed these stanzas. Therefore, this inscription cannot be cited as evidence that at one time the religion of the Cham was thoroughly Indianized.

50. Smith and Watson, *Early South East Asia*, 242ff.; *Encyclopedia of Religion*, vol. 9, 336–46.

51. See Day, *Great Tradition and Little Tradition*, which provides a summary of important research on this topic. Even though Day's writing style is terse and difficult, the work is still useful despite the fact that much of his information appears to be gleaned primarily from book reviews written by other scholars, without much analysis on his part.

52. E. R. Leach, *Dialectic in Practical Religion*, 1, has summarized the situation quite well:

> In studies of comparative religion a failure to take into account this distinction between philosophical religion and practical religion has often led to grave misunderstanding. Thus Western interpretation of Buddhism has, until very recently, been derived almost exclusively from a scholarly study of ancient Pāli texts glossed by the modern commentaries of professional Buddhist theologians; very little attention has been paid to the ordinary practice of Buddhism in the parishes of its indigenous homeland in Ceylon, Burma, Thailand or elsewhere.

While studies of the practical side of Buddhism or the lived tradition have certainly grown in recent years, it still remains accurate to say that the practical side is primarily studied in order to demonstrate the contrast or tension with the textual side.

53. Marriott, "Little Communities in an Indigenous Civilization," 171–222.

54. Quoted in Day, *Great Tradition and Little Tradition*, 8–13.

55. Ibid.

56. There are many theories about the rise of Mahāyāna. In *A Short History of Buddhism*, 41, Conze suggests that Mahāyāna Buddhism

> . . . was prepared by the exhaustion of the old impulse which produced fewer and fewer Arhats, by the tensions within the doctrines as they had developed by then and by the demand of the laity for more equal rights with the monks. Foreign influences also had a great deal to do with it. The Mahāyāna developed in North-West India and South India, the two regions where Buddhism was most exposed to non-Indian influences, to the impact of Greek art in its Hellenistic and Romanized forms and to the influence of ideas from both the Mediterranean and the Iranian world. This cross-fertilization incidentally rendered the Buddhism of the Mahāyāna fit for export outside India.

For Conze, Mahāyāna emerges as a result of both inside and outside influences. Akira Hirakawa, having rejected the theory that Mahāyāna originated only from the Mahāsāṅghikas, shows that the Sarvāstivādins also contributed to the development of Mahāyāna. He links the origin of Mahāyāna to the cult of the *stūpa* which, he proposes, developed among the laity. See Hirakawa, "The Rise of Mahāyāna Buddhism," 57–106. Gregrory Schopen, however, thinks that monks also contributed to the development of Mahāyāna. The cult of the *stūpa*, in his view, should not be seen as a lay movement in opposition to a monastic community. See the articles by Schopen: "Two Problems in the History of Indian Buddhism," 9–47; and "On Monks, Nuns and 'Vulgar' Practices," 153–68.

57. See Lamotte, *Histoire du bouddhisme indien*, 597–600. If the accounts of Chinese pilgrims are to be believed, by the seventh century Mahāyāna monks in India numbered around 60,000, and Hīnayāna monks, 134,800.

58. The Pāli canon, which according to tradition, was compiled as early as the first century BCE, already included the *Vibhaṅga*, a commentary on monastic rules, as well as part of the *Niddesa*, which provides a commentary on the *Aṭṭhakavagga* and the *Pārāyanavagga* of the *Suttanipāta*. At this time, the canon shows a tendency toward the style of the *Abhidhammapiṭaka*. *Suttas* such as *Dasuttarasutta* of the *Dīghanikāya*, and the arrangement of the *Aṅguttaranikāya* by the number of dharmas are forerunners of the Abhidharmic literature that followed.

59. In addition to the two articles cited in note 56 above, Schopen has written other useful pieces on this point. See "The Phrase 'sa pṛthivīpradeśaś caityabhūto bhavet' in the Vajracchedikā" (1975); "Sukhāvatī as a Generalized Religious Goal" (1977); "Mahāyāna in Indian Inscriptions" (1979); and "The Inscription on the Kusān Image of Amithābha" (1987).

60. See Jaini, "Śramaṇas," 39–82.

61. See *Bṛhadāraṇyaka Upaniṣad* 2.1ff.; and the second *sutta* of the *Dīghanikāya*.

62. See Bollée, *Pādas of the Suttanipāta*; and Bollée, *Reverse Index of the Dhammapada*.

63. Monastic institutionalization seems to have had a great impact on the Brahmanical world, to be followed later by Śaṅkara. See Pande, *Origins of Buddhism*, 326ff.

64. In the *Taittiraya* and *Bṛhadraṇyaka Upaniṣad*, early efforts were made to systematize the names given to the senses and sense organs, as in the theory of the five *kośas*, which can be compared with the Buddhist theory of the five *skandhas*. In the *Bṛhadāraṇyaka Upaniṣad* 2.1.17, the *vijñānamaya puruṣa* can be compared to the *manomaya kāya* of Buddhism. There is also a reference to the concept of *grāhaka* and *grāhya*, which later becomes one of the main tenets of the Vijñānavāda school of Buddhism. Seen in this light, one cannot pursue a careful study of Hinduism without studying Buddhism and Jainism and vice versa.

65. The study of Buddhism has been mainly a study of the canonical literature, which accounts for the emphasis on philosophical ideas. As a result, secular elements in the canon are often overlooked, and if any leaning toward popular practice is detected, it is described as a remnant of Brahmanism. Other studies have emphasized asceticism in Buddhism over the Brahmanical tradition. This is an inaccurate contrast because ascetics were a part of Indian society. The general populace could be characterized as Brahmanical, yet they gave food to these ascetics. It is quite common to find passages where the Buddha or his disciples go on their begging rounds to brahman households. The Buddha's style of preaching and teaching is akin to the teachers in the *Upaniṣads*. Both used similar methods and metaphors.

66. Knowledge is usually emphasized in the *Upaniṣads*. One cannot simply perform a ritual; one has to "know" it as well. For examples, see the *Bṛhadāraṇyaka*; and also Staal, "Substitutions de paradigms."

67. On this point, see Yuyama, "'Jūni innenju' oboegaki," 445nn26–27. The stanza is also found on images of Avalokiteśvara, Kubera, and Mañjuśrī, for instance.

68. Nidhi Aeusrivongse, "The Devarājā Cult," 114ff.

69. Quoted in Filliozat, "Sur le çivaïsme," 85. The inscription is dated 946 CE and has two parts, Sanskrit and Khmer; the Khmer part mentions only Śiva and Viṣṇu, and not the Buddha. Filliozat asks the pertinent question of whether these were exclusively regarded as different foreign religions in terms of how they were organized and administrated, or whether Buddhism was, in reality, in accord with Śaivism. He proposes another interpretation of the inscription when he points out that apart from the name "Buddha" there is nothing else in the inscription that would make the Śaivites feel uneasy or hostile to the content of this inscription. The Śaivites also wear the yellow robe of the *yati,* and attributes given to Buddha, such as *vītarāga,* apply to Śiva as well.

70. In *Kāraṇḍavyūha* (ed. P. L. Vaidya, *Mahāyāna-sūtra-saṅgraha*), 265, the Buddha describes Avalokiteśvara to the bodhisattva named Sarvanīvaraṇaviṣkambhin as follows: *bhagavān āha cakṣusoś candrādityav utpannau, lalāṭān maheśvaraḥ, skandhebhyo brahmādayaḥ, hṛdayān nārāyaṇaḥ,* [and so on]. The same kind of identification occurs in Upaniṣadic literature.

71. The author of this quote, Anuman Rajadhon, in *Popular Buddhism in Siam,* 99–100, goes on to say:

> The generic word *phii* therefore degenerated into restricted meaning of bad *phii.* It now means a ghost, a devil or an evil spirit. Nevertheless the old meaning of *phii* in certain cases is not yet dead and still lingers in some expressions in the language. For instance, of any evil deed done in secret, we sometimes say as a warning, "men never see the evil deed done but the *phii* does." In order not to divulge the source of any formula, especially a medicinal prescription which is effective, the owner will say that the formula is "*phii bok*", or told by a *phii,* so as to give it a sacred and mystical effect. The *phii* here is a good *phii* or a *thevada.*
>
> The dividing line between gods and devils, like men, is a thin one which is a matter of varying degrees. Some gods are bad and some devils are good. There are, in fact, almost as many kinds of good and bad *phii* as there are of men. It follows therefore, that out of these *phii* there emerges a class whose position is on a border line between the gods and the devils. They are called "*Caw phi*" which means a lord or prince *phii* but is sometimes also called *thevada* . . .

72. Porée-Maspero, *Étude sur les rites agraires,* vol. 3, 701–3.

73. Ibid. Porée-Maspero tends to regard all rites concerning agriculture in Cambodia or Thailand as either indigenous or Chinese in origin, rather than Indian.

74. For a study of different views on religion and critiques of methodologies see, Geertz, "Religion: Anthropological Study;" *Encyclopedia of Religion,* vol. 12, 282–333; and Leach, *Dialectic in Practical Religion,* 1ff.

75. See Ibid. for references.

76. See Nidhi Aeusrivongse, "The Devarājā Cult," 107–49.

77. Griswold and Prasert na Nagara, "Epigraphic and Historical Studies No. 9," 214.

78. Griswold and Prasert na Nagara, "Epigraphic and Historical Studies No. 14," 233.

79. Ibid., 234n7.

80. Swearer, "Myth, Legend, and History," 75ff. For other studies of these legends in Thailand, see Wyatt, "Thai Historiography." For Burma see, Muang Htin Aung, *Folk*

Elements in Burmese Buddhism; U Tet Htoot, "Nature of the Burmese Chronicles;" and Hazra, *Buddhist Annals*.

81. For a discussion of Fa Xian, see Giles, *Travels of Fa-Hsien*, 13. Giles translates this entry from Fa Xian's diary:

> Formerly when Buddha was visiting this country in company with ten of his disciples, he said to Çnanda, "When I have passed away, a king of this country by name of Kaniòka, will raise a pagoda at this spot." Subsequently, when king Kaniòka came into the world and was travelling about to see things, Indra, God of Heaven, wishing to originate in him the idea, caused the appearance of a little herd-boy building a pagoda in the middle of the road. "What are you making there?" said the king. "I am building a pagoda for Buddha," replied the boy. "Splendid!" cried the king; and he forthwith built a pagoda, over four hundred feet high. . . .

See also *Epigraphia Birmanica*, vol. 1, pt. 2 (1919): 113ff.

82. Two of the chronicles that relate the story of Cāmadevī were edited and translated into French by George Cœdès in "Documents sur l'histoire politique et religieuse du Laos occidental." The *Jinakālamālinī* was edited into roman script by A. B. Buddhadatta in 1962 and translated into English in 1968 by N. A. Jayawickrama. The proper title should be the *Jinakālamālinī*, not *Jinakālamālī* as changed by Professor Manavidur. Judging from the names in the Pāli commentaries, the preferred form is in the feminine case, as in, for example, the *Sumaṅgalavilāsinī* or the *Manorathapūraṇī*. Chronicle titles that do not end in *vaṃsa* also have a name in the feminine case, as in the *Vaṃsatthapakāsinī*. For the role played by *rishis*, see *Inscriptions of Pagan*, 15; and *Epigraphia Birmanica*, vol. 1, pt. 2 (1919): 113ff.

83. Staal, "Substitutions de paradigms," 23–24.

84. Śivaliṅgas are found in many Thai monastery compounds, even in royal monasteries such as Wat Phra Chetuphon in Bangkok. On a hill near Lopburi, Śivaliṅgas have been found in such numbers that the hill was given the name, Khau Sapphalinga (Sarvaliṅga). King Rāma IV later changed the name to Sapphanimita (Sarvanimita) in order to avoid using the word "*liṅga*."

85. See Souyris-Rolland, "Contributions à l'etude du culte des génies tutelaires," 161–73; Tambiah, "Ideology of Merit," 53–56; and Anuman Rajadhon, *Popular Buddhism in Siam*. We cannot totally agree with Tambiah that the *phii* and *thewadā* are "two opposed supernatural categories." For the Thai understanding, see Anuman Rajadhon cited herein.

86. *Inscriptions of Pagan*, 34; see also 14, 15, 22, 48.

87. Anuman Rajadhon, *Popular Buddhism in Siam*; and Tambiah, "Ideology of Merit," 53ff.

88. In Thailand, the ascendancy of ritual can be seen as beginning with the establishment of the present dynasty. In the ceremony for taking the oath of loyalty to the king, Brahmanism and ancestor worship, in the earlier period, played more prominent roles. In the first reign of this present dynasty, the king ordered all officials to worship the *Triratna* above the other two creeds. This custom grew stronger during subsequent reigns, especially during the reign of Rāma IV or King Mongkut, when Buddhist ceremonies were prefixed onto all Brahmanic ones. In the sixth reign, this custom led to the enactment of the Palace Law, which states that the king of Thailand must be a Buddhist.

89. See Jacob, "Pre-Angkor Cambodia," 406–26. Jacob summarizes the details, mostly Śaivite, found in the Khmer inscriptions during the pre-Angkorian period as follows: (1) date or name of the reigning king; (2) title and names of donors; (3) name of the god; (4) names of those from whom the donor obtained land as an offering for the building of the structure; (5) the amount paid to those who provided land for the structure; (6) size, location, and harvest capacity of the donated rice fields; (7) names of the donated slaves along with their specific duties; (8) details of the subsidies given to the religious personnel; (9) details of other land given for the structure: orchards, market gardens, and so on; (10) list of precious objects given for the structure; (11) statement that the revenues should be combined with those of another structure; and (12) warning that anyone using or abusing the contents of the structure will be punished. The absence of any mention of meritorious aspirations or the transfer of merit is remarkable. The same point holds true in subsequent periods for Brāhmanic and Mahāyānistic inscriptions in this tradition.

90. Bechert, "Theravāda Buddhist Sangha," 766.

91. For extended discussions on this topic, see Dupont, "Études sur l'Indochine ancienne II;" Filliozat, "Sur le çivaïsme;" Kulke, *Devarājā Cult*; Kulke, "Southeast Asian History;" and Mabbett, "Kingship in Angkor."

92. The two epics, *Rāmakirti* and *Unaruddha* (the story of Aniruddha from the *Mahābhārata*) were considered by Rāma I as essential national epics, even though they are not Buddhist. In a postscript to the texts, the king warns that while they are important epics, they are secondary to the Buddha's teaching.

93. There is no study of the titles of kings in Southeast Asian languages, and it would appear that most modern states in the region have essentially lost the importance of the institution of kingship. I conducted interviews with informants from different cultures of Southeast Asia regarding the meanings of various titles for kings. The data presented below is only preliminary, however, and needs to be verified through further research.

Burma (Informant: Kyaw Soe, East-West Center, University of Hawaii)

In normal conversation, the king is referred to as Ba Yin, Shin Ba Yin (with Shin = owner and master), while officially and in historical documents, the king is called:

1. Ba Yin Min Myat (Myat signifies higher or nobler status)
2. Ba Yin Min Tayar Gyi (Min = king; Tayar = just; Gyi = great)
3. Min Gyi = The Great One (the most common term found in history books)

Malaya (Informant: Chris Ng, East-West Center, University of Hawaii)

1. Rāja (Sanskrit)
2. Sultan
3. Agung = the king of kings, the best, the first
4. Tuan ku = the master (Ten gu = the king's son)

Indonesia (Informant: Hedina Utarti, East-West Center, University of Hawaii)

1. Rāja
2. People referred to the king as Gusti, which the informant thinks is a Sanskrit word (with Gusti Allah = God; Gusti Panguan = the prince, my master)
3. Officially, the king is referred to as Sri Sultan; Sri Susuhuna (the one that I lift) (suhun = to lift)

4. In court language, Sihunan means the one who was lifted (compare this to Thai court language, with Thun Kramom = the one whom I place above my head).

Cambodia (*Charuek nai Prathet Thai*, vol. 3, 78, 96, 128, 151, and so on)

1. Kamrateṅ añ; Vrah Påd (påda) Kamrateṅ añ
2. Dhulī Vrah Dhulī Jeṅ Vrah Kamrateṅ añ; (Jeí = Påda)
3. Vrah Pād kamrateṅ Kamtuan añ

Thailand

1. Pho Khun (The Chief who is the Father; this title was used in the thirteenth century during the Sukhothai period. One also finds Cambodian titles used for Thai kings in inscriptions, often written in Khmer.)
2. Khun Luang (The Great Chief; this was a common title during the Ayutthaya period in the fourteenth century)
3. Phra Chao Phendin (The Lord of the Land); Phra Mahākasat (Mahākṣatriya)
4. Chao Chiwit (The Lord of Life); Chao Nuea Hua (The Lord Above the Head)
5. Officially, Phra Bāt (*pāda*) Somdet Phra Chao Yu Hua (The Lord Above the Peoples' Heads)

Most of these titles appear in vernacular languages. If the inscription is in Sanskrit, the king's name is usually preceded by *śrī*, without any additional title.

94. See K. Hall, *Maritime Trade*; and Welch, "Late Prehistoric and Early Historic Exchange Patterns."

95. Welch, "Late Prehistoric and Early Historic Exchange Patterns," 14.

96. Srisakra Vallibhotama, "Dvarati Sites," 234–35.

97. Cœdès, *Indianized States*, 97.

98. Mabbett, "Buddhism in Champa," 289–314.

99. See, e.g., Aung-Thwin, *Pagan*; Guillon, "Jalon pour une histoire bouddhisme;" and Saddhātissa, "Pāli Literature of Thailand."

100. Cœdès, *Indianized States*, 33.

101. Only after Christian and Western concepts of "religion" began to penetrate Southeast Asian culture did purist movements arise. The issue was taken seriously in Thailand, where several movements to purify Buddhism have come into being. Only then did Thais declare themselves as Buddhists as a reaction to a declaration by the Roman Catholic Church that conversion was its goal. These recent religious developments are unprecedented.

Chapter 6

1. See Leach, *Dialectic in Practical Religion*, 1–6.

2. Spiro, *Buddhism and Society*, 6–9. I quote further from Spiro at length to illustrate the kinds of misunderstandings that, at times, accompany discussion of Buddhism:

> *Materialism.* Contrary to almost every other religion, one of the foundation stones of Buddhism is the doctrine of nonsoul. Man is an aggregate of five material factors and processes which, at death, disintegrate without residue. The belief that behind these material processes there exists some spiritual or incorporeal essence—a soul—which

guides and directs behavior and which survives the dissolution of the physical body, is a Buddhist heresy. The building block of the world, and of man, is the atom. Man, like the rest of the world, consists of atoms in motion.

Atheism. Buddhism is a religion without a God. Just as the body has no soul which guides and directs its action, so the universe has no Creator who brought it into being, who guides its course, or who presides over the destiny of man. More important, there is no Being—no savior God—to whom man can turn for salvation. Each man, as it were, must save himself. Durkheim (1954:29-32), it will be recalled, was so impressed with the Buddhist example that he argued that the belief in God could not be used as a defining characteristic of "religion." Other scholars, themselves the products of the eighteenth-century Enlightenment and of nineteenth-century rationalism, found the precursor of these latter movements in Buddhism . . .

Nihilism. The doctrine of no-soul is intimately associated with a second building stone—the doctrine of impermanence. According to Buddhism everything in the universe, including the universe itself, is impermanent. There can be no supreme reality because anything that is "real"—anything that exists—is in a perpetual flux, in a constant state of creation and dissolution, of coming into and passing out of existence. But Buddhism makes an even more radical claim—and this is a second meaning of Buddhist nihilism: even if there were some permanent reality, perhaps some condition of immortality, it is not a condition to which man ought aspire. Rather than aspiring to an eternal existence, the Buddhist (in theory) aspires to the extinction of existence . . .

Pessimism. Buddhist nihilism is reasoned, not capricious. Just as Calvinism teaches that there is no conceivable act of even the most righteous man which is not sinful (in the sight of God), so Buddhism teaches that there is no conceivable act of even the happiest man which is not painful (when analyzed in the crucible of Buddhist meditation). Associated with the doctrines of no-soul and impermanence, the doctrine of suffering forms the third of the famous Buddhist trinity. From the lowest hell to the highest heaven suffering is an inescapable and essential attribute of life. Since so long as there is life there is suffering, the only reasonable goal to aspire to, according to Buddhism, is the extinction of life as we ordinarily understand it.

Renunciation. Religions not only take different attitudes to the world, but these attitudes vary systematically with their basic doctrines, and especially with their doctrines of salvation. Thus, religion may accept the world, viewing it as not incompatible with its soteriological goal; it may be indifferent to the world, viewing it as irrelevant to that goal; it may reject the world, viewing the latter as the major obstacle to attainment of that goal. The last attitude, the rejection of the world, may lead, as Weber has shown, to such diverse responses as innerworldly asceticism, mysticism, and otherworldly asceticism (Weber 1946:323-58). Buddhism is a religion, par excellence, of otherworldly asceticism. . . . By renouncing the world, the Buddhist aspires to detachment from persons, from material possessions, and even from himself.

Spiro's statement on the "nihilism" found in Buddhist teachings fails to recognize that for ordinary people reflection on "impermanence" applies to daily situations to remind themselves not to become attached to material things and thus not inflict their thoughts with such attachments. These are functional coping strategies, and do not refer to reality per se. Moreover, attaining *nirvāṇa* (what Spiro terms the "extinction of existence") is, in Spiro's view, nihilistic as compared to the ideal of "eternal existence." Yet the Indian concept of the ending of the soul's transmigration should not be confused with the extinction of life, but, rather, it means the extinction of continual becoming or continual rebirth. In Indian philosophy, the life of every being is endless, unless the wheel of *saṃsāra* is broken. Spiro's word choices are rather misleading.

3. See, e.g., Bellah, "Sociology of Religion," 412–13; and Staal, "Substitutions de paradigms," 41–42.

4. The misconception persists in Damien Keown's *Buddhism: A Very Short Introduction,* 11, with his emphasis on the difference between Mahāyāna and Theravāda. Keown states: "Individual Buddhists would identify themselves as belonging to one or another of these two 'families', in a way that Muslims would regard themselves as Sunni or Shiite, or Western Christians would think of themselves as either Protestant or Catholic." Keown has only to visit a Theravāda monastery in Thailand to realize how wrong his statement is. How would he respond when he saw the variety and sizes of Guanyin images in the most important monastery of Thailand?

5. Staal, "Substitutions de paradigmes," 46.

6. See, e.g., Horner, *Book of the Discipline*, vol. 1, xxix: "Historically, the success of the Early Buddhist experiment in monasticism must be in great part attributed to the wisdom of constantly considering the susceptibilities and criticisms of the laity."

7. Lester, *Theravada Buddhism in Southeast Asia*, chaps. 5 and 6; see also Lester, *Buddhism: The Path to Nirvana*, chap. 4.

8. Spiro, *Buddhism and Society*, 11.

9. Spiro, *Burmese Supernaturalism,* 271.

10. *Dīghanikāya* II, 253–62; *Dictionary of Pāli Proper Names*, vol. 2, 564–65.

11. The *Ratanasutta* occurs twice in the canon: in the *Khuddakapāṭha,* and the *Suttanipāta* (verses 222–38).

12. *Dīghanikāya* III, 194ff.

13. Masson, *La religion populaire.*

14. Spiro, *Burmese Supernaturalism,* 271.

15. The following stanzas, recalled from memory, are usually recited before the actual *paritta* recitation begins:

> sagge kāme ca rūpe girisikharataṭe cantalikkhe vimāne
> dīpe raṭṭhe ca gāme taruvanagahaṇe gehavatthuṃhi khette
> bhummā cāyantu devā jalathalavisame yakkhagandhabbanāgā
> tiṭṭhantā santike'yaṃ munivaravacanaṃ sādhavo me suṇantu.

16. Bechert, *Buddhism in Ceylon*, 221. See also Ames, "Magical-animism," 21–52; Bechert, "Contradictions in Sinhalese Buddhism," 7–17; Pfanner, "Theravada Buddhism," 341–61; and Piker, "Relations of Belief Systems," 384–99.

17. Lester, *Theravada Buddhism in Southeast Asia*, chap. 6; and Tambiah, *World Conqueror and World Renouncer*, chap. 14.

18. Spiro, *Buddhism and Society*, 11–14.
19. See Tambiah, *Buddhism and the Spirit Cults*, chaps. 14–15.
20. Ibid., 252.
21. Tambiah, "The Ideology of Merit," 52–53.
22. Ibid., 53.
23. Ibid. Compare Tambiah to B. J. Terwiel, "Study of Thai Buddhism," 393, who states:

> During the first months of fieldwork, it became clear that questions with regard to the division or the syncretism of Buddhist and non-Buddhist practices presented informants with severe problems. Though in general no reticence was met when discussing religious belief or practices, as soon as the question arose whether this was in accordance with the teachings or contravened the doctrine, a variety of reactions was observed. *The more sophisticated person usually brought forward the view that the Lord Buddha had never forbidden ancient ritual to take place. Others hesitatingly made up their minds with regard to the orthodoxy of a ritual, but on subsequent occasions contradicted their own judgment. Many were at a loss to classify rituals or beliefs under headings such as "Buddhist" and "non-Buddhist." It soon appeared that informants were classifying merely to please the researcher; the categories under discussion had little relevance in their minds* (italics are mine).

24. Bechert cited in Day characterizes Buddhism in Sri Lanka and Southeast Asia as having the following components: monastic Buddhism of the Theravādin school; the Great Tradition, either canonical or literary Buddhism; popular Buddhism having its foundation characterized by localized Great Tradition Buddhist elements combined with a cult of gods and magical rites; a non-Buddhist cult of gods; and court Buddhism or state religion composed of a Buddhicized version of regional *vaiṣṇavite-brāhmanism* or modern Theravāda Buddhism. See Day, *Great Tradition and Little Tradition*, 80ff.
25. Schopen, "On Monks, Nuns and 'Vulgar' Practices," 153–68.
26. Terwiel, "Study of Thai Buddhism," 391–403.
27. Ibid., 392.
28. For a detailed study of these schools, see Bareau, *Les sectes bouddhisques du Petit Véhicule.*
29. For relations between these two regions, see Hazra, *History of Theravāda Buddhism*; Paranavitana, "Religious Intercourse;" Sirisena, *Sri Lanka and South-East Asia.*
30. Cœdès, "Une Roue de la Loi," 226.
31. The term "Theravāda" appears first in the *Majjhimanikāya* I, 164; see also *Dīpavaṃsa* IV, 6, 13.
32. Aung-Thwin, *Pagan*, 17–19. Parenthetical material is Aung-Thwin's.
33. Lamotte, *Histoire du bouddhisme indien*, 571ff.; Bareau, "Les sectes bouddhiques," 40–41.
34. Aung-Thwin may be basing his statement on Blagden's article, "Notes on Talaing Epigraphy," but Aung-Twin neglects to take into account N. R. Ray's *Theravāda Buddhism in Burma.* The evidence Ray presents overrides Blagden's thesis.
35. See Guillon, "Jalon pour une histoire du bouddhisme," 123–24:

> Pour résumer l'ensemble de ce parcours historique, on pourrait fixer cinq étapes qui aboutissent, à la fin de notre XVième siècle, à une unification à peu près complète du bouddhisme de l'Asie du Sud-Est péninsulaire sous l'égide du Mahavihara:

1/ une période—encore presque inconnue—où apparaissent ici et là, notamment en Birmanie et en Thaïlande, des traces d'un bouddhisme directement issu de l'Inde mais encore mal identifié. Cette période correspond aux IIème–VIème siècle de notre ère.

2/ le fleurissement du bouddhisme de Dvāravati, du petit véhicule mais non-pāli, qui va féconder les cultures suivantes.

3/ Parallèlement se constituaient en Birmanie des royaumes Pyu, à la religion syncrétique, et un ensemble Môn influencé par ou héritier des communautés bouddhiques de l'estuaire de la Kṛṣṇa, en Inde.

4/ L'apparition ensuite, au Xème - XIIème siècle de notre ère, en Birmanie, d'un bouddhisme en liaison avec Kāñcipuram mais également, via les communautés de l'actuel Bangladesh, avec les royaumes Pāla du Bihar.

5/ les débuts, au XIIème siècle, de la lente montée du Mahāvihāra, qui aboutira, trois siècles plus tard, à son installation presque complete.

36. See Dohanian, *Mahāyāna Buddhist Sculpture*, 8; *Encyclopedia of Religion*, s.v. "Sinhalese Buddhism," "Theravāda Buddhism;" *Dictionary of Pāli Proper Names*, vol. 2, 147–50; and Bechert, "Theravāda Buddhist Sangha."

37. Saddhātissa, "Pāli Literature of Thailand," 211.

38. N. R. Ray, *Sanskrit Buddhism.*

39. Blagden, "Notes on Talaing Epigraphy."

40. See introduction of *Epigraphia Birmanica*, vol. 1, pt. 2 (1920); D. E. Smith, *Religion and Politics in Burma*, 23.

41. *Tamnān Mūlasāsanā*, 15.

42. See *Encyclopedia of Religion*, s.v. "Theravāda Buddhism."

43. Cœdès, *Indianized States*, 150, and chaps. 12–14.

44. See, e.g., Ibid., where Cœdès writes: "The political result of the conquest of Thaton was the submission of the whole delta and its Indian principalities, thus opening a window on the sea for the Burmese; the cultural result was the conversion of Pagan to Theravāda Buddhism and the decline of Tantric Mahāyāna." Actually the sovereignty of the Burmese over the Mon and other groups in Burma constantly waxed and waned. There were times when the Mon gained their independence from the Burmese.

45. Ibid., 189.

46. Luce, "Early Syām," 126.

47. See, e.g., Manit Vallibhotama, *Suvarnabhûmi yu thi nai.*

48. Ibid., 62–201.

49. This date is as claimed in the chronicles. Archaeological evidence, however, does not appear until the tenth century. See *Borankhadi si phak*, 35ff.

50. Luce, "Early Syām," 124–25.

51. N. R. Ray, *Theravāda Buddhism in Burma*, 254.

52. The English translation is mine. See *Sāsanavaṃsa*, 56:

> Amhākaṃ hi Marammamaṇḍale Tambadīparaṭṭhe Arimaddananagare Sammutirājā nāma bhūpālo rajjaṃ kāresi. Tato paṭṭhāya yāva Anuruddharaññā Samati-nāmake dese nisinnānaṃ tiṃsasahassamattānaṃ samaṇakuttakānaṃ saṭṭhisahassamattānaṃ sissānaṃ ovādaṃ datvā cariṃsu.

Tesaṃ pana samaṇakuttakānaṃ ayaṃ vādo:

Sace yo pāṇātipātaṃ kareyya so īdisaṃ parittaṃ bhaṇanto tamhā pāpakammā parimuñceyya. Sace pana yo mātāpitaraṃ hantvā anantariyakammato parimuccitukāmo bhaveyya īdisaṃ parittaṃ bhaṇeyya. Sace pi puttadhītānaṃ āvāhavivāhakammaṃ kattukāmo bhaveyya ācariyānaṃ paṭhamaṃ niyyādetvā āvāhavivāhakammaṃ kātabbaṃ. Yo idaṃ cārittaṃ atikkameyya bahu apuññaṃ pasaveyyā ti.

In the introduction to the *Sāsanavaṃsa*, the editor, Mabel Haynes Bode, explains *samaṇakuttaka* as follows (pp. 16–17): "With regard to the name Samaṇakuttaka: from the analogy with *kuttima* = artificial (derived by Childers from Skt. *Kṛtṛma*), *kuttaka* seems to be the Skt. *Kṛtaka* = false, artificial, simulated. *Samaṇakuttaka* would therefore simply mean: simulating (the life of) the Samaṇas." These *samaṇakuttakas* have been identified with the *ari* of Burma. See also Duroiselle, "Aris of Burma."

53. *Sāsanavaṃsa*, 57–58.
54. The English translation is mine. Ibid., 59:

Tadā rājā theraṃ pucchi: Ko pana tvan ti.

Aham mahārājā Gotamassa sāvako ti.

Puna rājā pucchi: Tiṇṇaṃ pana ratanānaṃ kīdiso ti.

Thero āha: mahosadhapaṇḍito viya mahārājā buddho daṭṭhabbo; ummaggo viya dhammo; Videhasenā viya saṃgho ti. Evaṃ upamāhi pakāsito rājā puna pucchi: kin nu kho ime Gotamassa sāvakā ti.

Na kho maharājā ime Gotamassa sāvakā, ime pana amhehi visabhāgā samaṇakuttakā yevā ti evaṃ vutte tato paṭṭhāya te samaṇakuttake vijahi. Tiṇaṃ nātimaññi pāṭalirukkhasusirato pi laddhaṃ tesaṃ gandhaṃ laddhaṭṭhāne yeva agginā jhāpesi.

55. Ibid., 59–60.
56. Ibid., 60.
57. Ibid.:

Evaṃ nānācariyānaṃ vādo nānākārena dissamāno pi Arahantatherassa Arimaddananagare sāsanaṃ anuggahetvā patiṭṭhānatā yev' ettha pamāṇan ti katvā nāvamaññitabbo.

Sabbesaṃ hi ācariyānaṃ vāde pi Arahantathero Arimadddananagaraṃ āgantvā sāsanaṃ patiṭṭhāpesī ti attho icchitabbo yevā ti, Arahantathero pana mālanāmena Dhammadassī ti pākaṭo Sudhammapuravāsī Sīlabuddhitherassa sisso ti daṭṭhabbo.

So ca thero pubbeva pabbajjakālato catāsu vedesu sikkhitasippo.

Pabbajitvā pana sāṭṭhakathaṃ piṭakattayaṃ uggaṇhitvā pāraṃ gantvā sabbattha pākaṭo. Sokkatayanagaraṃ ānetvā manussā pājenti.

Tattha dasa vassāni vasitvā puna Sudhammapuraṃ āgantvā araññavāsaṃ samādayi.

Tato pacchā jinacakke ekasaṭṭhādhike pañcasate sahasse ca sampatte . . . Anuruddharājā rajjaṃ pāpuṇi.

Tadā Arimaddananagare samaṇakuttakā mayaṃ Gotamasāvakā ti vatvā . . . Anuruddharājā ca tesaṃ samaṇakuttakānaṃ āgāriyābrahmacariyādīni sutvāna pasīdi. Evam pi paveṇiyā āgatattā na pajahi.

Arahantam pana theraṃ passitvā tato paṭṭhāya tesaṃ samaṇakuttakānaṃ nibaddhavattāni bhinditvā sāsane pasīdi.

58. Ibid., 80.

59. When the new ordination lineage was introduced from Sri Lanka, the old lineage was still in place throughout the entire Sangha. See N. R. Ray, *Theravāda Buddhism in Burma*, 110ff. The same thing was true in Sukhothai, where the new Sri Lankan lineage formed the *araññika* or forest monks as a separate monastic community, but they still belonged to the same Sangha. See Prince Damrong Rajanubhab, *Tamnān Khana Song*, 5–41. For a discussion of the forest monk tradition in Sri Lanka, see Rahula, *Buddhism in Ceylon*, chap. 10, 196ff., 215ff.

60. For different versions of the legend of Aśoka, see Strong, *Legend of King Aśoka*, 18ff.

61. See Duroiselle, "Aris of Burma," 83ff., in which he produces new data and gives a different account from the one in the Burmese chronicles, writing:

Another point worthy of remark is that contrary to all we are told in the chronicles about the intense enmity between the Arī and the professors of the newly implanted Theravāda faith from Thaton, the two communities seem to have lived on a footing of amity; for, as the inscription tells us, Shin Arahan, the staunch Theravādī, goes to Tenasserim in Lower Burma to bring back a Buddha-relic for enshrinement in the Nandamaññā, an avowedly Arī temple. The fact no doubt is that, at Pagan as well as in India and elsewhere, Mahāyānism and Hināyānism, at that period and probably long after, lived peaceably side by side, as I-tsing and Tārānātha tell us was the case.

62. *Sāsanavaṃsa*, 62ff.

63. See Ibid., 39:

Tato pacchā chasatādhike sahasse sampatte pubbe vuttehi tīhi kāraṇehi sāsanassa uppattiṭṭhānabhūtaṃ Rāmaññaraṭṭhaṃ dāmarikacorabhayena pajjararogabhayena sāsanapaccatthikabhayena cā ti tīhi bhayehi ākulitaṃ ahosi.

Tadā ca tattha sāsanaṃ dubbalaṃ ahosi yathā udake mande tatra jātaṃ uppalaṃ dubbalan ti.

Tattha bhikkhä pi sāsanaṃ yathā kāmaṃ pāretum na sakkā. Säriyakumārassa nāma Manohārirañño pana kāle sāsanaṃ ativiya dubbalaṃ ahosi. Jinacakke ekasaṭṭhādhike vassasate sampatte ... Arimaddananagare Anuruddho nāma rājā tato saha piṭakena bhikkhusaṃghaṃ ānesi.

64. The relevant passages of the inscription that contain religious elements: include

The people of this city of Sukhodai like to observe the precepts and bestow alms. King Rāma Gaṃhèṅ, the ruler of this city of Sukhodai, as well as the princes and princesses, the young men and women of rank, and all the noblefolk without exception, both male and female, all have faith in the religion of the Buddha, and all observe the precepts during the rainy season. At the close of the rainy season they celebrate the Kaṭhina ceremonies, which last a month, with heaps of cowries, with heaps of areca nuts, with heaps of flowers, with cushions and pillows: the gifts they present [to the monks] as accessories to the Kaṭhina [amount to] two million each year. Everyone goes to the Araññika over there for the recitation of the Kaṭhina. When they are ready to return to the city they walk together, forming a line all the way from the Araññika to the parade-ground . . . As this city of Sukhodai has four very big gates, and as the people always crowd together to come in and watch the King lighting candles and setting off fireworks, the city is filled to the bursting point.

Inside this city of Sukhodai, there are *vihāras*, there are golden statues of the Buddha, there are statues eighteen cubits in height; there are big statues of the Buddha and medium-sized ones; there are monks, Nissayamuttas, Theras and Mahātheras.

West of this city of Sukhodai is the Araññika, built by King Rāma Gaṃhèṅ as a gift to the Mahāthera Saṅgharājā, the sage who has studied the scriptures from beginning to end, who is wiser than any other monk in the kingdom, and who has come here from Möaṅ Srī Dharmmarājā. Inside the Araññika there is a large rectangular *vihāra*, tall and exceedingly beautiful, and an eighteen-cubit statue of the Buddha standing up. East of this city of Sukhodai there are *vihāras* and monks . . . North of this city of Sukhodai there is the bazaar, there is the Acan statue [of the Buddha of Acala, Acanā?] . . . South of this city of Sukhodai there are *kutīs* with *vihāras* and resident monks, there is the dam . . . there is Braḥ Khabuṅ. The divine sprite of that mountain is more powerful than any other sprite in this kingdom. Whatever lord may rule this kingdom of Sukhodai, if he makes obeisance to him properly, with the right offerings, this kingdom will endure, this kingdom will thrive; but if obeisance is not made properly or the offerings are not right, the sprite of the hill will no longer protect it and the kingdom will be lost.

In 1214 saka . . . King Rāma Gaṃhèṅ, lord of this kingdom of Śrī Sajjanālai and Sukhodai, who had planted these sugar-palm trees fourteen years before, commanded his craftsmen to carve a slab of stone and place it in the midst of these sugar-palm trees. On the day of the new moon, the eighth day of the waxing moon, the day of the full moon, and the eighth day of the waning moon, [one of] the monks, *theras* or *mahātheras* goes up and sits on the stone slab to preach the Dharma to the throng of lay-people who observe the precepts. When it is not a day for preaching the Dharma, King Rāma Gaṃhèṅ . . . goes up, sits on the stone slab, and lets the officials, lords and princes discuss affairs of state with him. On the day of new moon and the day of the full moon, when the white elephant named Rūcaśrī has been decked out with howdah and tasseled head cloth, and always with gold on both tusks, King Rāma Gaṃhèṅ mounts him, rides away to the Araññika to pay homage to the Saṅgharājā, and then returns . . .

In 1207 saka . . . he caused the holy relics to be dug up so that everyone could see them. They were worshipped for a month and six days, then they were buried in the middle of Śrī Sajjanālai, and a *cetiya* was built on top of them which was finished in six years. A wall of rock enclosing the Braḥ Dhātu was built which was finished in three years.

See Griswold and Prasert na Nagara. "Epigraphic and Historical Studies No. 9," 209–17.

65. Keyes, *Thailand*, 33; and Rong Syamananda, *History of Thailand*, 25.

66. The term "*araññika*" refers to one of two components of the Sangha: *araññavasī* or *vanavasī* (forest-dwelling) as opposed to *gāmavāsī* (city-dwelling). The *araññavāsins* usually take up the study of meditation (*vipassanādhura*), and the *gāmavāsins* focus on the study of scripture (*ganthadhura*). It seems that all schools in Sri Lanka had an *aññikavāsin* faction, but that it was not considered as a separate *nikāya*. The tradition seems to have been established from about the sixth century. The *araññika* monks are referred to in canonical works, and are thus not particular to Sri Lanka. However, the distinction between the forest-dwelling monks and the city-dwelling monks seems more important in the Sinhalese organization of the Sangha. The fact that the word in this inscription is in a Pāli form could be interpreted as influence from the Pāli tradition of Sri Lanka. See Rahula, *Buddhism in Ceylon*, 196–97.

67. *Encyclopedia of Religion*, vol. 2, 392.

68. Prathip Chumphon in *Raingan Kansammana Prawattisat Nakhon Si Thammarat*, 355–75.

69. Paranavitana, "Epigraphical Summary," Section G1, part 4; Section G2, parts 1–3.

70. See *Raingan Kansammana Prawattisat Nakhon Si Thammarat*, 439–73.

71. Bizot in *Premier Symposium Franco-Thaï*, 387–402.

72. Ibid., 388.

73. Ibid., 390ff.

74. *Encyclopedia of Religion*, vol. 2, 395ff.

75. Ibid., vol. 14, 476–77.

76. Writing in French, Bizot prefaces his remarks with: *"Le Mahāvihāra ne s'est véritablement implanté et étendu en Asie du Sud-Est que lorsqu'il a pu s'y maintenir intact, c'est-à-dire beaucoup plus tard, à partir du XIXe siècle seulement. Le Siṅhalapakkha (ou 'branche cinghalaise'), le représenta et transmis ses idées dès le XIIe siècle en Birmanie et dès le XVe siècle au Siam, mais ne lui fut pas affilié comme on l'a généralement cru."* See Bizot in *Premier Symposium Franco-Thaï*, 387–402.

77. See Jaini, "Story of Sudhana and Manoharā;" and Jaini, *Paññasa-Jātaka*. See also K. R. Norman, *Pāli Literature*, 177–79.

78. The *Vyāghrī Jātaka* is found in the *Jātakamāla* and the *Jātakastava*, with the latter in summary form only. See Cummings, *Lives of the Buddha*, 85–93.

79. Liebenthal, "Sanskrit Inscriptions from Yunnan I;" and Liebenthal, "Sanskrit Inscriptions from Yunnan II."

80. Luce, *Old Burma-Early Pagan*, vol. 1, 16ff.

81. *Charuek nai Prathet Thai*, vol. 5, 53–57.

82. Ibid., 43–46.

83. The English translation is mine. See Ibid., 62–67:

> pathamaṃ sakalakkhanam ekapadam
> dutiyādipadassa nidassanato
> samanidunimā samadū sanidū
> vibhaje kamato paṭhamena vinā.

For another example of a "cryptic" or acronymic stanza, see *Charuek nai Prathet Thai*, vol. 5, 47ff. These inscriptions date from approximately the fourteenth century on. It is unknown whether a text existed from which these inscriptions were drawn, but it was common practice for such stanzas to be explained in written manuscripts. Even if these manuscripts come from a later date than the inscriptions, it is reasonable to assume that they were copied from older ones, or put in written form from an earlier oral tradition. The script used is Khmer, or a type of Khmer used in Thailand.

84. *Prachum silacharuek,* vol. 3, no. 54:

sabbaññutañāṇapavarasīsaṃ nibbānārammaṇapavaravilasita-
kesaṃ catutthajjhānapavaralalātaṃ . . .

aññesaṃ devamanussānaṃ buddho ativirocati
yassa tam uttamaṅgādi ñāṇaṃ sabbaññutādikaṃ
dhammakāyamataṃ buddhaṃ name taṃ lokanāyakaṃ.

imaṃ dhammakāyabuddhalakkhaṇaṃ yogāvacarakulaputtena
tikkhañāṇena sabbaññubuddhabhāvaṃ patthentena
punappunaṃ anussaritabbaṃ.

85. Ibid., vol. 3, no. 46. Note that *satrū* is a quasi-Sanskrit form of the Pāli, *sattu.*

86. Ibid., vol. 4, no. 86.

87. *Inscriptions of Pagan, Pinya, and Ava,* 5.

88. See, e.g., the inscriptions cited in notes 89 and 90 below and also *Charuek nai Prathet Thai,* vol. 5, 155. For inscriptions in Burma, see *Inscriptions of Pagan, Pinya, and Ava,* 21.

89. See, e.g., *Charuek nai Prathet Thai,* vol. 5, 83, 84, 187; *Inscriptions of Pagan, Pinya, and Ava,* 2–3.

90. See, e.g., *Prachum silacharuek,* vol. 3, no. 77 (p. 225):

nibbānapaccayo hotu no anāgate kāle niccaṃ imasmiṃ
attabhāve āyuvaṇṇādivḍḍhidhammāvahaṃ.

See also *Charuek nai Prathet Thai,* vol. 5, 170.

91. See, e.g., Ibid., 106–8. See also Ibid., 159–64:

sirinandavhayo dhīro saddho saddhammadāyako
tipumayaṃ buddhabimbaṃ karomi nahutādhikaṃ.

puññenānena so' haṃ amitabhavabhavaṃ yāva
sandhāvamāno

medhāvī cārurūpo madhuratarasaro sabbasatthāticheko
metteyyo sīladhāro varavividhadhano'nomadānādadāyo
mocento tāva vajje kusalaratirato'nāgate homi buddho.

siddhir astu
yo yojjharājaparamo paramoracakka-
vattīti nāma vidito imam ettha thūpaṃ
kārāpayaṃ ṭhapayi mārajidhātuyanto
assāpi kālavikalo ayam āsi thūpo.

tassoraso sakalabhūtalarājarājo
rājādhirājapavaro puna kārayāno
thūpaṃ purādhikataraṃ imam assa canto
gabbhe ṭhapeti munino varadhātuyomā.

thūpe pasanno vararājarājā
hemādipūjāhibhipūjiyetaṃ
puññena me tena anāgatatehaṃ
buddho bhaveyyanti varaṅkaro'ti.

92. Ibid., 188, 190; *Inscriptions of Pagan, Pinya, and Ava*, 7, 9, 14, and 22ff.
93. *Prachum silacharuek*, vol. 4, no. 93, face 2 (pp. 52–53):

iminā puññakammena mama mātāpitā ubho
sāmiko me mahādhammarājādhirājanāmako
sridhammarājamātā ca ye ca ñātī añātikā
sabbeva sukhitā hontu niddukkhā nirupaddavā
mama puññānubhāvena sabbe te tidivaṅgatā
chasu saggesu sampattiṃ anubhuñjantu kāmato
mama puññānubhāvena puriso homanāgate
metteyyasseva buddhassa aggadhammaṃ suṇāmahaṃ
tassāpi puññasambhāraṃ muddhāraṃ pacināmahaṃ
parisāgaṇamajjhamhi so maṃ buddho pasaṃsatu
dānādinā samo añño rūpenāpi yasena vā
āyunā dhanarāsihi mā me hotu bhave bhave
mesaṃ nādātukāmassa koci sakkotu gaṇhituṃ
apica mama santasaṃ daliddānaṃ payojanaṃ
gambhīrāpāradānādi sāgarehi susitale
nimujjitvā munindā va sambodhiṃ pāpuṇāmahaṃ
imasmiṃ nagare rajjaṃ kāressanti anāgate
khattiyā ceva uggā ca dhammikā ye mahāyasā
sabbe te anumodantu puññakamme mayā kate
pūjāvatthūni vaḍḍhantu puññakammarattā idhā'ti.

94. Caldarola, *Religions and Societies*, 401–2n1.
95. Bechert, "Theravāda Buddhist Sangha," 773.
96. *Khuddakapāṭha.*, 6.
97. A valid research topic would be an examination of how in a single ceremony people bring together different types of cults, rituals, and practices. Such investigation may yield insight into how these supposedly contradictory beliefs have worked together for the benefit of the peoples of Southeast Asia.
98. Cœdès, *Indianized States*, 33ff.
99. Tambiah, *Buddhism and the Spirit Cults*, 253ff.
100. Luce, *Old Burma-Early Pagan*, vol. 1, 49.

Bibliography

Aiyangar, Krishnaswami. "The Buddhism of Manimekhalai." In *Buddhistic Studies*, edited by Bimala Churn Law, 3–25. Calcutta: Thacker, Spink & Company, Ltd., 1931.

Aiyappan, A. and P. R. Srinivasan, eds. *Story of Buddhism with Special Reference to South India*. Madras: Government of Madras, 1960.

Ames, Michael M. "Magical-animism and Buddhism: A Structural Analysis of the Sinhalese Religious System." *Journal of Asian Studies* 23, no. 3 (1964): 21–52.

Anan Ganjanapan. "Wai Pii Muang and the State's Power in Lanna." In *Thailand: Culture and Society*, 149–61. In Thai with abstract in English.

Anuman Rajadhon, Phya. *Essays on Thai Folklore*. Bangkok: Thai Inter-Religious Commission for Development and the Sathirakoses Nagapradipa Foundation, 1987. First published 1968 by the Social Science Association Press of Thailand.

———. *Popular Buddhism in Siam and Other Essays on Thai Studies*. Bangkok: Thai Inter-Religious Commission for Development and the Sathirakoses Nagapradipa Foundation, 1986.

Archaeological Survey of Burma. *Annual Reports of the Archaelogical Survey, Burma Circle*. Rangoon: Office of the Superintendent, Government Printing, 1901–1926.

Archaeological Survey of India. *Annual Reports of the Archaeological Survey of India*. Simla and Delhi: Archaeological Survey of India, 1901 and following.

Asian Review. Bangkok: Institute of Asian Studies, Chulalongkorn University. 1980 and following.

Auboyer, Jeannine, Jean Boisselier, Michel Beurdeley, Huguette Rousset, and Chantal Massonaud. *Oriental Art: A Handbook of Styles and Forms*. Translated by Elizabeth and Richard Bartlett. New York: Rizzoli International Publications, Inc., 1980.

Aung Thaw. *Historical Sites in Burma*. Rangoon: Ministry of Union Culture, Government of the Union of Burma, 1972.

Aung-Thwin, Michael. *Pagan: The Origins of Modern Burma*. Honolulu: University of Hawai'i Press, 1985.

Ba Maw. "The First Discovery in the Evolution of Anyathian Cultures from a Single Site in Myanmar." *Myanmar Historical Research Journal* 2 (June 1998): 97–105.

Ba Shin, Jean Boisselier, and A. B. Griswold, eds. *Essays Offered to G. H. Luce By His Friends and Colleagues: In Honour of his Seventy-fifth Birthday (EOGHLUCE)*. AA Supplementum 23. 2 vols. Ascona, Switzerland: Artibus Asiae, 1966.

Bandaranayake, Senake. *Sinhalese Monastic Architecture: The Vihāras of Anurādhapura*. Edited by J. E. Van Lohuizen-de Leeuw. Studies in South Asian Culture. Leiden: E. J. Brill, 1974.

Bareau, André. *Les sectes bouddhiques du Petit Véhicule*. Publications de l'École Française d'Extrême-Orient Paris, vol. 38. Saigon: École Française d'Extrême-Orient, 1955.

Basak, Radhagovinda, ed. *Asokan Inscriptions.* Calcutta: Progressive Publishers, 1959.

Basham A. L. *The Wonder That Was India.* Vol. 2, *A Survey of the History and Culture of the Indian Sub-Continent from the Coming of the Muslims to the British Conquest.* London: Sidgwick and Jackson, 1987.

Bayard, Donn. "The Roots of Indo-Chinese Civilization: Recent Developments in the Prehistory of Southeast Asia." *Pacific Affairs* 53, no. 1 (1980): 89–114.

Beals, Alan R. "Conflict and Interlocal Festivals in a South Indian Region." *Journal of Asian Studies* 23 (June 1964): 99–114.

———. *Village India: Studies in the Little Community.* Edited by McKim Marriot. Comparative Studies of Cultures and Civilizations, Memoir No. 83 of the American Anthropology Association. Chicago: University of Chicago Press, 1969.

Bechert, Heinz. "Aspects of Theravāda Buddhism in Sri Lanka and Southeast Asia." In *The Buddhist Heritage*, edited by Tadeusz Skorupski, 19–28. Tring: The Institute of Buddhist Studies, 1989.

———, ed. *Buddhism in Ceylon and Studies on Religious Syncretism in Buddhist Countries.* From the Series Symposien zur Buddhismusforchung, I. Göttingen: Vandenhoech & Ruprecht, 1978.

———. *Buddhismus, Staat und Gesellschaft in der Ländern des Theravāda-Buddhismus.* Frankfurt and Berlin: Metzner, 1966.

———. "Contradictions in Sinhalese Buddhism." In Smith, *Tradition and Change in Theravada Buddhism*, 7–17.

______. "Some Sidelights on the Early History of Pāli Lexicography." In *Añjali: Papers on Indology and Buddhism: A Felicitation Volume Presented to Oliver Hector de Alwis Wijesekera*, edited by J. Tilakasiri. Peradeniya: Felicitation Volume Editorial Committee, University of Ceylon, 1970.

———. "Theravāda Buddhist Sangha: Some General Observations on Historical and Political Factors in its Development." *Journal of Asian Studies* 29 (1970): 761–78.

Bechert, Heinz, and Richard Gombrich, eds. *The World of Buddhism.* London: Thames and Hudson, 1984.

Bekker, Sarah M. "Transformations of the *Nats*: The Humanization Process in the Deception of the Thirty-Seven Lords of Burma." Special Burma Studies Issue. *Crossroads* 4, no. 1 (fall 1988): 40–45.

Bellah, Robert. "Religion: The Sociology of Religion." In *International Encyclopedia of the Social Sciences.* New York: Macmillan and Free Press, 1968.

Benda, Harry. *Continuity and Change in Southeast Asia: Collected Journal Articles of Harry J. Benda.* Yale University Southeast Asian Studies. Monograph Series, No. 18. New Haven: Yale University Southeast Asian Studies, 1972. First published as "The Structure of Southeast Asian History: Some Preliminary Observations," *Journal of Southeast Asian History* 3, no. 1 (1962): 106–38.

Bhattacharya, Kamaleswar. *Les religions brahmaniques dans l'ancien Cambodge.* Publication de l'École Française d'Extrême-Orient, vol. 49. Paris: École Française d'Extrême-Orient, 1961.

Bizot, François. *Le Bouddhisme des Thaïs: Brève histoire de ses mouvements et de ses idées des origines à nos jours.* Bangkok: Éditions des Cahiers de France, 1993.

Blagden, C. O. "Notes on Talaing Epigraphy." *Journal of the Burma Research Society* 2, no. 1 (June 1912): 38–43.

———. "Shan Buddhism." *Journal of the Royal Asiatic Society* 2 (1912): 495–96.

Bodhi, Bhikkhu, trans. *The Discourse on the All-Embracing Net of Views: The Brahmajala Sutta and Its Commentaries.* Kandy: Buddhist Publication Society, 1978.

Boelès, J. J. "Two Yoginis of Hevajra from Thailand." In Ba Shin, et al., *EOGHLUCE*, AA, Supplementum 23, vol. 2, 14–29.

Boisselier, Jean. *Le Cambodge.* Manuel d'Archéologie d'Extrême-Orient (première partie). Paris: Éditions A. et J. Picard et Cie, 1966.

———."Un fragment inscrit de Roue de la Loi de Lop'buri." *Artibus Asiae* 24, no. 1 (1961): 225–31.

———. "Nouvelles données sur l'histoire ancienne de la Thaïlande." In *Boranwitthaya rueang mueang U Thong.* Bangkok: Department of Fine Arts, 1966.

———. "U Thong et son importance pour l'histoire de Thaïlande." In *Boranwitthaya rueang mueang U Thong.* Bangkok: Department of Fine Arts, 1966.

Bollée, Willem B., ed. *The Pādas of the Suttanipāta. With Parallels from the Ayāranga, Sūyagada, Uttarajjhāyā Dasaveyāliya and Isibhāsiyāim.* Studien zur Indologie und Iranistik. Monographie 7. Reinbek: Verlag für Orientalistische Fachpublikationen, 1980.

———., ed. *Reverse Index of the Dhammapada, Suttanipāta, Thera- and Therīgāthā Pādas with Parallels from the Ayāranga, Sūyagada, Uttarajjhāya Dasaveyāliya and Isibhāsiyāim. Studien zur Indologie und Iranistik.* Monographie 8. Reinbek: Verlag für Orientalistische Fachpublikationen, 1983.

Bongard-Levin, G. M. "Fragment of Saka Version of the *Dharmaśarīra-sūtra* from the N. F. Petrovsky Collection." *Indo-Iranian Journal* 11, no. 4 (1969): 269–80.

Borankhadi si phak [Archaeological discoveries in four regions of Thailand]. Bangkok: Department of Fine Arts, 1988.

Boranwitthaya rueang mueang U Thong [Archaeology concerning U Thong]. Bangkok: Department of Fine Arts, 1966.

Brac de La Perriere, Benedicte. *Les rituels de possession en Birmanie: du culte d'État aux cérémonies privées.* Paris: Éditions Recherche sur les Civilisations, 1989.

Briggs, Lawrence Palmer. "The Hinduized States of Southeast Asia: A Review." In *South and Southeast Asia: Enduring Scholarship Selected from the Far Eastern Quarterly and the Journal of Asian Studies, 1941–1971*, edited by John A. Harrison, 181–96. Tucson: The University of Arizona, 1972. Originally published in the *Far Eastern Quarterly* 7, no. 4 (1948): 376–93.

———. "The Syncretism of Religions in Southeast Asia, especially in the Khmer Empire." *Journal of the American Oriental Society* 71, no. 4 (1951): 230–49.

Brohm, John. "Buddhism and Animism in a Burmese Village." *Journal of Asian Studies* 22, no. 2 (1963): 155–67.

Bukkyō daijiten [Encyclopedia of Buddhism]. 7 vols. Edited by Mochizuki Shinkō. Tokyo: Bukkyō Daijiten Hakkojo, 1932–1964.

Bussho kaisetsu daijiten [Encyclopedia of Buddhist literature]. 12 vols. Edited by Ono Genmyō. Tokyo: Daitō Shuppan, 1936.

Caldarola, Carlo, ed. *Religions and Societies: Asia and the Middle East.* New York: Mouton, 1982.

Cambridge History of Southeast Asia. 4 vols. Edited by Nicholas Tarling. Cambridge: Cambridge University Press, 1999.

de Casparis, J. G. "Palaeography as an Auxiliary Discipline in Research on Early Southeast Asia." In R. B. Smith, *Early South East Asia,* 380–94.

———. *Prasasti Indonesia I.* Bandung: A. C. Nix and Company, 1950.

———. *Prasasti Indonesia II.* Bandung: Masa Baru, 1956.

Charnvit Kasetsiri. *The Rise of Ayudhya: A History of Siam in the Fourteenth and Fifteenth Centuries.* Kuala Lumpur: Oxford University Press, 1976.

Charuek Boran Run Raek phop thi Lopburi lae klai khiang [Ancient inscriptions found in Lopburi and its vicinity]. Bangkok: Department of Fine Arts, 1981.

Charuek nai Prathet Thai [Inscriptions in Thailand]. 5 vols. Bangkok: National Library of Thailand, 1986.

Charuek samai Sukhothai [Inscriptions of the Sukhothai period]. Bangkok: Department of Fine Arts, 1983.

Chavannes, E. *Mémoire composé à l'époque de la grande dynastie T'ang sur les religieux éminents qui allèrent chercher la loi dans les pays d'Occident.* Paris: Ernest Leroux, 1894.

Chhabra, Bahadur Chand. *Expansion of Indo-Aryan Culture during Pallava Rule (as evidenced by inscriptions).* Delhi: Munshiram Manoharlal, 1965.

Chihara, Daigoro. *Hindu-Buddhist Architecture in Southeast Asia.* Translated by Rolf W. Giebel. Leiden: E. J. Brill, 1996.

Cœdès, George. "Documents sur l'histoire politique et religieuse du Laos occidental." *Bulletin de l'École Française d'Extrême-Orient* (*BEFEO*) 25 (1925): 1–204.

———. *The Indianized States of Southeast Asia.* 3d ed. Edited by Walter F. Vella. Translated by Susan Brown Cowing. Honolulu: The University of Hawai'i Press, 1968 (1st French ed. 1962).

———. "Les langues de l'Indochine." *Conférence de L'Institut de Linguistique de l'Université de Paris* 8 (1940–1948): 63–81.

———. *The Making of South East Asia.* Translated by H. M. Wright. Berkeley: University of California Press, 1966.

———. "Les Mōns de Dvāravatī." In Ba Shin, et al. *EOGHLUCE,* AA, Supplementum 23, vol. 1, 112–16.

———, ed. and trans. *Prachum silacharuek phak thī 2: Charuek Krung Thawarawadi Si wichai Lawo lae mueang prathetsarat khuen kae Krung Si Wichai = Recueil des Inscriptions du Siam: Inscriptions de Dvāravatī, de Çrīvijaya et de Lavo.* Bangkok: Department of Fine Arts, 1961. In Thai and French.

———. *Recueil des inscriptions du Siam. Première Partie: Inscriptions de Sukhodaya.* Bangkok: Bangkok Times Press, 1924.

———. *Recueil des inscriptions du Siam. Duexième Partie: Inscriptions de Dvāravatī, de Çrīvijaya et de Lavo.* Bangkok: Bangkok Times Press, 1929.

———. "Une Roue de la Loi avec inscription en pāli provenant du site de P'ra Pathom." *Artibus Asiae* 19, no. 3–4 (1956): 221–26.

———. "Le substrat sutochtone et la superstructure indienne au Cambodge et à Java." *Cahiers d'Histoire Mondiale* 1 (1953): 368–77.

———. "Tablettes votives bouddhiques du Siam." In *Études Asiatiques, I.* Paris: L'École Française d'Éxtrême-Orient, 1925.

———. "Une vie indochinoise du Bouddha: la Pathamasambodhi." In *Mélanges d'Indianisme.* 40e Anniversaire de la Fondation de L'Institut de Civilisation Indienne de l'Université de Paris, 217–28. Paris: Éditions E. de Boccard, 1968.

Condominas, George G. *Le bouddhisme au village. Notes ethnographiques sur les pratiques religieuses dans la société rurale Lao (plaine de Vientiane).* Vientiane: Éditions des Cahiers de France, 1998.

Conze, Edward. *A Short History of Buddhism.* London: Allen and Unwin, 1980.

Cousins, L., A. Kunst, and K. R. Norman, eds. *Buddhist Studies in Honour of I. B. Horner.* Dordrecht: D. Reidel Publishing Company, 1974.

Crossroads: An Interdisciplinary Journal of Southeast Asian Studies. DeKalb: Center for Southeast Asian Studies, Northern Illinois University, 1983 and following.

Cummings, Mary. *The Lives of the Buddha in the Art and Literature of Asia.* Michigan Papers on South and Southeast Asia, No. 20. Ann Arbor: University of Michigan, Center for South and Southeast Asian Studies, 1982.

Damais, Louis-Charles. "Études d'épigraphie indonésienne II: La date des inscriptions en ère de Sañjaya." BEFEO 45, fasc. 1 (1951): 1–41.

———. "Études d'épigraphie indonésienne III: Liste des principales inscriptions datées de l'Indonésie." BEFEO 46, fasc. 1 (1952): 1–105.

———. "Études d'épigraphie indonésienne IV: Discussion de la date des inscriptions." BEFEO 47, fasc. 1 (1955): 7–290.

———. "Études d'épigraphie indonésienne V: Dates des manuscrits et documents divers de Java, Bali et Lombok." BEFEO 49, fasc. 1 (1958): 7–29.

Damrong Rajanubhab, Prince. *Monuments of the Buddha in Siam.* 2d ed. Translated by Sulak Sivaraksa and A. B. Griswold. Bangkok: The Siam Society, 1973.

———. *Tamnān Khana Song* [Accounts of the Sangha]. Bangkok: Sophonphiphatthanakon, 1923.

D'Ancona, Mirella Levi. "Amarāvatī, Ceylon, and Three 'Imported Bronzes.'" *Art Bulletin* 36, no. 1 (1952): 1–18.

Dani, Ahmad Hasan. *Indian Palaeography.* Oxford: Clarendon Press, 1963.

Day, Terence P. *Great Tradition and Little Tradition in Theravāda Buddhist Studies.* Studies in Asian Thought and Religion, No. 7. Lewiston, NY: The Edwin Mellen Press, 1988.

Dhammapada, The. Edited by S. Radhakrishnan. London: Oxford University Press, 1950.

Dhanit Yupho. *Dharmacakra or the Wheel of Law,* 4th ed. Bangkok: Department of Fine Arts, 1974.

———. *Suvarnabhûmi.* Bangkok: Department of Fine Arts, 1967.

Dictionary of Pāli Proper Names. Edited by G. P. Malalasekera. 2 vols. London: Pali Text Society, 1974.

Diffloth, Gérard. "Reconstructing Dvāravatī-Old Mon." In *Recent Discoveries from the Period of Early Indian Influence,* edited by P. Bhumadon. Lopburi: Lopburi Museum Publications, 1981.

Dohanian, Diran K. *The Mahāyāna Buddhist Sculpture of Ceylon.* New York, London: Garland Publishing Inc., 1977.

Dupont, Pierre. "Études sur l'Indochine ancienne II: Les débuts de la royauté angkorienne." *BEFEO* 46 (1946): 119–76.

———. *L'archéologie mône de Dvāravatī.* Publications de l'École Française d'Extrême-Orient, vol. 41. Paris: École Française d'Extrême-Orient, 1959.

———. "Les Buddha dits d'Amarāvatī en Asie du Sud-Est." *BEFEO* 49 (1949): 631–36.

Duroiselle, Charles. "The Aris of Burma and Tantric Buddhism." *Annual Report of the Archaeological Survey of India* (1915–1916): 79–93.

———. "Inventaire des inscriptions pālies, sanskrites, mōn et pyū de Birmanie." *BEFEO* 12, no. 8 (1912): 19–33.

———. "Place-Names in Burma." *Annual Report of the Archaeological Survey of India* (1922–1923): 173–74.

Dutt, Nalinaksha. *Buddhist Sects in India.* 2d ed. Delhi: Motilal Banarsidass, 1978.

———. *Gilgit Manuscripts.* Vol. 1. Srinagar, 1939.

Elder, Joseph W., ed. *Chapters in Indian Civilization,* Vol. 1. Dubuque, Iowa: Kendall/Hunt Publishing Company, 1970.

Encyclopedia of Buddhism. 13 vols. Edited by M. G. Chikara. New Delhi: A. P. H. Publishing Corp., 1999.

Encyclopedia of Religion. 16 vols. Edited by Mircea Eliade. New York: Macmillan Publishing Co., 1987.

Epigraphia Birmanica: Being Lithic and Other Inscriptions of Burma. 4 vols. Edited by Charles Duroiselle. Rangoon: Office of the Superintendent, Government Printing, 1919–1936.

Epigraphia Indica. 5 vols. New Delhi: Archeological Survey of India. 1898–99 and following.

Epigraphia Zeylanica: Being Lithic and Other Inscriptions of Ceylon. 5 vols. Edited by Martino de Zilva Wickremasinghe, H. W. Codrington, and S. Paranavitana. London: H. Frowde for the Govt. of Ceylon, 1912–1933.

Études birmanes en hommage à Denise Bernot. Études thématiques 9. P. Pichard and F. Robinne, éds. Paris: École Française d'Extrême-Orient, 1998.

Études épigraphiques sur le pays Cham. Louis Finot, Edouard Huber, George Cœdès, et Paul Mus, éds. Paris: École Française d'Extrême-Orient, 1995 [Réimpression de l'École Française d'Extrême-Orient 7].

Filliozat, Jean. "Sur le çivaïsme et le bouddhisme du Cambodge à propos de deux libres récents." *BEFEO* 70 (1981): 59–99.

Finot, Louis. "Le plus ancien témoignage sur l'existence du Canon Pāli en Birmanie." *Journal Asiatique* (July–August 1913): 193–95.

———. "Un nouveau document sur le bouddhisme birman." *Journal Asiatique* 20 (July–August 1912): 121–36.

Fontein, Jan. "Notes on the *Jātakas* and *Avandānas* of Barabudur." In Gomez and Woodward, *Barabudur: History and Significance of a Buddhist Monument,* 85–108.

Forest, Alain. *Le culte des génies protecteurs au Cambodge: Analyse et traduction d'un corpus de textes sur les neak ta.* Paris: Editions L'Harmattan, 1992.

Foucher, Alfred C. A. *La vie du Bouddha d'après les textes et les monuments de l'Inde*. Bibliothèque historique. Paris: Payot, 1949.

Geertz, Clifford. "Religion: Anthropological Study." In *International Encyclopedia of the Social Sciences*, edited by David Sills, et al., 399–406. New York: Macmillan and Free Press, 1968.

Giles, H. A., trans. *The Travels of Fa-Hsien*. Cambridge: Cambridge University Press, 1923.

Gombaz, Gisbert. "L'Évolution du stūpa en Asie: Étude d'architecture bouddhique." *Mélanges chinois et bouddhiques 2*. Bruxelles: Institut Belge des Hautes Études Chinoises, 1932/1933.

Gombrich, Richard. "Merit Transference in Sinhalese Buddhism: Case Study of the Interaction between Doctrine and Practice." *History of Religions Journal* 11, no. 2 (November 1971): 203–19.

Gomez, Luis, and Hiram W. Woodward, Jr., ed. *Barabudur: History and Significance of a Buddhist Monument*. Berkeley Buddhist Studies Series, No. 2. Berkeley: Asian Humanities Press, 1981.

Goonaratne, Edmund R., ed. "*Telakaṭāhagāthā*." *Journal of the Pali Text Society* 1 (1884): 49–68.

Grimes, A. B. "The Journey of Fa-Hsien from Ceylon to Canton." *Journal of the Royal Asiatic Society, Malaya Branch* 19, no. 1 (1941): 76–92.

Griswold, A. B. "Imported Images and the Nature of Copying in the Art of Siam." In Ba Shin, et al., EOGHLUCE, AA Supplementum 23, vol. 2, 37–73.

Griswold, A. B., and Prasert na Nagara. "Epigraphic and Historical Studies No. 9: The Inscription of King Rama Gamhen of Sukhodaya (1292 A.D.)." *Journal of the Siam Society* 59 (1971): 179–228.

———. "Epigraphic and Historical Studies No. 14: Inscription of the Siva of Kāmben Bejra." *Journal of the Siam Society* 62 (1974): 223–39.

de Groot, J. J. M. *The Religious System of China: Its Ancient Form, Evolution, History and Present Aspect*. Vol. 2, Book 1, *Disposal of the Dead*. 1894. Reprint, Taipei: Chengwen, 1969.

Groslier, Bernard Philippe. "La cité hydraulique angkorienne: exploitation ou sur exploitation du sol?" BEFEO 66 (1979): 161–202.

Guillon, Emmanuel. "Jalon pour une histoire du bouddhisme en Asie du Sud-Est." *Peninsule* 15, nos. 8–9 (1984): 113–36.

———. *The Mons: A Civilization of Southeast Asia*. Bangkok: The Siam Society, 1999.

Gunawardana, R. A. H. L. "Buddhist Nikāyas in Medieval Ceylon." *Ceylon Journal of Historical and Social Sciences* 9 (1966): 55–66.

Hall, D. G. E. *A History of South-East Asia*. 3d ed. 1968. Reprint, Hong Kong: The Macmillan Press, 1977.

Hall, Kenneth. *Maritime Trade and State Development in Early Southeast Asia*. Honolulu: University of Hawai'i Press, 1985.

Halliday, Robert. *The Mons of Burma and Thailand*. 2 vols. Edited by Christian Bauer. Bangkok: White Lotus, 2000. First published as *The Talaings* in 1917 by Rangoon Government Printing.

Harley, J. B. and David Woodward, eds. *The History of Cartography*. Vol. 2, Book 2: *Cartography in the Traditional East and Southeast Asian Societies*. Chicago: University of Chicago Press, 1994.

Hazra, Kanai Lal. *The Buddhist Annals and Chronicles of South-East Asia*. New Delhi: Munshiram Manoharlal, 1986.

———. *History of Theravāda Buddhism in South-East Asia: With Special Reference to India and Ceylon*. New Delhi: Munshiram Manoharlal, 1982.

Heine-Geldern, Robert von. *Conceptions of State and Kingship in Southeast Asia*. Southeast Asia Program Data Paper, No. 18. Ithaca: Cornell University, 1956.

Higham, Charles. *The Archaeology of Mainland Southeast Asia from 10,000 B.C. to the Fall of Angkor*. Cambridge World Archaeology. Cambridge: Cambridge University Press, 1989.

———. *The Civilization of Angkor*. London: Weidenfeld and Nicolson, 2001.

Higham, Charles, and Rachanie Thosarat. *Prehistoric Thailand: From Early Settlement to Sukhothai*. Bangkok: River Books, 1998.

Hirakawa, Akira. "The Rise of Mahāyāna Buddhism and Its Relationship to the Worship of Stupas." *Memoirs of the Research Department of the Toyo Bunko* 22 (1963): 57–106.

Horner, I. B. *The Book of the Discipline*. Vol. 1. London: Pali Text Society, 1938.

Horsch, Paul. "The Wheel: An Indian Pattern of World Interpretation." *Sino-Indian Studies* 5, nos. 3–4 (1957): 62–79.

Htin Aung, Maung. "Burmese Buddhist Historiography." *International Association of Historians of Asia* 2 (n.d.): 1123–36.

———. *Folk Elements in Burmese Buddhism*. London: Oxford University Press, 1962. First published 1959 by Department of Religious Affairs, Rangoon, Burma.

I-Tsing. *A Record of the Buddhist Religion as Practised in India and the Malay Archipelago, A.D. 671–695*. Translated by J. Takakusu. Oxford: Clarendon Press, 1896.

Indrapala, K. "Buddhism among the Tamils A.D. 1000–1500." *In Proceedings of the 5th International Conference-Seminar on Tamil Studies*. Madras: International Association of Tamil Studies, 1981.

Inscriptions du Cambodge. Collection de Textes et Documents sur l'Indochine: III. 8 vols. Edited and translated by George Cœdès. Hanoi and Paris: École Française d'Extrême-Orient, 1937–1966.

Inscriptions of Pagan, Pinya, and Ava: Translation, with Notes. Rangoon: The Superintendent, Government Printing, Burma, 1899.

International Association of Historians of Asia. *Proceedings of the 7th IAHA Conference August 22–26, 1977*. Bangkok: Chulalongkorn University Press, 1977.

Irwin, John. "'Asokan' Pillars: A Reassessment of the Evidence, Part I." *Burlington Magazine* 115 (November 1973): 706–20.

———. "'Asokan' Pillars: A Reassessment of the Evidence, Part II: Structure." *Burlington Magazine* 116 (December 1974): 712–27.

———. "'Asokan' Pillars: A Reassessment of the Evidence, Part III: Capitals." *Burlington Magazine* 117 (October 1975): 631–43.

———. "'Asokan' Pillars: A Reassessment of the Evidence, Part IV: Symbolism," *Burlington Magazine* 118 (November 1976): 734–53.

Ito, Shoji. "On the Date and Analysis of Stone Dharmacakra Found in Thailand." In *Proceedings of the 7th IAHA Conference August 22–26, 1977*. Vol. 2.

Jacob, J. M. "Pre-Angkor Cambodia: Evidence from the Inscriptions in Khmer Concerning the Common People and their Environment." In R. B. Smith, *Early South East Asia*, 406–26.

Jacques, Claude. "'Funan,' 'Zhenla': The Reality Concealed by These Chinese Views of Indochina." In R. B. Smith, *Early South East Asia*, 371–79.

Jaini, Padmanabh S., ed. *Paññasa-Jātaka or Zimme Pannāsa*. Vol. 1 (*Jātakas* 1–25). London: Pali Text Society, 1981.

———, ed. *Paññasa-Jātaka or Zimme Pannāsa*. Vol. 2 (*Jātakas* 26–50). London: Pali Text Society, 1983.

———. "Śramaṇas: Their Conflict with Brahmanical Society." In Elder, *Chapters in Indian Civilization*, vol. 1, 39–82.

———. "The Story of Sudhana and Manoharā: An Analysis of the Texts and the Borobudur Reliefs." *Bulletin of the School of Oriental and African Studies* 29, no. 3 (1966): 533–58.

Jayawickrama, N. A., trans., A. B. Buddhadatta, ed. *The Sheaf of Garlands of the Epochs of the Conqueror: Being a Translation of Jinakālamālipakaranam of Ratanapanna Thera of Thailand*. London: The Pali Text Society, 1968.

Jenner, Philip N. *A Chrestomathy of Pre-Angkorian Khmer*. Southeast Asia Paper, No. 20, Part 1. Honolulu: Southeast Asia Studies, Asian Studies Program, University of Hawai'i, 1980.

———. *A Chronological Inventory of the Inscriptions of Cambodia*. Southeast Asia Paper, No. 19. Honolulu: Southeast Asia Studies, Asian Studies Program, University of Hawai'i, 1980.

Jinakālamālī. Transcribed from a Siamese text and edited by A. P. Buddhadatta. London: Luzac & Co., 1962 (published for the Pali Text Society).

de Jong, J. W. "The Background of Early Buddhism." *Indogaku bukkyōgaku kenkyū* [Journal of Indian and Buddhist Studies] 12 (1964): 34–47 (437–424) [English translaton of no. 105].

Kāraṇḍavyūha. In *Mahāyana-sūtra-saṅgraha*. Buddhist Sanskrit Texts, No. 17, Part 1, edited by P. L. Vaidya. Dharbhanga: The Mithila Institute, 1961.

Kempers, Bernet, and August Johan. *The Kettledrums of Southeast Asia: A Bronze Age World and Its Aftermath*. Rotterdam and Brookfield, VT: Balkema, 1988.

Keown, Damien. *Buddhism: A Very Short Introduction*. Oxford: Oxford University Press, 1996. Reprint, New York: Oxford University Press, 2000.

Keyes, Charles F. *The Golden Peninsula: Culture and Adaptation in Mainland Southeast Asia*. New York: Macmillan, 1977.

———. *Thailand: Buddhist Kingdom as Modern Nation-State*. Boulder: Westview Press, 1986.

Klausner, William J. *Reflections on Thai Culture*. Bangkok: The Siam Society, 1993.

Klin Khongmuaenphet. "From the West to the East: Following the Route of Villages along the Krabi Shore." *Muang Boran* 4, no. 3 (1988): 51–58. In Thai with English abstract.

Kongkeaw Veeraprajak, "Inscriptions from South Thailand." *SPAFA Digest*, 7, no. 1 (1986): 7–21.

Konow, Sten. "Remarks on the Khotanese Jātakastava." *Indian Historical Quarterly* 16, no. 2 (1940): 255–67.

Kulke, Hermann. *The Devarājā Cult.* Translated by I. W. Mabbett. Southeast Asia Program Data Paper, No. 108. Ithaca, NY: Southeast Asia Program, Department of Asian Studies, Cornell University, 1978.

———. "The Early and the Imperial Kingdom in Southeast Asian History." In Marr and Milner, *Southeast Asia in the 9th to 14th Centuries,* 1–22.

Lamotte, Étienne. *Histoire du bouddhisme indien des origines à l'ère Śaka.* Bibliothèque du Muséon, Vol 43. Louvain: Publications Universitaires, Université de Louvain, Institut Orientaliste, 1958.

———. "Le traité de l'acte de Vasubandhu: Karmasiddhiprakarana." *Mélanges chinois et bouddhiques 4.* Bruxelles: Institut Belge des Hautes Études Chinoises, 1935/1936.

Law, Bimla Churn, ed. *Buddhistic Studies.* Calcutta: Thacker, Spink & Company Ltd., 1931.

———. *On the Chronicles of Ceylon.* Bibliotheca Indo-Buddhica, No. 40. Delhi: Sri Satguru Publications, 1987.

———, tr. "*Telakaṭāhagāthā.*" *Indian Culture* 5 (1938–1939): 25–39.

Leach, E. R., ed. *Dialectic in Practical Religion.* Cambridge Papers in Social Anthropology, No. 5. Cambridge: Published for the Department of Archaeology and Anthropology at the University Press, 1968.

Lester, Robert C. *Buddhism: The Path to Nirvana.* Religious Traditions of the World Series, edited by H. Byron Earhart. San Francisco: Harper and Row, 1987.

———. *Theravada Buddhism in Southeast Asia.* Ann Arbor: University of Michigan Press, 1973.

Lévi, Sylvain. "Ptolémée, le Niddesa et la Bṛhatkathā." In *Études Asiatiques II,* 1–55. Paris: Publications de l'École Française d'Extrême-Orient, 1925.

Liebenthal, Walter. "Sanskrit Inscriptions from Yunnan I." *Monumenta Serica* 12. (1947): 1–40.

———. "Sanskrit Inscriptions from Yunnan II." *Sino-Indian Studies* 5, nos. 3/4 (1955): 1–23.

Luce, Gordon H. "The Advent of Buddhism to Burma." In Cousins, *Buddhist Studies in Honour of I. B. Horner,* 119–38.

———."The Early Syām in Burma's History." *Journal of the Siam Society* 46, no. 2 (1958): 123–213.

———. "The 550 Jātakas in Old Burma." *Artibus Asiae* 19, nos. 3–4 (1956): 291–307.

———. *Old Burma-Early Pagan.* 3 vols. Locust Valley, NY: J. J. Augustin, 1969–70.

Lunet de Lajonquière, Étienne Edmond. "Le domain archéologique du Siam." *BEFEO* 9 (1909): 351–68.

———. "Le domain archéologique du Siam." *Bulletin de la Commission Archéologique de l'Indo-Chine* (1909): 188–262.

———. "Essai d'inventaire archéologique du Siam." *Bulletin de la Commission Archéologique de l'Indo-Chine* (1912): 100–27.

Mabbett, Ian W. "Buddhism in Champa." In Marr and Milner, *Southeast Asia in the 9th to 14th Centuries,* 289–314.

———. "The 'Indianization' of Southeast Asia: Reflections on the Historical Sources." *Journal of Southeast Asian Studies* 8, no. 2 (1977): 143–61.

———. "Kingship in Angkor." *Journal of the Siam Society* 60, no. 2 (1978): 1–58.

Macdonell, Arthur A. *The Vedic Mythology.* Varanasi: Indological Book House, 1963. First edition Strassburg 1898.

Mahāyana-sūtra-saṅgraha. Buddhist Sanskrit Texts, No. 17, Part 1, edited by P. L. Vaidya. Dharbhanga: The Mithila Institute, 1961.

Majumdar, R. C. *Ancient Indian Colonies in the Far East,* Vol. 1, *Champā.* The Punjab Oriental (Sanskrit) Series, No. 16. Lahore: The Panjab Sanskrit Books Depot, 1927.

———. *The Classical Accounts of India.* Calcutta: Firma KLM, 1960.

———. *Hindu Colonies in the Far East.* Calcutta: General Printers and Publishers, 1944.

———. "India and Ceylon." *Indo-Asian Culture* 1 (July 1952): 17–25.

———. "The Indian Epics in Indo-China." *Indian Historical Quarterly* 22 (1946): 220–22.

———. *Inscriptions of Kambuja.* Calcutta: The Asiatic Society, 1953.

———. "King Sūryavarman I of Kambuja." *Journal of the Greater Indian Society* 10 (1943): 136–44.

———. "La paléographie des inscriptions du Champā." *BEFEO* 32 (1932): 127–39.

———. "Les rois Cailendra de Suvarnadvīpa." *BEFEO* 33 (1933): 120–46.

———. "Some Aspects of Indo-kambuja Culture." *Indo-Asian Culture* 2 (1953): 247–54.

———. *Suvarṇadvīpa.* Dacca: Ashoka Kumar Majumdar, 1937.

Malleret, Louis. *L'Archéologie du delta du Mékong.* Paris: École Française d'Extrême-Orient, 1959–1963.

Manit Vallibhotama. *Suvarnabhûmi yu thi nai* [Where is Suvarṇabhūmi?]. Bangkok: Karawek Publishing Company, 1978.

Marr, David G., and A. C. Milner, eds. *Southeast Asia in the 9th to 14th Centuries.* Singapore: Institute of Southeast Asian Studies and the Research School of Pacific Studies at the Australian National University, 1986.

Marriott, McKim. "Little Communities in an Indigenous Civilization." In *Village India: Studies in the Little Community,* ed. McKim Marriott, 171–222. Chicago: The University of Chicago 1955.

Masson, Joseph. *La religion populaire dans le canon bouddhique pâli.* Louvain: Bureux du Muséon, 1942.

Minakshi, C. "Buddhism in South India." In *South Indian Studies II,* edited by R. Nagaswamy, 83–131. Madras: Society for Archaeological, Historical, and Epigraphical Research, 1978.

Modelski, George. "Kautilya: Foreign Policy and International System in the Ancient Hindu World." *American Political Science Review* 58, no. 3 (1964): 549–60.

Muang Boran Journal. Bangkok: Muang Boran. 1974 and following. In Thai with some English text and/or abstracts.

Mulder, Niels. "Concepts of Power and Moral Goodness in the Contemporary Thai World-View." *Journal of the Siam Society* 67, no. 1 (January 1979): 111–31.

Mus, Paul. *Barabudur: Esquisse d'une histoire du bouddhisme fondée sur la critique archéologique des textes.* 2 vols. Hanoï: Imprimarie d'Extréme-Orient, 1935.

———. *India Seen from the East: Indian and Indigenous Cults in Champa.* Translated by I. W. Mabbett. Monash Papers of Southeast Asia, No. 3, edited by I. W. Mabbett and D. P. Chandler. Clayton, Victoria, Australia: Centre of Southeast Asian Studies, Monash University, 1975. Originally published as "Cultes indiens et idigenes au Champa," in *BEFEO* 33 (1933): 376–410.

Myanmar Historical Research Journal. Yangon: Universities Historical Research Centre, Ministry of Education, 1995 and following.

Nagao, Gadjin. "On the Theory of the Buddha-Body (Buddha-kāya)." *The Eastern Buddhist* 6, no. 1 (1973): 25–53.

Nandana Chutiwongs. "On the Jataka Reliefs at Chula-Pathon Cetiya: Review of *Buddhist Folk Tales Depicted at Chula Pathon Cedi* by Piriya Krairiksh." *Journal of the Siam Society* 66, no. 1 (1978): 133–51.

Ng, R. C. Y. "The Geographic Habitat of Historical Settlement in Mainland South East Asia." In R. B. Smith, *Early South East Asia*, 262–72.

Nidhi Aeusrivongse, "The Devarājā Cult and Khmer Kingship at Angkor," in *Explorations in Early Southeast Asia: The Origins of Southeast Asian Statecraft.* Papers on South and Southeast Asia No. 11, ed. Kenneth R. Hall and John K. Whitmore, 107–49. Ann Arbor: University of Michigan, 1976.

Norman, K. R. "The Pāli Language and Scriptures." In *The Buddhist Heritage*, edited by Tadeusz Skorupski, 29–54. Tring: The Institute of Buddhist Studies, 1989.

———. *Pāli Literature: Including the Canonical Literature in Prakrit and Sanskrit of all the Hīnayāna Schools of Buddhism.* A History of Indian Literature Series, No. 7, Fasc. 2. Wiesbaden: Otto Harrassiwitz, 1983.

———. "The Role of Pāli in Early Sinhalese Buddhism." In Bechert, *Buddhism in Ceylon and Studies on Religious Syncretism in Buddhist Countries*, 28–47.

O'Connor, Richard A. "Agricultural Change and Ethnic Succession in Southeast Asian States: A Case for Regional Anthropology." *Journal of Asian Studies* 54, no. 4 (November 1995): 968–96.

Oertel, F. O. "Excavations at Sârnâth." *Annual Report of the Archeological Survey of India 1904–5.* Calcutta: Superintendent Government Printing, 1908, 59–106.

Pachow, W. "The Voyage of Buddhist Missions to South-East Asia and the Far East." *Journal of the Greater Indian Society* 17, nos. 1–2 (1958): 1–22.

Pals, Daniel L. *Seven Theories of Religion.* New York: Oxford University Press, 1996.

Pande, Govind Chandra. *Studies in the Origins of Buddhism.* New Delhi: Motilal Banarsidass Publishers, 1983.

Pandey, L. P. *Sun-Worship in Ancient India.* Delhi: Motilal Banarasidass Publishers, 1971.

Paññāsāmīsirikavividhaja, Maungduang Saya. *The History of the Buddha's Religion.* 2d ed. Translated by B. C. Law. Bibliotheca Buddhica Series, No. 29. Delhi: Sri Satguru Publications, 1986.

Paranavitana, Senarat. "Epigraphical Summary." *Ceylon Journal of Science*, section G1, part 4 (February 1928): 165–74.

———. "Epigraphical Summary." *Ceylon Journal of Science*, section G2, part 1 (December 1928): 17–30.

———. "Epigraphical Summary." *Ceylon Journal of Science* , section G2, part 2 (August 1930): 99–128.

———. "Epigraphical Summary." *Ceylon Journal of Science*, section G2, part 3 (October 1933): 175–228.

———. "Mahāyānism in Ceylon." *Ceylon Journal of Science*, section G2, part 1 (December 1928): 35–71.

———. "The Religious Intercourse between Ceylon and Siam in the Thirteenth and Fifteenth Centuries." *Journal of the Royal Asiatic Society, Ceylon Branch* 32, no. 85 (1932): 190–212.

Paṭissambhidāmagga: The Path of Discrimination. Translated by Ven. Ñāṇamoli. Bristol: Pali Text Society, 1982.

Pelliot, Paul. "Deux itinéraires de Chine en Inde à la fin du 8e siècle." *BEFEO* 4 (1904): 131–413.

Pfanner, David E., and Jasper Ingersoll. "Theravada Buddhism and Village Economic Behavior: A Burmese and Thai Comparison." *Journal of Asian Studies* 21, no. 3 (1962): 341–61.

Pham Huy Thông. *Dong Son Drums in Vietnam.* Hanoi: Vietnam Social Science Publishing House, 1990.

Pichet Suypan. "Nam Tao Pung: The Structural Analysis of the Myths of Origin." In *Thailand: Culture and Society*, 116–36. In Thai with abstract in English.

Piker, Steven. "The Relations of Belief Systems to Behavior in Rural Thai Society." *Asian Survey* 8, no. 5 (1968): 384–99.

Piriya Krairiksh. *Buddhist Folk Tales Depicted at Chula Pathon Cedi.* Bangkok: Prachandra Printing Press, 1974.

Porée-Maspéro, Eveline. *Cérémonies privées des cambodgiens.* Phnom-Penh: Éditions de l'Institut Bouddhique et Commission des Mœurs et Coutumes, 1958.

———. "La cérémonie de l'appel des esprits vitaux chez les cambodgiens." *BEFEO* 45, fasc. 1 (1951): 145–83.

———. *Étude sur les rites agraires des cambodgiens.* 3 vols. Paris: La Haye, Mouton & Co., 1962–1969.

Prachum silacharuek [Collection of inscriptions]. 7 vols. Bangkok: Department of Fine Arts, 1924–1993.

Pranee Wongthet. "Ancestor Worship among the Khamu." In *Thailand: Culture and Society*, 137–48. In Thai with abstract in English.

Premier Symposium Franco-Thaï: La Thaïlande des débuts de son histoire au XVème siècle. Bangkok: Université de Silapakorn, 18–20 Juillet 1988.

Radhakrishnan, S., ed. and trans. *The Principal Upanisads.* The Muirhead Library of Philosophy Series. Edited by H. D. Lewis. London: George Allen and Unwin Ltd., 1953.

Rahula, Wapola. *History of Buddhism in Ceylon.* Colombo, Ceylon: M. D. Gunasena and Company, 1956.

Raingan Kansammana Prawattisat Nakhon Si Thammarat [Proceedings from the conference on the history of Nakhon Si Thammarat]. Edited by Witthayalai Khru. Bangkok: Witthayalai Khru Nakhon Si Thammarat, 1978.

Rajani, M. C. Chand Chirayu. *Towards a History of Laem Thong and Sri Vijaya.* Asian Studies Monographs, No. 34. Bangkok: Institute of Asian Studies, Chulalongkorn University, 1987.

Ray, Himanshu Prabha. "Early Maritime Contacts between South and Southeast Asia." *Journal of Southeast Asian Studies* 20, no. 1 (1989): 42–54.

———. *Monastery and Guild: Commerce under the Sātavāhanas.* Delhi and New York: Oxford University Press, 1986.

Ray, Nihar Ranjan. *Brahmanical Gods in Burma.* Calcutta: University of Calcutta, 1932.

———. *An Introduction to the Study of Theravāda Buddhism in Burma.* Calcutta: University of Calcutta, 1946.

———. *Sanskrit Buddhism in Burma.* Calcutta: University of Calcutta, 1936.

Recherches nouvelles sur le Cambodge. Études thématiques 1. F. Bizot, éd. Paris: École de Française d'Extrême-Orient, 1994.

Research Conference on Early Southeast Asia, Bangkok and Nakhon Pathom, 8–13 April 1985. Bangkok: British Institute in South-east Asia and Silapakorn University, 1988.

Reynolds, Frank E. "From Philology to Anthropology: A Bibliographical Essay on Works Related to Early Theravāda and Sinhalese Buddhism." In *The Two Wheels of Dhamma: Essays on the Theravada Tradition in India and Celyon*, edited by Gananath Obeyesekere, Frank Reynolds, and Bardwell L. Smith, 107–21. American Academy of Religion, No. 3. Chambersburg, PA: American Academy of Religion, 1972.

———."Totalities, Dialectics, and Transformations: Review of *World Conqueror and World Renouncer* by S. J. Tambiah." *History of Religions* 18, no. 1 (1978): 258–68.

———. "Tradition and Change in Theravāda Buddhism: A Bibliographical Essay Focused on the Modern Period." In Smith, *Tradition and Change in Theravāda Buddhism*, 94–104.

Richman, Paula. *Women, Branch Stories, and Religious Rhetoric in a Tamil Buddhist Text.* Foreign and Comparative Studies, South Asian Series, No. 12. Syracuse, NY: Maxwell School of Citizenship and Public Affairs, Syracuse University, 1988.

Rodrique, Yves. *Nat-Pwe: Burma's Supernatural Sub-culture.* Gartmore, Scotland: Kiscadale, 1992.

Rong Syamananda. *A History of Thailand.* Bangkok: Chulalongkorn University, 1977.

Saddhātissa, Hammalawa. "Pāli Literature of Thailand." In Cousins, *Buddhist Studies in Honour of I. B. Horner*, 211–25.

Sarkar, H. B. *Cultural Relations between India and Southeast Asian Countries.* New Delhi: India Council for Cultural Relations and Motilal Banarsidass, 1985.

Sāsanavaṃsa. Edited by Mabel Haynes Bode. London: Pali Text Society, 1897.

Sastri, K. A. Nilakanta. "Ancient Indian Contacts with Western Lands." *Diogenes: A Quarterly Publication of the International Council for Philosophy and Humanistic Studies* 28 (1959): 40–62.

———. "Dvīpāntara." *Journal of Greater Indian Society* 9, no. 1 (1942): 1–4.

———. *A History of South India: From Prehistoric Times to the Fall of Vijayanagar.* 3d ed. Bombay: Oxford University Press, 1966. 2nd Impression 1971.

Saunders, E. Dale. *Mudrā: A Study of Symbolic Gestures in Japanese Buddhist Sculpture.* Bollingen Series, No. 58. Princeton, NJ: Princeton University Press, 1960.

Schopen, Gregory. "The Inscription on the Kusān Image of Amithābha and the Character of the Early Mahāyāna in India." *Journal of the International Association of Buddhist Studies* 10, no. 2 (1987): 99–134.

———. "Mahāyāna in Indian Inscriptions." *Indo-Iranian Journal* 21 (1979): 1–19.

———. "On Monks, Nuns and 'Vulgar' Practices: The Introduction of the Image Cult into Indian Buddhism." *Artibus Asiae* 49, nos. 1–2 (1988–1989): 153–68.

———. "The Phrase 'sa pṛthivīpradeśaś caityabhūto bhavet' in the *Vajracchedikā*: Notes on the Cult of the Book in Mahāyāna." *Indo-Iranian Journal* 17 (1975): 147–81.

———. "Sukhāvatī as a Generalized Religious Goal in Sanskrit Mahāyāna Sūtra Literature." *Indo-Iranian Journal* 19 (1977): 177–210.
———. "Two Problems in the History of Indian Buddhism: The Layman/Monk Distinction and the Doctrine of the Transference of Merit." *Studien zur Indologie und Iranistik* 10 (1985): 9–47.
Schwartzberg, Joseph E. "Cosmography in Southeast Asia." In *The History of Cartography*. Vol. 2, Book 2, *Cartography in the Traditional East and Southeast Asian Societies*, edited by J. B. Harley and David Woodward, 701–40. Chicago: University of Chicago Press, 1994.
———. "Introduction to Southeast Asian Cartography." In Harley and Woodward, *The History of Cartography*, 689–700.
Shizutani, Masao. *Indo bukkyō himei mokuroku* [Catalog of Indian Buddhist inscriptions]. Kyoto: Heirakuji Shoten, 1979.
Shorto, H. L. "The Linguistic Protohistory of Mainland South East Asia, with Comment by D. T. Bayard." In R. B. Smith, *Early South East Asia*, 273–80.
Siam Society. *The Archaeology of Peninsular Siam: Collected Articles from the Journal of the Siam Society, 1905–1983*. Bangkok: The Siam Society, 1986.
Silapakorn Journal. Bangkok: Department of Fine Arts, 1970 and following.
Siraporn Nathalang. "An Analysis of the Creation Myths of the Tai Speaking Peoples." In *Thailand: Culture and Society*, 88–15. In Thai with abstract in English.
———. "Conflict and Compromise between the Indigenous Beliefs and Buddhism as Reflected in Thai Rice Myths." In Siraporn Nathalang, *Thai Folklore*, 99–122.
———. "Tai Creation Myths: Reflections of Tai Relations and Tai Cultures." In Siraporn Nathalang, *Thai Folklore*, 81–98.
———, ed. *Thai Folklore: Insight into Thai Culture*. Bangkok: Chulalongkorn University Press, 2000.
Sircar, D. C. *Indian Epigraphy*. Delhi: Motilal Banarsidass, 1965.
———. *Inscriptions of Asoka*. New Delhi: Publications Division, Ministry of Information and Broadcasting, Government of India, 1957.
———. "Inscriptions in Sanskritic and Dravidian Languages." *Ancient India* 9 (1953): 212–32.
Sircar, D. C., and A. N. Lahiri. "Footprint Slab Inscription from Nagarjunikonda." *Epigraphica Indica* 33 (1959–1960): 247–50.
Sirisena, W. M. *Sri Lanka and South-East Asia: Political, Religious, and Cultural Relations from A.D. c. 1000 to c. 1500*. Leiden: E. J. Brill, 1978.
Smith, Bardwell L., ed. *Tradition and Change in Theravada Buddhism: Essays on Ceylon and Thailand in the 19th and 20th Centuries*. Contributions to Asian Studies, vol. 4. Leiden: E. J. Brill, 1973.
Smith, Donald E. *Religion and Politics in Burma*. Princeton, NJ: Princeton University, 1965.
Smith, R. B., and W. Watson, eds. *Early South East Asia: Essays in Archaeology, History and Historical Geography*. New York and Oxford: Oxford University Press, 1979.
Snellgrove, David L., ed. *The Image of the Buddha*. Tokyo: Kodansha International, 1980.
Snodgrass, Adrian. *The Symbolism of the Stupa*. Studies on Southeast Asia. NY: Southeast Asia Program, Cornell University, 1985.

Souyris-Rolland, André. "Contribution à l'étude du culte des génies tutélaires ou 'Neak Ta' chez cambodgiens du sud." *Bulletin de la Société des Études Indochinoises* 26, no. 2 (1951): 161–73.

Spiro, Melford E. *Buddhism and Society: A Great Tradition and Its Burmese Vicissitudes.* 2d ed. Berkeley: University of California Press, 1982.

———. *Burmese Supernatrualism.* Expanded Edition. Edison, NJ: Transaction Publishers, 1996. First published in 1967 by Prentice-Hall.

Srisakra Vallibhotama. *Borankhadi Thai nai thotsawat thi phan ma* [Thai archaeology in the past decade]. Bangkok: Muang Boran Publications, 1982.

———. "Political and Cultural Continuities at Dvāravatī Sites." In Marr and Milner, *Southeast Asia in the 9th to 14th Centuries,* 229–38.

Staal, J. Frits. "Substitutions de paradigmes et religions d'Asie." *Cahiers d'Extrême-Asie* 1 (1985): 21–57.

Stargardt, Janice. *The Ancient Pyu of Burma.* Cambridge: PACSEA and Singapore: In association with the Institute of Southeast Asian Studies, 1990.

Strong, John S. "The Buddhist Avadānists and the Elder Upagupta." In *Tantric and Taoist Studies in Honour of R. A. Stein,* edited by Michael Stickmann, *Mélanges chinois et bouddhiques* 22, no. 3 (1985): 862–81.

———. *The Legend of King Aśoka: A Study and Translation of the Aśokāvadāna.* Princeton, NJ: Princeton University Press, 1983.

Swearer, Donald K. "Myth, Legend and History in the Northern Thai Chronicles." *Journal of the Siam Society* 62, no. 1 (1974): 67–88.

Tai Culture. Berlin: Southeast Asia Communication Centre (SEACOM). 1996 and following.

Takushi, Sugimoto. "Buddha called Mahādeva and Pitāmaha." In *Proceedings of the 31st International Congress of Human Sciences in Asia and North Africa,* edited by Yamamoto Tatsuro, 24–25. Kyoto–Tokyo: The Tōhö Gakkai, 1984.

Tambiah, Stanley. J. *Buddhism and the Spirit Cults in North-east Thailand.* Cambridge Studies in Social Anthropology 2. London: Cambridge University Press, 1970.

———. *The Buddhist Saints of the Forest and the Cult of Amulets: A Study in Charisma, Hagiography, Sectarianism, and Millennial Buddhism.* Cambridge Studies in Social Anthropology, No. 49. Cambridge: Cambridge University Press, 1984.

———. "The Ideology of Merit and the Social Correlates of Buddhism in a Thai Village." In *Dialectic in Practical Religion,* edited by E. R. Leach, 41–121. London: Cambridge University Press, 1968.

———. *World Conqueror and World Renouncer: A Study of Buddhism and Polity in Thailand against a Historical Background.* Cambridge Studies in Social Anthropology, No. 15. Cambridge: Cambridge University Press, 1976.

Tamnān Mūlasāsanā [Chronicles of the origins of the teaching]. Bangkok: Department of Fine Arts, 1987.

Terwiel, B. J. "A Model for the Study of Thai Buddhism." *Journal of Asian Studies* 35, no. 3 (1976): 391–403.

Tet Htoot, U. "The Nature of the Burmese Chronicles." In *Historians of South East Asia,* edited by D. G. E. Hall, 50–62. London: Oxford University Press, 1961.

Tha Myat, U. *Pyu Reader: A History of the Pyu Alphabet.* Rangoon: National Printing Works, 1963. In Burmese.

Thai Culture, New Series. Bangkok: Department of Fine Arts, 1962 and following. Reprint of *Thailand Cultural Series*, Bangkok: National Culture Institute, 1950–56.

Thailand: Culture and Society [Sangkhom lae Wattanatham nai Prathet Thai]. Edited by Sanit Samakkan. Published on the occasion of the opening of Princess Maha Chakri Sirindhorn Anthropology Centre by Her Royal Highness Princess Maha Chakri Sirindhorn, March 9, 1999. In Thai with abstracts in English.

Thani Nayagam, Xavier S. "Earliest Jain and Buddhist Teaching in Tamil Country." *Tamil Culture* 8, no. 4 (1959).

Thapar, Romila. *Ancient Indian Social History: Some Interpretations.* New Delhi: Orient Longman, 1978.

Tucci, Giuseppe. *Indo-Tibetica.* Vol. 1, *Stupa: Art, Architectonics, and Symbolism.* Edited by Lokesh Chandra. Translated by Uma Marina Vesci. Sata-Pitaka Series, Indo-Asian Literatures, vol. 347. New Delhi: Aditya Prakashan, 1988. First published 1932 by Reale Accademia d'Italia.

Vickery, Michael. "Some Remarks on Early State Formation in Cambodia." In Marr and Milner, *Southeast Asia in the 9th to 14th Centuries*, 95–116.

Vogel, J. Ph. "Prakrit Inscriptions from a Buddhist Site at Nāgarjunakonda." *Epigraphia Indica* 20, no. 1 (1929): 1–37.

Wales, H. G. Quaritch. "Archaeological Researches on Ancient Indian Colonization in Malaya," *Journal of the Royal Asiatic Society, Malaya Branch* 18, part 1 (February 1940): 1–85.

———. *Divination in Thailand: The Hopes and Fears of a Southeast Asian People.* London: Curzon Press, 1983.

———. *The Making of Greater India.* London: B. Quaritch, 1951.

———. *The Mountain of God: A Study in Early Religion and Kingship.* London: B. Quaritch, 1953.

———. *Prehistory and Religion in South East Asia.* London: B. Quaritch, 1957.

Waterson, Roxana. *The Living House: An Anthropology of Architecture in South-East Asia.* New York: Whitney Library of Design, 1997.

Wayman, Alex. "Reflections on the Theory of Barabudur as a Mandala." In Gomez and Woodward, *Barabudur: History and Significance of a Buddhist Monument*, 139–72.

Welch, David J. "Late Prehistoric and Early Historic Exchange Patterns in the Phimai Region, Thailand." *Journal of Southeast Asian Studies* 20, no. 1 (1989): 11–26.

Wheatley, Paul. *The Golden Khersonese: Studies in the Historical Geography of the Malay Peninsula before A.D. 1500.* Kuala Lampur: University of Malaya Press, 1961.

Williams, Lea E. *Southeast Asia: A History.* New York: Oxford University Press, 1976.

Wolters, O. W. *History, Culture and Region in Southeast Asian Perspectives.* Singapore: Institute of Southeast Asian Studies, 1982. Revised edition published by Southeast Asia Program Publications, Southeast Asia Program, Cornell University, 1999.

Wyatt, David K. "Chronicle Traditions in Thai Historiography." In *Southeast Asian History and Historiography: Essays Presented to D. G. E. Hall*, edited by C. D. Cowan and O. W. Wolters, 107–22. Ithaca, NY: Cornell University Press, 1976.

Xinru Liu. *Ancient India and Ancient China: Trade and Religious Exchanges, A.D. 1–600.* Delhi: Oxford University Press, 1988.

Yuyama, Akira. "'Jūni innenju' oboegaki" [Notes on the *Pratītyasamutpādagāthā*]. *Indogaku bukkyōgaku kenkyū* [Journal of Indian and Buddhist Studies] 20, no. 1 (1971): 48–52 (448–44). In Japanese.

———. *Kacchapa-Jātaka: Eine Erzūhlung von der Schildkröte und dem Kranzwinder.* Studia Philogica Buddhica, Occasional Paper Series, No. 5. Tokyo: The International Institute for Buddhist Studies, 1983.

———, ed. *Prajñā-pāramitā-ratna-guna-samcaya-gāthā.* Cambridge: Cambridge University Press, 1976.

Zimmer, Heinrich. *The Art of Indian Asia.* Princeton, NJ: Princeton University Press, 1955.

Index

Abhayagiri school, 6, 90, 103, 170, 171. *See also* Sri Lankan Buddhism
Abhidhammapiṭaka, 6, 80, 161, 173, 229n58
Abhidhammatthasaṅgaha, 80
acronymic texts, 174
Aeusrivongse, Nidhi, 132
afterlife beliefs, 33
Agastya, 89
Aggaññasutta, 36
agricultural societies, 8–10, 21, 27, 39, 42, 118, 124, 145
Ajātaśatru, King, 129
Amarāvatī
  period, 67
  region, 20, 108
  style of art, 67, 68, 91, 93, 108, 188
  Stūpa, 92, 104
amulets and charms, 41–42, 57, 153, 179
ancestor worship, 28, 33, 35, 38, 42–43, 113, 116, 120, 123, 137
Andhra Pradesh, 67, 92, 93, 102, 109, 159, 187
Angkor Empire, 8, 17
Angkor Thom, 93
Angkor Wat, 20, 22, 122
Angkorian *maṇḍala*, 20, 21, 53, 87, 94
Aṅguttaranikāya, 79
anicca, 177, 178
animism, 37, 113–14, 124, 147
Aniruddha, King (Anawrahta)
  "conversion" to Buddhism, 162, 164–69, 99, 170, 183
  nat cult and, 39
  "introduction" of Buddhism to Burma, 1, 3, 111–12, 163, 191
  use of Buddhism as political strategy, 173, 180, 181
Anurādhapura
  city of, 86, 87, 92, 103, 187
  period, 91
  style of art, 91, 93, 108, 111, 188
Appamāda-vagga, 166
Arahanta, 166–69
araññika, 170, 191, 239n59, 241n66
architecture (ancient), 12, 20, 22, 67, 91–93, 122, 188
Ari cult, 105, 111, 239n61
Arimaddana, 165, 166, 167, 169. *See also* Pagan
ariyasacca, 76–77, 81. *See also* Four Noble Truths
Aryanization, 10
asceticism, 151, 229n65
Aśoka, Emperor, 1, 59, 143, 166, 168, 180, 192
  invasion of Kalinga, 15
  mission to Suvarṇabhūmi, x, 45, 54, 55, 59–63, 159, 169, 201n2
  Third Buddhist Council under, 60, 63, 105, 190
Aśokan Buddhism, 195n3
Āṭānāṭiyasutta, 56, 152
Aung-Thwin, Michael, 107, 160
Avadāna, 87, 92, 96, 97, 98, 112. *See also individual texts*
Avadānaśataka, 97, 221n109
Avalokiteśvara, 94, 133, 136, 138, 230n70
Avanti, 59
Ayutthaya, 17, 182, 224n141

Ban Don Ta Phet, 30, 34
Barabudur, 20, 22, 93, 95, 97, 122, 221n112
Bareau, André, 109
Basham, A. L., xix
bas-reliefs, 65, 67, 92, 97–99, 112, 187
Bateson, J. H., 150
Bechert, Heinz, xviii, 141, 143, 153, 154, 157, 178
Beiktano, 20
Benda, Harry J., 4
bhakti, 130
Bharhut, 57
Bhattarcharya, Kamaleswar, xvii